# Conservation Politics

# Conservation Politics
## The Senate Career
## of Clinton P. Anderson

*Richard Allan Baker*

University of New Mexico Press / Albuquerque

Library of Congress Cataloging in Publication Data

Baker, Richard A.
   Conservation politics.

   Based on the author's thesis (Ph. D.)—University of
Maryland, 1982.
   Bibliography: p.
   Includes index.
   1. Conservation of natural-resources—Law and
legislation—United States—History. 2. Conservation
of natural resources—Government policy—United States—
History. 3. Anderson, Clinton Presba, 1895–
I. Title.
KF5505.B35   1985      346.7304′4      85-8748
ISBN 0-8263-0821-X

Designed by Stephanie Jurs

To the memory of Walter Rundell, Jr.

# Contents

# Preface

Two events occurred in the fall of 1975 that led me to write this book. In September, on the eve of the American Revolution bicentennial, the United States Senate established a Senate Historical Office and appointed me to be its director. Party leaders Mike Mansfield and Hugh Scott were determined that the office provide effective assistance to senators, scholars, and the general public in search of access to a rich documentary record of the Senate's history and traditions.

Several weeks later, on November 11, 1975, former United States Senator Clinton P. Anderson succumbed to a stroke at his home in Albuquerque, New Mexico. Under provisions of a deed, executed a decade earlier, the Library of Congress opened to researchers a massive 1,112-box collection containing the office files and personal papers that documented Anderson's twenty-four-year Senate career.

One of my early responsibilities as the Senate's historian was to advise members on techniques for identifying and separating from the increasing bulk of their routine correspondence those files that most specifically demonstrated their roles in shaping federal policy at the state and national levels. After several months of exploring Clinton Anderson's newly opened collection, I determined that it was of outstanding quality—a gold mine for researchers and a worthy model for senators wishing to improve the quality and structure of their own collections. Culled of repetitive, single-issue constituent correspondence, the collection abounds in candid assessments of major policy issues from Anderson's staff, congressional colleagues, executive agency officials, and interest groups. The collection is particularly rich in executive branch and interest group documentation not otherwise accessible to researchers at this relatively early date. Anderson wisely planned for disposition of his permanent files well in advance of retirement, avoiding the possibility of misguided efforts by staff and associates to remove materials they might perceive to be sensitive or otherwise embarrassing.

By any measure, Clinton Anderson ranks as one of the most powerful and effective members of the United States Senate during the 1950s and early 1960s. By 1965, his chronically poor health finally began to get the best of him. Although he enjoyed a secure power base in New Mexico and on Capitol Hill, illness took an increasingly heavy toll, and Anderson became largely dependent on his capable staff to initiate and pursue substantive legislative activity. Even at the height of his legislative effectiveness from 1949 to 1965, the news media and other observers, assuming that one of Anderson's many health problems would soon remove him from the national arena, paid less attention than his contributions merited. Almost as if to prove them wrong, Anderson survived to celebrate his 80th birthday, dying three weeks after that anniversary.

Clinton Anderson's imprint appears on a wide range of major post World War II legislation, including measures promoting health care for the elderly, peaceful uses of atomic energy, and exploration of outer space. He entered the Senate in 1949 to lay claim to New Mexico's full entitlement to the vital waters of the Colorado River. Within six years he had largely achieved that objective and his focus had shifted to the related field of natural resources policy. As he told a 1964 meeting of the Sierra Club, "I did not initially seek membership in the Senate to provide or push legislation for those who love nature in its various forms, but along the way I have found myself intrigued by side interests alien to my early desires, but of such an appealing nature that they have commanded more and more of my time until now the side shows have swallowed up the circus."[1] Throughout his rich and productive public career, Anderson's greatest satisfaction came from his success in forging new directions in America's natural resources policy. Summing up a decade and a half of Anderson's conservation policy achievements, his aide Claude Wood observed, "I always believed that the Senator had from the beginning of his Senate service a general plan in mind for a conservation program. Even though I have never seen anything in writing, it is evident that the Senator has put together—one piece at a time—legislative acts that fit as though they were planned a long time in advance. I believe that the Senator's success in this field can be attributed to the fact that he knew where to start and how to tie his conservation proposals together."[2]

My five-year journey through Anderson's manuscript collection justified my initial optimism and the accuracy of Claude Wood's observation. At the outset, I had hoped to advance my own training as the Senate's historian by analyzing the methods with which a key modern era senator shaped a major domestic policy issue. Anderson's papers, used in conjunction with mountains of congressional hearings, reports, and floor proceedings, spiced by interviews with key staff and associates, provided me with an unparalleled opportunity to do so. The result is a case study of the way in which one powerful, well-positioned, and highly intelligent member of Congress influenced national policy at a time when the executive branch was unable to respond realistically to post war demands on the nation's natural resources inventory. Seldom in recent times has a member of Congress pursued such a course over a decade and a half to such great effect.

Shortly after I took on responsibility for developing the Senate Historical Office, I turned for assistance to Professor Walter Rundell, Jr., then chairman of the history department at the nearby University of Maryland. Rundell had been a major promoter of federal agency historical programs for nearly two decades, and he quickly grasped the potential for a constructive program within the Senate. Believing that the Senate deserved as its official historian a scholar rather than a civil servant, he encouraged me to complete my doctoral studies at the University of Maryland and generously agreed to direct my dissertation. Late in 1982, as I was preparing to defend that dissertation, Walter Rundell died unexpectedly at the age of fifty-three. This book grew out of his skillful guidance and inspiration. Where it succeeds, I wish it to stand as a tribute to his genius as a teacher, scholar, and friend.

Others at the University of Maryland shared their wisdom and experience. Professors Horace Samuel Merrill, Wayne S. Cole, Keith Olson, and Phillips Foster assisted in the painful process of converting a dissertation to a book manuscript. Senator Frank E. Moss examined the entire work with the insight of one who had shared many of Clinton Anderson's committee assignments and legislative successes. Anne M. Butler, the first person to complete a doctorate under Rundell's direction, and my collaborator in completing Rundell's biography of historian Walter Prescott Webb, read the full text in several versions. With great insight, she offered the incisive analysis that so clearly informs her own scholarship.

To my colleagues Donald A. Ritchie, Kathryn Allamong Jacob, John O. Hamilton, Karen Dawley Paul, and Elizabeth Ann Hornyak in the Senate Historical Office, I owe special thanks for their patience and support. Elsewhere in the Senate, James Roe Ketchum, Francis R. Valeo, J. S. Kimmitt, Marilyn Courtot, and William F. Hildenbrand underwrote this work in the most fundamental manner.

Clinton Anderson's immediate family, for reasons that one must respect, neither impeded nor advanced this study. His close staff associates were uncommonly generous with their time and insight. My special thanks and deepest appreciation go to Ruby Hamblen who opened many doors in the early stages, to Claude E. Wood who did all within his power to keep me from stumbling into errors of fact and interpretation, and to the late Richard Pino, who congenially guided the New Mexico phase of my research.

Many others have supported this study in a less direct but equally important way. I am especially indebted to Donald J. Pisani of Texas A & M University, Harry James Brown of Michigan State University and the late John Neal Waddell of Columbia University. I can never fully repay the sacrifice of my parents, H. Allan and Eleanor Baker and of my grandmother, Agnes E. Baker. Patricia K. S. Baker has generously and actively assisted my work for more than two decades, recently at the expense of her own scholarly labors, while my children, Christopher Allan and David Richard deserved vastly greater amounts of their father's attention than they received.

Richard Allan Baker
*Washington, D.C.*

# Introduction

By constitutional design and historical precedent, Congress and the president formulate public policy in a tentative and fragmentary manner. As Woodrow Wilson pointed out a century ago, making legislation is an aggregate process, not a simple production. American political history, as written over the past fifty years, is replete with examples of the role of the executive branch in the policy process, as the never-ceasing tide of New Deal era studies demonstrates. Focused accounts of the congressional role appear only infrequently. The basic fragmentation and complexity of the legislative process compound the difficulties of tracking the Senate and House's contributions to policy development. Contrary to popular stereotypes, Congress has played a powerful role in initiating as well as validating new directions in public policy. This has been particularly true when three factors coincide. They include a demonstrated need for change, presidential apathy or preoccupation, and the availability of independent and articulate legislators dedicated to achievement of change regardless of adverse political consequences.[1]

This study seeks to demonstrate the range and depth of constructive public policy accomplishments within the grasp of a single well-placed and well-equipped member of the United States Congress. The policy issue examined here is natural resources conservation during the two decades following World War II. The principal legislative actor under scrutiny is Sen. Clinton P. Anderson, a Democrat of New Mexico. Anderson's approach to the issues associated with the conservation of natural resources, during the years 1949 to 1964, resulted in significant long term contributions. Although he was but one of Congress's 535 members, Anderson marshaled his creative intellect, his unsurpassed sense of legislative timing, and his stature among peers and subordinates in a campaign to ensure preservation and measured use of the natural resources of his state, region, and nation. An entrepreneurial legislator, Anderson made a profound difference and in so doing, he provided further proof of Congress's capacity for dominance in federal policy development.

Clinton Anderson arrived in the United States Senate in 1949 intending to stay for only a single six-year term. He remained for nearly a quarter century. The first decade and a half of the New Mexico Democrat's service, the period of this study, coincided with a massive reorientation of public policy approaches to resources conservation. Western states, while guarding local prerogatives, looked to the federal government for leadership and relief in their efforts to stake out secure claims to diminishing land and water resources. Meanwhile, programs and traditional attitudes within federal executive branch agencies were faltering under the weight of nationwide post World War II demands on water, timber, and recreation resources. Conservation interest groups struggled to achieve an effective and lasting coalition to revise outmoded federal policies. The principal forum for that battle was the Congress of the United States.

The Senate, with its longer terms for members, its guarantee of equal representation for each state regardless of population, and its expanded staff resources in the postwar period to reduce reliance on an often uncooperative executive branch, became the central arena for adjustment and experimentation. There, policies that would preserve and develop the less populous West for the rest of the nation's benefit received sharpest scrutiny. There, Clinton Anderson demonstrated his powerful intelligence and his intelligent use of power. His ability to concentrate on the important while avoiding the trivial combined with his strategically key committee assignments to yield a rich harvest of resources legislation. By 1964, among the fifty major conservation bills that he had sponsored, half that number had become public law, and others would soon find their way to the statute books.

Anderson's philosophy of conservation and the opportunities for its application evolved over nearly a half century. At the age of twenty-two, he moved from South Dakota's fertile plains to New Mexico's starkly beautiful mountains, mesas, and desert flatlands. Cured of tuberculosis, the gregarious young man fell under the influence of the indefatigable naturalist Aldo Leopold. Anderson did not take for granted, as a native son might have, the attractions of the Gila wilderness and the Sangre de Cristo Mountains. As he turned to those places within his adopted state for renewal of his fragile health, he developed a lasting animosity toward those who sought to despoil its natural timber and recreation resources for unbridled commercial gain.

In 1922 at Santa Fe, he witnessed the feverish efforts of representatives from Colorado River Basin states to stake out claims to a share of that river's vital water resources. In the years that followed, he watched as California harnessed its own allocation as well as that which the upper basin states, including New Mexico, paralyzed by internal disputes, allowed to flow unclaimed into the Golden State's waiting reservoirs. Elected to the U.S. House in 1940 and appointed Secretary of Agriculture five years later, Anderson had the opportunity to test and expand his ability to balance the requirements of natural resources preservation with those of measured and wise use, developing an impressive inventory of legislative and administrative skills in the process.

In 1949, Anderson's initial interest in the Senate centered on development of New Mexico's fullest possible entitlement to the Colorado River's waters. A chain of statutes, extending from legislation confirming the 1948 Upper Colorado Basin Compact to the 1962 law authorizing construction of the Navajo Indian Irrigation Project and the San Juan-Chama Transmountain Diversion, testified to his success. In the process, he drew on skills of mediation and diplomacy that in 1932 had elevated him to the presidency of Rotary International at the age of thirty-six. He fashioned timely coalitions of preservationists and recreationists, easterners and westerners, upper and lower Colorado River basin interests, as well as senators and representatives to ensure passage, in 1956, of the Upper Colorado Storage Project Act. The largest reclamation project ever authorized by Congress to that time, the Colorado project opened the way to man's redesign of nature's water plan for New Mexico.

With authorizing and funding statutes firmly in place, Anderson set his sights on a broader, nationally oriented program of wilderness preservation, outdoor recreation planning, and water resources research and development that resulted in a burst of legislative energy culminating in the remarkable "Conservation Congress" of 1963–64. Among the principal legislature monuments erected under his leadership were the Wilderness Act, the Land and Water Conservation Fund, the Outdoor Recreation Act, and additional statutes to preserve seashores and parklands.

The evolution of Anderson's principal orientation from securing water resources for his state and region to a broader program of national resources conservation paralleled a major reassessment of the federal role in resources protection and development. These shifts, concurrent in their timing and pace, proved to be interrelated. The Hoover Commission on the Organization of the Executive Branch issued its landmark report on natural resources policy in 1949. A year later a special study commission on federal water policy, chaired by former Rural Electrification Administrator Morris Cooke, released its findings. Both reports pointed to the necessity of modernizing federal resources agencies. The Reclamation Bureau within the Department of the Interior came under increasing pressure to move from traditional irrigation agriculture where the simple projects had already been developed to more complex multiple purpose projects providing water for recreation and industry where costs and benefits could be more broadly distributed.

During World War II, outlays for federal park and recreation facilities had evaporated. By 1949, as millions of Americans searched for outdoor recreation, they found crowded, outmoded and dilapidated sites, many of which were located far from population centers. Postwar housing booms intensified demands on the nation's timber resources, and lumber companies turned to more efficient methods of clearcutting to improve yields while keeping costs at a minimum. Public interest groups became more vocal and began to form coalitions with like-minded constituencies to push for a more effective federal response.

These pressures, turned aside by the Truman administration preoccupied with its war in Korea, increased in 1953 as a new Republican administration continued its predecessor's policy of passivity. At lower levels in the federal bureaucracy, sniping continued between the Agriculture Department's Forest Service and the Interior Department's National Park Service, "the most celebrated interbureau rivalry in all government."[2] The Park Service with its "Mission '66" program sought aggressively to regain control of federal recreation policy through a long-term congressional funding commitment. The Forest Service, choked with ambivalence, wished to compete with the Park Service as a recreation agency while also promoting increased timber yields. It responded with a pale imitation labeled "Operation Outdoors." Such was the mid-decade agency response to the crisis in recreation resources.

Outside the federal government forceful and articulate new leadership arose to bring a degree of unity to a recreation-minded public frustrated by federal pace and direction. David Brower of the Sierra Club, Howard Zahniser of the Wilderness Society, and Joseph Penfold of the Izaak Walton League turned the broad objectives of their organizations into specific legislative proposals and sought well-placed allies on Capitol Hill. Zahniser in 1951 unveiled his first plan for legislation to give greater protection to wilderness areas under Forest Service jurisdiction. Penfold followed suit with his outline for a federal study commission to review recreation resources.

The decade of the 1950s began with the Hoover and Cooke commission reports. It ended with passage of the Multiple Use–Sustained Yield Act of 1960, which redefined and consolidated the Forest Service's mandate in the face of escalating user group pressure. As one observer noted, the act was "a fitting monument to gradual changes in value and perspective regarding resources management that had found their political feet in the postwar years."[3] As leadership of natural resources management slipped from Eisenhower era executive agencies under pressure from preservationists, recreationists, and developers, Congress moved to take up its constitutional role as mediator and innovator.

Political scientist James Sundquist evaluated the consequences, for the decade following 1955, of an inversion in the traditional roles of Congress and the presidency. "As long as presidential and congressional majorities were of the same party—which until the mid 1950's was the normal state of affairs—this relationship [the president as planner and Congress as deliberator] was acceptable enough." In 1955, however, Democrats took control of both houses of Congress while the Republicans held the White House. This split lasted until 1961, whereas earlier divisions of this nature had occurred only twice before in the twentieth century and had extended for only two-year intervals. Sundquist observed that "when the branches were under control of opposing parties, the Congress re-

jected the president as its leader and legislative planner, and the
weakness of Congress in trying to set its own course became glar-
ingly apparent. Then the legislators came to comprehend the importance to them of the function of agenda setting that they had
given up, and the consequences of their failure to develop the institutional capacity for planning."[4]

By 1955 Clinton Anderson was well positioned to command a
congressional review of outmoded resources conservation policies.
In that year he became chairman of the Senate Interior Committee's powerful Subcommittee on Irrigation and Reclamation. Simultaneously, he assumed the helm of the prestigious Joint Committee
on Atomic Energy. His close colleague from the southwest, Lyndon Johnson (D-TX), had just risen to the post of Senate majority
leader and Anderson, despite his unyielding independence, had become a member of the Senate's storied "inner club." As a former
New Deal administrator and as Secretary of Agriculture he had sharpened his managerial skills. As a legislator, he drew on the expertise
and innate resourcefulness that had made him a successful businessman. He appreciated the value of precise cost accounting and
efficient administrative policies. He recognized, for instance, that
water projects, vital to the West's economic future, were becoming prohibitively expensive, so he applied his business skills to push
for separate capital budgets divorced from routine operating outlays. He insisted that the cost of borrowing be tied to prevailing
interest *rates* on long term government securities rather than on
their less predictable and generally higher long term *yields*—a critical distinction on which rested the ultimate feasibility of many proposed water projects. He worked to assign a portion of a water
project's value to its recreation potential, thus reducing the burden for project cost repayment that would otherwise have been
borne by the direct user. In the Colorado River Storage Project,
Anderson was quick to recognize the benefit to New Mexico of
main system electric power revenues to finance smaller irrigation
dams such as the Navajo.

Anderson's flexibility in directing the legislative reexamination
of federal conservation policy contrasted starkly with the iron-clad
rigidity of his legislative counterpart in the House of Representatives, Colorado's acerbic Wayne N. Aspinall (D). As chairman of
the House Interior Committee, Aspinall argued that the particular-
istic interests of his urban-oriented chamber placed special con-

straints on his flexibility. Early in his chairmanship, he exhibited a paralyzing pride in never having a bill, approved by his committee, killed on the floor of the House of Representatives. The need for this caution, coupled with the anti-preservation sentiments of his vocal coal mining constituency, hobbled the House chairman and led to his demands on Anderson that the Senate slow its pace or see its handiwork buried.

Ultimately, the Senate Interior Committee became the testing ground for new proposals. From 1955 through 1964 Anderson exercised great influence within that powerful Senate panel. Few resource bills traveled from the Interior Committee to the Senate floor without first passing his active scrutiny. When they arrived for House consideration, they frequently had been propelled to that side of the Capitol by decidedly large margins of Senate approval.

As chairman of the Senate Interior Committee, in 1961 and 1962, Anderson spoke from within the very heart of the upper house as a defender of its prerogatives and traditions. He was particularly sensitive to executive agency efforts to misconstrue congressional intent, and he repeatedly assaulted the mighty Bureau of the Budget as it sought to reshape the Interior Department's legislative mandate. He lectured young President John Kennedy, his former Senate colleague, on the realities of congressional-executive relations. Outwardly deferential to the chief executive, Anderson left no doubt as to what he considered proper resources policy and the surest road to its implementation.

As his committee's top ranking member even after he turned over its chairmanship to Henry Jackson (D-WA) in 1963, Anderson routinely shaped legislation drafted within the Kennedy and Johnson administrations. This was the case in 1962 when Kennedy aides suddenly presented him with a major water resources planning bill more comprehensive than his own, on which extended hearings had just concluded. Nonetheless, he dropped his own plans and reservations to move ahead in the role of the president's legislative lieutenant. He recognized, however, that the road from introduction to enactment was lengthy and perilous. Along that tortuous course, he took command of strategic and tactical decisions within the Senate, deciding when to report a measure out of his committee, when to move it to the floor for debate, when to apply pressure on counterparts in the House of Representatives, when to seek

White House intervention, when to move behind the scenes, and when to go public.

A veteran Washington lobbyist for liberal causes characterized Anderson as a "protean legislator . . . a sixteen-cylinder senator."[5] His Senate campaign for natural resources legislation, waged with studied determination between 1949 and 1964, demonstrated that he was above all a master legislative strategist and a pragmatic politician. To label him a "conservationist" is as meaningless as that overworked and ill-defined term. In search of a more precise definition, one must also reject "preservationist." Anderson strongly sympathized with preservationist leaders such as David Brower, Joseph Penfold, and Howard Zahniser. He drew on their fervor and support when it reinforced his immediate legislative objectives. He stopped short, however, of unreflective and open-armed commitment common to those in Congress who sought to build reputations on fervent espousal of single issues.

At the other end of the conservation policy spectrum, Anderson certainly advocated development and wise use of natural resources, placing him at odds with those preservationists accused of wanting to lock up the nation's remaining store of untouched wilderness and parklands. In this, he appeared to be making common cause with miners, grazers, and lumbermen. Yet, a review of his outspoken opposition to these interests helps to clarify his practical and philosophical positions. As a businessman with a New Deal education in the value of federal intervention in resources development, Anderson believed that unchecked adherence to the alleged dictates of the market economy would ultimately cripple enjoyment of these resources by those participating in the fruits of an industrialized economy as well as those seeking relief from its rigors.

Clinton Anderson served New Mexico in the Senate of the United States at a time when issues that traditionally had been associated with the West—those involving management of energy, land, and water resources—rapidly evolved into national issues. Anderson's distinction as a legislator of great stature came because he was able to reconcile and balance the interests of his state and region with those of the country at large. When he advocated legislation of obvious value to his state, he did so in terms that colleagues from other regions found difficult to deny.

Sympathetic to those who feared that the price of federal involvement was federal domination, Anderson nonetheless worked from a nationalist perspective. He believed that the federal government had the duty to intervene to guarantee achievement of congressionally mandated national conservation goals. These objectives required expenditure of vast sums of federal money. Management of that investment provoked a high-stakes struggle between the respective defenders of national and local sovereignty. The ultimate issue centered on whether the nation's increasingly threatened public lands and waters would be administered for local or national advantage. In this fierce struggle, Anderson's mediatory skills proved decisive.

The two decades since 1964, following the end of Clinton Anderson's active involvement in natural resources policy, have severely tested the statutes he played such a major role in fashioning. In their essentials, however, those laws have proven to be lasting monuments to his creative legislative genius applied to policy issues of overriding national importance.

# *1*

# Senator from New Mexico

On the evening of May 20, 1963 the main ballroom of Washington's Statler Hilton Hotel resounded to the animated conversation of a festive dinner party for United States Senator Clinton P. Anderson. As the 650 guests settled back from their meal of braised beef and turned their attention to the head table, itself thronged with eighty dignitaries, representatives of twelve leading American conservation organizations stepped forward to bestow on the New Mexico Democrat the National Conservation Award. Among those present on that mild spring evening were one-third of the Senate's membership, three cabinet officers, dozens of House members, and scores of federal officials, lobbyists, and private citizens engaged in the advancement of the nation's natural resources conservation policies.

Earlier in the day, President John F. Kennedy, in a Rose Garden ceremony, saluted the sixty-seven-year-old senator for a lifetime of dedication to conservation. Vice President Lyndon Johnson had engineered a delay in the Washington arrival of Astronaut L. Gordon Cooper so that the scheduled celebration of his return from a pioneering space flight would not conflict with the Anderson festivities. Four days earlier, Senate and House negotiators had quickly compromised their differences over legislation to establish a major federal program to accelerate development of outdoor recreation facilities. They hoped to have the measure ready so that the president could sign it at the time of the tribute to Anderson, its principal architect. Numerous speakers at the evening banquet cited this act, as well as dozens of Anderson's other conservation achievements. These ranged from development of New Mexico's vital water entitlements to a broad, nationally oriented program of wilderness preservation, water resources research, and land use planning.[1]

Anderson's philosophy of conservation and the skills he fashioned to implement it sharpened over the half century that preceded his 1948 election to the United States Senate. Born in Centerville, South Dakota, on October 23, 1895, Clinton Presba Anderson spent his formative years in the nearby town of Parker. His father moved frequently between careers as storekeeper, sheriff, farmer, and agricultural equipment supplier in the pioneer South Dakota communities to which the great Scandinavian migrations of the 1880s had brought him.[2]

As Clinton, youngest of the Anderson's three children, entered his teen years, his father took a relatively lucrative position with International Harvester in Mitchell, South Dakota. Compared with Parker's dirt streets and wooden sidewalks, Mitchell, a town of 8,000 fifty miles northeast in the rich corn belt, impressed young Anderson as a thriving metropolis. Following graduation from high school in 1913, and without firm career plans, Anderson enrolled at Mitchell's Dakota Wesleyan University. There he came under the influence of Clyde Tull, a dynamic professor of English who nurtured his nascent writing skills. Tull later recalled that his student "was the best speaker in the college and an able debater. He had a definite journalistic ability which we encouraged and he turned out a number of stories of the O. Henry type."[3]

After two years in the small South Dakota college, Anderson decided to apply to a major university. Columbia University rejected his application, despite Anderson's promising grades and success in acquiring the typing and shorthand skills necessary for a program in journalism. Concluding that the eastern university considered him "too much of a hick to make good in New York," Anderson set his sights on the University of Michigan, entering in the fall of 1915 to undertake studies in journalism and law.[4] There, he joined the staffs of the *Michigan Daily* and the campus humor magazine. At Ann Arbor, Anderson's career prospects brightened when a visiting editor from *The New York Sun* read his article about two students who had been killed by a passing train. On the spot the editor offered the twenty-year-old a job in New York City, and Anderson quickly accepted.[5]

As the young South Dakotan prepared to move east, he received word that his father had suffered a disabling accident. So, in 1916, he abruptly ended his university career, foreclosed his opportunities as a big city journalist, and dutifully returned home. In Mitchell he accepted a position as the lone reporter for that town's *Daily Republican,* a vigorously Democratic organ in spite of its name. Life as a small town reporter had its moments of peril, as Anderson quickly discovered in a confrontation with Arthur Townley, the Non-Partisan League's fiery organizer. When the agrarian radical sought to instruct the young reporter on proper coverage of the League, an argument ensued and the 6 foot 2 inch Anderson knocked the larger man down a narrow flight of stairs.[6] His independence and volatile temper remained distinguishing characteristics throughout Anderson's lifetime.

Anderson seldom experienced long periods of good health after his adolescent years. While a student at Dakota Wesleyan, he suffered pleurisy. At Michigan, doctors discovered an active case of tuberculosis but declined to inform their young patient. Shortly thereafter, in the spring of 1917 as the United States entered the World War, Anderson failed an Army physical exam and a family doctor told the senior Anderson that his son had less than six months to live. Treatment of Clinton's tuberculosis at one of the high priced sanatoriums in Colorado Springs or Tucson was simply beyond the reach of the family's meager income. Recalling that a local Methodist minister had told him of his brother-in-law who was a clergyman and trustee of the Methodist sanatorium in Albuquerque, New Mexico, Anderson asked his help in finding a place in that modestly priced facility. The Albuquerque minister responded that he would do his best.[7]

In October 1917, faced with imminent death, Clinton Anderson gathered his small savings and cast his fate to the climate and medical facilities of the distant town on the Rio Grande. On the day he arrived in Albuquerque Anderson weighed a mere 133 pounds, his body temperature registered 104°, and his pulse beat at a rate too fast to be accurately measured. The city's four hospitals were filled and each had a long waiting list. Anderson contacted the minister who told the South Dakotan to check out of the Alvarado Hotel and go immediately to the Methodist sanatorium. He was instructed to sit in the lobby and await the death of another patient. The minister used his influence with the hospital superintendent, and within two hours Anderson entered his newly fumigated room. His doctors expected him to survive no longer than five days.[8]

Anderson received excellent medical care, and within a month his recovery was assured. During his nine-month convalescence, Anderson used his idle time to read widely, including every book available on the game of bridge. Throughout his remaining years, Anderson maintained his intense love of books and his skill at bridge. A fellow patient described him as a "very friendly sort who spent most of his time talking to other patients." Anderson also worked on his writing skills, preparing short stories, poetry, and magazine articles in an effort to keep his mind busy and defray his medical expenses. He later recalled that his labors cost him "a lot of postage and brought a wonderful collection of rejection slips."[9]

As Anderson prepared to return to South Dakota in November 1918, the editor of the *Albuquerque Evening Herald* urged him to join the paper's staff, recently depleted by that year's devastating influenza epidemic. Anderson agreed to fill in temporarily, but he intended to return to Mitchell to pursue his budding romance with Henrietta McCartney whom he had met in February 1917. His reporting tenure extended into 1919 when he drew an assignment to cover the state legislature's January–March session. In Santa Fe he received his first direct exposure to the tumultuous world of New Mexico politics. After filing his daily dispatches, the journalist turned his creative mind and skillful pen to the service of the legislature's beleaguered Democratic minority. He drafted amendments and devised strategy to frustrate Republican efforts at strengthening their already substantial power base.[10]

When the legislature adjourned in March, Anderson resigned from the *Herald* and planned his return home. Again illness intervened. Smallpox forced him into quarantine. While recovering he accepted an invitation to serve as executive secretary of the New Mexico Public Health Association, which he had helped found in 1917. His experience in that body, the political contacts he had developed in Santa Fe, and his willingness to take on tasks others shunned all contributed to his effectiveness and increasing prominence. His health restored, Anderson travelled east in the fall of 1919 for a six-week course at the New York School of Social Work's Tuberculosis Institute. With this training, he then conducted a successful campaign to establish a much-needed public health department for New Mexico.[11]

In 1921, at the age of twenty-six, Anderson finally abandoned plans to return to South Dakota. His parents had moved to California, and Henrietta McCartney had agreed to join him in New Mexico. His enjoyment of newspaper work led him to accept a post (as managing editor and chief investigative reporter) on the *Albuquerque Journal*. In that capacity Anderson uncovered shady dealings between California oilman Harry Sinclair and Interior Secretary Albert Fall. He observed that unusually high quality cattle were being delivered to Fall's New Mexico ranch, and he learned from a disgruntled ranch foreman that the secretary had received a $25,000 race horse from a mysterious source. Early in 1922, after the articles began to appear, a confrontation reportedly took place between the cabinet secretary and the young editor. The enraged Fall stormed into the *Journal*'s offices and is said to have demanded of Anderson, "Are you the son-of-a-bitch who has been writing those lies about me?" Anderson drew himself up to his full height and characteristically responded, "I may be a son-of-a-bitch, but I'm not a liar." Anderson's reporting led to the broader investigation of irregularities in private leasing of U.S. naval oil reserves that became known as the "Teapot Dome" scandal and resulted in Fall's conviction and imprisonment.[12]

In June 1921, Clinton and Henrietta were married after he promised her mother they would never reside in Santa Fe, a town the elder woman considered a sink of sin. The union proved of great benefit to Anderson as his strong-willed bride spent a lifetime guarding his health and serving as his thoughtful and determined alter ego. After the newly-weds settled in Albuquerque, they harnessed available family resources to assist the *Journal* and its owner, Carl Magee, in raising operating capital to stave off efforts of Albert Fall's state Republican machine to gain control of the spunky paper. When Magee finally capitulated and sold the *Journal* in June 1922, he repaid the Andersons' sizable investment.

With the unexpected windfall, Clinton decided to revise his career plans and buy a share of a local banking enterprise that seemed to offer promising investment opportunities. After a year of running the mortgage side of the New Mexico Loan and Mortgage Company, he had a falling out with the firm's principal owner. Perceiving greater potential in the local insurance business, he arranged to purchase the company's insurance division and in 1923 established the Clinton P. Anderson Agency.[13]

By early 1923 highway construction had become a major activity in New Mexico. State law required contractors to purchase workman's compensation insurance. Most turned to agents in Denver or El Paso, as the insurance industry in Albuquerque was virtually nonexistent. Over the next three years Anderson sold policies on a door-to-door basis. Building on his already wide circle of business and political acquaintances, he prospered and became increasingly active in the city's community life. In 1925 the local Rotary Club chose him as its tenth president in recognition of his effective service as that body's secretary. Popular with Albuquerque's business establishment, Anderson seemed to have limitless energy for the many burdensome tasks that came his way.[14]

During this period of his early life, Anderson's interest in natural resources conservation deepened. Raised on South Dakota's fertile plains, he grew to love New Mexico's forested mountains, bold mesas, and high desert flatlands. Recuperating in the Methodist sanatorium, he looked eastward daily to the rugged Sandia peaks, standing in dramatic contrast to Albuquerque's level plain along the Rio Grande. As he turned to these places for renewal of his fragile health, Anderson came under the influence of Progressive Era conservation doctrine and of one of its principal apostles, naturalist Aldo Leopold.

The Progressive Era during the first two decades of the twentieth century nourished the development of a conservation philosophy that emphasized rational planning to promote efficient use of the country's natural resources. Despite the veneer of emotionalism associated with the struggle to protect virginal resources against the lustful designs of greedy corporate despoilers, this conservation movement rested on a hard-headed scientific base. Over the course of his subsequent public career, Anderson consistently displayed his Progressive faith in the scientific approach to resources problems. As one historian observed of the conservation movement that flourished during Anderson's formative years, "The new realms of science and technology, appearing to open up unlimited opportunities for human achievement, filled conservation leaders with intense optimism. They emphasized expansion, not retrenchment; possibilities, not limitations."[15]

Anderson met Aldo Leopold when the latter served as secretary of the Albuquerque Chamber of Commerce. As early as December

1918, Leopold had brought the Progressive conservation message to members of that city's Rotary Club, urging them to consider the economic value to New Mexico of a "businesslike policy of game propagation." The business community could appreciate an approach based not on an attack against greedy corporate interests, but on an appeal to scientific efficiency. At this time, the consequences of random development had become readily apparent. As newly built roads into National Forest areas facilitated public and commercial access, Anderson, with Leopold, developed a lasting animus for the consequences of unregulated timber harvesting and indiscriminate recreation use.[16] Establishment of the National Park Service in 1916 and the parallel growth of the U.S. Forest Service during the post–World War I period testified to increasing concern at the national as well as local level over management of the West's natural resources.

Throughout the late 1920s, Anderson's insurance business prospered, and his activity within the state Democratic party increased. In 1922 he had been elected secretary of the Bernalillo [Albuquerque] County party organization. Six years later, in 1928, he became his party's state chairman in time to preside over the defeat of all but one of its slated candidates. The presidential candidacy of New York Governor Al Smith, a "wet" Catholic, cost the Democrats their traditional stronghold of New Mexico's eastern Baptist counties.[17] With the election behind him, he turned to politics of another sort, serving in a succession of national and worldwide offices for Rotary International. In 1932, at age thirty-six, Anderson achieved the presidency of that organization, becoming the youngest chief executive in Rotary's history to that time. He took full advantage of the opportunity his Rotary duties gave him to travel widely, visiting many of the organization's 3500 clubs in sixty-eight countries.[18]

During this active period of Anderson's life, he never failed to keep his home base well covered. He had campaigned vigorously in 1932 to win New Mexico's endorsement for Democratic presidential contender Franklin D. Roosevelt. Shortly after Roosevelt's election, the New Mexico state treasurer died. Governor Arthur Seligman turned to the prospering insurance executive to secure bonding for a designated successor. Anderson reported that the governor's candidate lacked the financial resources to qualify for the required $1 million bond. He added that a Hartford insurance firm would be willing to bond him for the post. The governor agreed and Anderson became state treasurer.[19]

Tom Popejoy, Anderson's longtime political associate and later president of the University of New Mexico, observed that the presidency of Rotary International assured Anderson's subsequent political success. Prior to 1932 the young insurance executive had been known only locally. Through Rotary, Anderson met "thousands of influential men and developed into an excellent speaker." Anderson's maturing connections in the nation's capital accounted for his selection, upon expiration of his term as treasurer, as New Mexico state director of the Federal Emergency Relief Administration. Within a year he advanced to the posts of Mountain States relief coordinator and then Western States field coordinator. In the latter position, Anderson earned a reputation as a bold administrator, firing 156 California employees in a single day. Soon thereafter, he ran afoul of national relief director Harry Hopkins and was himself fired.[20]

In 1937, while serving as chairman of the New Mexico Unemployment Compensation Commission, Anderson decided the time had come to expand his insurance business. Large insurance underwriters were beginning to refuse to issue workman's compensation policies due to a dramatic growth in claim volume. Anderson learned of a state law permitting five or more employers to band together to handle their own compensation insurance. He approached five of the state's largest road contractors and offered to create a new firm to handle their insurance needs. He promised, "If I don't save you money, I will not charge you one cent for the operation of the business." They agreed, and Anderson established the Mountain States Mutual Casualty Company. During its first six months of operation, the firm assessed its five clients the customary premium, paid a twenty-five percent dividend, and realized a $500 profit. From that point, Anderson's financial success was assured.[21]

In 1940, the New Mexican's career took another major turn as he concluded his duties as executive director of the United States Coronado Exposition Commission. His work in obtaining funding for and directing that activity of great importance to the southwest strengthened his reputation for effectiveness with both state and national party leaders. Among his Washington allies were First Lady Eleanor Roosevelt and House Democratic Leader Sam Rayburn.

As that year began, state Democratic chieftans, seeking to ward off an impending and potentially disastrous intraparty battle, viewed

Anderson as just the person to help them. At issue was selection of a party candidate for the forthcoming U.S. Senate race. Six years earlier, incumbent Sen. Bronson Cutting had narrowly defeated Rep. Dennis Chavez in a contest that fell in the mainstream of the state's long tradition for political chicanery. Chavez protested the outcome, forcing Cutting to travel to New Mexico to defend his victory. On the return trip to Washington, the popular senator died in a plane crash. The governor then appointed Chavez to the vacancy.[22]

As the 1940 Senate campaign approached, bitter followers of Cutting sought to deny Chavez a second term, blaming him for their leader's tragic death. To spearhead their strategy, they selected the state's lone member of the U.S. House of Representatives, John Dempsey, to challenge Chavez in the Democratic primary. Meanwhile, senior party leaders devised a plan to maintain peace within the factions by reserving Dempsey's House seat in 1942 for the loser of the 1940 Dempsey-Chavez Senate primary. Recalling Clinton Anderson's frequent expressions of disinterest in elective office, particularly after his 1926 defeat by local mortician Chester French for a seat on the Bernalillo County Commission, party leaders prevailed on him to run for Dempsey's seat with the understanding that he would step aside in 1942. With assurances from both camps that he would have their active support, and with the reluctant assent of his wife and his physician, Anderson accepted the assignment.[23]

The senatorial campaign predictably degenerated and before long both candidates turned to Anderson for his endorsement, in violation of the earlier agreement that he would remain out of the battle. The Chavez faction even demanded that Anderson contribute $15,000 to the race against Dempsey. When he refused, each side produced its own candidate for the House seat, leaving Anderson to fend for himself. Betrayal and concerted opposition merely strengthened Anderson's determination. He waged a difficult primary race against several well-known New Mexico figures, emerging with a narrow victory. In the general election, he won handily, outpolling President Franklin Roosevelt and Chavez, the senatorial winner.[24]

Anderson arrived in the nation's capital in January 1941 as lawmakers and members of the Roosevelt administration struggled with the implications of the worsening European war situation. Against this grim backdrop, New Mexico's lone House member decided to depart from the tradition of congressional apartment living by purchasing a large house. The residence on fashionable Bradley Lane in suburban Bethesda, Maryland, provided sufficient room for three domestic servants and his two young children, son Sherburne and daughter Nancy. Surrounding the house were extensive grounds for the family's beloved riding horses, of which Anderson noted, "You just can't keep house without them." Back in New Mexico political foes attempted to call attention to the new congressman's efforts to put down roots in alien soil. With his customary scorn for such attacks, Anderson observed, "Everyone told me that it was political suicide for a congressman to own his own home in or near Washington, but then I'm enjoying life and my political fortunes are not worrying me as much as the privilege of living my life in the same manner. I believe I can serve my people better by living in this way."[25]

As he prepared to take his oath on January 3, 1941, Anderson discovered that his predecessor, John Dempsey, had told House leaders that Anderson's election was a fluke and that he surely would be only a one-term member. Anderson believed that Dempsey's hostility, along with his own failure to cultivate Sam Rayburn, newly elected as Speaker, cost him seats on the more desirable committees. Despite his frustration, Anderson received assignments to three panels whose jurisdiction related directly to his state's interests: the committees on Indian Affairs, Irrigation and Reclamation, and Public Lands. In addition, the freshman solon drew a seat on the Census Committee, widely considered among the "nits and lice" of House panels.[26]

Under the chairmanship of an obscure third-term Pennsylvania Democrat, the Census Committee nonetheless assumed particular importance in 1941 as a result of impending reapportionment of House districts following the 1940 Census. Anderson quickly involved himself in a contest between the states of Michigan and Arkansas over an additional seat. Painstakingly he wrestled with conflicting mathematical systems proffered as foundation for the states' respective claims. After appropriate consideration, Anderson decided that Michigan had the stronger case and should gain the disputed seat. Impressed by Anderson's careful homework and logical arguments, the remainder of the Census Committee agreed, as did Speaker Rayburn, and Anderson's legislative star began to rise.[27]

The New Mexico representative's friendship with Rayburn matured quickly. On several occasions the bachelor Speaker came to Anderson's home for dinner and brought along another junior southwestern congressman, Lyndon Johnson of Texas. Anderson became a member of Rayburn's inner circle, regularly stopping by in Room 9 of the Capitol's House wing, the exclusive "Board of Education," after a daily House session for a round of bridge or poker and drinks with the Speaker's proteges. Anderson carefully noted Rayburn's ability to remember political favors as well as political slights. He observed, "When the opportunity arrived for settling a score, he would settle it fairly and squarely."[28]

In 1942, as a result of the Census redistricting, New Mexico added a second at-large seat in the House of Representatives. This brought out a large field of contenders in the Democratic primary, but Anderson, who had earlier abandoned plans to be a one-term member, easily retained his right to run in the general election, outpolling his nearest rival by a two-to-one margin. Like others before him, Anderson had succumbed to "Potomac Fever." Unable to enlist for wartime military service because of his chronically poor health, Anderson viewed congressional service as a suitable alternative. Following his 1942 reelection, the New Mexico representative received a coveted assignment to the powerful House Appropriations Committee.

In 1943, Anderson gained national prominence through his campaign to guarantee absentee ballots to all military personnel. The House Rules Committee, actively hostile to the Roosevelt administration, believed that such a move would only serve to inflate the number of votes in 1944 for the commander-in-chief. Eventually Anderson forced consideration by the full House on the committee's delaying tactics, but he lost by a 233–160 margin.

A year later, following the 1944 spring primaries, Rayburn appointed Anderson to chair a special committee to investigate campaign spending irregularities. There he found himself in a crossfire between supporters of three conservative congressmen who had been defeated with the help of funds from the Congress of Industrial Organization's (CIO) Political Action Committee and, on the other side, from liberal members with similar charges against the right-wing Committee for Constitutional Government. Anderson conducted the inquiry with fairness and firm determination not to allow it to serve partisan purposes.[29]

In 1943 and early 1944 the New Mexico press speculated that Anderson would give up his House seat to challenge John Dempsey for a second term as governor. Dempsey had incurred widespread wrath among New Mexico citizens for his decision to send the entire state National Guard regiment to the Philippines because its members were fluent in Spanish. In April 1942 the 200th and the 515th Coastal Anti-aircraft Artillery regiments took enormous casualties when the Bataan peninsula fell to the Japanese. Local political observers believed that Anderson intended to use the governor's chair as a platform from which to challenge Dennis Chavez in 1946 for his U.S. Senate seat. Anderson fueled speculation by selling his Maryland home and shipping his riding horses back to New Mexico.

By April 1944 Anderson ended this uncertainty by filing for reelection to the House and announcing his support of Dempsey for a second term. Anderson reportedly believed that his continued presence on the ticket would shore up Roosevelt's sagging prospects for securing New Mexico's electoral votes.[30] In November Anderson easily out distanced all rivals, coasting to a third term victory. Nonetheless, by the beginning of 1945, Anderson's associates recognized that he had lost his fire for continued service in the House.

In recognition of the independence that accompanied Anderson's limited ambitions for advancement within the House, and recalling his successful chairmanship of the campaign expenditures investigating committee, Speaker Rayburn named him to head a House investigation of wartime food shortages. In this capacity, Anderson gained immediate national recognition as he launched a series of hard hitting hearings in major cities across the country. His panel found evidence of extensive violation of meat pricing and rationing regulations. The committee, in reports on meat and sugar shortages, recommended production incentives, increased storage facilities, and federal administrative restructuring.[31]

During the course of the Anderson food inquiry, on April 12, 1945, President Roosevelt succumbed to a cerebral hemorrhage, and Harry Truman moved to the White House. Within seven weeks of his accession, Truman acted to place his own stamp on executive branch operations. In mid-May, the chief executive requested the resignations of Labor Secretary Frances Perkins, Attorney General Francis Biddle, and Agriculture Secretary Claude Wickard. In one sweep, Truman shifted the geographical balance of his cabinet, replacing these predominately eastern members with Lewis Schwellenbach of Washington for Labor, Tom Clark of Texas for Attorney General, and Clinton Anderson of New Mexico for Agriculture.

Anderson expressed complete surprise at his own appointment.

He had gone to a May 23, 1945, White House meeting with the president "expecting to get romped on" as a result of his committee's criticisms of administration food policies. While the *Washington Post* speculated that Anderson's appointment served as a vehicle for reorienting the administration food policies that his committee had attacked, others in Washington shared Anderson's surprise, noting that his agricultural experience consisted of his brief service on the food inquiry committee, operation of a dairy farm in Albuquerque, and ownership of a grain farm in South Dakota. The *Chicago Tribune* reported that his friends in New Mexico described the new secretary as "genial and hearty, amiable with the ladies but primarily a man's man."

Columnist Will Harrison of the *Santa Fe New Mexican* had observed Anderson carefully over the years. He aptly commented, "Although the appointment makes one wonder what President Truman was thinking about, it is a pretty good bet that Anderson will get along all right in the cabinet. He is a good executive in utilizing the knowledge and energy of others and he knows where to apply his charm to make it produce the greatest benefit. He has no political label, being a conservative, a liberal, or a New Dealer as the occasion demands."[32]

The president, however, thought that Anderson's business acumen and his decisive investigative style were exactly what was needed in the Agriculture department. The two men had become acquainted several years earlier during Truman's Senate service. Both were active in local Masonic affairs and, as devotees of gin rummy and poker, had sized each other up on numerous occasions around the card table. In accepting the president's offer on the spot, the man whom Assistant Secretary of State Dean Acheson called "the nice congressman from New Mexico" became the first person from an irrigation farming region to be Agriculture secretary and the first cabinet member directly appointed from the House since 1918.[33]

Anderson's three years in the Department of Agriculture proved to be stormy. His credentials as a successful businessman and poker partner of the president were stronger than his skills for administering a sprawling bureaucracy or his expertise in agricultural policy. As he moved to the department's helm in the summer of 1945, with plans for curbing wartime production to preserve farmers' price levels, a serious wheat crisis was brewing. Over the following six months, a 19 million ton wheat surplus simply disappeared as farmers responded to meat shortages by feeding grain to their animals rather than selling it at depressed prices. Meanwhile, war torn Europe rolled ominously toward famine. By mid-1946, after periods of indecision and frantic experimentation, Anderson's department broke the European famine's grip by arranging for overseas shipment of one in every six pounds of the nation's food supply.[34]

His department's chronic inefficiency spurred Anderson to prepare a reorganization plan that in turn brought enraged protests from farmers and consumers as well as agency bureaucrats. Although effective timing was to become one of Anderson's most distinguishing legislative traits, he failed to exercise it in this instance. He acted on the eve of the 1946 midterm congressional elections when severe meat shortages and the removal of price controls without concurrent lifting of wage restraints strengthened Republican protests. Although Truman ignored intensifying calls for Anderson's ouster, he suspended his secretary's plan, leaving both men embarrassed and angry. To make matters worse, the November election, in which farm issues played a major role, gave Republicans control of both houses of Congress for the first time since 1931 and served as a clear repudiation of the outspoken new president's stewardship.[35]

Anderson's leadership of the department moved into calmer waters after the 1946 election. Although he was tiring of the position's burdensome demands and recognized its threat to his precarious health, he agreed to remain until the end of Truman's term in 1948. During 1947 and 1948 he served an important political role by traveling throughout the nation touting the administration's contributions to agricultural prosperity and seeking to keep agriculture from becoming the volatile issue it had been in the 1946 campaign.[36]

Early in 1948 the political situation in New Mexico forced Anderson to reconsider his promise to remain in the cabinet through the November elections. Senator Carl Hatch, veteran of nearly fifteen years in the upper chamber, learned in February that there would soon be a vacancy on the federal bench in Albuquerque. His deteriorating health and the attractions of his state's more favorable climate convinced Hatch to ask his old friend the president for nomination to the post. When Truman questioned Hatch about which of New Mexico's Democrats would pursue the party's Senate nomination, Hatch responded that he thought Anderson would be the strongest candidate. The president reacted sharply. He feared that the public would construe Anderson's departure as further confirmation that cabinet members were abandoning his ailing administration.[37]

Hatch had obtained assurances from other potential Democratic contenders that they would not challenge Anderson if he decided to enter the primary. This was designed to sweeten the proposition for Anderson, allowing him to remain in his cabinet post through mid-summer while avoiding the demands on his health of a contested race. On March 11, 1948, in response to rumors of Anderson's planned departure, the president told a press conference that he hoped the secretary would remain. The following day the New Mexican went to the White House to assure Truman that he would not enter the primary. As he left the president's office, however, Anderson received a phone call from Leslie Biffle, secretary to the Senate's Democrats and the chief executive's leading congressional strategist. Biffle told him that the party's Senate leadership wanted him to enter the race as part of a plan to select strong candidates to ensure return of the Senate to Democratic control regardless of how the Truman candidacy fared. Anderson put down the phone and asked the president's advice. According to the New Mexican's account, Truman experienced a change of heart and said, "Oh, why don't you go on and run? You would like the Senate—it is the best job in the world. You have worn yourself out working for me, and if you want to run, go on and run." Anderson considered the situation overnight and announced his candidacy the following day.[38]

Contrary to Hatch's optimistic assurances, Anderson found himself locked in a bitter primary battle with his old party foe, former Representative and Governor John Dempsey. He had hoped to conserve his energies for the general election battle against Republican Patrick Hurley, secretary of war in the Hoover administration and unsuccessful contender against Dennis Chavez in the 1946 Senate race. Anderson resigned from the cabinet on May 7 and defeated Dempsey by a three-to-two margin in the June 9 primary.[39]

Hurley enjoyed unusually strong support from the national Republican party and was confident of capturing the White House and continuing its control of Congress. During most of the race, however, Anderson considered his own prospects of victory to be excellent. The suave and facile Hurley left a generally favorable initial impression with his audiences. Anderson believed, however, that image would dissolve as the campaign intensified. He considered Hurley, an Oklahoma native, ill prepared to offer constructive solutions to New Mexico's problems.

Hurley charged that, as agriculture secretary, Anderson was to blame for the conservation policies of the forestry, soil conservation, and grazing services that restricted grazing to the point that cattle ranchers and sheep farmers could no longer earn a fair living. Anderson regarded that charge as campaign rhetoric, noting that, if elected, Hurley would be lucky to extract from the Agriculture Department grazing permits for even one hundred additional head of livestock. He remained confident that the majority of New Mexico's voters sympathized with the need for grazing controls rather than the policies of depletion that his opponent seemed to espouse.[40]

The aging Hurley lived up to Anderson's expectations of ineptitude. At one point in the campaign he attempted to convert a Mississippi land development plan to New Mexico's needs and pass it off as an original proposal. After blanketing the state with a descriptive brochure, Hurley discovered to his horror that his campaign staff had neglected to delete references to harbor construction from the Mississippi document. Anderson took great delight in touring the driest areas of his landlocked state and pointing to implausible sites for Hurley's docks and shipping canals. Anderson also paid individuals to infiltrate Hurley's rallies to shout, "Tell us about Yalta." Hurley's favorite theme was that the United States had sold out to communism at the 1945 Yalta Conference and he would respond with delight, using his allotted time to discourse on foreign policy matters of little interest to New Mexico voters. Anderson also managed to rebut Hurley's charges that he had violated a federal statute prohibiting use of government employees for campaign purposes.[41]

As election day dawned, many New Mexico observers saw the Anderson-Hurley race as too close to call. The state's newspapers had supported Hurley on the assumption that Republican Thomas Dewey would capture the White House. They reasoned that the state should have at least one senator of the president's party. Some journalists also expressed irritation with what they perceived to be Anderson's patrician attitude that he could simply have the Senate seat for the asking. On his own behalf, Anderson turned for editorial support to syndicated columnist Drew Pearson, risking inevitable charges of outside meddling in internal political matters. Another nationally syndicated writer, Walter Lippmann, defended Anderson's claim to the seat, arguing that a Democratic senator would work more effectively with Dewey than Republican Hurley. On November 2, 1948, unseasonably mild weather and a heated campaign produced a record voter turnout across New Mexico. Although Anderson had earlier advised a friend that "no one but a fool would bet that he would win by more than 15,000 votes," he triumphantly amassed nearly double that number.[42]

Within several days of his election, Clinton Anderson returned to Washington. From temporary quarters in the Department of Agriculture library, he began the crucial process of staff selection. The senator-elect possessed an instinctive ability to recognize competent people, and he made outstanding choices. Stability, loyalty, and efficiency were characteristics that most senators hoped to build in their staff, but few matched Anderson's ultimate success.

For guidance in the Senate's peculiar folkways, he retained Carl Hatch's personal secretary, Virginia Flanary. For personal administrative continuity, he brought with him from the Agriculture Department Luna Diamond, a highly efficient secretary who had also served on his House staff. Completing the secretarial force was Eloise de la O, a native of Lordsburg in southwestern New Mexico. Hired in November 1948 and paid out of Anderson's personal funds until his office allowance began in January, she set to work to answer the growing pile of congratulatory mail. She quickly impressed Anderson with her ability to take his dictation accurately. Within two weeks the skills acquired over fifteen years of government service placed her in second position among his clerical staff. She became his personal secretary and remained his entire twenty-four-year Senate career.[43]

Shortly after the election, Anderson turned his attention to recruiting a chief administrative aide. While lying in bed late one night, he decided on a particularly suitable candidate. Anderson had known Claude Wood for more than two decades. The son of a southwestern New Mexico goat rancher, Wood had become an expert in the highly charged issues of that state's land development and had served as chief clerk of the New Mexico Board of Land Commissioners. In the 1948 primary election, Wood narrowly lost a race for the influential post of public land commissioner. Anderson respected Wood's valiant efforts in the face of overwhelming opposition from the Democratic party's Chavez faction.[44]

The senator-elect summoned Wood to his Albuquerque insurance office and went to great lengths to assure him that he and his family would enjoy life in the nation's capital. He told Wood that he intended only to serve a single six-year term and, on its conclusion, he would help reestablish him in the insurance business. The former agriculture secretary then asked Wood to accompany him to a meeting of federal officials representing the Forest Service, the Soil Conservation Service, and the Indian Bureau. There they discussed plans to establish a forest research station at the University of New Mexico and the need to relieve unemployment among the state's Indian population. As the session concluded, Anderson turned to Wood and said, "Claude, I asked you to sit in on this meeting because this is the type of thing I would want you to work on. You understand the land business and you know what it means to take care of these resources. I hope that we could have a program developed to see that New Mexico makes full use of its water and other natural resources, but they must be protected by conservation and reasonable use." Wood agreed and reported for work on January 3, 1949. He retired with Anderson on January 2, 1973.[45]

Initially, Wood and the other new staff members found Anderson to be a difficult taskmaster. Like other senators of his generation, he expected their round-the-clock commitment. This included predawn calls for airport transportation and requests to run personal errands. The new senator expected his workers to remain in the office as long as necessary each day to satisfy legislative and constituency demands. That schedule often extended to Saturdays, Sunday afternoons and holidays. Suspecting that his staff was not working up to standards of the general federal workforce, Anderson once directed Wood to obtain a copy of the appropriate civil service regulations. When Wood informed him of the nine-to-five, five-day-a-week norm, the senator sheepishly told him to leave the office schedule as it was. Anderson also considered coffee breaks to be a serious encroachment on office efficiency. Shortly after becoming secretary of agriculture, he had encountered a long line of employees waiting at a window to buy coffee for their morning break. Immediately, he decreed an end to that custom, suggesting that each office install its own coffeepot. New members of Anderson's Senate staff quickly learned to forego the ritual visit to the

Office Building cafeteria, a site of useful, but time-consuming social interaction. Even within the office, trouble soon developed over
the use of the coffeepot. When staff began to leave dirty cups on
their desks and forget to turn off and clean the pot at day's end, the
senator quickly had it removed.[46]

Anderson took no vacation other than his four yearly trips to New
Mexico during congressional recesses. While there, he plunged into
the details of local constituent case work, ignoring veiled staff suggestions that he spend at least the first day of his stay resting at his
farm in Albuquerque's South Valley. No matter how ill or exhausted
he became in Washington, a journey to New Mexico and time with
his family brought a resurgence of Anderson's seemingly limitless
stamina.[47]

In the early Senate months, Anderson tended to play off staff members against each other, occasionally assigning a single project to
several key individuals. In determining staff salaries, the senator displayed the deliberation common to those whose personal wealth
was of their own making. He routinely compared notes with Senate colleagues Robert Kerr (D-OK) and Earle Clements (D-KY)—
men whom some considered to be notorious "tightwads." He set
salaries and working hours according to individual personal situations, favoring men with families above others. Once he told an
aide who had just transferred to Washington from Albuquerque that
she should compute her additional living costs and he would raise
her salary accordingly. The strong-willed assistant retorted that she
wished to be paid on merit and not for what she spent on
"toothpaste."[48]

Despite Anderson's efforts at frugality and his often gruff manner, his staff grew to regard him as essentially softhearted and, in
matters of genuine merit, uncommonly generous. On one occasion
he asked Edward Triviz, a former Hatch staffer who was studying
for a graduate degree while working in Anderson's office, to prepare a report by the next day. Triviz hurried to the Library of Congress just as it was closing for the evening. He convinced a library
aide to allow him to work after hours, and he stayed into the early
morning hours. After getting a brief rest, Triviz arrived in the office
and triumphantly presented the completed report to Anderson. The
senator glanced at him, nodded, and casually dropped the document onto a pile of correspondence. Triviz exploded with rage. He
stormed out of the office and resigned. Stunned, Anderson called

him and, with a display of affection, apologized. Triviz accepted the apology and returned.[49]

Near the end of Anderson's Senate career, another aide described him as "very emotional, very sensitive, a man who has compassion for human beings but no patience with irresponsibility."[50] Staff member Richard Pino, assigned to the Albuquerque office, fully experienced that trait in 1953 when he failed to transmit an urgently needed report to Anderson in Washington as quickly as the senator believed he should have. On learning that his boss was furious at the delay, Pino raced to the Albuquerque Post Office. There, he retrieved the just-mailed document and headed for the airport and a night flight to Washington. On his arrival, other staff told Pino that the senator intended to fire him for his irresponsibility. A forthright man, Pino decided to confront the senator, and he set out to deliver the document in person to Anderson at a meeting of the Senate Agriculture Committee.

Pino walked up to Anderson, who had stopped in mid-sentence, and thrust the report before him. Pino's impertinence infuriated the senator, but he pretended to take no notice of him. On returning to his office, Anderson told his secretary to obtain Pino's airline ticket receipt so that he could be reimbursed and fired. Pino refused to surrender the receipt to anyone but the senator. For the next three days, Pino later recalled, the two men played a cat-and-mouse game. Anderson went out of his way to avoid Pino, slipping in and out of his private office through a separate entrance. When a secretary approached Pino in tears, begging him to turn over the ticket to end the unpleasant standoff, he refused. Finally, on a quiet Saturday afternoon, the men met. Pino explained his side of the story and Anderson relented. Pino suspected that his boss' ill feelings persisted. Another four months passed before the senator and his aide cleared the air. Anderson told him, "I expected you to take responsibility."[51]

As an effective administrative assistant, Claude Wood served as mediator and Anderson surrogate. Junior to Anderson by eleven years, Wood possessed a no-nonsense demeanor that made him seem older and brought respect from staff and outsiders. Wood shared Anderson's sense of frugality. His abstinence from alcohol permitted him to push ahead with office tasks into the early evening while the senator and other aides paused to unwind over a scotch or two. Once a host offered Wood a drink in Anderson's presence. The senator, considering the business implications of the cocktail hour jokingly retorted, "I do the drinking for the office."[52]

Wood learned to anticipate Anderson's needs and attitudes. He became skilled at planting ideas with the senator despite the latter's justifiably strong resentment of staff efforts to guide his actions. Wood made his suggestions in a nondirective manner. One of his favorite approaches was to ask in a memo whether Anderson wanted to consider a particular matter. Wood added that if the senator was interested, he would get to work on it. Or he would take an even more successful negative approach, saying, "You probably do not want to do anything about this, but I just wanted you to know it was brought to my attention."[53]

Anderson was at his best when he permitted a staffer to work out the details of a proposal while he stood ready to suggest persons who might help overcome a particular problem, or to make helpful telephone calls. At the beginning, Anderson assumed that his staff knew as many people in Washington's executive branch bureaucracy as he did. Often, he would suggest as helpful sources prominent officials that Wood and others new to the city had never heard of. With equal frequency, staff found these officials, willing to accommodate Anderson personally, were not always the most appropriate references for a particular substantive problem. Gradually, the small staff developed its own routine contacts, but always with the realization that they would not have gotten to first base with most agencies without Clinton Anderson standing behind them. In his own dealings with outsiders, Anderson had a successful businessman's ability to look for the hidden agenda and to recognize ulterior motives that his staff would have missed.[54]

A difficult taskmaster within the office, Anderson displayed great charm and finesse to friends, lobbyists, and constituents on the outside. His large physical stature, broad smile, and friendly manner made him widely popular. From the back rooms of the state legislature to the Rotary Clubs of the world, he had developed an impressive array of effective political and social skills. On the arrival of an important visitor to his Senate office, Anderson made a practice of spending several intense minutes with the guest. Then he summoned Claude Wood, correctly assuring the visitor that his top aide would give the matter at hand his careful attention and would keep Anderson closely informed of developments. Unwilling to commit himself to a course of action on the spot, Anderson was able to make even nominal subsequent actions appear to be the product of special and dedicated effort.[55]

When discussing substantive matters on the phone, Anderson always had a secretary monitor the conversation. When a question was raised that required additional information, the secretary would make the necessary call while the senator continued the conversation. Often the secretary was able to report back to the senator in time for him to convey the information to the caller and take appropriate action.[56]

A similar approach guided Anderson's highly successful constituent service operation in his Albuquerque office, under the direction of Lorella Montoya, the sharp-witted and plain-spoken sister of New Mexico's lieutenant governor and later U.S. senator, Joseph Montoya. Visitors to the Anderson office in the downtown Federal Building would generally find a line of constituents awaiting Montoya's attention. She sought to handle as many cases as possible on the spot to minimize subsequent calls and correspondence. While the constituent waited, she would call the appropriate federal agency with a summary of the particular grievance. Over the years she had developed an ability to listen to a case and tell instantly where the weak points were and how it could be most effectively presented. Even in marginal cases, her attitude was to give it a try, as it was "better for the agency to laugh at us than for us to laugh at the constituent." She customarily asked agency representatives to send the constituent a follow up letter with a copy to the Anderson office. Then she would instruct the grateful constituent to call her if the agency failed to respond.[57]

Once Anderson offhandedly asked Montoya what she did all day. She answered that it was difficult to be specific, but that she certainly spent a lot of time on the phone. Reflecting on his question, Montoya became angry at what she perceived to be its insinuation. On the following day, she presented the senator with a detailed list of incoming calls. Surprised and defensive at her forthright response, Anderson sheepishly inquired, "Am I not allowed to make a mistake?"[58]

In his legislative dealings, Anderson made few mistakes of consequence. When he entered the Senate in 1949, he was fifty-three years old. Far from a novice in public life, he had developed a profound understanding of the operation of the American governmental system. Unlike younger and less seasoned colleagues, Anderson was not bound by fears of a fickle constituency. Independently wealthy and in unstable health, he could easily have yielded to his wife's urging to forsake Washington for the quieter life of horse-back riding and cattle raising at his Albuquerque farm. For his en-tire twenty-four-year Senate career, his electoral base was secure. Enormously popular, virtually an institution within New Mexico, Anderson deftly adjusted his style to fit a diversity of audiences. To the farmer, he was a former secretary of agriculture. To the small businessman, not only was he a self-made millionaire, but also a former president of Rotary International. To liberals, he had been a New Deal relief administrator. Displaying a politician's flair for being all things to all people, Anderson once described his broad experi-ence with organized religion as follows. "I was born of Lutheran parents, baptised by immersion to become a Baptist, exposed to education in a Methodist college, married to a Congregational girl by an Episcopal rector and we and our children are Presbyterians."[59] His charming, witty manner created a lasting favorable impression on constituents and congressional colleagues alike.

The Senate freed Anderson from the cabinet's daily administra-tive and political rigors, while offering him an elevated platform to develop as a regional and national spokesman for issues that he judged vital. He used that platform effectively, selecting his issues carefully, and pursuing them with quiet determination. At the 1948 Democratic National Convention, he turned aside budding efforts to draft him as the vice presidential nominee to pursue the Senate seat for which he had just received his party's nomination. Later he observed, "I don't have very good health, and I try to take easier jobs than I otherwise would. I have wanted to have membership in the United States Senate for a long, long time, as a boy almost."[60]

In the Senate, Anderson earned his colleagues' respect for his intellect, experience and legislative style. He resembled Lyndon Johnson, his companion in the Senate class of 1948, in his ability to set up issues in such a way that other senators found it difficult to vote against him. His command of topics that interested him in-spired committee aides to hours of careful preparation before brief-ing him. They knew he was capable of absorbing complex new information quickly and recalling it in proper context weeks later. He was generally ahead of staff experts on subjects of major inter-est, maintaining that lead by taking home bulging briefcases of ma-terial that he rose early in the morning to read.[61]

Unlike Senate classmates Lyndon Johnson and Robert Kerr, Anderson displayed little interest in acquiring power for its own sake. A master legislative mechanic, he possessed an inner confidence and an understanding of his range of options that permitted him to use available power constructively. He had the rare ability to conserve his shots and mediate positions that appeared irreconcilable. When mediation failed, he deftly applied pressure. He never hesitated to call on a vast network of peers and subordinates to move a worthwhile proposal that he believed had been studied sufficiently. Whether the objective was crucial legislation or a friend's request to have a son admitted to law school despite marginal credentials, Anderson adroitly pulled the strings of senatorial influence.[62]

Anderson took enormous pride in his own intellectual capacity and his breadth of experience. He owed his financial and legislative achievements to his ability to apply those gifts to changing conditions. He remained open to new information, soaking up its essence and discarding the peripheral. When he encountered those whom he believed where lying or deliberately trying to mislead him, a darker side of his character emerged. Under such circumstances, he became petty and vindictive, following Speaker Rayburn's teachings of tenacity in pursuit of settling old scores.

Although he referred to himself in his memoirs as an "Outsider in the Senate," by 1961 Anderson was very much a member of the Senate's "inner club."[63] At the beginning of his Senate career, there was some justification for his feeling of exclusion. In 1951, 1953, and 1957, he led campaigns to liberalize that body's famed cloture rule governing the size of the majority necessary to cut off filibusters, the favorite tactic of members opposed to civil rights legislation. For this, the southern-dominated party leadership excluded him from a desired seat on the Democratic Policy Committee and until 1956, a place on the Finance Committee. By 1961, Anderson was an outsider only in the sense of his customary independence. He was by no means a maverick or an outcast.

Anderson's legislative resourcefulness appeared most forcefully in committee hearings and subsequent sessions to markup or redraft legislation. There, as a well-briefed member and, after the mid 1950s as chairman of the Interior Committee's Reclamation subcommittee, he kept deliberations within his intellectual and procedural grasp. One veteran observer referred to Anderson's committee style as the "old lion syndrome." He would permit the other "lions" on the committee to frolic and spar for a while, but when he called a halt, they listened and complied.[64] He loved to sandbag hostile witnesses, leading them along a sympathetic line of questioning only to deliver the fatal query when their defenses had been cast aside. He grew particularly irritated when lawyers tried to suggest that there was an immutable legal reason to follow a desired course when in fact the only barrier to contrary action, in his judgment, was prevailing policy. He never tired of reminding opponents of the distinction between the small body of law that had a constitutional base and the much larger volume of statutes that were policy based.[65]

In the vital markup sessions that followed committee hearings, Anderson was at his most effective. His command of issues and his engaging personality often served to convince less well prepared members of the merit of his position. Yet, as chairman, he remained scrupulously fair, striving to protect the rights of other members, even against their own ineptitude. After one particularly tumultuous session, Senator Ernest Gruening (D-AK) approached Anderson to ask whether, in the confusion, his own amendment had survived. Anderson viewed the Alaskan as a whiner and testily responded, "If you don't know, you don't need it."[66] The amendment had survived and, despite the chairman's instinctive wish to punish Gruening's inattentiveness by dropping it from the subsequent committee report, he retained the desired language.

On the Senate floor, Anderson exercised his effectiveness through careful preparation and quiet conversation with potential adversaries, rather than with frequent and longwinded speeches. He spoke only rarely, but when he did, other members paid more than customary attention. When presenting a committee-approved bill, Anderson schooled himself in arguments likely to build consensus among wavering colleagues. In 1959, for example, he demonstrated masterful advance preparation in setting forth the case for a home state water diversion project from a variety of alluring perspectives. They included an appeal to congressional prerogatives, Democratic hostility toward the Republican administration's program, the nation's obligations to its exploited Indians, demands of national security, and an altruistic sense that the bill's value transcended the mere interests of New Mexico.[67]

On another occasion, he presented a tightly constructed case for a measure to provide water research centers in every state of the nation. After describing the crisis in compelling terms, he laid out his proposed solution. His remedy had the endorsement of two prestigious federal research panels, a select Senate study group, and the test of three quarters of a century's experience for the program from which it was copied. To make the proposal even more palatable, Anderson documented its relatively modest cost and its design to draw largely from existing resources.[68]

Throughout Clinton Anderson's Senate career, he displayed characteristics of balance and perspective that came to few legislators. With a sharp eye on New Mexico's needs, this unusually complex man never lost sight of the broader national agenda for natural resources conservation. In effectively advancing the nation's interests, he created an environment in which his state could also flourish. The 1963 National Conservation Award confirmed the singularity of this achievement.

# 2

## Setting the Stage
### The Eighty-First Congress, 1949–1951

I am not particular as to which person picks our pocket, but I just want to be sure you realize we understand we are about to have it picked.

Clinton P. Anderson
March 23, 1949

Time, experience, and long study of the United States have taught me how valuable courage and integrity are in public office, and how rarely we get public officials with so much of both as you. It would be of great satisfaction to me if an occasion should arise when my pen could be of service to you. If one ever does, a word from you will instantly adjourn whatever I may be doing.

Bernard DeVoto to Anderson
October 19, 1950

Writing from Washington late in 1949, at the end of Clinton Anderson's first year in the Senate, Texas newswoman Sarah McClendon reported that the junior senator from New Mexico's record of accomplishment was "nothing short of phenomenal." Observing that his somewhat unorthodox manner "frequently gets him in dutch momentarily" with his colleagues, she attested to his effectiveness and praised his personal legislative agenda as being "as broad as the nation." In her view, "Clinton Anderson looms as presidential or vice presidential material." She continued, "You can write that down in your books now. The Anderson boom is on."[1]

Natural resources policy ranked high on Anderson's personal legislative agenda from the very start of his Senate career. During his first two years in the upper chamber, the period of the 81st Congress from January 1949 through January 1951, he established positions on issues including reclamation project funding, Colorado River Basin development, Navajo Indian water rights, and protection of forests and parklands. Anderson's previous congressional and cabinet experience combined with his personal leadership skills and a postwar climate decidedly favorable to a thoroughgoing reevaluation of natural resources policy quickly propelled him to a position justifying Sarah McClendon's hearty assessment.

Eight years had brought many changes to the structure and outlook of the United States Congress and to the legislative stature of Clinton Presba Anderson. Back in January 1941, as he took his oath as a freshman member of the House of Representatives, Anderson found himself virtually unknown and without a trace of power among his 434 colleagues. As the flames of war engulfed Europe, Congress focused almost exclusively on the nature of the country's likely involvement in that rapidly expanding conflict. The administration of Franklin Roosevelt and an opposing coalition of conservative southern legislators firmly controlled the congressional agenda.

By contrast, in January 1949 the war had ended and winds of change stirred through both legislative chambers. Long weary of executive branch domination, congressional leaders had sanctioned major structural reforms under the provisions of the 1946 Legislative Reorganization Act. That statute provided expanded staff expertise and improved political party apparatus to both houses of Congress to deal more constructively with the burgeoning array of policy issues confronting postwar America.

Clinton Anderson entered this promising environment, at the age of fifty-three, in the company of one of the most remarkable freshman classes in the Senate's modern history. His new colleagues included Hubert Humphrey, the crusading Minneapolis mayor; Paul Douglas, the liberal economist from the University of Chicago; Robert Kerr, the millionaire former Oklahoma governor; Tennessee progressive Estes Kefauver; Maine's Margaret Chase Smith; Russell Long, the thirty-year-old son of Huey Long; and Texas's Lyndon Baines Johnson. With the exception of Johnson, whose eighty-seven-vote margin clouded his claim to victory, most of the fourteen Democrats among the Senate's eighteen new members had significantly outpolled President Harry Truman in their respective states. Truman's razor-thin victory led many in Congress to attribute his election to his opponent's inept campaigning rather than as a mandate for continuation of administration policies. Columnists Roland Evans and Robert Novak later observed that the Senate class of 1948, "perhaps the most publicized band of freshmen in Senate history," consisted of "independent personalities whose ambitions, idiosyncracies and rivalries were to shape the history of the Senate and the nation for the next decade." The Senate of 1949, with a party ratio of fifty-four Democrats to forty-two Republicans contained nine more Democrats than in the Republican-controlled Senate of 1947. Among its members were twenty-six former House members and twenty-six former governors. Solidly in Democratic control, with fresh and tested new troops who enjoyed the independence of their six-year terms, the Senate of 1949 was positioned to assume a vital policy leadership role.[2]

Shortly after taking his Senate oath, Anderson received assignments to the committees on Agriculture and Interior— constituency-oriented panels with jurisdiction vital to New Mexico's interests. From his position on these committees, the new senator sharpened his skills to devise legislative solutions to his state's problems of natural resources conservation while casting those solutions in the context of broader national interest. A review of his strategies and achievements during the 1949 and 1950 congressional sessions sets the stage for an evaluation of his expanded efforts, during the following decade and a half, to devise effective and enduring resources policy legislation.

During Anderson's first month in the Senate, postwar conservation policies fell under the scrutiny of three separate and powerful federal authorities. They included the blue ribbon Hoover Commission on Executive Organization, a joint congressional panel consisting of members of the House and Senate Interior committees, and the president of the United States. Each authority found these policies and their supporting structures in need of fundamental overhaul.

Early in 1949, the study commission under the direction of former President Herbert Hoover was completing a two-year review of the executive branch's organizational structure. Creation of a cabinet-level Department of Natural Resources ranked near the top of the commission's pending recommendations. That panel's members believed that such an agency would significantly reduce bitter and crippling competition among government resources bureaus.[3]

A second initiative was launched on January 5, 1949, when President Truman, in his annual State of the Union address, called for imaginative new federal programs to ensure wise and timely use of the nation's land, water, and mineral resources. Asserting that "the task of conservation is not to lock up our resources, but to develop and improve them," the president placed his administration in the camp of those within the American conservation movement who advocated a utilitarian or "wise use" approach to natural resources policy.[4]

The third and most significant conservation policy review of 1949 began on January 31. As western states staggered under the weight of severe winter snow storms that threatened disastrous spring flooding in the southwest, senators, representatives, and senior officials from the Interior Department gathered in the splendidly ornate Caucus Room of the Senate Office Building. In that formal setting, they launched an unprecedented inquiry into the bases for "an improved policy for the conservation, development and administration of the natural resources of the United States." Under the chairmanship of Wyoming senator Joseph O'Mahoney (D), the joint panel took up the challenges embodied in the Hoover and Truman reports.[5]

On that winter morning the prospect of flooding in New Mexico along the Rio Grande undoubtedly troubled Anderson. The danger was particularly acute in Albuquerque, where the river bed lay at an elevation above the surrounding terrain and where sand levees proved of marginal value against the river's sustained pounding.[6] This unwelcome water surplus, combined with its predictable shortage during the late spring and summer growing months, further strengthened Anderson's belief in the federal government as the only practical agent of relief and redirection. The Interior Committee's joint hearings reflected Congress' desire to begin a fundamental reevaluation of existing executive agency conservation programs in order to eliminate the ineffective and reinforce those with records of solid accomplishment.

The committee's review began with testimony from Interior Secretary Julius "Cap" Krug. Krug had taken over the department's reins following the celebrated resignation in February 1946 of Harold Ickes, who had held the post since the beginning of the Franklin Roosevelt administration thirteen years earlier. A protegé of Bernard Baruch and David Lilienthal, Krug served in the 1930s as chief engineer of the Tennessee Valley Authority and in the mid-1940s as chairman of the War Production Board. Considered "able but indolent," the secretary had been a close friend of Anderson's during the time of their joint service in the Truman cabinet. Somber hues predominated in the picture Krug painted for the joint panel. Seeing "no basis for complacency" in the condition of the nation's natural resources development, he spoke of forest harvesting practices that removed timber at twice its natural restorative capacity while leaving behind as waste one third of the available supply. Krug documented the squandering of the nation's electric power generating capacity and of nonrenewable coal, oil, and gas supplies. He called for a concerted program to harness the country's major rivers to bring in vitally needed new supplies of electricity. Turning to reclamation of the nation's arid lands, the secretary reported that half the range lands of the West required extensive revegetation. He estimated that development of the Colorado, Rio Grande, Columbia, and Missouri river basins would add 17 million acres of land to productive use and supplemental water supplies would increase crop yields on another 9 million.[7]

The success of developmental programs within and between river basins depended largely on the leadership of the Interior Department's Bureau of Reclamation. In 1949, of that department's ten divisions, the Reclamation Bureau commanded the largest budget and its 17,800 employees made up nearly one third of the Interior's total workforce.[8] Following the testimony of Secretary Krug, Reclamation Commissioner Michael Straus explained to the panel a major shift in the focus of his agency's objectives. Straus, a former Chicago newspaperman, had served during the 1930s as publicist for Secretary Ickes. In 1946 he gave up his position as assistant secretary of interior to take over as chief of the Reclamation Bureau. One associate observed that Straus was "principally interested in obtaining work and jurisdiction and is not greatly interested in the social and economic problems." Under his leadership, the bureau took on a spirit of unbridled ambition. In that spirit, he reported to the joint congressional committee that "nearly all the simple, low cost irrigation projects have now been developed." In the face of the West's rapid population growth, and the resulting necessity for continuing water resources development, Straus proclaimed that a new era was at hand. He asserted that future reclamation projects would be characterized by their vastness, expense, and multiplicity of functions.[9]

Straus urged Congress to shift its frame of reference from individual projects to the broader "basin wide" concept. Beyond harnessing water for irrigation and power supply purposes, the Reclamation Bureau henceforth would need to consider additional uses including flood control, municipal water supply, silt control, saline repulsion, as well as recreation and protection of fish and wildlife development.[10] Straus also advocated a rethinking of the means of financing these larger projects. Under the emerging basin wide concept, a project's feasibility no longer ought to be judged strictly on its individual merits, but rather on its contribution to the larger system. Within a single system, projects designed to generate power would produce revenues from the sale of that power to finance smaller associated projects providing only irrigation water.[11]

Clinton Anderson listened sympathetically as Straus advocated revision of the forty-seven-year-old system of project cost allocation in recognition of the shift to enormously expensive multipurpose projects. At that time, the direct beneficiaries of a project's water and power resources shouldered the principal burden of its costs. The federal government stepped in only to assume such "nonreimbursable" expenses as flood control and navigation improvement where the benefit clearly accrued to the public at large. Considering the tremendous costs of systems such as those designed to transfer water as far as 450 miles across the Continental Divide, Straus sought ways to distribute the financial burden more broadly. He recommended inclusion, among the costs that the federal government might assume, of fish and wildlife development, recreation, salinity abatement, and silt control.[12]

Anderson had a businessman's appreciation for the value of effective cost accounting. He also had a politician's understanding that his home state's need for such expensive water projects greatly exceeded users' ability to finance them. He strongly endorsed Straus' arguments for expanding the categories of nonreimbursable costs. Speaking with the authority of a former secretary of agriculture, the New Mexico senator emphasized to his colleagues on the joint panel that the expansion of farming, through reclamation, to previously arid lands, benefited not only the West, but the nation at large. Citing projections of dramatic population increases by 1975, Anderson urged his colleagues not to allow existing short term crop surpluses to distract them.[13]

Anderson asked Secretary Krug to provide a written analysis of the increasing costs of power development in the face of the shrinking inventory of desirable water project sites. The senator's strategy was to set the stage for expected legislative battles over project financing. He wanted congressmen from outside the public lands states of the West to understand that traditional irrigation costs were about to double. Consequently, he urged relief through an extension of the payoff period, which was then set at forty years. In a new era of multiple purpose projects designed to last a century or more, Anderson believed the payoff time should be extended accordingly. By lengthening the repayment period and reducing the proportion of expenses paid by direct beneficiaries, Anderson and Straus sought to ease congressional resistance to high cost, complex projects that under existing benefit-to-cost formulas would have been branded unfeasible. In the Reclamation Bureau's campaign to bring millions of additional acres into production, Anderson was becoming a valued and resourceful ally.[14]

The Hoover Commission's Natural Resources task force, in its 1949 report, confirmed the Reclamation Bureau's plea for a new financing system and called for creation of a "Board of Impartial Analysis" to keep track of project costs. The board would help minimize chances for major cost overruns such as occurred in Montana's "Hungry Horse" project, which soared from its initial estimate of $6.3 million to an actual cost of $93.5 million. The board would also protect the Interior Department against pressures of strategically placed congressmen for approval of preferred homestate projects despite their being premature, unsound, or duplicative.[15]

The Hoover Commission cited, as an example of the contradictory mandates that led to conflict among federal resources agencies, the diverse purposes of dam operation. These purposes included flood control, electric power generation, and irrigation. Flood control required empty storage space prior to the high water season, storage during the flood season, and discharge during dry spells. Hydroelectric power generation demanded an even level all year. By contrast, irrigation required storage of water in winter months and release in summer. The commission strongly endorsed the Reclamation Bureau's call for a major updating of the laws it administered, calling the 803 pages of statutes "indefinite, complex, and contradictory."[16]

Clinton Anderson's campaign to pass legislation authorizing construction of New Mexico's Vermejo Project illustrated the complexities of the federal reclamation bureaucracy and his effectiveness in directing its latent force to his home state's resources needs. In this effort he appeared as the classic "pork barrel" politician, a role that did not seem to him inconsistent with the principles underlying his broader regional and national conservation objectives. Since 1888, settlers in the semiarid agricultural region of northeastern New Mexico, on the upper reaches of the Canadian River, had struggled with a succession of reclamation projects to capture a crop yield sufficient to ensure their survival. Over the intervening years the network of reservoirs, dams, canals and supporting diversion facilities had fallen into disrepair. The greatest enemy of this and other long-established reclamation projects was excessive accumulation of silt on reservoir bottoms, significantly reducing their storage capacity.[17]

In 1946 the Bureau of Reclamation, at the urging of New Mexico's influential senior senator Carl Hatch (D), began an extensive inquiry into the possibility of rehabilitation. Two significant obstacles lay in the path of federal assistance. The existing project was privately owned, and individual land holdings greatly exceeded the 1902 Reclamation Act's 160-acre assistance limitation. This provision was designed to ensure that assistance went only to "family farms" and not to monopolistic or speculative ventures. Nonetheless, the Bureau went ahead with its study, propelled in part by realization that the simple, low cost irrigation projects, those clearly within the scope of its mandate, were mostly completed. To continue operation at its prewar level of funding and vitality, the Bureau needed to expand the frontiers of the possible, whether by bureaucratic assertion, administrative regulation, or statutory license.[18]

The Bureau completed its study in February 1949, shortly after Anderson took his Senate oath. Known as the "Vermejo Project," after one of the Canadian River's principal tributaries, the plan became a bellwether for the agency's agenda of the 1950s. In 1949, the existing facility was capable of supplying water to only one-fourth of the 12,780 acres in its reclamation district. The Bureau proposed to double the irrigable area at a cost of slightly under $3 million and at a presumed benefit that exceeded the project's cost by a ratio of 1.76 to 1.[19]

Three factors were necessary to ensure the success of a reclamation proposal: a favorable benefit-to-cost ratio, a period of repaying capital costs to the federal treasury of not more than forty years, and support of Senate and House members who were well placed in the respective authorizing and appropriating committees. Those members needed a sufficient store of credit with eastern and urban colleagues to cement the necessary alliances. In the absence of a credible benefit-to-cost ratio, however, little else was possible. Accordingly, the Bureau and a project's legislative supporters paid very close attention to the calculations lying behind the ratios.[20]

Computation of project "benefits" engendered heated challenges from reclamation's foes outside western states. Unquestionably a matter of considerable conjecture, calculation of Vermejo's benefits, set at $193,600 on an annual basis, proceeded as follows: "Direct" irrigation benefits were figured at $99,800 (52%). "Indirect" benefits accruing to the sale of irrigated crops from wages, interest and profits amounted to $60,200 (31%). The yearly value of flood control in preventing property damage was $2,830 (1%). Finally, using figures supplied by its sister agencies, the Fish and Wildlife Service and the National Park Service, the Reclamation Bureau set the wildlife and recreation benefits at $30,800 (16%) per year. When this plan reached Capitol Hill, its supporters incorporated, over the project's lifetime, benefit charges of $220,000 for "sediment control," a significant departure from the Bureau's customary list of permissible benefits. Cutting through the higher mathematics, on the cost side, was the reality that user fees would meet only one-quarter of operating expenses and capital costs. The federal treasury would underwrite the remaining costs for the unprecedented sixty-seven-year life of the project.[21]

Realizing limitations of the Bureau's plan, but aware of the political benefits of its legislative enactment, Anderson introduced the plan in the Senate on March 23, 1949.[22] His assignment to the Senate Interior Committee facilitated the bill's smooth journey through the upper house. An identical House version also moved quickly and, five months from the date of its introduction, the act was presented to the president.

To Anderson's consternation, President Truman vetoed the measure on the grounds that it established, in piecemeal fashion, a precedent for aiding private projects at a time when the administration was preparing its own broader, more systematic plan. The chief executive, reflecting opposition from the Bureau of the Budget, noted the violation of the 160-acre assistance limitation and objected to the specific calculation of non-reimbursable costs. The Bureau had planned to set aside, within the project, 5,200 acres in its low-lying portion for a waterfowl resting and nesting area. The federal Fish and Wildlife Service had earlier endorsed this plan as the project was situated along a major waterfowl flyway. The president believed, however, that the specific proposal went beyond a policy of basic protection by creating a major wildlife management area "not required for the operation of the irrigation project or for protection of existing wildlife resources of this specific area." Further, Truman declared that the sixty-seven-year repayment period set an unwelcome precedent far in excess of the generally accepted forty-year term.[23]

Finally, the president asserted that this measure would provide preferential treatment to a private venture at the expense of federally owned projects of equal or greater merit. Truman urged Congress to wait until its 1950 session when he would submit a more systematic and coordinated administration proposal. He also claimed that the Interior Department had not properly consulted the Department of Agriculture—a tip off to behind-the-scenes interagency squabbling. Reclamation Bureau officials hotly denied this contention, and it fueled their fears that Agriculture, in alliance with the Budget Bureau, was getting the best of their longstanding rivalry.[24]

The New Mexico press swiftly targeted Anderson as the culprit. One editorial writer noted that the freshman senator had spent the weekend prior to the veto on the presidential yacht and wondered why he had not capitalized on that opportunity to sidetrack the veto. The paper suggested that the people of New Mexico would have been better served by resorting to the so-called influence peddlers whose activities were subject to searching press attention at the time.[25]

With characteristically combative sarcasm, Anderson responded that he was "surprised and a little disgusted" by the reaction. He observed that such comments seemed to be the "usual reward for passing a tough piece of legislation." Privately, he acknowledged that the bill violated "all the usual stipulations laid down for federal reclamation projects." He admitted that the assignment of $718,590 over the project's life to fish and wildlife benefits was "greatly exaggerated," with the actual expense but a "tiny fraction" thereof. On inclusion of the sediment control benefit figure, Anderson acknowledged that "we put it in because had we not done so, it would have made the repayment period seventy-six years instead of sixty-seven years and made it just that much more difficult to justify the project."[26] He was particularly upset by the local press assessment that only freshman Representative John E. Miles (D-NM) could save the legislation. He suggested that such an attitude "only stirs up trouble" for Miles and "doesn't make the rest of us feel too kindly."[27]

As Anderson was defending himself and considering his next move, the president made a decision that immediately offered new ammunition to Vermejo's supporters. On August 30, 1949, Truman signed Utah's Weber Basin bill which authorized construction of a $69 million reclamation project in that state. This action further inflamed Anderson's wounds. Not only had the New Mexico Democrat been embarrassed in his public speculations on the day before the Vermejo veto that the act would be signed, but it also appeared that his views had less force on the president than did the blandishments of Utah's irascible Republican senator, Arthur Watkins. Anderson hurriedly expressed to Truman his unhappiness over the president's seemingly inconsistent treatment of such apparently similar bills. Anderson noted that the Weber bill had three times the amount of nonreimbursable charges, including recreation funding similar to that which the White House had found objectionable in the Vermejo bill.[28]

Three weeks passed before the president responded, a delay suggesting extensive internal inquiry into the Reclamation Bureau's actions. In an apparent effort to curry favor with Anderson, the Bureau earlier had neglected to clear its recommendations with the White House, thus embarrassing the president and incurring Anderson's wrath. Before Truman sent a formal response, his aide, David Bell, assured Anderson that pressure from within the Utah delegation had come from Democratic Senator Elbert Thomas, not Republican Watkins. In his reply, the president expressed his frustration at Congress's "premature" action on water resources legislation. He acknowledged that the Reclamation Bureau had been unduly anxious to cater to Congress's desires. Defensively, the president stated that Utah's project was economically sound while New Mexico's was not. By administration calculations, forty percent of Vermejo's costs were nonreimbursable, whereas Weber's amounted to only fifteen percent.[29]

Anderson attributed the president's veto to poor White House staff work and interagency feuding. His suspicions were partially substantiated on November 12, 1949, with the resignation of Interior Secretary Krug. Reflecting his own disenchantment with the president, Anderson told the Associated Press that there was "no question that Krug was let out because he was pressing for reclamation projects." In a slap at an agency he despised, Anderson said he was sorry that Krug was "blamed for asking for appropriations and projects which were not approved by the Bureau of the Budget." He concluded that he would hate to see the secretary "crucified for asking for things which, in the 1948 campaign, he said he stood for. He went about the country telling people that Truman stood for progress and reclamation."[30]

On May 1, 1950, midway through the second session of his first Senate term, Anderson introduced a revised version of the Vermejo bill. It included a face-saving upward adjustment in the proportion of costs that local water users would pay the federal government. Both houses of Congress again acted quickly and, without hesitation, the president signed the act in September.[31] The Vermejo Project underscored Congress's emerging leadership in forcing a reevaluation of reclamation policy. While executive agencies responsible for water resources development feuded with one another in the face of escalating demands for effective management of increasingly limited resources, pressure from Capitol Hill slowly but steadily forced a fundamental policy shift.

A second confrontation during Anderson's first two years in the Senate, over authorization of the Canadian River Project, demonstrated tensions within the congressional arena. This dispute not only pitted the New Mexico and Texas congressional delegations against each other, but it also reinforced animosity between New Mexico's two senators.

Rising in the Sangre de Cristo Mountains of northeastern New Mexico, the Canadian River crosses the Texas Panhandle just north of Amarillo and then traverses most of Oklahoma before entering the Arkansas River. Early in 1949, the Reclamation Bureau, responding to demands from the Texas delegation, undertook a survey of water resources and needs of the Texas Panhandle-South Plains region. After a three-month study, the Bureau recommended an $85 million multiple purpose project to supplement the diminishing ground water supplies in that area. The Bureau proposed a rolled earth dam and reservoir with a storage capacity of nearly two million acre feet.[32] A 275-mile-long system of pipeline would provide water for the 260,000 residents of the area's eleven cities and towns.[33]

Worthy of particular notice in the Bureau's proposal was its emphasis on water supply for municipal and industrial uses rather than for irrigation purposes. Of the project's $85 million cost, less than $2 million would be required for irrigation of an estimated 20,000 acres. The Bureau assigned a benefit cost ratio of 1.7 to 1, indicating that over a fifty-year period, the federal treasury would realize $157 million on its initial investment. Reclamation officials emphasized that the project was not designed to "make the desert bloom," but rather to "save the bloom that has been brought to the desert by decades of industrious labor."[34]

In its legislative form, the Canadian Project moved quickly through Speaker Sam Rayburn's (D-TX) House where the Texas delegation outnumbered New Mexico's by a ratio of more than ten to one. In the Senate, where the ratio was even, both New Mexico senators recognized their obligation to ward off a potential threat to their state's water interests. Texas's attempt to slip the measure through the Interior Committee without proper consultation with New Mexico and without formal hearings particularly irritated Anderson. Neither he nor New Mexico state engineer John Bliss saw the Bureau's report until more than two months after it had reached the Texas delegation.[35]

Aside from the project's feasibility, the major issue for New Mexico was its neighbor's efforts to apply a double standard to congressional authorization of the two states' respective projects. Earlier, in May 1949, Texas Senator Tom Connally (D) had blocked Senate approval of New Mexico's Fort Sumner Rehabilitation Project, claiming that no action could be taken until both states had agreed to a compact protecting Texas water rights in the Pecos River Valley. That compact was quickly drafted and approved. Shortly thereafter, the Fort Sumner Project was agreed to. When the Texas delegation, in turn, sought action on its Canadian River Project, it reaped a harvest of New Mexico's ill feelings. Not to be so easily outmaneuvered, Anderson, as a precondition for action, called for a similar compact to protect his state's rights. Given the longstanding climate of suspicion between the two states, Anderson agreed with state engineer Bliss that a compact should precede approval of the Canadian River Project to prevent Texas from claiming priority rights to that river's water.[36]

In February 1950, the Senate Interior Committee, with Anderson's assent, favorably reported legislation establishing a Canadian River compact and set a date for hearings on the actual project. By mid-July, the committee had given its blessing to the project, sending it to the full Senate for action. On September 20, 1950, as the Senate raced toward a preelection recess, Texas Senator Lyndon Johnson (D) made a routine motion to bring up the bill for consideration and passage. Without warning, New Mexico's Dennis Chavez (D) moved to block the bill and threatened to derail recess plans with a filibuster.[37] Although the two states' differences were quickly reconciled, Chavez's surprise action angered and stunned Anderson. He found his senior colleague's effort to assume the role of New Mexico's water champion particularly annoying. Chavez's assertion that it was time to put an end to Texas's piracy of New Mexico's water led Anderson to observe that Chavez had been in Congress for twenty years and if he had intended to protect the state, "that would have been a good time to do it."[38]

Both states signed the Canadian River Compact in Santa Fe, New Mexico, on December 6, 1950. Anderson did not learn of this action until nearly a week later. Press accounts of the event quoting Chavez's expressions of approval made Anderson furious. He asked state engineer Bliss why he had not been notified. Bliss sheepishly replied that due to a "clerical" error, the informing telegram had not been sent. When the president signed the Canadian Project act later that month, Anderson privately noted his satisfaction for that measure's success and its likely benefits for New Mexico. The experience, however, had confirmed his distrust of Chavez and had taught the state engineer to keep the assertive junior senator fully informed in the future.[39]

Despite the regional value of the Vermejo and Canadian projects, their importance for New Mexico paled in comparison to projects for development of that state's entitlements to the Colorado River's vital flow. Clinton Anderson's experience with efforts to allocate the Colorado's resources among the seven states of its upper and lower basins dated back more than a quarter century to 1922. As a young reporter for the *Albuquerque Journal,* he covered negotiations that led to signing that year of the Colorado River Compact, apportioning the river's erratic flow between upper and lower basin states. While the lower basin states of California, Arizona, and Nevada set out immediately to harness their portions, the upper states failed to do so. After more than two decades of squabbling, New Mexico, Colorado, Utah, and Wyoming, in the upper basin, finally devised an allocation plan that they signed in October 1948.[40]

The Gila and the San Juan served as New Mexico's major Colorado tributaries. As of early 1949, efforts to develop these vital waterways depended totally on solution of a long festering water rights dispute between California and Arizona. For California, adoption of the 1922 compact had been a major first step toward harnessing the Colorado, particularly for the rapidly growing Los Angeles metropolitan area. Six years later, Congress passed the Boulder Canyon Act authorizing construction of a major lower basin dam and allocating the lower region's average annual entitlement of 7.5 million acre feet between California (4.4 million), Arizona (2.8 million), and Nevada (300,000).[41]

California moved quickly to capture its share under the compact. Arizona, however, claimed that since half of the Colorado's entire course lay along its own western border, the time honored western water doctrine of "prior appropriation," or "first in time, first in right" entitled it to as much water as it could consume without regard to surrounding states' claims. This set the stage for an Arizona-California confrontation of unprecedented dimensions.[42]

By 1944 Arizona's overdevelopment of its existing water resources and the consequent need for federal assistance in harnessing its share of the Colorado led that state to petition the Reclamation Bureau for a study to determine the most effective delivery of its 2.8 million acre foot share. The Bureau responded in 1946 with a plan known as the "Central Arizona Project." At a staggering estimated cost in excess of $700 million, the project would remove water from the Colorado at the southern tip of Lake Havasu, elevate it nearly one thousand feet, and send it by gravity flow through aqueducts nearly 150 miles eastward to Phoenix and then south to Tucson. The water was intended to serve as supplemental supply for approximately 700,000 acres in Arizona's Gila and Salt River valleys.[43]

California officials immediately set out to block Arizona's plans. They argued that Arizona was already consuming most of its 2.8 million acre foot allocation by drawing that amount from the Gila River, a major Colorado tributary that flowed westward from New Mexico across south central Arizona. Arizona rejected that interpretation, claiming the 1922 compact framers had intended its allocation be measured from the Colorado's main stream rather than its tributaries. Each of the basin states feared that uncertainties over the river's apportionment could seriously delay all future development plans. The Reclamation Bureau agreed. In a September 1948 report to Congress, the Bureau recommended that the project proceed, but only after Arizona had fully justified its claims.[44]

The Central Arizona Project dispute provided Clinton Anderson his first opportunity to deal with the broader issues of river basin development. Throughout the Senate Interior Committee's six-week inquiry, beginning in March 1949, the freshman senator performed impressively. Demonstrating a reverent awareness of the Central Arizona Project's complexities, he nonetheless established himself as a vigilant guardian of New Mexico's water interests. Anderson perceptively and shrewdly engaged the issues, forcing potentially hostile witnesses to answer the questions he wished them to answer rather than the questions they wished him to ask. He challenged their arithmetic down to the last decimal, testing both their assumptions and their conclusions. Wryly conceding that he was neither a lawyer nor an engineer, he proceeded to demonstrate the skills of both.

Anderson's familiarity with the 1948 Reclamation Bureau report drew admiration from California's chief engineer, who commented that not only had the senator shown diligence in attending most of the hearings, but he had also "taken the trouble to read a lot of rather boring material." Anderson insisted on knowing how the data had been gathered and how they had been analyzed. He refused to accept unsubstantiated conclusions. He carried over from his successful insurance business a determination to obtain statistical summaries expressed in clear language. At one point he noted, "I have a set of books on my business. The individual books contain all the information that I want. But they are not brought together in a single balance sheet until the accountant does it and sends it to me."[45]

Committee chairman Joseph O'Mahoney had reason to be grateful for Anderson's insistence that the experts from both sides simplify and refine their statements. In the early phases of the twenty-day probe, the proceedings seemed to elude the chairman's ability to control them. When other commitments kept O'Mahoney from presiding, he turned the chair over to the freshman senator from New Mexico, a gesture confirming his regard for Anderson's mastery of the issues and personalities before the committee.[46]

Anderson's primary concern at the outset of the hearings was to establish precisely the source of the Central Arizona Project's water. He feared that if California succeeded in protecting its rights to lower basin waters, Arizona, by virtue of a court decision, might be awarded priority rights to water intended for the upper basin states. He quipped, "I am not particular as to which person picks our pocket, but I just want to be sure you realize we understand we are about to have it picked."[47] He was especially bothered by reports that the total flow of the Colorado had decreased substantially since the 1922 apportionment due to increased evaporation resulting from higher average temperatures and a decline in precipitation.

Anderson pressed his case, arguing that the central issue was whether there would be any water at all for New Mexico. He observed that a recent New Mexico request for a water project requiring an annual flow of only three thousand acre feet had been denied over the lack of assured water supply. At the hearings' conclusion, Anderson joined with the Interior Committee's majority, over California's vigorous objections, in voting to recommend Senate authorization for the Central Arizona Project. Early in 1950 the Senate agreed to the committee's bill and sent it to the House where it died under the weight of the Truman administration's refusal to endorse the project until California and Arizona resolved their differences.[48]

As the Arizona–California feud provided an external threat to New Mexico's development of its Colorado River allocation, an equally formidable challenge came from within the state over the issue of Indian water claims. Late in April 1949 New Mexico state engineer John Bliss alerted Anderson to the growing likelihood of a conflict over apportionment of the waters from the state's largest Colorado tributary, the San Juan River. When New Mexico officials signed the Upper Colorado compact in 1948, they expected that 300,000 of the state's 800,000 acre-foot entitlement would be available for diversion from the San Juan in the state's northwestern corner eastward across the Continental Divide to the Rio Chama with a major portion to be sent down the Rio Grande to the rapidly growing Albuquerque metropolitan region.[49]

Engineer Bliss and other state planners recognized that a maze of litigation awaited them, as nearly eighty percent of the potential project sites in the San Juan Basin were located on Navajo Indian lands. Four decades earlier, in 1908, the nation's Indians had won a major legal battle as a result of the U.S. Supreme Court's ruling in the so-called Winters Case. That decision marked a major turning point in the intensifying battle between the federal and state governments over control of water use in nonnavigable western streams. During the drought of 1904–05 white settlers had diverted water from the Milk River in northern Montana, leaving none for the Fort Belknap Indian Reservation located downstream. The settlers contended in the ensuing litigation that their use was protected under Montana's adherence to the western water doctrine of prior appropriation. That doctrine gave priority rights to the first persons taking water from a stream as long as they continued to put their water to a beneficial use. Subsequent users could have access to the stream flow only so long as it did not interfere with the needs of the earlier arrivals. In opposition to this position, the Supreme Court determined that the federal government's treaty power gave it the right to reserve water for Indian use. This federally guaranteed right, implicit in the 1888 treaty that established the reservation, was superior, the court contended, to the state's right to allocate water usage through the prior appropriations doctrine. The Winters decision affirmed Indian rights to priority claim on all irrigation water within their reach, regardless of when they put it to use. The decision stipulated that ambiguities surrounding allocation of irrigation water were to be resolved in the Indians' favor. Ultimately, however, the Winters decision did "as much to cloud the meaning and nature of Indian water rights as it did to assert the right's existence."[50]

Bliss warned Anderson that the Indians' proposed Shiprock Project, if not carefully defined, could tie up water intended for diversion to Albuquerque. Designed in 1945 to irrigate 70,000 acres of Navajo lands in the San Juan Basin, the project's estimated scope had grown in direct proportion to the increasing likelihood of actually obtaining the long-desired Colorado water. At one point, Anderson compared the troublesome project to the New Mexico state motto: "It grows as it goes."[51]

Bliss pointed out that the Shiprock Project could irrigate up to 90,000 acres without auxillary pumping facilities. With the aid of such devices, the project could reach as many as 160,000 acres, an area that encompassed nearly the entire land holdings of the region's Navajo tribes. If the Shiprock Project were permitted to transcend the limits of its gravity flow capacity, however, there would be insufficient water remaining for the San Juan–Chama diversion to the Albuquerque region in central New Mexico.[52]

Early in the 1949 congressional session, Anderson met with representatives of the involved federal agencies, including the Indian Irrigation Service. He discovered that the state engineer's concerns were fully justified. Indian Service officials made clear their intention to assert full claim to the San Juan's flow, leaving an insignificant residue for "white" projects. They contended that the recent "San Carlos" case in Arizona confirmed the right of Indians living in the vicinity of a river to use its water for irrigation at any time, including for future projects not yet conceived, irrespective of past usage.[53] Anderson viewed this claim, with its foundation in the Winters Doctrine, as enormously troublesome. Acknowledging that Navajos had the right to develop the first San Juan project, he cautioned that under no circumstances should the facility exceed its originally specified 90,000 acre range. Agency representatives promised to offer more detailed plans and accompanying justifications as soon as specific surveys had been completed.[54]

After several months of prodding Interior Secretary Krug, Anderson received a formal reply. The secretary cautioned the senator that as many as 170,000 acres within the Shiprock Project's area met the standards set for arable land and thus were subject to inclusion. Krug suggested, however, that the Indian representatives might agree to a 100,000-acre limitation, leaving barely enough water to make the San Juan–Chama diversion to Albuquerque feasible. This would occur, Krug warned, only if the Indians were guaranteed a "water right priority senior to any other development made subsequent to the 1948 Colorado River Compact." The secretary further advised Anderson that, in addition to the Shiprock and San Juan–Chama facilities, the Interior Department had under study a third potential project known as the "South San Juan." If completed, it would irrigate 75,000 acres in the San Juan Valley, northwest of Cuba, New Mexico, leaving insufficient water for the San Juan–Chama diversion.[55]

Anderson launched a spirited offensive against the Reclamation Bureau's interest in promoting the South San Juan Project, which he felt was "located out in the middle of a desert waste." He emphasized to the Bureau's acting director that the project's lands were largely at a high elevation, promising a restricted annual growing season and he calculated the cost of irrigating the project's 75,000 acres to be $500 per acre. Considering the brevity of the growing season and the land's relative inaccessibility, Anderson concluded "that there isn't a chance" that the land would be worth more than $200 an acre." He continued, "We know the project is no good and yet the Bureau is going to spend another $150,000 to prove it, thereby wasting the money in the Colorado River Development Fund when we could be using it to make surveys for the dams and the structures that would permit us to develop the waters of the San Juan River."[56]

When Anderson returned to New Mexico early in September 1949, he met with state engineer Bliss and attorney Fred Wilson, a member of the Interstate Stream Commission, to prepare a case against the Interior Department's apparent willingness to support the Shiprock and South San Juan projects. Wilson, who had participated in the 1948 compact negotiations, sought to assure Anderson that in spite of the often cited Winters decision, subsequent court decisions had undercut the Indians' sound legal basis for "preferential or reserved right to the use of any quanity of water different from that of the white owners." Bravely, he argued that at the time the treaties were negotiated in the nineteenth century, "there was no thought or intent, either on the part of the United States or of the Indians, that enormous storage facilities would be constructed along the Colorado River and that miles of canals, tunnels, and aqueducts would be built to convey the water to the place of use." Adopting a highly selective interpretation of the confused and bitterly contested realm of Indian water law, Wilson counseled Anderson to assume a firm stance with the Reclamation Bureau. He urged the senator to tell the Bureau that 300,000 acre feet "will be diverted" for use either in the Rio Grande or in the South San Juan project and that the agency should conduct its planning for the potentially expensive Shiprock project with that reality clearly in mind.[57]

The matter remained in abeyance for nearly a year until July 1950 when Anderson arranged a meeting between Interior secretary Oscar Chapman, who had succeeded Krug, and influential New Mexicans including members of the state's congressional delegation, state engineer Bliss, and attorney Wilson. Chapman called to the meeting his senior reclamation officials and for nearly two hours both sides scrutinized the political and engineering feasibility of the pending New Mexico projects. Assistant secretary William Warne ultimately acknowledged that the Shiprock project could be kept within the 90,000 acre limits of its gravity flow irrigation capabilities, leaving sufficient water for other New Mexico projects.[58]

The discussion then turned to alternative plans for the San Juan–Chama to Albuquerque diversion. They ranged from an annual maximum of 290,000 acre feet to a low of 175,000. With the Korean conflict less than a month old, Anderson emphasized the special requirements of the area's growing defense establishments and expressed willingness to settle for a "middle option" of 279,000 acre feet. He recognized that not only must the diversion include enough water to supplement existing projects and establish new ones, but there must also be sufficient water to share with the neighboring states of Colorado and Texas. Without such a gesture of neighborliness, combined with the project's military potential, Anderson doubted that he could interest those states' congressional delegations in his campaign to move the project off the Reclamation Bureau's drafting tables.[59] Subsequently, Secretary Chapman directed his department's Reclamation Bureau and Indian Service to agree on the magnitude of the San Juan–Chama diversion. This was the first occasion on which the Interior Department had openly addressed the *amount* of the diversion, as opposed to its feasibility.[60]

In September 1950, the *Farmington Times*, the principal newspaper of northwestern New Mexico in the vicinity of the San Juan River, bitterly attacked Anderson. The paper charged that the senator's efforts to divert water from the San Juan to Albuquerque region were motivated by a need to obtain irrigation for his own "529 arid acres" along the Rio Grande. The editorial suggested that the "little people of the state should rise up in wrath and make life so miserable for Senator Anderson that he would never run for office again."[61]

Anderson responded quickly to the editorial, which he characterized as "vicious and violent." In a statewide radio broadcast, he reminded his constituents of his efforts during his first two years in the Senate to secure projects benefiting all regions of New Mexico. He added that his own farm was well watered and, although producing beautifully, would be even more productive financially if he sold it to the area's rapidly encroaching real estate developers. He defended Albuquerque's need for increased water and hydroelectricity to supply its population, which had more than tripled over the past decade, and for the adjacent defense installations. In this instance, Anderson shrewdly capitalized on the traditional hostility of New Mexico's northwestern region to enumerate his own legislative initiatives and to rise above intersectional bickering, appearing in the role of a statewide conciliator and provider.[62]

Although Anderson's conservation policy activities during his first two years in the Senate focused primarily on the West's water resources, he also took an interest in the forest and parkland protection. On those issues, he placed himself in the middle of a well-established conflict between advocates of federal involvement in natural resources development and those who favored exclusive reliance on local control and private enterprise. He decisively cast his lot on the federal side.

Within a week of taking his Senate oath, Anderson introduced a bill to protect the timber resources of New Mexico's Santa Fe National Forest from indiscriminate cutting by mining companies whose mineral rights allowed them to take surface timber. His bill attracted considerable home state attention, reinforcing his conservationist sympathies. "People wrote me letters and I wrote back," he later observed. "I began to know that I had constituents and that they cared for the golden color of the aspens on the slopes of the Sangre de Cristo Mountains in October. They did not want ugly sign boards to obstruct the view. They cared for the little brooks that tumbled along the roadway. They cared that I cared. I would not forget that." Within six months, Anderson's timber protection bill was law.[63]

Early in the 1949 session, Anderson introduced a related measure providing for reforestation and revegetation of forest and range lands. It too became public law during his first year in the Senate. Sponsored in the House by Representative Mike Mansfield (D-MT), the joint resolution authorized an accelerated fifteen-year grant program with annual appropriations of up to $13 milllion to complete replanting of four million national forest acres. Under this program, Agriculture Secretary Charles Brannan estimated that depleted range

and watershed areas could be restored within three years of planting, supporting up to ten times the number of livestock then possible. The so-called Anderson-Mansfield Act received the full Senate's
approval on April 11, 1949.[64]

Several weeks later, Anderson introduced a far more controversial forest management measure. He needed little education into
the deficiencies of forest conservation practices, particularly within
the private sector. Frugal in his personal and business affairs, the
senator was particularly concerned by the wasteful clear-cutting
practices and inadequate fire-control programs of small, frequently
irresponsible holders of commercial forest lands. The U.S. Forest
Service had worked for nearly a half century to assist commercial
operators with research, financial aid, and technical support in growing, marketing, and harvesting their timber. Despite this effort, nearly
100 million commercial acres remained without benefit of such
planning and protection. In 1947, of the more than 300 million
acres that received organized fire control protection, only one percent suffered fire damage. By contrast, nearly one-fifth of the 100
million unprotected acres were destroyed.[65]

Anderson agreed with Forest Service chief Lyle Watts that the
time had come to clothe public aid to commercial growers with
public regulation of their cutting, fire control, and other management practices. Observing that fourteen states already had regula-
tory laws in force, Anderson felt that there was ample precedent
for public supervision of private forestry. He agreed with the Forest Service's strategy of developing forest management standards
for voluntary adoption by individual owners. Where volunteerism
failed to work, the state, or ultimately the federal government would
intervene. In situations where commercial forests could no longer
be operated profitably, or where public interests overrode private
considerations, as with watershed protection, Anderson believed
that the state or federal governments should be in a position to
purchase them.[66]

Anderson's Forest Practices Act provided for specific conservation measures such as fire and insect control and regulation of cutting, grazing, and replanting. The New Mexico senator was quick
to point out that his bill was in no way tantamount to nationaliza-
tion of the forest industry and it surely did not sound the death
knell of private enterprise. He observed that such "protective regulation" was common within the railroad, public utility, broadcast-

ing and meat packing industries. The bill, he said, did no more than "impose such regulations as are necessary to safeguard the collective public interest."[67]

Despite Anderson's disclaimers, commercial foresters, wood products manufacturers, saw mill operators, and sheep and cattle interests angrily launched a counteroffensive. The June 1949 issue of the *New Mexico Stockman* carried a prominently headlined article warning its readers that the Anderson bill would establish the Secretary of Agriculture and the Forest Service chief as "czars of all privately owned timber and watershed grazing lands." The article took particular exception to the bill's provision allowing the Agriculture Secretary to withdraw "any type of federal aid under his jurisdiction" to any state that failed to develop a satisfactory plan. The writer saw this provision as the entering wedge in a paternal bureaucracy's campaign of coercion under the threat of losing all federal aid, regardless of its connection to the forest industry. The author quoted a "New Mexico citizen" to the effect that the bill "might work behind the Iron Curtain, but it is certainly a radical departure from the American way of life."[68]

Anderson demonstrated in full measure a politician's aversion to press criticism. During his earlier years in the Senate, he saw no need for a press secretary, preferring to handle media relations directly. His usual response to journalistic attacks was to compose strongly worded detailed rebuttals. In this instance, he sent a testy three-page letter to the editor, charging him with blatant dishonesty. "People just don't believe the trash you print," he thundered. Warming to the challenge, he accused the editor of cowardice in not spelling out the "Iron Curtain" charge. "You are smart enough to know that if you applied the term "communist" to me, I would have a ready-made suit for libel against you." Anderson cited Forest Service chief Watts's observation that the "threat to our democratic way of life lies in depleted resources, not in a strong and reasonable plan to conserve them." Calling the assertion that noncomplying states would lose all federal aid a "wholly manufactured lie," Anderson declared that the writer "ought to be ashamed of himself."[69]

Late in May 1949 the Senate Agriculture Committee held hearings on six bills, all of which were designed to increase the federal role in private forestry. Anderson's bill, introduced only two weeks earlier, was not among them, as there had been insufficient time to receive the required executive agency comments. In any event, there would have been little hope for his measure. A milder version had passed the House and, in the face of vigorous private sector opposition, the Senate settled for its more permissive language.[70]

Meeting from January 1949 to January 1951, the 81st Congress stayed in session longer and appropriated more funds than any previous peacetime Congress. Although it willingly responded to administration requests for accelerated funding of defense and foreign assistance programs, the legislature displayed a striking new independence of White House dictation. The President's "Fair Deal" package of domestic policy initiatives was deliberately rejected or ignored. Admittedly, domestic programs took a back seat to the Korean Conflict after June 1950, and the newly strengthened Democratic majorities in the Senate and House sought to exercise their independence on issues not closely associated with national security. Natural resources policy provided one significant outlet for that independent approach. Although the 81st Congress produced no legislative monuments in that field, it certainly laid the groundwork for future accomplishments. These two years proved to be a time of training for legislative field commanders. Clinton Anderson moved quickly to the forefront of those ranks. He engaged issues through sustained study and through initiatives limited chiefly to his southwestern constituency. He brought together the legislative skills of his previous service in the House with the bureaucratic and substantive experience gained as Secretary of Agriculture. By the time the 81st Congress passed into history, Anderson had successfully engaged the natural resource-related issues of reclamation, river basin development, Indian water rights, and forest management. That Congress had provided a valuable education for the New Mexico freshman and the result confirmed Sarah McClendon's optimistic prediction: "The Anderson boom is on."

# 3

# "Over My Dead Body"

## The Navajo Dam and The Politics of River Basin Development, 1951–1956

I have a feeling of obligation to the state of New Mexico. It gave me my health. I am loyal to it. I do not mind standing on the Senate Floor day after day participating in the filibuster against the bill which sought to do damage to the state of my adoption. If that be treason, you will just have to make the most of it.

Clinton P. Anderson
July 28, 1955

When he entered the Senate in 1949, Clinton Anderson's principal goal was to end the stalemate threatening development of New Mexico's 800,000 acre-foot entitlement to the Colorado River's annual flow. Nearly half that amount was earmarked for the rapidly growing Albuquerque metropolitan area with its expanding defense establishments. To bring this about, legislation was required to authorize a costly transmountain diversion of water from the San Juan River in New Mexico's northwest corner, eastward across the Continental Divide to the Rio Grande and south to Albuquerque. Before the vital plans for that diversion could leave the federal Reclamation Bureau's drafting tables, however, a major water rights dispute with the state's Navajo Indians had to be resolved. The Navajos were insisting on development, in the area of the San Juan River, of two irrigation projects that could, if not carefully delineated, drain away the minimum flow necessary for the diversion to Albuquerque.

Between 1949 and 1956, Anderson labored mightily to bring these potentially conflicting projects into balance. One of his principal strengths as a United States senator was his ability to act as forceful mediator. He negotiated between his state's Indians and whites, between residents of the San Juan and Rio Grande basins, between intransigent state engineers and stubborn Reclamation Bureau officials, between developers and preservationists, and between the House and the Senate.

The results of his labors were contained in the 1956 Colorado River Storage Project Act, the largest reclamation project ever authorized by Congress to that time. That statute included a provision for a $40 million Navajo Dam in New Mexico's San Juan basin. With a less dedicated and skilled patron than Anderson, that dam would never have emerged from the Reclamation Bureau. Crucial to the future authorization of the Navajo irrigation projects and the transmountain diversion, the dam was merely New Mexico's entering wedge, its nose under the tent, its guarantee that the state would have a project financed from revenues of larger power producing dams included in the Colorado Storage project. Taken by itself, the project could not have earned an acceptable cost-benefit rating. Therefore, Anderson's objective was to keep it attached to the larger project plan. On several occasions, between 1950 and 1955, it was removed. In January 1954, the senator warned a House subcommittee that if the dam were taken out of the larger plan, "the bill will pass over my dead body." When the commissioner of Reclamation asked him what New Mexico intended to do with the dam in the light of his willingness to defer a request for associated irrigation and diversion projects, which he recognized were then of questionable economic and political feasibility, Anderson replied, "We can suggest what to do with the water after we get the dam."[1]

In 1955, Anderson became chairman of the influential Senate Subcommittee on Irrigation and Reclamation. From that position, he was able to ensure inclusion of the Navajo Dam as he negotiated a larger dispute between conservationists and developers over a proposed dam at Echo Park in western Colorado, near the federally protected Dinosaur National Monument. The Echo Park controversy raised old questions of the ability of developers to encroach on presumably inviolate national parklands, and Anderson feared in 1955 that the growing storm of conservationist outrage over the issue would blow away the entire Colorado storage bill, including

New Mexico's projects. Accordingly, he took on an active mediatory role that led to abandonment of the Echo Park site and inclusion in the final law of a provision forbidding for all time construction of dams and reservoirs inside national parks or monuments.

Passage of the Colorado River Storage Project Act proved to be a pivotal event in the postwar development of American conservationism. For the heterogeneous collection of interest groups drawn together to preserve Echo Park, it marked a moment of unprecedented solidarity. For Congress, and especially the Senate, it represented an assertive victory over a recalcitrant presidential administration and hidebound resources agencies. Finally, for Clinton Anderson, the 1956 enactment brought a shift in focus from the narrow pork barrel politics associated with allocation of Colorado River water resources to broader natural resources considerations of wilderness preservation and outdoor recreation planning.

In December 1950 the Reclamation Bureau issued its long awaited development plan for the Upper Colorado River Basin.[2] At an unprecedented estimated cost of $1.5 billion, the plan included a network of six high dams and seventeen subsidiary projects for water storage, power generation, flood control, and irrigation of nearly a half-million semi-arid acres. Missing from that proposal were specific provisions for New Mexico's San Juan River projects. Bureaucratic infighting and administrative inefficiency within the state government, resistence to the spectre of federal control, and the impasse over Indian water rights prevented submission of data essential to determining project feasibility. The Bureau, however, was not about to foreclose opportunities for development of future facilities. Its administrators realized that New Mexico's congressional delegation, including Senate Public Works Committee chairman Dennis Chavez (D) would hardly remain indifferent to being excluded from a plan designed to set the upper basin's development for the next quarter century. Accordingly, the Bureau added a general provision for irrigation dams on the San Juan River on the grounds that it would be necessary to regulate the flow of this major Colorado tributary and to reduce the accumulation of sediment downstream in a larger power-producing dam. In passing, the Bureau noted that the San Juan dam would eventually be used to assure continuous water supply for the proposed Shiprock Irrigation project, the South San Juan project, and as replacement storage for the San Juan–Chama Diversion project.[3]

During 1951, the basin states affected by the Reclamation Bureau's Colorado River Storage Project plan examined its local implications, while the national government's attention centered on the conflict in Korea. Early in 1952, Utah's two senators, with their state's water development needs firmly in mind, contacted Senate colleagues from the other Colorado basin states, to enlist their cosponsorship of legislation embodying the Bureau's 1950 project plan. The New Mexico state administration's difficulties with its own bureaucracy and its continuing legal battle with the Navajos over water rights placed Clinton Anderson in a difficult position. Responding to the Utah senators, Anderson lamented, "Until I can find out from my state what they want done with the Shiprock Project and the San Juan Transmountain Diversion, I can't put my name on the bill."[4]

As it turned out, the Utah bill went nowhere during the 1952 session. It did, however, serve its sponsors' purposes of "smoking out" the Truman administration with regard to its likely support for the project. Preoccupied with the Korean situation and the forthcoming presidential and congressional election campaigns, Truman indicated that he was unwilling to invest the political capital necessary to underwrite such an unprecedented and regionally exclusive program. The initiative would remain in legislative hands.

The Eisenhower election landslide in November 1952 profoundly changed the climate, replacing established legislative-executive relationships with the uncertainties of new programs and untested administrators. In January 1953, for the first time since 1948, both houses of Congress reverted to Republican control. The new administration boasted of its "partnership concept," a rhetorical blanket for future programs that would shift to the private sector those activities that it was presumably best equipped to manage with minimal assistance from the national government. Eisenhower observed, "The federal government can help, but it should stimulate State and local action, rather than provide excuses for inaction."[5]

To direct his Interior Department, the president selected Oregon governor Douglas McKay, a party stalwart and automobile dealer. McKay was well known for his support of private development of natural resources and his criticism of the federal bureaucracy's role in the administration of those resources. An Idaho newspaper cheerfully greeted the news of his appointment with the prediction, ". . . there will be the long-needed cleaning of the Interior Department. The fuzzy haired boys will be gone. So will their aims and ideas. The great Northwest's natural resources may now be developed under American principles, and through the cooperation of the states."[6]

The possibility that the Colorado project might summarily be placed into private hands served as a powerful force for cohesion among New Mexico's legislators, state officials, and Indian leaders, emphasizing their mutual interest in the Bureau's plans for the Colorado basin. In April 1953, as a reflection of his state's newly found unity, Anderson joined nine other senators from the five affected states in introducing the Colorado River Storage Project Act (S.1555), embodying the Bureau's plan. The measure included within the initial construction program a dam on the San Juan and provided for later authorization of the Shiprock and San Juan—Chama projects on completion of further design studies and approval by neighboring states and Congress.[7]

Anderson supported this latter provision. He recognized that Texas' powerful congressional delegation was prepared to battle any project that threatened to reduce water flow in the Rio Grande. Specifically, the Texans feared that a power producing dam on the San Juan would leave a smaller volume of water for diversion out of that river and into the Rio Chama and then into the Rio Grande to augment flows passing through New Mexico and into Texas. In Sam Rayburn's (D-TX) House of Representatives, even a hint of a reduction on the Rio Grande promised to consign the entire project to the backmost pages of the legislative calendar.[8]

Following introduction of the Colorado Storage Project bill, Interior Secretary McKay directed the Reclamation Bureau to reevaluate its 1950 project plan in the light of the new administration's emphasis on local initiative. Not surprisingly, the dam-building agency concluded late in 1953 that its earlier recommendations retained their validity. With the benefit of additional engineering data for the New Mexico facilities, the Bureau certified the "acute" need for the transmountain diversion project "to relieve pressing and impending water shortages both for irrigation and for municipal and industrial purposes in New Mexico and to provide an important bloc of hydroelectric power in a power-short area." The Bureau also recommended merging the Shiprock and South San Juan projects and tying both to a storage facility on the San Juan to be known as the Navajo Dam. In an unexpected deviation from its earlier plans, the Bureau advocated transferring the entire Navajo project, including the central dam and the dependent projects, to its sister agency within the Interior Department, the Bureau of Indian Affairs.[9]

Anderson reacted quickly and with frustration to this changed scenario. From his first days in the House of Representatives, a decade earlier, Anderson had worked on building strong relationships within the labyrinthine Reclamation Bureau, an agency adept at creating favorable benefit-cost ratios for desired water projects. He was now prepared to collect the interest on that investment and the first step was to block the transfer of New Mexico's most valued projects to the less familiar agency. Accordingly, he wasted no time in requesting an opportunity to testify at the House Irrigation Subcommittee's hearings on the Colorado River Project set for January 1954.

In his late January appearance, Anderson carefully laid out his views on New Mexico's participation in the Colorado project. He quickly got to the point. The Navajo Dam and subordinate units must remain within the larger storage project proposal under the Reclamation Bureau's control. Sensitive to the farm bloc's opposition to measures that would contribute to an already severe crop surplus, accelerating the downward price spiral, Anderson focused on the project's national defense applications. Speaking as an influential member of the joint congressional committee on atomic energy, the New Mexico senator left little doubt as to the consequences of less than generous support for his state's nuclear industry. He underscored the importance of dependable water supplies for the nuclear laboratories at Los Alamos and the White Sands Proving Grounds. The depth of Anderson's determination appeared inadvertently at the end of his formal testimony when, in response to a colleague's question, he promised that if New Mexico's projects failed to appear in the final legislation the bill would pass over his "dead body."[10]

As originally designed by the Reclamation Bureau, the Navajo dam, reservoir, and associated projects would provide irrigation for 151,000 acres of semi-arid land lying to the south of the San Juan River. Of this land, 122,000 acres were located on the Navajo Indian reservation. According to the Bureau's design, the project would consist of a storage dam, a reservoir, and a main highline canal to divert water to a point twenty-eight miles downstream "where water would be dropped through a direct-connected turbine pumping plant to a lower main canal that would extend westerly about sixty miles to serve the major portion of the project lands by gravity." The Bureau's engineers anticipated that the project would deplete the San Juan's flow by approximately 341,000 acre feet per year. The Bureau further estimated that most of the project's $232,000 million cost would be allocable to irrigation.[11] Although direct beneficiaries would pay a small amount of that cost, the portion chargeable to Indian users would be paid from the federal treasury under the provisions of a twenty-year-old statute designed to provide free irrigation on Indian reservations. Additionally, according to the Bureau's careful calculations, the overwhelming majority of the construction costs would be financed by revenues from the sale of power from "workhorse dams" located elsewhere in the Colorado basin. Such calculations, offering maximum return for a minimal investment, proved irresistable to public land states' politicians, particularly during an election year.

On March 20, 1954, nearly two months after the House subcommittee concluded hearings on its version of Anderson's Senate bill, President Eisenhower announced his support of the Colorado plan. To the chagrin of Anderson and other basin representatives, however, the president recommended that only two of the originally proposed six dams be authorized for initial construction. The favored projects were to be located at Echo Park in western Colorado and at Glen Canyon in northern Arizona. The president's statement neglected to mention the New Mexico projects. Concluding that they were to be shelved indefinitely, Anderson responded with a verbal barrage.[12] The angry senator told one associate that if "the president believes he can put through this Congress a billion dollar Upper Colorado River bill [without New Mexico projects], he may reckon without our ability to fight." He continued that "As long as I am in the Senate of the United States, I will battle from daylight to dark this effort to let New Mexico's share of the Colorado River flow down to the great state of California."[13]

The Republican-controlled House committee, by a 13–12 vote, dropped its own earlier version in deference to the president's wishes and adopted the administration's plan. Anderson remarked that the "congressional battle for our right to use our own water is now on in earnest," as he recognized that if the state's projects remained outside the scope of the Colorado river plan, those facilities would be ineligible to share the power revenues from the Echo Park and

Glen Canyon dams and would have little chance at a later date of linkage with comparable revenue producing sources. Sniffing a plot within the administration to exclude New Mexico and its Democratic congressional delegation, Anderson acknowledged that his only hope of reinserting his state's projects lay within the more sympathetic Senate and in the House–Senate conference committee that ultimately would reconcile differences between the two bodies.[14]

Late in June 1954, the Senate Irrigation and Reclamation subcommittee began a week-long series of hearings on a bill similar to the original House version. As the subcommittee's senior minority member, Anderson insisted that the Senate version include the Navajo Dam as an initial project and that the state's smaller irrigation projects appear on a "provisional" basis until local engineers had completed their long delayed feasibility studies. He bluntly told one administration official that "New Mexico gets nothing out of the recommendations you have made." He noted that, due to the delicate cost accounting system, the projects' slim positive benefit-to-cost ratio would quickly evaporate without the assistance of the larger dams' power revenues. Citing the Navajo Indians' vested interest in the matter, Anderson left little doubt as to his own feelings, declaring "I want the Navajo Dam put into the bill as an initial project!" When the Reclamation Bureau's commissioner asked him what he would do with the water in the light of the senator's proposal to defer immediate authorization of the two supporting irrigation projects, Anderson snapped that he would concern himself about what to do with the water after he got the dam.[15]

As the Senate hearings ran their week-long course, it became clear that the legislation's supporters faced opposition from three significant interest groups. They included conservationists, Californians, and a coalition of eastern and midwestern congressmen who had little appetite for costly reclamation projects of no immediate benefit to their regions. Individually, Anderson believed, they could be neutralized. In combination, however, he knew their forces would easily undercut the bill's chances. An examination of Anderson's relationships with these three groups sheds light not only on his tactics for the Navajo project, but more broadly on the strategy he would employ throughout the remainder of his public life in working for natural resources conservation legislation.

The conservationists, broadly defined, commanded the largest and most vocal constituency in opposition to the Colorado River

Storage Project. Organizationally, they belonged to a variety of single and multi-issue organizations including the Sierra Club, the Wilderness Society, and the National Parks Association. Philosophically, they included "aesthetic preservationists" arguing for an untouched wilderness and the so-called "wise use" proponents supporting a measured and "reasonable development" of natural resources. The one provision of the administration's proposal that brought these diverse groups together was the plan for a major dam and reservoir at Echo Park in northwestern Colorado.

For at least a decade, the Echo Park site had been among the Reclamation Bureau's most favored for possible future development. Its wilderness location insured that the Bureau would not have the politically unpopular task of uprooting residents to flood out their homelands. From an engineering perspective, the site was nearly perfect. The Green River, a major tributary of the Colorado, sharply narrowed between three-thousand-foot-high cliffs below Echo Park. This setting offered maximum protection of the water below against the sun's evaporating rays. Those walls would require virtually no reinforcement, eliminating a potentially costly undertaking. The site's proponents argued that the reservoir would elevate the river a mere three hundred feet, hardly noticeable in a gorge ten times as high. The resulting placid reservoir would permit easy access to one of the nation's most colorful, least explored regions without destroying its beauty. Previously, undeveloped roads and murderous rapids had excluded all but the most intrepid explorers.[16]

The conservationists argued that these theoretical advantages paled in the face of one overriding reality. The proposed dam site was situated well within the boundaries of a federally protected preserve known as Dinosaur National Monument. In 1938 President Franklin Roosevelt had authorized the expansion of an eighty-acre site surrounding a quarry containing dinosaur bones to more than 200,000 acres. Echo Park, not a traditional "park" under the terms of federal statutory protection, was located far from the original excavation site in the added area.

The project's tortuous course, in the years immediately following World War II, through the Interior Department's bureaucracy only served to inflame conservationist sentiments. Early in 1950 Interior Secretary Oscar Chapman mediated a dispute over the Echo Park site between his department's developmentally minded Reclamation Bureau and the preservationist-spirited National Park Service. He decided in favor of the Reclamation Bureau's position that Echo Park offered the best protection against major water losses through evaporation. His decision unleashed a torrent of opposition from the conservationists. This resulted in further delay, ultimately passing the decision in 1953 to the incoming Eisenhower administration. Finally, in December 1953, Interior Secretary McKay approved the Echo Park dam on the basis of studies demonstrating that alternative sites would lose to evaporation an additional 100,000 to 200,000 acre feet of water per year. This decision set off a firestorm of criticism among the conservationists.[17]

One of their foremost spokesmen to appear before the Senate subcommittee was General U.S. Grant, III. In 1954, Grant had completed forty-three years of service with the U.S. Army Corps of Engineers, the federal government's principal dam-building and flood-control agency. As president of the American Planning and Civic Association, Grant was the conservationists' lead-off witness. Assuring the senators that conservationists generally had no objection to the other provisions of the Colorado River bill, he tore into the Echo Park proposal. Grant's principal argument was that the dam at Echo Park would violate the integrity of the national park system. He feared that Echo Park was to be only the first in a long series of developers' assaults on previously immune national parks. He evoked images of the wild Green and adjoining Yampa river valleys flooded beyond recognition and drew on his engineering experience to prove that other sites would be less subject to water loss through evaporation. The subcommittee's peppery Utah Republican Arthur Watkins declared full scale war on the courtly general. He challenged him on every point, reducing Grant to incoherence.[18]

Similar treatment awaited David Brower of the Sierra Club. Watkins shouted. Brower persisted. He successfully challenged the Reclamation Bureau's evaporation figures and introduced photographs showing the ugly consequences of the federal government's 1913 decision to convert California's beautiful Hetch Hetchy Valley into a water supply for San Francisco. The Hetch Hetchy decision fired the determination of conservationists never again to allow the government to invade areas previously set aside as park and wilderness preserves. The Echo Park provision evoked memories of this earlier violation and elevated the Colorado River bill to the status of a national *cause celebre*. Its opponents believed that if the developers prevailed at Echo Park, the entire national park system would become vulnerable to their insatiable demands. Conservationist leaders such as Brower and Howard Zahniser of the Wilderness Society made clear to the subcommittee their intent to seek common cause with the bill's other foes if Congress failed to remove the Echo Park provision.[19]

Anderson took this threat seriously. He believed that with the aid of sympathetic Reclamation Bureau experts, he could neutralize each group's specific arguments. His overriding concern was to avoid driving the opposing groups into a "marriage of convenience." Such an alliance, he surmised, would surely doom the bill and New Mexico's chances to move ahead with the development of the San Juan and, consequently, its entire Colorado River allocation.

While the conservationists were vociferous but imperfectly organized, a second major opposition group moved into the fray with quiet and well-financed determination. The Californians' threat to the bill proceeded from a far less idealistic base. California's chief concern was that the upper basin's storage project would seriously deplete the Colorado's flow into the lower basin. Put more boldly, that state's representatives feared that the project would put an end to the flow of water in excess of their entitlement, water rightfully belonging to the upper basin but heretofore unharnessed, and thus an unintentional gift of the upper basin to the lower.[20] Many supporters of the Echo Park project feared that the Californians were using the more idealistic conservationists, particularly the California-based Sierra Club, as a front for their greedy designs on Upper Basin water.

The membership of Anderson's subcommittee was heavily stacked against the California position. Accordingly, that state's representatives found the panel had alloted them only several hours at the end of the week-long hearing, beginning at five o'clock on Friday afternoon. While Anderson's subcommittee colleagues were fleeing the Capitol for the attractions of a pleasant summer weekend, the New Mexico senator assumed responsibility for questioning the Californians.

Unlike Watkins, Anderson treated dissenting witnesses respectfully, patiently allowing that state's water counsel, prominent Washington attorney Northcutt Ely, to rehearse California's familiar objections. Ely disputed Anderson's claim that the 1922 compact entitled the upper basin states to all the river's water in excess of seventy-five million acre feet per decade. He argued that both basins were to divide the flow evenly, with the lower states receiving no less than seventy-five million acre feet over any ten-year period. In vain, Ely sought to scrap the entire bill, claiming that its assumptions would greatly reinforce and expand the mass of water rights litigation to which California was then a party. Anderson listened attentively. He sympathized with the predicament wherein California had allowed itself to become dependent upon the upper basin's unused water in expanding the power capacity of Hoover Dam to meet Los Angeles' growing requirements. In his opposition to the well-schooled Ely, Anderson displayed impressive expertise with a carefully targeted point-by-point rebuttal.[21]

At the conclusion of the subcommittee's hearings on July 13, 1954, Anderson viewed the Colorado Storage Project bill's future with skepticism. Senator Joseph R. McCarthy's irresponsible four-year campaign to rout suspected Communists from the government had finally exceeded the Senate's capacity to tolerate excesses in its members' behavior. Arthur Watkins, Anderson's irascible and effective ally, was rapidly becoming the point-man for those in the Senate who had concluded that the time had come to call McCarthy to account. Anderson became preoccupied with his own reelection campaign, and recognized that more than twenty-five of his Senate colleagues faced similar distractions.

In mid-July, several influential New Mexico newspapers criticized Anderson for his apparent reluctance to move S.1555 out of committee and onto the Senate floor. Bristling at the papers' display of impatience, Anderson declared that the subcommittee's chairman, Colorado Republican Eugene Millikin, was then heavily involved with a major tax bill before the Senate Finance Committee, which he also chaired. Aging and sick, Millikin moved at his own pace. Anderson, a master of legislative timing, recognized that premature interference could prove fatal. "I could come charging in like a bull in a china shop and I might be able to pressure some of my colleagues on the subcommittee into reporting the bill. With that, I could pin medals on myself and go around feeling good." He added, however, that without the chairman's cooperation, S.1555 would never reach the Senate floor and his victory would be hollow indeed.[22]

Key to Anderson's strategy was the final conference between the House and Senate to hammer out points of disagreement. The rest was window dressing. He felt certain that his subcommittee's agreement to include the New Mexico projects would prevail in the Senate. If the House would pass any bill bearing the title "Colorado River Storage Project Act," Anderson believed he could take care of the discrepancies in the final reconciliation conference between the two houses.

On July 22, 1954, the Interior Committee met to examine its subcommittee's handiwork. With California's Republican senator Thomas Kuchel offering the lone dissent, the committee quickly approved S.1555 for the Senate's consideration. As reported, the measure included authorization of $68 million for the Navajo Dam and $318 million for the Navajo Irrigation and the San Juan–Chama projects.[23] Four days later in a Senate floor speech, Anderson praised Millikin's leadership in guiding the bill. Privately, the New Mexican suspected that Millikin was a reluctant champion and that the White House was pressuring the Colorado Republican out of its hostility to the subcommittee's addition, five days earlier, of the New Mexico projects. He feared that Millikin would do nothing to hasten the bill's consideration. Anderson tied Millikin's reluctance to Colorado's incomplete plans for the use of its own portion of the river. In the absence of such plans, Millikin feared that New Mexico and other upper basin states would preempt Colorado's allocation for their own uses.[24]

After delivering verbal bouquets to his chairman, Anderson proceeded on the Senate floor to characterize the bill as an important vehicle for allowing the upper basin states to meet their delivery obligations to the lower states. In the absence of the proposed holdover storage facilities, he argued, the upper states would find it impossible, during low water years, to increase their consumptive uses without interfering with the established rights of the lower states. He stated that the upper basin's goal was to add two million acre feet to its existing usage, bringing the total to four and a half million acre feet, three million short of its entitlement under the 1922 compact. For the California senator's benefit, Anderson reminded his audience that it would take the upper basin states at least seventy-five years to harness their full allotment of the river's flow. He concluded by noting that the upper basin reservoirs, by retaining the huge volume of silt that would otherwise flow into the lower basin, would prolong the Hoover Dam's life by at least one hundred years.[25]

Despite Anderson's efforts, time ran out on S.1555. He was able to do little more than obtain pledges from both parties' Senate leadership that the bill would receive a high priority in January 1955, at the beginning of the next congressional session.

As the Senate turned its attention exclusively to censure proceedings against Senator McCarthy, Anderson continued to ponder effective strategy against the third major opposition group, the industrialized states of the east and mid-west. Their representatives in Congress had already launched an attack on the Colorado River bill's anticipated billion-dollar price tag, charging that the stated figure was merely the "tip of the iceberg." They estimated that hidden costs could increase the ultimate expenditure fivefold. Anderson was keenly aware of the not-so-silent fraternity of the House's urban members, dedicated to stopping reclamation projects hatched in the Senate where the thinly populated western states' influence was proportionally greater.[26]

Anderson recognized that a full-scale educational campaign would be required to reach the vital majority of uncommitted congressmen. For that reason, he agreed to cooperate with the newly established "Upper Colorado Grass Roots Committee." Under the leadership of thirty-six-year-old Tom Bolack, a politically ambitious San Juan basin Republican who in the early 1950's had turned `$600 borrowed on his automobile into a quick fortune in gas and oil, the committee took on the external trappings of a vigilante organization. Calling its members "Aqualantes," the group sought to enlist 100,000 members nationwide. In return for a one dollar initiation fee, members received a blue plastic sheriff's badge and a sense of service as protectors of their country's water resources. Under the credo "To be ever alert and to stand ready to serve as we are needed," the Aqualantes attracted a sizable membership extending far beyond the upper basin's borders. By the end of 1954, Bolack's committee had distributed thousands of booklets, maps, and speakers' kits and had prepared a film entitled "Birth of the Basin," and a recording called "Song of the Aqualantes."[27] Although skeptical of the committee's techniques and sensitive to the political motives of its Republican coordinator, Anderson appreciated Bolack's apparent willingness to follow his own lead.

The 1954 congressional elections by a slim margin returned the House and Senate to Democratic control. In January 1955, Anderson, fresh from his own impressive reelection victory, succeeded Millikin as chairman of the Senate Irrigation subcommittee. Concurrently, he assumed the chairmanship of the prestigious Joint Committee on Atomic Energy. He suspected that the latter post would make severe demands on his frail health and already over-committed schedule. Nonetheless, Anderson wasted little time setting a date for a new round of hearings on the Colorado River bill. The specific bill, S.500, was identical to the version the subcommittee had approved six months earlier.

To underscore the bill's importance, Anderson decided to conduct the initial hearing in the Senate's ornate Caucus Room, familiar to millions of television viewers as the site of the 1954 Army–McCarthy hearings. On February 28, a dozen senators and scores of spectators looked on as the chairman, good-humored and gracious in his new role, wielded the gavel and stepped up the pressure behind S.500. Wishing to expedite the committee's deliberations, he admonished the witnesses, most veterans of earlier hearings on the subject, to be brief and avoid duplicating previous testimony.[28]

Anderson's objective was clear. He sought to push the bill quickly onto the Senate's calendar for floor consideration, avoiding competition later in the session with other priority legislation. Wyoming Senator Joseph O'Mahoney (D), once chairman of the full Interior Committee, reflected the confident attitude of his subcommittee colleagues in asking to hear "whatever possible argument can be made against the bill." He said he awaited anxiously "those who would prefer to see the Upper Colorado River basin exist forever as a desert made by the floods of a thousand years rather than develop the [region's] wonderful mineral and water resources."[29]

Colorado's governor, former senator Edwin Johnson (D), sounded the first discordant note. The large, ruddy-complexioned chief executive arrived with a list of eighteen Colorado projects that he wished added to the bill. His projects' estimated cost was $218 million, and they would appropriate 400,000 acre feet of water annually. Johnson threatened to sink the bill unless the subcommittee corrected the inequity wherein Colorado "provided" 72 percent of the river's flow while receiving an allocation of only 51 percent. He was particularly upset at the bill's projected division of power revenues. Over a seventy-one year period, Colorado was to receive a mere 5 percent, while Anderson's New Mexico would have taken more than 60 percent.[30]

Despite Anderson's warning, most of the subsequent witnesses duplicated testimony of the previous year. After six days of hearings, in which the Californians and conservationists received only perfunctory attention, the subcommittee approved S.500, sweeping it through the full Interior Committee and onto the Senate floor.[31] True to his word, Lyndon Johnson, savoring his new role as Senate Majority Leader, set April 18 as the opening day of debate for the Colorado River bill.

Clinton Anderson moved directly to the majority leader's front-row desk to take command as floor manager of S.500. In a brief opening address, designed to reassure his industrial state colleagues, Anderson noted that Congress over the past half century had appropriated $2.5 billion for western reclamation projects.[32] He quickly added that the West had more than repaid this amount to the treasury in the form of project-derived taxes. The payback principle, observed Anderson, was the cornerstone of S.500, wherein power revenues would flow into the treasury over a period of fifty years, paying off most of the construction costs with interest.[33]

The first substantive objection came from Illinois Senator Paul Douglas (D), an able proponent of the eastern–midwestern opposition bloc. Douglas, a former University of Chicago economist, suggested sardonically that the upper basin states could more profitably use the $1.5 billion to erect on Pike's Peak hothouses in which to grow bananas. He repeated the familiar charge that sixteen percent of the Senate, representing three percent of the nation's population, was seeking to enrich its region at the expense of the rest of the country. He presented a detailed and convincing benefit-cost analysis showing that the cost of construction at Echo Park would be $640 per kilowatt hour compared with the Tennessee Valley Authority's average of $166. He concluded by addressing the fears of a nation that saw itself falling prey to the developer's bulldozer. The projects, in his view, "would cripple the recreational features of the country and tend to transform the nation physically, into a placid, tepid place, greatly unlike the wild and stirring America . . . from which we draw inspiration."[34]

Anderson viewed Douglas as a formidable adversary and decided to deliver his own principal speech immediately following that of the Illinois Democrat. On the Senate floor, Anderson conducted himself as he had during the committee hearings, as a non-ideological conciliator, principled, yet not unbending. Addressing the Echo Park issue, the New Mexican underscored his own credentials as a conservationist. He recalled his unsuccessful fight in the House during

World War II to protect the beleaguered National Park Service from crippling budget cuts. He reminded other senators of his central role in the transfer of New Mexico's Carlsbad Caverns from state to federal ownership at no cost to the United States government. He expressed pleasure that the Caverns' large annual proceeds went to support other, less popular, sites under the Park Service's jurisdiction. Anderson inserted into the *Congressional Record* his September 1954 address, delivered at the invitation of the Wilderness Society to commemorate one of its founders, Aldo Leopold. The senator regarded Leopold as his mentor during the 1924 battle to save New Mexico's Gila River wilderness region from the grasping hands of private speculators.

Anderson turned next to the food surplus issue, so worrisome to the nation's farmers and their representatives. Speaking in his customary low key, barely audible fashion, he cited his past service as secretary of agriculture, chairman of the World Food Board, the nation's War Food Administrator, and as a long time member of the Senate Agriculture Committee. He predicted significant food shortages would appear within a decade in the face of natural population growth, increased per capita consumption and chronic drought. He cited an Agriculture Department study calling for the development of thirty-five million new acres of crop land by 1962. Anderson admitted that S.500 would provide only 600,000 acres over twenty-seven years, but that it would help compensate for the large amount of prime acreage that airport and highway builders were removing from production. Finally, Anderson noted hopefully that the anticipated power gains could transform the entire upper basin into a "vast inland empire," based on its virtually unlimited mineral, timber, and agricultural resources.[35]

After three days of debate, during which the bill's supporters were clearly dominant in their organization and strategy, the Senate passed S.500 by a 58–23 vote. Anderson and his upper basin colleagues had succeeded in avoiding a battle of the sections, picking up votes from every region and political persuasion. Although he had few doubts about the bill's capacity to attract a sufficient majority, Anderson had worried about the impact of failing to obtain a resounding victory on his future bargaining with House negotiators.[36]

As the focus shifted to the bill's uncertain future on the House floor, Anderson spent more time with his friend Tom Bolack. On May 9, he presided at the opening in the United States Capitol of an Aqualantes exhibit designed to emphasize the Colorado River project's benefits to the upper basin's Indians, as well as to the nation's defense and reclamation programs. Two weeks later, the senator appeared with Bolack on a New Mexico radio program to describe the bill's progress and accelerate regional pressure on undecided House members.

On the following day, the Upper Colorado River Commission, the river's administrative agency, met in Denver and made a crucial decision. The body endorsed Anderson's earlier private suggestion to eliminate from S.500 the controversial Echo Park Dam provision to avoid jeopardizing the bill's wider benefits. As a direct result of the commission's actions, House sponsors moved to strike Echo Park from their own bill. The Interior Department's admission that their evaporation figures were incorrect made the sponsors' action easier. Undersecretary Ralph Tudor told a House subcommittee further study had led to the conclusion that use of alternate sites would bring an additional loss of only 25,000 acre feet per year, as opposed to earlier estimates of 200,000 acre feet. Although Tudor continued to support Echo Park, the House committee had found a convenient justification for dropping the troublesome site. The House Interior Committee then began work on a formal report clearing the measure for floor consideration. The *Washington Post* editorially praised the removal of Echo Park, calling the modified House bill "a conservation bill in the largest sense of the word."[37]

As the Senate's version had already passed with Echo Park intact, Anderson felt that action in the upper chamber to delete the offending provision would be premature. He decided to wait, hoping that by midsummer the House would pass its revised bill. Anderson believed he could then drop the offending provision in the subsequent House–Senate conference.

The New Mexico senator did not move fast enough to suit the conservationists. Energized by their victory in the House, they moved in for the kill. Intolerant of poorly grounded opposition, Anderson deeply resented outside pressure once he had arrived at his own tactical decisions. A letter from Horace Albright, an acquaintance of long standing, ignited Anderson's anger and led to a revealing and intemperate exchange.[38]

Albright, formerly a superintendent of Yellowstone National Park and a director of the National Park Service, was among the nation's leading conservationists. As board chairman of Resources for the

Future, Inc., Albright had organized an important "Mid-Century Conference on Resources for the Future" in December 1953. His enormous credibility grew from his dual role as long time conservationist and successful corporation president. In the decade after 1945, his firm, the United States Potash Company, had doubled its annual sales, and its net income had grown by 70 percent. No fuzzy-minded extremist, Albright assumed a position of command in the war against the proposed dam at Echo Park.[39]

Albright wrote Anderson in July 1955 to enlist his aid in dislodging from the Senate Interior Committee a bill establishing a national park in the Virgin Islands. Anderson quickly responded that "it is going to be a long time before any more national parks are created . . . after the rather difficult experience with Dinosaur National Monument and the Echo Park Dam." Albright countered that, in his long Washington experience, he had never seen anything quite like the senator's behavior in this instance. The exchange shifted to Anderson who replied that Albright should know better than to write him on the letterhead of the United States Potash Company which had extensive production facilities in New Mexico. The senator thought it "strange" that a firm that had benefited so heavily from New Mexico's resources would use the money from those resources to take away the state's water and send it into California. Anderson surmised that influence of Albright's California shareholders might account for his "puzzling" betrayal of New Mexico. Albright responded, in a tone of sadness and disbelief, that Anderson was putting words into his mouth. At this, Anderson took the opportunity to remind the conservationist of his own successful efforts while serving in the House to add to the nation's tax code a depletion allowance for potash, and thus for Albright![40]

The disagreement with Albright and the bill's dim prospects in the House affected Anderson's already marginal health and forced him to bed for several days. Word had reached him that the bill's managers in the House were unable to line up enough Republican votes to ensure passage. In the face of the impending August recess, they had decided to wait until early 1956.

Regaining his strength, Anderson set out to mend his fences with the conservationists. He confided to an associate that Albright, "more than any one man, ruined us." Referring to the increasingly bothersome Aqualantes, Anderson observed that due to Albright's "fine reputation, a lot of people believed what he had to say, more than they would believe the petty propagandists." He conceded that they could not win the fight as long as Albright remained their most active opponent.[41]

A strategy session was clearly in order. On October 11, 1955, Anderson, Millikin of Colorado, Watkins of Utah, and O'Mahoney of Wyoming invited their states' governors and congressional delegations to a November 1 meeting in Denver. Under Anderson's skillful chairmanship, the four governors and seventeen congressmen who assembled at Denver's Brown Palace Hotel passed a series of key resolutions. They formally pledged to drop Echo Park from further legislative consideration, and they agreed to add New Mexico's Navajo Dam to the House bill. After a grueling day, during which Colorado's Governor Johnson proved to be the greatest obstacle to accord, Anderson left Denver, tired and drawn, but with renewed hopes for the Colorado River bill's chances in the new year.[42]

The conservationists still sought Anderson's personal assurance that under no circumstances would Echo Park slip back into a final bill. On January 4, 1956, Howard Zahniser of the Wilderness Society asked Anderson to add to the bill a stipulation forbidding the construction of dams or reservoirs within the boundaries of any national park or national monument. Insertion of this statement represented a major substantive victory for the newly consolidated cadre of seasoned conservation lobbyists. If not overridden, it would mark the end of the need for continued defensive actions on behalf of individual wilderness areas. Although Anderson believed such statements to be gratuitous, and not binding upon the action of future Congresses, he readily agreed. In return, he suggested that the conservationists issue a strong endorsement of the revised bill. Anxious to renew his previously positive relationship with Anderson, Horace Albright released a statement praising the project as a conservation measure that "created new, and protected existing, recreational facilities . . . conserving the West's most valuable resource, water."[43]

On March 1, President Eisenhower called a press conference to announce that he would be a candidate for reelection and to urge the immediate passage of the Colorado River bill. That afternoon the House completed a roll call vote, passing its version of the bill by a margin of 256 to 136. In an editorial the following day, the *Farmington* [New Mexico] *Daily Times* promised that the event "will be remembered as long as there is a New Mexico." Papers throughout New Mexico were quick to acknowledge Anderson's vital role.[44]

Back in Washington, however, Anderson knew that the battle was not yet over. On March 8, as chairman of the House-Senate conference committee, Anderson sat down behind closed doors with four Senate colleagues and five House members to reconcile S.500 with its House counterpart. True to his Denver pledge about Echo Park, Anderson blocked Arthur Watkins' repeated attempts to reinsert the dam. Watkins' persistence underscored a reality in campaigns to maintain wilderness in an untouched state. Victories could prove to be temporary, while defeats were irreversible.[45] After four difficult sessions, over the course of a week, the House conferees yielded to most of the Senate's points. The bill then moved swiftly to win the approval of both chambers and the president's signature.[46]

The turning point in Anderson's bid to save the Navajo Dam had come during the November 1955 Denver conference at which he engineered the agreement to drop the Echo Park Dam. This action effectively destroyed the conservationist opposition to his bill and also opened the way for the addition of one or more major projects to replace Echo Park. By that time the Eisenhower administration had placed its support solidly behind the concept of a Colorado River storage project. With a presidential election campaign looming ahead, the administration was not willing to sustain a defeat on this legislation. Moreover, opponents of the Navajo Dam within the Interior Department recognized that there was a great difference between authorizing a project, which was the purpose of S.500, and securing the actual appropriations. By yielding on the authorization, they could return after the election to fight against the appropriation. Anderson realized this and laid his battle plans accordingly.[47]

Anderson's campaign to include New Mexico projects in the Upper Colorado development plan succeeded because the larger plan, delayed by intrabasin squabbling and wartime distractions, was long overdue and because he brought to the task determination, experience and an unsurpassed sense of timing. During the eight-year battle, leadership in natural resources conservation policy passed from the executive branch to Congress, and particularly to the Senate. In the upper chamber, where each western state had an equal voice and could barter its influence with northern and southern states over issues that traditionally separated those two regions, the climate for constructive action promoted Anderson's effectiveness. From 1949 to 1956, he helped define the issues and mapped the feasible solutions. Over the following eight years, his leadership would largely determine the shape of those solutions for New Mexico, the West, and the nation.

Newly appointed Secretary of Agriculture Clinton P. Anderson poses outside his Albuquerque home on May 28, 1945. From left: son Sherburne, daughter Nancy, Anderson, and his wife, Henrietta. *(Acme Photos)*

Anderson receiving congratulations on his 1948 Senate election from his predecessor, Sen. Carl Hatch. *(Library of Congress)*

As secretary of agriculture, Anderson shares a light moment with President Harry Truman. *(Library of Congress)*

Three freshman members of the Senate "class of 1948." Lyndon B. Johnson (D-TX), Robert S. Kerr (D-OK), and Anderson. *(Wide World)*

Victorious Democratic members of the Senate "class of 1948" pose with party national chairman Sen. J. Howard McGrath, Secretary of the Senate Leslie Biffle, Senate Majority Leader Scott Lucas, and Chicago Mayor Martin Kennelly. Standing from left: Estes Kefauver (TN), Anderson, Russell Long (LA), McGrath, Matthew Neely (WV), Robert Kerr (OK), Lester Hunt (WY), Paul Douglas (IL), Biffle. Seated from left: Guy Gillette (IA), Hubert Humphrey (MN), Kennelly, Lucas, J. Allen Frear (DE), Virgil Chapman (KY), Bert Miller (ID), and Garrett Withers (KY). Missing was Lyndon B. Johnson (TX). *(Library of Congress)*

Anderson joins other members of the Senate Interior Committee in a 1949 formal portrait.
*(Library of Congress)*

Top and above: Anderson's 1954 reelection campaign. *(Library of Congress)*

New Mexico's senators, Dennis Chavez and Anderson, July 12, 1954. *(Library of Congress)*

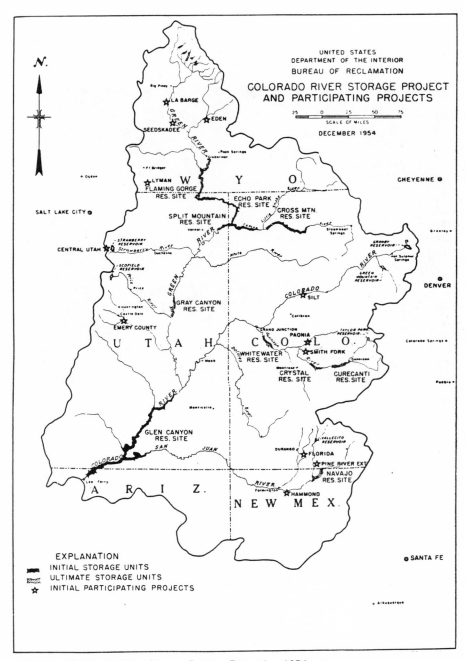

Proposed Colorado River Storage Project, December 1954.

Above: Anderson dedicates Aldo Leopold
Marker in New Mexico's Gila Wilderness
Area, September 12, 1954. *(Library of Congress)*

Right: Claude E. Wood, Anderson's
administrative assistant, November 1955.
*(Courtesy Claude E. Wood)*

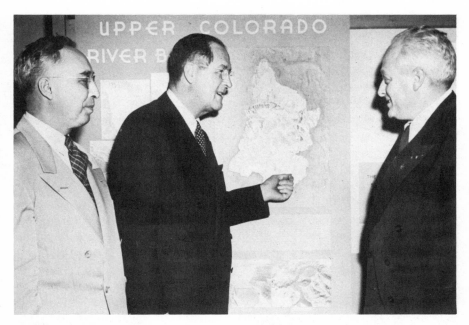

Facing page and above: Anderson with members of the Upper Colorado Basin Commission. *(Library of Congress)*

Anderson poses with Secretary Eloise de la O in 1956 publicity photo for National Foundation for Infantile Paralysis. *(Library of Congress)*

# 4

# From Regional Spokesman to National Advocate
## 1956–1961

There is a spiritual value to conservation, and wilderness
typifies this. Wilderness is a demonstration by our people that
we can put aside a portion of this which we have as tribute to
our Maker and say—this we will leave as we found it.

Clinton P. Anderson
September 5, 1961

Authorization of the Colorado River Storage Project allowed Clinton Anderson to shift focus from allocation of Colorado River basin water resources to related natural resources considerations of wilderness preservation and outdoor recreation planning. In the five years immediately following 1956, Anderson subtly but perceptably merged his role as regional spokesman for the water-deficient West with that of mediator and advocate for a responsive national conservation policy. In so doing, he further associated solutions to western resources problems with nationally based policies for natural resources protection and development.

During the period from 1956 to 1961, Anderson held life-or-death power in the Senate over three major legislative proposals for furtherance of national conservation policy. His sense of timing and ability to distinguish the possible from the desirable led him to a fundamental strategic decision. That decision accounted for the success in 1958 of the first of these proposals—the Outdoor Recreation Resources Review Act. It also led to postponement until 1961 of action on the second major proposal—the Wilderness Act. A third measure, the Multiple Use–Sustained Yield Act of 1960, represented a way station between the first and the second, bringing a fundamental readjustment of the U.S. Forest Service's traditional orientation in the face of intensifying user group pressure. An analysis of Anderson's role in the evolution of each measure demonstrates his growing effectiveness in the legislative forum as a shaper of national conservation policy.[1]

In 1956, when sponsors first circulated preliminary versions of the three bills, Anderson decided to support only the outdoor recreation legislation. His decision represented his wish to acknowledge the federal government's role in directing a revitalization of the nation's over used and inadequately planned inventory of recreational resources. At the same time, however, he had more immediate objectives. He believed the measure would help justify substantial write-offs for the general recreation value of water projects. These could be taken on the grounds that construction expenses directly assignable to recreation features of water projects, as well as other public benefits such as flood control, fish and wildlife enhancement, navigation improvement and silt retention, should be financed out of the federal treasury rather than by agricultural interests principally seeking irrigation benefits. The concept of a review commission, with its emphasis of state and local fact finding, particularly appealed to him. Anderson was unwilling to load the congressional agenda with other broadly based bills seemingly in conflict with, or supplementary to, his recreation measure. He believed that bill would provide a crucial first step in building support among urban-based House members, traditionally skeptical of forest and reclamation legislation. Accordingly, he blocked all efforts to advance the various wilderness proposals until the recreation bill had become law and until he had moved to a position of influence within the resulting study commission.

As a former secretary of agriculture, Anderson was sympathetic to the desire within the U.S. Forest Service to promote the so-called Multiple Use–Sustained Yield Act. That agency wished to clarify its authority to establish and administer national forests in the face of conflicting claims by developers and preservationists. During World War II and the years immediately thereafter, the national forests had been opened for commercial logging and mining to a degree not anticipated in 1897 when the original governing statute had been fashioned. The Multiple Use–Sustained Yield bill was intended to set forth specific priority uses, including recreation, and to convey to the Forest Service unrestricted discretion to resolve conflicts as various groups competed for access to increasingly overburdened forest resources.[2] By 1960, as the bill's chances of enactment increased, it had become widely perceived as a substitute, in tandem with the recreation commission, to the proposed Wilderness Act. This led the wilderness bill's advocates to turn to Anderson for help in guiding their measure through the precarious shoals of the Forest Service bureaucracy at a time when the supporting coalition of conservationist organizations, united at Echo Park, appeared to be fragmenting under the weight of their differing objectives.

The version of the Wilderness Act that triumphantly passed the Senate in 1961 had endured a decade of scrutiny. The measure's substance first underwent public inspection at the Sierra Club's 1951 biennial wilderness conference. Over the following thirteen years, Howard C. Zahniser of the Wilderness Society vigorously served as the proposal's philosopher and legislative strategist. Executive secretary of the society since 1945, he brought to that position years of experience as a journalist and Department of Agriculture official. A man of modest means, the bald and bespectacled lobbyist served, in the assessment of a Forest Service historian, as "a more appropriate role model for the average wilderness lover than the wealthy, backpacking 'elitists' who figured prominently in the demonology created by wilderness opponents." Zahniser's soft-spoken manner cloaked a dogged persistence, prompting Anderson to recall that the "evangelical fervor" with which the lobbyist approached the challenges of conservation could be explained by his descent from a long line of clergymen.[3]

Zahniser rooted his plan for a national wilderness preservation system in a growing awareness among conservationists of the inconsistent preservation policies of the Forest Service, born of chronic jealousy between that agency and the National Park Service. Since the establishment of the National Park Service in 1916, the Forest Service had sought to earmark prime timber tracts for preservation from the increasing resource demands of a growing nation and from the Park Service's strengthened grasp. In the 1920s the Forest Service, to keep its lands from being transferred to Park Service jurisdiction, devised a new category of park preserves known as "primitive areas." By the beginning of World War II the Forest Service had managed, under the Secretary of Agriculture's administrative authority, to set aside primitive areas amounting to eight million acres.[4]

A decade later, in the early 1950s, many conservationists, including Zahniser and David Brower of the Sierra Club, had become suspicious of the Forest Service's ability to devise and enforce long-range preservation plans for these areas. The agency's decentralized organization worked against application of uniform policies for protection of wilderness resources. Each man also recognized that the secretary of agriculture could remove an area from the "primitive" category and open it to development as easily as a predecessor had set it aside. The Forest Service's action between 1954 and 1956 in Oregon's Willamette National Forest substantiated their fears. There, in the Three Sisters Primitive Area, the service agreed to open for logging at lower elevations 53,000 acres of prime timber previously accorded a protected status. That agency then compounded the situation by placing the opened area's boundaries along river beds rather than following the customary practice of setting them along ridges to shield the adjacent wilderness areas from the unsightly effects of timbering.[5]

Zahniser and Brower were also concerned about the shift in philosophy evident in the National Park Service's leadership. The service had grown dramatically during the two previous decades. In 1930, it had custody of only fifty-five areas spread over ten million acres, and it played host to three million visitors. By 1948, that agency had added 125 areas. Its twenty-four million acres accommodated ten times the number of visitors, largely as a result of the greater availability of automobiles and leisure time in the postwar years.

Newton Drury, who had served as the Park Service's director since 1940, had participated in the Senate's early 1949 review of Interior Department activities. On that occasion, he urged the committee members to assist in his agency's badly needed modernization by funding expanded field staffs, improved road systems, and acquisition of 800,000 acres of private lands to round out the nation's park system. He argued that through adequate funding Congress could ensure not only the preservation of nationally significant scenic lands in the form in which they were created, but also could promote the spiritual well-being of a citizenry caught up in an increasingly urbanized and mechanized society.

In his testimony Drury identified several obstacles to the Service's efficient operation. He warned that cattle and lumber interests were intensifying their campaign for relaxation of restrictions against grazing and logging. Taking up the preservationists' long standing grievance against the Reclamation Bureau and the Army Corps of Engineers, Drury complained that the agencies' respective programs of dam and waterway construction threatened to flood scenic areas and drastically reduce the flow and recreation potential of major rivers.[6]

In its land acquisition program, the Park Service faced particularly strong opposition from western states unwilling to suffer the loss of tax revenues. Unlike the Reclamation Bureau, the Park Service was not permitted to reimburse local governments for their tax losses. Citing the nationwide benefits of the Service's facilities, Drury urged the committee to approve a system for sharing revenues with local areas and to bear a greater share of the purchase costs of suitable areas, particularly those private lands within the system's exterior boundaries.[7]

In June 1950 Interior Secretary Chapman recommended congressional approval of the Echo Park reservoir proposal. This action came within a few days of the outbreak of hostilities in Korea. Developers interpreted the decision as a green light for access to other federally protected preserves. The Defense Department rejected a proposal that Everglades National Park be turned into a bombing range. Stockmen tried without success to obtain grazing permits in units of the national park system for the duration of the war emergency. These growing assaults on the integrity of the park system were at the base of a growing dispute between Park Service Director Drury and Interior Secretary Chapman. Drury stoutly opposed Chapman's Echo Park decision, seeing it as the entering wedge against the principle of park inviolability. When subsequent events made it clear that the Reclamation Bureau had gotten the upper hand over the Park Service in the interagency struggle for Chapman's support, Drury hardened his attitude. As a result Chapman asked for and received his resignation.[8]

In 1951 Conrad Wirth replaced Drury as Park Service director. The new chief, a landscape architect, lost no time in expressing his intention to make the national parks more accessible to the public through improved road systems and other tourist conveniences. Under Wirth, development would undoubtedly take precedence over Drury's preservationist sentiments.[9]

Between 1951 and 1955 Zahniser toured the country seeking to

build a constituency for his wilderness proposals among conservationists of all varieties. On May 24, 1955, he unveiled his completed
draft at the Washington, D.C. meeting of the National Citizens' Planning Conference on Parks and Open Spaces. In his address, Zahniser articulated the preservationists' classic view of the wild state.
In distinguishing the wilderness from other settings for outdoor
recreation, Zahniser observed that in the wilderness the impres-
sions on the sojourner would more likely be "joyous than merry,
more refreshing than exciting, more engrossing than diverting." The
wilderness offered not an escape from society, but a setting in which
to find oneself and also to know a "profound humility, to recognize one's littleness, to sense dependence and interdependence,
indebtedness and responsibility . . . as members of a great community of life." Several years later, Zahniser put it more succinctly,
noting that wilderness, like chastity, is defined by that which it
negates.[10]

Hubert Humphrey eagerly accepted Zahniser's invitation to serve
as the Wilderness bill's chief Senate sponsor. The Minnesota Democrat sought to quiet developers' fears that the measure would lock
up the nation's most promising virgin lands. If enacted, he explained,
the bill would simply extend uniform statutory protection to 165
specifically designated wilderness areas that were already under
some form of federal supervision. Humphrey emphasized that the
bill would not rearrange agency jurisdiction of wilderness areas,
require new expenditures, extend to areas then outside of federal
control, or interfere with established mining and grazing operations.
On the positive side, he observed that the measure would bring
under control excessive road construction and, most importantly,
would provide congressional review of agency decisions to open
previously restricted wilderness preserves.[11]

The Humphrey bill's principal targets were the extensive land
holdings of the Forest Service. It specifically listed portions of eighty
of the country's 149 national forests, covering fourteen million acres
within the Service's 181 million acre domain. Of the eighty sites,
fifty-two were then classified as primitive areas. The bill gave the
Agriculture Department ten years to review each area for inclusion
either as permanent wilderness or for reversion to routine forest
status. The measure further provided that either house of Congress
could reverse a departmental decision to downgrade any of the
primitive areas. The bill's overriding purpose was to end two de-

cades of uncertainty over the future of Forest Service primitive areas and to keep them from being arbitrarily removed from their protected status.

In addition to Forest Service lands, the Humphrey Wilderness bill addressed the control and development of lands assigned to Interior Department's Park Service, Bureau of Land Management, and Bureau of Indian Affairs. To coordinate wilderness policy development between these diverse agencies, Zahniser included in his proposal a National Wilderness Preservation Council whose membership would be drawn from the affected agencies, Congress, and the general public.[12]

Anderson was unwilling to support the Humphrey bill and unable to ignore it. The measure singled out for protection five New Mexico tracts including the San Pedro Wild Area, the Gila Wilderness Area, the Pecos Wilderness Area, Carlsbad Caverns, and the White Sands National Monument. Anderson knew that the boundaries of several of these areas were subject to ongoing local disputes, that New Mexico mining and grazing interests would interpret the measure as a threat to the expansion of their activities, and that the Navajo Indians would view the bill as another unwarranted extension of federal control over their affairs.

New Mexico state engineer Steve Reynolds' negative evaluation of the Humphrey bill impressed Anderson. Reynolds argued that it threatened the long standing right of states to control water resources on federal lands that lay within their boundaries. He asserted that officials of the state of New Mexico were best qualified to determine where boundaries that might affect water development in New Mexico ought to be located.[13] He cited a report of his predecessor, John Bliss, to the effect that the bill was a thinly disguised effort to give legal standing to administrative orders of the past two decades that were in conflict with an 1897 statute guaranteeing that "all waters within boundaries of national forests may be used for domestic, mining, milling, or irrigation purposes under the law of the state wherein such national forests are situated." In addition to frustrating water development, the legislation, in Bliss' view, would effectively prohibit "for all time" development of strategic minerals, including gas and oil. He recommended that the legislation be delayed until affected states and federal executive agencies had a reasonable opportunity to evaluate its long-term effects.[14]

By mid-1956, Anderson concluded that he must sidetrack the Humphrey bill. To accomplish this, he seized upon the time-honored device of a study commission that would spend several years examining the relevant issues from the state and local perspectives as well as from the national. Joseph Penfold, conservation director of the Izaak Walton League, provided the New Mexico senator an appropriate vehicle.

During the 1956 presidential election campaign, Penfold completed work on a proposal to establish the National Outdoor Recreation Resources Review Commission. Anderson respected the sandy-haired Penfold whose easygoing outdoors image belied the strength with which he held to his convictions. His plan satisfied the senator's twin objective of buying time against increasingly severe developmental pressures on the country's park and wilderness lands and of focusing on the problems from the local and regional, as well as the national levels.[15] The measure also had the potential to establish the tangible recreational value that would be a by-product of the increasingly expensive western water projects. Anderson hoped that the data assembled by the Commission would support his arguments for reducing direct user costs by assigning more of those charges to recreation benefits, which were categorized as non-reimbursable and thus paid by the federal treasury.

Early in 1957, at the beginning of the Eighty-fifth Congress, Anderson introduced Penfold's proposal in the Senate. Noting that the bill's (S.846) purpose was to preserve the longstanding tradition of the "healthful and alluring appeal of the great outdoors," Anderson warned that the nation could no longer take its natural resources for granted. Rather, he insisted, they must be "protected and developed only by sound planning intelligently based upon the fullest understanding of all the pertinent facts and requirements." Anderson claimed that his bill would lead to a "comprehensive inventory and evaluation of outdoor recreation resources [and] project, as scientifically as possible, the known trends of population and recreation habits and desires of the public in order to estimate our future needs for continued outdoor recreation opportunity."[16]

Shortly after introducing S.846, Anderson addressed the annual convention of Penfold's Izaak Walton League. Preaching to the converted, he took issue with the U.S. Chamber of Commerce's argument that his bill would duplicate the objectives of resource surveys already planned by the Departments of Agriculture and Interior.

He asserted that the proposed commission would have a broader focus, giving "each community in America an opportunity to participate in a program that will assist in providing recreation where, in many instances, none existed before." He remarked, with a view toward building broad senatorial support, that the legislation would do as much for the East as for the West, where "lakes and streams, fish and wildlife refuges, marsh and wet-lands, and coastal areas" were in a similarly great need of development.[17]

On May 15, 1957, members of the Senate Interior Committee convened to hear testimony on the Anderson recreation bill. Committee chairman James Murray (D-MT) turned over the proceedings to Anderson, and the New Mexico senator began the familiar process of calling friendly witnesses, first from the Interior and Agriculture departments and then from the major conservation organizations. Representatives of the Park and Forest services endorsed the bill with minor reservations, and Joseph Penfold came forward to spread onto the hearing record a thick blanket of supportive documentation.

The first deviation from this comfortable scenario occurred when Harlean James, long time executive secretary of the American Planning and Civic Association, took her place at the witness table. She noted that her views were essentially those of two figures very familiar to Anderson and the Interior Committee, Horace M. Albright, her organization's chairman, and General U.S. Grant III, its president. Stating that her association, the sponsor of the 1955 forum at which Howard Zahniser had introduced the original wilderness proposal, was in favor of a "competent survey" of the nation's recreational resources, James unwisely volunteered that she would not be upset if the Anderson bill failed to pass. She contended, as had the Chamber of Commerce, that the National Park Service, under its existing statutory authority and programs, could just as easily accomplish those goals.[18]

Anderson's surprise at James' ambivalence quickly dissolved to anger and frustration. When James reiterated that she spoke for Albright and Grant, Anderson sharply told her that with Congress in an economizing mood, she could not have done a more effective job of lobbying against his bill than by saying it was not necessary. James begged Anderson not to call her a "lobbyist." The senator responded that he recognized a lobbyist when he saw one and that it was too bad that her group felt it had to join with the Chamber

of Commerce to kill his bill. Anderson continued that existing statutes permitted surveys only by the Interior Department's National
Park Service, specifically excluding participation of the Department
of Agriculture. He asked how she proposed to conduct a comprehensive survey without such a major component as the latter department's Forest Service. James sought in vain to argue that the
Forest Service would certainly cooperate and suggested that "legal
authorities" within the Interior Department supported her view.
When James proved unable to identify those "authorities," Anderson abruptly moved on to other witnesses.[19]

Several weeks later, Anderson received a letter from Horace Albright. Beginning with the observation that "it looks as though maybe
I am in your 'dog house' again," the former National Park Service
director attempted to explain the context of James's testimony. He
claimed that the American Planning and Civic Association thought
it was supporting the Interior Department's position that it already
had sufficient authority and funding for a recreation survey. Albright
explained that the Interior Department had subsequently changed
its stand to accommodate the Anderson bill, but had neglected to
tell his association. He confessed if that was the view of the Department, it was also his own and that he stood ready to join forces
with Anderson.[20]

Anderson believed that Albright characteristically was trying to
"play both sides" of the issue. He told Albright that "to be perfectly
frank with you, I was thoroughly shocked when your organization
testified against a bill to survey the recreation facilities of this country." The irate senator claimed that he had "tried hard in this bill to
be responsible to the requests and requirements of good people. I
have no apologies," he said, "for offering the bill and know how
disappointed you have been with the fact that I did not and could
not appreciate what I regarded as an unnecessary opposition to the
Upper Colorado project, but thank God, it is now law and I have
every hope that my survey bill will also become law."[21] Albright
responded that in the light of their thirty-year-long friendship, it
was hard to understand "how you could write me a letter like that."
In a gesture of conciliation, he promised Anderson that he would
work in his capacity as chairman of the Boone and Crockett Club's
conservation committee to generate appropriate support.[22]

Anderson's frustration stemmed in part from his apprehensions
that the Park Service, with whom Albright, as its former chief, was

firmly allied, was bent on "gutting" his bill. He believed that Director Conrad Wirth's strategy was to praise the bill faintly while allowing the Budget Bureau, an agency Anderson roundly despised, to raise potentially fatal questions with respect to the duplication of existing resources. In its report, issued two weeks after the Senate Interior Committee's May hearings, the Budget Bureau confirmed Anderson's suspicions by gently suggesting that the National Park Service alone could do the job. The Bureau also opposed the Anderson bill's provision for a lump sum multi-year appropriation, which the senator had seen as essential for entering into agreements for long-range studies with private contractors.[23]

To counter the Budget Bureau's report, Penfold advised the Interior Committee that a recreation survey such as Anderson's bill authorized would be beyond the capacity of a single bureau to conduct and that the resulting report would be valueless if it were too closely tied to a specific agency with known program biases. He noted that fish and game departments across the nation "pretty generally disagree with the wildlife policies of the Park Service," and that they were not at all likely to support its recommendations. Penfold concluded with a statement that mirrored Anderson's views. He said, "If the Park Service wants to be the sole voice for recreation policy and program planning at the federal level, I can understand that ambition, but I have no sympathy with it. There are altogether too many varied and diverse and conflicting elements in the national picture for such an arrangement ever to work out."[24]

In a closed meeting of the full Interior Committee on June 18, 1957, Anderson announced that Albright had dropped his previous opposition. He went on to tell his colleagues of his own first visit to the Grand Canyon three decades earlier at a time when only a handful of visitors made the risky trip to the Canyon's bottom. He compared this placid setting with the traffic jams and limited accommodations that confronted the one million visitors in 1956. Without the coordinated planning that the commission would encourage, Anderson warned that the situation would only deteriorate.

Wyoming's Sen. Joseph O'Mahoney (D) agreed with Anderson and praised the proposed commission's composition, which included eight members of Congress and seven individuals appointed by the president. O'Mahoney, a dogged defender of congressional prerogative, hoped that the legislative members would resist temptation to allow control of the commission to fall into the hands of less

distracted executive appointees. In that fighting spirit, the committee voted unanimously to report the bill favorably to the full Senate.[25]

A week later, on June 26, Anderson called up S.846 for Senate
debate. New Hampshire's Norris Cotton (R), fearing that the bill
would serve as the "entering wedge" for those western state senators who sought to include recreational benefits as part of the non-
reimbursable cost calculations in public works projects, nearly
crushed Anderson's hopes for speedy approval. Senators from both
parties and all regions assured Cotton that in this instance his suspicions were unfounded. The crusty New Englander accordingly
withdrew his objection, and the Senate quickly agreed to the bill.[26]

With Senate passage accomplished, Anderson began to suspect
that the National Park Service had a specific diversionary tactic in
mind. Several months earlier Park Service Director Wirth chose the
occasion of the annual American Pioneer Dinner, held at the Interior Department with sixty members of Congress present, to un-
veil his ambitious new project, "Mission 66." Wirth's proposal,
essentially a public relations campaign, would have committed $787
million to the revitalization of the nation's deteriorating and over-
used park system by 1966, the Park Service's fiftieth anniversary.
Although it was clear that the Park Service had sufficient statutory
authority, and appropriations, to launch "Mission 66," Wirth wanted
a long-term congressional guarantee for continued funding of his
program. Accordingly, he sent to the Park Service's supporters on
Capitol Hill a draft of the appropriate legislation.[27]

Conrad Wirth by mid-1957 had established himself as a determined and resourceful bureaucratic infighter. He served as the National Park Service's point man in the continuing struggle with the
Forest Service on one hand and the preservationist conservation
groups on the other. His chief antagonist in the latter camp was
David Brower of the Sierra Club. Once characterized as an "archdruid" who would sacrifice human beings to the worship of trees,
Brower exhibited an engaging smile and a handsome, delicately chis-
eled face somewhat out of proportion to his large, prepossessing
frame. He had spent his life protecting mountain ranges and wild-
lands against the designs of development-minded planners in the
Reclamation Bureau and the forest and park services.[28]

In the early 1950's Wirth, with the assistance of Horace Albright,
had attempted to have the troublesome Brower fired. Again in 1957
the two came to blows over the Wilderness bill and the Outdoor Rec-

reation Commission proposal. Brower charged Wirth with duplicity in his handling of a confidential draft of the wilderness measure. A year earlier, he had visited Wirth to discuss the Zahniser proposal. On three subsequent occasions, Wirth told Brower that he had not had the opportunity to study the bill. In the meantime, Brower suspected that the Park Service director had leaked the Zahniser draft to the hostile American Mining Congress, giving that well-funded opponent ample time to develop an effective counteroffensive. Declaring that he was "stunned" by Brower's allegations, Wirth urged the Sierra Club board of directors to fire their impolitic executive director. Recalling that Wirth recently had used similar tactics to unseat Devereux Butcher, editor of the National Parks Association's magazine, the board quickly affirmed its support of Brower.[29]

Anderson knew of Wirth's behind-the-scenes efforts to generate adverse Interior Department reports on his own recreation bill as well as on the Humphrey Wilderness bill. From Anderson's point of view, one of the most troublesome provisions of S.342, the Senate version of Wirth's "Mission 66" proposal, was a section which would establish a "National Recreation Survey" within the Interior Department. Anderson feared that if S.342 arrived on the president's desk before his own recreation bill, it would provide sufficient basis for the Interior Department to recommend that Eisenhower subsequently veto the Anderson bill. He contacted Senator Arthur Watkins (R-UT), a co-sponsor of his recreation bill and the sponsor, by request, of the "Mission 66" bill and asked him to intercede with Interior Secretary Fred Seaton, who had replaced Douglas McKay in 1956. Watkins reported that he would gladly call Seaton and "tell him that we are not going to have Conrad Wirth trying to run through a special program."[30]

Meanwhile, the House of Representatives' version of Anderson's bill encountered difficulty in that body's Interior Committee. Despite the efforts of committee chairman Clair Engle (D-CA) and the second-ranking Democrat, Wayne Aspinall (D-CO), Nebraska Republican Arthur Miller blocked the measure citing its duplication of Park Service prerogatives. That resistance promised to side-track the bill for the remainder of the 1957 congressional session.[31]

In frustration, Anderson, second in seniority on the Senate Interior Committee, wrote to Secretary Seaton, observing that the situation before the House committee left the "impression that the Park Service was secretly trying to gut the bill, and simultaneously in the Senate, Senator Watkins was prompted and urged to bring out S.342." He bluntly asked Seaton if he should "regard this as a declaration of war" on his bill. "If so," he wondered, "do we have to try to cut down appropriations to "Mission 66" in order to keep them from preempting the field which we believe should be occupied by another group?"[32] At the same time, Anderson asked Senator Interior Committee Chairman Murray to block action on S.342, hoping to delay the measure until S.846 was safely written into public law.[33]

In mid-August, shortly before the congressional adjournment, Wirth wrote to assure Anderson that his fears were without foundation. Recalling that the Interior Department had submitted a favorable report on S.846, Wirth lamely volunteered that the Park Service actions "will be guided at all times by the views of the Department." Consequently, the bill moved quickly through the House in the early months of 1958, receiving that body's final approval in mid-June and the president's signature shortly thereafter.[34]

On June 19, 1957, the day following its approval of Anderson's recreation bill, the Senate Interior Committee convened the first formal hearings on Humphrey's wilderness proposal. The timing of those hearings coincided with Senate floor debate on the controversial 1957 Civil Rights Act. Consequently, Anderson and most of his committee colleagues were unable to devote time or attention to them, and the hearings became largely a staff controlled exercise in record building. In the course of testimony, it became clear that the Humphrey bill would need substantial modification to obtain committee approval. Humphrey himself conceded that the bill was the work of dedicated conservationists rather than of skilled legislative draftsmen. As he took his place at the committee's witness table, he acknowledged that he appeared as an "advocate" who sought to work with the opposition and those more familiar than he with the technicalities of the issue to achieve a version that would respond to their major objections.[35]

The bill's need for substantive revision became painfully obvious when the Department of Agriculture voiced its opposition to the measure's legislative veto provision allowing a single house of Congress to override secretarial decisions downgrading primitive areas to forest status. The Department also objected to the bill's provision for a National Wilderness Preservation Council, seeing it as a needless bureaucratic buffer between itself and Congress and also as a potential lobby for wilderness issues within the federal government. Finally, the Agriculture Department argued that the bill violated the Forest Service's multiple-use policy and would impose highly restrictive "wilderness" standards in conflict with large scale recreational uses, as well as effective timber, watershed, wildlife, and range management.[36]

The Interior Department outlined similar reservations, noting that the bill's provisions ran counter to Anderson's Outdoor Recreation bill that it had already endorsed. It observed that the provision allowing either house to overrule departmental decisions would thrust Congress into the day-to-day management of national parks, wildlife refuges, Indian reservations, and similar "wilderness" regions. By attempting to set standards for non-park areas, which in the Department's opinion did not lend themselves to easy definition and a uniform management scheme, the bill threatened to stimulate controversy needlessly eroding the Park Service's already secure statutory foundations.[37] The Department argued that wildlife refuge areas required various forms of alteration, such as water impoundment and timber management, to maintain their usefulness to the species seeking refuge therein. Officials from the Department's Bureau of Indian Affairs complained that the bill contradicted the expressed national policy of turning over to private Indian ownership income-producing federal lands that would promote tribal self-sufficiency. In the Bureau's opinion, the bill would only serve to "lock-up" such lands. Other significant opponents included the Chamber of Commerce, the Upper Colorado River Commission, the National Reclamation Association, the Navajo Indian tribe and representatives of the cattle, lumber, and wood processing industries.[38] Among the bill's most active advocates was the Wilderness Society's Howard Zahniser, who contributed testimony, articles, maps, and charts that filled more than a quarter of the 450-page hearing record.[39]

Upon conclusion of the 1957 hearings, the sponsors of the wilderness bill agreed to incorporate many of the suggestions put forth during the two days of testimony. This process consumed exactly one year. On June 18, 1958, several weeks before the recreation commission bill itself was signed, Senator Humphrey introduced a revised bill. His new version, however, created as many difficulties as it eliminated. One of the most vexing was the provision that the Secretary of the Interior need only *consult* with the Indians before including their lands within the wilderness system. This represented a backward step, as the earlier bill had required their full consent. The new measure also permitted grazing and confirmed the use of power boats in National Forest areas where those uses were already well established. To further mollify critics, its backers added provisions affirming the applicability of state water laws to federal lands and providing for the construction of secondary roads to permit the control of fires, insects and diseases. Finally, they downgraded responsibilities of the proposed National Wilderness Preservation Council to that of a mere coordinating body and removed the stipulation that executive agencies receive the Council's clearance in their dealings with Congress.[40]

With the aid of Interior Committee staff, the Wilderness Society's Zahniser was chiefly responsible for fashioning the revisions. Zahniser attempted on several occasions to meet with Anderson to discuss these changes and enlist his support. The New Mexico senator found it inconvenient, however, to see the lobbyist until the Recreation bill was safely enacted. He agreed with his chief aide, Claude Wood, who advised, "too much legislation of this type all at one time is likely to arouse opposition and could ruin the chances of passing any of it."[41]

Shortly after President Eisenhower signed the Recreation Commission act on June 28, 1958, Anderson and Wood met with Zahniser. At that session Anderson promised to give the revised Humphrey bill his serious attention. Subsequently, Wood reported to Anderson that Zahniser was pressuring Chairman Murray to have the Interior Committee act on the bill without further hearings. This, Wood felt, would be unwise due to the substantial revisions from the first bill and the intense opposition of the Navajos, the cattle-growers, the National Reclamation Association and, of course, the Departments of Agriculture and Interior. Anderson agreed and urged the chairman to schedule an additional hearing. Accordingly, the committee met on July 23, 1958, less than four weeks before the end of the Eighty-fifth Congress. Anderson was unable to attend, but directed Wood to sit in on his behalf.[42]

The hearings produced clarification on the revisions and cautious support from the Agriculture and Interior departments. The chief point of contention centered around the newly created Outdoor Recreation Commission. Supporters of the Wilderness bill argued that its passage would significantly aid the commission in reaching its objectives. The measure's opponents, on the other hand, seized upon the commission's existence as an excuse to delay the bill's progress. They argued, often with less than complete sincerity, that it would be well to wait until the commission had studied the broad field of recreation, of which wilderness was but a single component, before deciding upon legislative remedies. As the commission's report was not due until September 1961, this would have guaranteed a three-year delay. A less strenuously opposed group of senators, of whom Anderson was one, believed that the wilderness bill needed more study, particularly by those constituency groups that had so strongly opposed the original Humphrey bill.[43] This "airing" could best be achieved, they felt, in field hearings. Accordingly, hearings were scheduled for the week following the November 1958 congressional elections in Richard Neuberger's Oregon, Thomas Kuchel's California, Arthur Watkin's Utah, and Clinton Anderson's New Mexico.

With the wilderness bill safely on the back burner, Anderson turned his attention to the organizing, funding, and staffing of the Outdoor Recreation Commission. On July 10, 1958, the Senate's president named four senators to the commission. As the bill's chief sponsor, Anderson was a certain choice. Joining him on the new panel were Richard Neuberger (D), Arthur Watkins, and Frank Barrett (R-WY). The House also selected four of its leading conservationist members, including Gracie Pfost (D) of Idaho, Al Ullman (D) of Oregon, John Saylor (R) of Pennsylvania, and Harold Collier (R) of Illinois.[44]

President Eisenhower received a great deal of advice from conservationists and members of Congress as to which individuals would best serve in the seven positions he had to fill. Anderson shared his own recommendations with Joseph Penfold. Writing in mid-July to the man who more than any other had nurtured the commission from idea to reality, Anderson told Penfold that "very confidentially someone came to see me about people who might be appointed and I gave them the name of Horace Albright as a likely chairman since he is now retired and included in the four or five names the name of a fellow named Penfold from Denver, since I think highly of him." Anderson concluded, "I hope the president may think as highly." Penfold responded that as a "realistic kind of guy, I must say I'd be about a million to one shot."[45]

On September 15, 1958, Eisenhower removed the basis for Penfold's pessimism by appointing him to the commission. Other seats went to a professor of forestry, a lumber company executive, a director of the American Forestry Association, an insurance company vice president, and a former Minnesota conservation commissioner. Eisenhower selected as chairman Laurance Rockefeller, one of the nation's leading philanthropists and conservationists.[46]

The crucial appointment that awaited the commission at its first meeting on September 25, 1958, was that of executive director. The commission's backers recognized that the success of the undertaking would depend heavily upon the enterprise and experience of the chief of staff. The wily and outspoken associate chief of the Forest Service, Edward Crafts, feared that a director too closely aligned with the rival Park Service, or the forest industry would foredoom the commission's work. Crafts, whom forest industry representatives viewed as a mortal enemy, took the liberty of sending Anderson a list of individuals who he believed intended to apply. Crafts volunteered his opinion of each of the potential candidates. One was the brother-in-law of a high administration conservation official, and that official had reportedly advised against his consideration because he lacked qualifications and was "mixed up in Republican politics." Several others on the list recently had been eased out of their high-profile positions and were "looking for work." A former state university president was identified as too close to the forest products industry and too old. Crafts did, however, suggest several individuals who were, in his estimation, well qualified.[47]

Meanwhile, with Congress in adjournment until the following January, Anderson returned to New Mexico, thereby missing the commission's initial meetings in September and November. It was clear by year's end that the commission was off to a slow start as neither its budget appropriation nor its staff director had been secured. Penfold feared the administration would try to frustrate the commission's work by recommending only a token appropriation and he urged Anderson to use his contacts at the Budget Bureau to sidetrack any such efforts.[48]

Back in New Mexico, Anderson's attention shifted once again to the pending wilderness legislation. On November 14, 1958, Anderson and two legislative aides presided over a well attended field hearing at the Albuquerque federal building. During the day-long session, the New Mexico senator listened to the wide ranging arguments with apparent judicial detachment. He acknowledged only that "the designation and use of some of our public lands for wilderness areas [is] a proper and desirable use for them." He hastened to add that "how large a system we should have, how far we should go in establishing wilderness areas, to what extent we should permit multiple use of wilderness areas, and what methods should be used in establishing and administering these areas" were all open to question.[49]

State Engineer Steve Reynolds led a long parade of witnesses and set the pace by arguing that the Wilderness bill, in a questionable effort to accommodate the interests of a tiny fraction of the population, would only lock up the state's natural resources and discourage tourism. Privately, Reynolds feared that the measure would frustrate New Mexico's efforts to receive authorization for construction of the Hooker Dam on the Gila River. That facility would back up water into the Gila Wilderness area, an action likely to be prohibited under the bill as then drafted. Livestock owners and wool growers added that the bill's restriction on road construction would make it impossible to control fires and would frustrate an effective program of predator control.[50] When a representative of New Mexico cattle interests suggested that the bill was the work of "Eastern dominated sportsmen, wildlife and historical organizations," Anderson briefly dropped his judicial mien to defend the sponsors' motives. He assured the witness that neither Senators Humphrey, Neuberger, nor Douglas was "dominated by any group of Eastern sportsmen." He explained that "we have a mutual defense society in the Senate. We look after each other, and they are not here to speak for themselves, so I presume to speak for them." Anderson agreed, however, with the witness' assertion that "they have been giving a lot of thought to this in the East."[51]

Paul Jones, astute chairman of the Navajo Tribal Council and Anderson's long time friend, took exception to the provisions restricting road development and permitting the federal government to take Indian lands without tribal consent. Without roads, Jones contended, Navajo children had been forced to attend boarding schools because school buses were unable to reach them on a daily basis. He argued that the lack of roads on Indian reservations was a principal contributor to continued poverty and ignorance. Anderson assured Jones that this provision for taking tribal lands without consent would be stricken from the bill, but patronizingly "reminded" him that the government in recent years had compensated Indians for lands taken at a rate far in excess of their market value. Anderson concluded with the assurance that "nobody is going to try to take this land away from you; so you quit worrying."[52]

Richmond Johnson, executive secretary of the Central Arizona Project Association, added his voice and influence to the opposition by focusing on the problem of the West's chronic water shortages. Noting the value of public lands as watersheds, he asserted that it was not sufficient to let nature take its course. In Johnson's view, those watersheds required active and sustained management if the West was to continue to grow and prosper, and he charged that the Wilderness bill would preclude that management.[53]

Elliott Barker of the New Mexico Wildlife and Conservation Association disagreed with Johnson, arguing that the bill would enhance the watershed values of the designated areas and that it would not interfere with such established uses as grazing of livestock. He attacked the introduction of roads, which he believed would facilitate excessive grazing and lumbering and would promote commercialization. This, in his view, would threaten all of the land's resources, including, most importantly, its watershed capabilities. The positions of Barker and the other conservationist witnesses were best summarized in one sentence from the testimony of an Izaak Walton League representative. "We like to feel," said the League's David Shaffer, "that the wilderness areas are like United States savings bonds, set aside, accruing interest, reassured that if there is a time of need, they are still there and increasing in value."[54]

At the beginning of the Eighty-sixth Congress in January 1959, Hubert Humphrey realized that his wilderness bill would have to win the endorsement of a wider range of senators to clear the crucial hurdle of the Senate Interior Committee. Chairman Murray nominally had sponsored the bill since 1957, but at the age of eighty-two and in poor health, he was increasingly passing leadership of the committee to Anderson as the second-ranking majority member. Murray had two years remaining in his Senate term and his ability to stand for reelection was in doubt. Accordingly, Humphrey told Anderson early in the session that his cosponsorship of the wilderness bill "would please me a great deal." Humphrey promised that he was still open to "concessions."[55]

Anderson still was not ready to join Humphrey's crusade. Claude Wood had studied the new bill and reported that it was not substantively different from the previous Congress' version. Wood concluded that "there is no real and pressing need for this legislation at the present time" and suggested that Congress might achieve the measure's principal goal of providing legislative sanction to the Forest Service's administrative management of wilderness areas by simply passing a joint resolution to that effect. Wood incorporated this proposal in Anderson's letter of response to Humphrey. He also questioned the logic of applying the multiple-use concept to wilderness areas. By definition, that concept implied a variety of uses and thus was inconsistent with the single-purpose intent of wilderness legislation.[56]

Although Humphrey thanked Anderson for his "frank response," he stated that he had invested too much time and energy to "back up all the way" at that point. Anderson expressed sympathy with his colleague's position, but felt that the Minnesota senator's overture was belated. In explaining his own position, he noted that the original bill was "far too extreme in the beginning and that prejudiced it badly." He continued pointedly, that "whether it prejudiced it so much that it cannot be revived in this session, I do not know. I only know that the people who took it up originally might have done well to have had the advice of those individuals who would have the responsibility of passing it."[57]

Anderson was aware that influential and highly vocal portions of his own constituency misunderstood or deliberately misrepresented the bill. At a meeting of the Catron County Farm and Livestock Bureau, speakers alleged that the measure would extend New Mexico's Gila Wilderness without limit. They also falsely claimed that it would end all grazing and also would wipe out programs for predator control. The state legislature, in a strongly worded memorial to New Mexico's congressional delegation, followed in this same vein.[58]

In April 1959 promoters of the Wilderness bill increased their pressure on Anderson to make a commitment. Howard Zahniser appeared as the principal force behind this effort. He urged Odd Halseth, a long time Anderson friend and director of the city of Phoenix, Arizona's division of archeology, to contact the New Mexico senator. Halseth wrote Anderson that "few people seem to know how you stand personally [on the bill] though I have personally had no doubt." Alluding to the senator's forthcoming 1960 reelection campaign, Halseth continued on an optimistic note, remarking "that while you may not have done much talking as far as I know, I am sure that you would never use the Wilderness bill for political campaign purposes of winning favor with the opposition, and that

I would bet my bottom dollar that you would vote for the bill when it comes out of committee."[59] Several days later Zahniser met with Claude Wood in a further attempt to resolve the issues that Anderson found troublesome. He told Wood that contrary to the argument that the measure was inconsistent with the multiple-use concept, it actually reinforced the idea by striking a balance between the need to permit grazing in those lands and the need to keep them in their untrammeled natural states. He suggested that the grazing interests opposing the bill be reminded that very few cattle and sheep grazed in the areas designated for inclusion within the wilderness system.[60]

For the first half of 1959 Anderson found little time to deal with conservation legislation. In January he began his second term as chairman of Congress's Joint Committee on Atomic Energy. That prospect, late in 1958, had led Admiral Lewis Strauss, chairman of the Atomic Energy Commission, to decline President Eisenhower's offer for reappointment. Relations between the admiral and the senator had been strained since 1953 when Strauss had opposed plans to have the Tennessee Valley Authority sell power to Atomic Energy Commission installations in the area and refused to support J. Robert Oppenheimer against Senator Joseph McCarthy's charges of disloyalty. Anderson had been a strong supporter of Oppenheimer, who had directed New Mexico's Los Alamos Scientific Laboratory. Anderson believed that Strauss had politicized the Atomic Energy Commission, and he told President Eisenhower early in 1958 that Strauss could expect "a penetrating examination" during his reconfirmation hearings. At the heart of Anderson's bitter and unyielding attitude toward Strauss lay his determination that Congress must take an active part in the work of executive branch agencies. Accordingly, he reacted angrily at Strauss' efforts to withhold information from the Joint Committee on Atomic Energy.

Not wishing to lose a trusted friend and adviser, Eisenhower nominated Strauss as Secretary of Commerce in October 1958. Confirmation hearings began in mid-March and by April 22, Strauss had managed to antagonize Commerce Committee Chairman Warren Magnuson (D-WA) to the point that he urged Anderson to testify. Magnuson believed that Anderson knew more about Strauss' fitness than any other senator. Anderson, not a member of the committee, initially had not intended to stand in Strauss' way, but the nominee's uncooperative attitude during the first month of his hearings convinced Anderson that the admiral was unfit for federal service of any kind. During the final days of April, Anderson and his aides spent many hours assembling a case against Strauss. On May 4, Anderson appeared before the Commerce Committee with a 66-page indictment. From that time until June 19, 1959, when the Senate voted 49-46 to reject the presidential cabinet appointment, the first such occasion since 1925, Anderson had little time for other initiatives. Furious at Anderson and Majority Leader Lyndon Johnson for this embarrassment, Eisenhower told his secretary the following morning, "This was the most shameful thing that had happened in the U.S. Senate since the attempt to impeach a President many, many years ago."[61]

Late in June, Claude Wood again turned his attention to the wilderness bill. He met with Hugh Woodward, a New Mexico resident who was a regional director of the National Wildlife Federation and for whom Anderson and conservationists across the country had great respect. Woodward was well aware of the objections of influential New Mexicans such as Steve Reynolds. Woodward believed he could address Reynolds' concerns by inserting language that would further affirm the primacy of state water laws in the face of apparently contradictory federal legislation. Woodward also proposed elimination of the controversial National Wilderness Preservation Council, substituting an inter-agency body constituted by the Departments of Agriculture and Interior. He inserted a provision to prevent "unwarranted expansion of wilderness areas without congressional consent."[62]

After discussing the changes with Anderson's aide, Woodward went to the offices of the National Wildlife Federation to present the modifications to key conservation leaders meeting there. Only Zahniser was reluctant, but in the face of an emerging consensus that the modifications were the price for Anderson's support and action in the Interior Committee, he went along with the others. Still, Wood continued to believe the bill was largely unnecessary and that it should remain in committee until 1961 when the Outdoor Recreation Commission was scheduled to make its final report. He advised Anderson that national parks and wildlife refuges should be removed from the bill and that it should be amended to permit Congress to veto agency actions designating individual wilderness tracts. The bill's language earlier had been changed to require a *joint* resolution of Congress to achieve that end. As the president had the authority to veto a joint resolution, he could, in effect, veto the congressional veto. Wood subsequently suggested the device of a *concurrent* resolution, not subject to executive approval, which would permit Congress to exercise its judgment without the possibility of a presidential veto.[63]

Wood sent the revised version of the bill to Steve Reynolds for further comment. Reynolds agreed that it was an improvement and recognized that Anderson was coming under great pressure to support "some sort of" wilderness bill. He commended the senator on his efforts "to develop something that we can live with." Nonetheless, he still opposed the bill, arguing that the pressures for increased resource development and the growing tourist industry in New Mexico made inevitable the conversion of much wilderness and primitive land in the years ahead. Reynolds agreed with Wood that the measure should deal only with Forest Service wilderness lands, deleting controls over Park Service and Bureau of Land Management tracts. He added that recent research substantiated his view that proper timber and vegetation management could materially increase watershed yields. Accordingly, he called for an amendment that would permit the construction of permanent roads when they were deemed necessary to promote watershed development.[64]

Late in July Anderson recognized that there was no chance that Congress would enact the Wilderness bill during 1959. The House committee had set aside its version, and there were a number of other measures further advanced in the legislative pipeline. Although Anderson "could see no reason why we should rush it through," he deferred to Chairman Murray's desire to bring up the bill at the committee's August 4th business meeting. That meeting proved inconclusive; consequently the chairman placed the much-amended bill on the committee's agenda for August 14th.[65]

At the subsequent meeting, the committee's Wilderness bill's opponents unveiled their strategy, which amounted to replacing the bill, by then a patch-work of compromise, with a new measure. Although the proposed replacement bore a superficial resemblance to the Humphrey version, it was actually a creation of the opposition mining, timber, and livestock coalition. The revised bill's principal Senate backers were Joseph O'Mahoney and Gordon Allott (R-CO). At the time of the August committee meetings, poor health had sidetracked O'Mahoney, so Allott carried the torch. He managed to offer so many new amendments that Chairman Murray reluctantly decided to postpone consideration until the 1960 session.[66] Several days later, O'Mahoney wrote to Murray, arguing that the original bill's vagueness would result in tying up valuable mineral resources, vital to the nation's defense. The measure's provision that placed decisions on wilderness site selection in the executive branch, presumably in the hands of a "faceless bureaucrat," clashed with O'Mahoney's support of congressional prerogatives. He compared this arrangement with the Soviet Union's decision-making processes and warned against an unnecessary surrender of congressional power.[67]

The Allott-O'Mahoney substitute set off a furious counterattack by the conservationist forces. Zahniser, Charles Callison of the National Wildlife Federation, and William Zimmerman of the Trustees for Conservation told Anderson and other sympathetic members that the proposed amendments would "emasculate the bill" and "provide the legal basis for the destruction of the wilderness." They feared that the technique of "committee filibuster," as Anderson called it, would work to delay the Wilderness bill indefinitely. The conservationists felt that delay would only encourage commercial interests who would redouble their efforts to seize potential wilderness lands before Congress could act.[68]

During the early days of the 1960 congressional session, two leading conservationists, Arthur Johnson of the Federation of Western Outdoor Clubs and David Brower of the Sierra Club, contacted Anderson to suggest a counter strategy. Their objective was to have Congress pass a resolution declaring a moratorium on the development of lands subject to study by the Outdoor Recreation Commission. These lands would presumably include potential wilderness tracts. Brower and Johnson argued that such a moratorium could facilitate the recreation commission's work and that the idea had been included in the original version of the recreation bill only to be dropped when Senator Arthur Watkins insisted that the appropriate agencies already had the necessary set-aside power. In subsequent meetings with Interior Secretary Seaton, the conservationists were unable to identify existing authority. Consequently, the Interior Department's solicitor set up procedures whereby agencies such as the recreation commission could request that choice lands be temporarily set aside.[69]

Anderson told Brower that he was "very much interested" in the moratorium idea but that he was reluctant because of his familiarity with excessive set asides in Alaska. He warned Brower that there would be "plenty of difficulty" if the Alaska pattern were duplicated, and suggested that many members of Congress would be alert to efforts to prevent mineral development in the guise of preserving "scenic values."[70]

Before proceeding with the moratorium idea, Anderson decided to survey the congressional delegations from those western states most likely to be affected by such a plan. Senator Magnuson's response was typical of most that he received. The Washington Democrat said that "it seems that we have enough legislation on this subject before Congress at the moment to take care of the situation." Magnuson's Washington colleague Henry Jackson agreed and expressed the fear that the resolution would be interpreted as giving the recreation commission additional power that could be used as an excuse to delay, or block, further consideration of the Wilderness bill.[71]

As the replies were arriving in Anderson's office, he learned to his great embarrassment that the recreation commission, two days before he sent his survey, had voted to oppose the moratorium plan. Although Anderson had attended a portion of that meeting, he had not recalled the discussion, and staff director Francis Sargent had neglected to tell him of the action. Representative Wayne Aspinall, who had been present at the meeting, later told Anderson that the commission thought it would be unwise to give priority status to any one of the issues then before it.[72]

As the second session of the Eighty-sixth Congress got underway in January 1960, Howard Zahniser, with leaders of the National Wildlife Federation, the Wildlife Management Institute and the Trustees for Conservation, set out to change O'Mahoney's mind and to negotiate with him the minimum alterations necessary to forge a broadly acceptable Wilderness bill. They met on January 27 with O'Mahoney, Chairman Murray and several committee aides. O'Mahoney seemed generally pleased with their detailed explanation of the revised measure. At one point the Wyoming senator's aide Jerry O'Callaghan suggested that they prepare a clean bill. Zahniser quickly responded that the major constituencies had finally come to understand the existing bill and that a new bill would certainly create additional confusion and delay. At the end of the meeting, O'Mahoney expressed his support and asked Zahniser to communicate their understanding to Wyoming Governor Leslie Miller.[73]

On the eve of the Interior Committee's February 16, 1960, meeting, the conservationists compared notes. William Zimmerman, Jr., the Washington representative of the Trustees for Conservation and a participant in the earlier O'Mahoney meeting, reported to David Brower that it was essential for Anderson and Henry Jackson to be present at that session. He counted Senators Frank Moss (D-UT), Barry Goldwater (R-AZ), and Gordon Allott (R-CO) as likely opponents. He noted that O'Mahoney had stated in a recent newsletter that he and the conservationists had reached an agreement on the bill. Zimmerman predicted that they had the necessary votes to report the bill to the full Senate and that the only apparent danger lay in "long arguments which would tire everyone."[74]

When the Interior Committee met in executive session on February 16, O'Mahoney confounded Anderson and others sympathetic to the Wilderness bill by presenting his own draft, despite earlier assurances that he would support the committee's version. He argued that the panel's compromise version was excessively "vague" and that it bound future Congresses to an unwise policy. Anderson believed that O'Mahoney and Allott, taking unfair advantage of Chairman Murray's advanced age and infirmities, "dissected every item in the proposal to the point of obfuscation." He remembered that "O'Mahoney was particularly irritating in insisting on pedantic definitions of 'historical,' 'educational,' 'recreational,' and 'scenic' in the context of the legislation." Anderson noted that their performance served as a reminder that "many of the Mountain States senators could not be persuaded to overlook the commercial attractions of their natural resources."[75]

The February 1960 committee meeting ended in deadlock as had those that preceded it. This meeting, however, marked a turning point in Anderson's own extensive course of involvement with legislation for preservation and measured use of the country's natural resources. For the past three years, others in the Senate, principally Humphrey and Murray, had shepherded the Wilderness bill from rough draft to a point where it had attracted a large, well informed and highly vocal following, both in support and in opposition. Now Humphrey was aspiring to the presidency and had decided to invest more of his seemingly limitless energy in the upcoming primary campaigns. Murray had at last yielded to the pressures of old age and poor health by making public on April 28th his departure from the Senate at the end of the 1960 session.

Throughout most of the spring of 1960, Anderson concentrated on his primary election race. On May 10, he easily won renomination and, along with most of his Senate colleagues, focused his attention on the forthcoming presidential nominating conventions. The Wilderness bill languished in the Interior Committee in spite of the conservationists' effort to dislodge it in the guise of a farewell gesture to Chairman Murray.[76]

In April 1960, parties on all sides of the Wilderness issue paused to witness House passage of the Multiple Use–Sustained Yield Act. A month later the act cleared the Senate, and on June 12 President Eisenhower signed it into law. As with the wilderness and recreation bills, the Multiple Use Act sought to provide clear statutory protection for wilderness quality lands in the face of intensifying pressure for their unrestricted development. The passage of the 1958 Outdoor Recreation Act and the apparent progress of various versions of the Wilderness bill galvanized the timber, mining, and cattle interests to pressure the Forest Service for protection against excessive "set-asides" of choice lands.[77]

The Multiple Use Act established as congressional policy that the national forests would be administered for five basic uses. They were "outdoor recreation, range, timber, watershed, and wildlife and fish purposes." The description and arrangement in the act of the five "purposes" occasioned heated controversy on all sides. Each constituency believed that the order of arrangement would reflect priority of treatment. The Forest Service's decision to list purposes in alphabetical order, to emphasize its recreation role, set off a vigorous battle. The grazing interests objected to the use of the word "range," preferring alphabetically superior words such as "grazing" or "forage." They and others were unhappy over the addition of "outdoor" to recreation, but Forest Service drafters argued that Congress had already established that usage with the passage of the 1958 act. The suspicions of at least one interest group about semantic manipulation were well founded. The Forest Service did not want the enumeration of national forests resources to begin with the word "fish," so it inverted the customary usage "fish and wildlife," relegating that purpose to the tail end of the list. Assistant Forest Service director Edward Crafts turned aside criticism for including recreation as a resource, explaining "we so badly wanted recreation included in our listing for strategic reasons in order to help us in our recreation activities and incidentally in our competition with the Park Service."[78]

As the Senate Agriculture Committee was putting the finishing touches on the bill, Howard Zahniser and the Audubon Society's Charles Callison surprised and angered the Forest Service's leadership by requesting that "wilderness" be specifically listed as a resource. The Forest Service argued that inclusion would hurt the Wilderness bill's chances for passage by giving its opponents the argument that the Multiple Use Act was all that was needed. Zahniser, recognizing that the Wilderness bill was going nowhere until the 1961 session, disagreed, in the belief that this first statutory recognition of wilderness would have a great precedential value.[79]

The Sierra Club split with Zahniser and the Wilderness Society over the Multiple Use Act. David Brower saw the bill as a Forest Service stratagem to destroy the Wilderness bill. He urged Zahniser to drop his support of the Forest Service bill and concentrate instead on getting the Wilderness bill, "even as presently weakened," enacted. He cautioned his long time associate that "the conservation alliance so long in the building—and so effective when it has gone well—is splitting, and doing so, I think, because of overdependency on the Forest Service." Brower reported to his organization's president they were not likely to get "the Forest Service's support of wilderness preservation the way it used to until it feels itself more directly under the gun, that gun being the threat that more national parks will be carved out of national forests."[80]

The passage of the Multiple Use Act represented a momentary truce in the escalating war between the developers and the conservationists. No single interest group was enthusiastic about the act but, for the first time, water and timber uses would have to share equal billing with recreation resources that had been accustomed to a distinctly secondary status. Interior Chairman Murray, in one of his final legislative acts, introduced a revised version of his committee's Wilderness bill and sought, in vain, to press for its consideration.[81] By mid-year, it was clear that the fate of the Wilderness bill would depend on new leadership. Assuming that Anderson was successful in his November reelection bid, he would become the committee's chairman, a much coveted post for a western senator. There he would no longer be able to sidestep the increasingly rapid momentum of wilderness legislation. Rather, he would have to draw upon his considerable substantive knowledge and negotiating skills, sharpened in his campaign for the Outdoor Recreation Commission, to fashion a system of wilderness preservation to last for countless generations.

# 5

# Wilderness and Shoreline Legislation
## *A Tenacious Advocacy, 1961*

When Clinton Anderson of New Mexico became chairman of
the Interior Committee in 1961, the Wilderness Bill had a
tenacious advocate who would not be denied.

Stewart Udall
May 1962

The decade of the 1950s witnessed deliberate study and cautious
reassessment of federal natural resources policy. In sharp contrast,
the first half of the 1960s brought a series of legislative enactments
unprecedented in the nation's history for their scope and perma-
nence. In 1961 the United States Senate served as the catalyst for
action. There, Clinton Anderson, newly elected chairman of the Committee on Interior and Insular Affairs, set the pace. While the newly
ascendant administration of John F. Kennedy struggled to set its
own policies across a broad and perplexing terrain of troublesome
issues, conservative elements within the House of Representatives
collectively decided to resist presidential dictation, a course that
brought stalemate. When Congress adjourned in September 1961,
the Senate handed the House and administration a carefully revised
Wilderness Act cleared by a decisive majority of its members. The
upper chamber also had shaped legislation on shoreline preservation and had addressed the broader question of how the administration would organize its natural resources bureaucracy.

Pres. John F. Kennedy established the natural resources policy for his new administration in a special message to Congress on February 23, 1961. Departing from the Eisenhower doctrine of local initiative for development of the nation's land and water resources, the president committed himself to an aggressive "sound resources program under the progressive principles of national leadership first forged by [Gifford] Pinchot and Theodore Roosevelt, and backed by the essential cooperation of state and local governments." Under the category of "recreation," the chief executive identified two "essential" goals for his administration: "a wilderness protection bill along the lines of S.174" and establishment of a system of "seashore and shoreline areas such as Cape Cod, Padre Island, and Point Reyes for the use and enjoyment of the public."[1] Clinton P. Anderson, newly elected chairman of the Senate Interior Committee, became the president's chief agent for accomplishing this program on Capitol Hill. The bill to which Kennedy referred, the only specific legislation mentioned in his message, was Anderson's carefully crafted compromise version of the Wilderness bill.

As Senate colleagues during the 1950s, Anderson and Kennedy had traveled in different circles. The New Mexico senator was a generation older than Kennedy and a recognized member of the Senate's inner club whose members included powerful southern and western senators such as Lyndon Johnson (D-TX), Richard Russell (D-GA), Carl Hayden (D-AZ), and Robert Kerr (D-OK).[2] Kennedy remained an outsider, devoting little time to his Senate duties while nursing ill-concealed aspirations to higher office. No one would have labeled the junior member from Massachusetts a "Senate Man."

During the 1960 presidential primary season, Anderson worked on behalf of Lyndon Johnson. He believed that the ascension of his Texas colleague to the White House would benefit New Mexico, and he admitted his "selfish motives," noting that "our state would be safe and we'd be in fine shape." On the morning after Kennedy won the Democratic nomination, he solicited Anderson's recommendations for a suitable running mate. The New Mexico senator suggested colleagues Stuart Symington (D-MO) or Henry Jackson (D-WA). Kennedy then asked Anderson for his opinion of Lyndon Johnson. The New Mexican responded with astonishment that House Speaker Sam Rayburn (D-TX) had made Johnson promise he would never accept the second position. Later that day, when Johnson told Anderson of his intention to accept Kennedy's offer, Anderson urged him to reconsider, counseling, "You're young, you'll be elected someday yourself. Don't take a chance on getting messed up now."[3]

On November 8, 1960, Clinton Anderson easily won a third term to the Senate by the greatest margin ever accorded any candidate in a New Mexico election. Kennedy, on the other hand, barely carried that state in the closest presidential race since 1884. Although in retrospect New Mexico's four electoral votes would not have proven decisive, Kennedy felt indebted to Anderson for his post-convention assistance. Within several weeks of his victory, the president-elect offered the senior senator his choice of two cabinet posts—Interior or Agriculture. The newly-reelected senator had no desire to resign and leave the appointment of his successor to New Mexico's new Republican governor. He told Kennedy, "You can get much better people in the first place, . . . I'm worn out, you shouldn't have a retread." Kennedy undoubtedly anticipated Anderson's response. His offer simply provided an opportunity to flatter an influential senator and to place a "reserved" sign on the positions until he could more thoroughly explore his options.

Anderson endorsed South Dakota Representative George McGovern (D) to be Secretary of Agriculture. During his own unsuccessful 1960 campaign to unseat Senator Karl Mundt (R-SD), McGovern had provided valuable support for Kennedy in the Coyote State. Kennedy barely knew either McGovern or former Minnesota governor Orville Freeman, the other frequently mentioned contender. In deference to members of the House Agriculture Committee and to Robert Kennedy's desire to repay Freeman for past political favors, the elder Kennedy selected the former governor, telling Anderson that his administrative experience made him preferable to McGovern.[4]

The president-elect was not well acquainted with Arizona representative Stewart Udall (D), but he was grateful for his support at the Democratic National Convention. At a crucial moment, Udall had led his state's delegation away from venerable Carl Hayden's pro–Lyndon Johnson slate by a single vote, delivering it, under the unit rule, to Kennedy. Udall badly wanted the Interior Department post and turned to veteran Washington lobbyist Maurice Rosenblatt for assistance. Rosenblatt arranged an appointment for Udall at Kennedy's Georgetown home. When the congressman arrived, the president-elect met with him briefly and concluded by telling him to "clear it with Clint." Udall, fearing Anderson had designs on the job for himself, approached him with trepidation. The Arizonan carried instructions from Rosenblatt that if Anderson mentioned the name of former agriculture secretary Charles Brannan, Anderson's successor in that agency and foe on the issue of price supports, Udall should avoid the bait and remain noncommittal. Anderson assured Udall of his support, noting that he intended to remain in the Senate where he would be of greater service to the administration as chairman of the Senate Interior Committee. During the coming year, Anderson would prove the soundness of his own advice.[5]

As John Kennedy completed plans for his new administration, Anderson was busy making his own arrangements to assume the reins of the Interior Committee. In 1953, when the Republicans took control of the Senate, the new chairman of the Interior Committee, Hugh Butler (R-NE) purged all Democratic staff members. In 1955, with the return of a Democratic majority, chairman James Murray (D-MT) repaid the favor. Under Murray's leadership, parallel staffs developed. A large number of patronage employees worked in a basement office and had little contact with the main professional staff. Among the latter were old time reclamationists such as Michael Straus, the reclamation bureau's director in the Truman years and his one-time deputy, Goodrich Lineweaver. They, along with other veterans of the decade-long Hells Canyon dispute over the role of the federal government in hydro-electric power production, offered the Democratic majority fertile new ideas for legislative campaigns. Their conservation orientation was decidedly utilitarian as they looked for ways to develop natural resources. While Murray remained chairman, staff were hired, but never fired. His son Charles and staff director Richard Callaghan managed the committee's day to day operations. During Murray's final years, poor health and advancing age forced him to yield considerable power and autonomy to his subcommittee chairmen. As head of the influential Subcommittee on Irrigation and Reclamation, Anderson benefited greatly from the opportunity and he was often called on to serve as acting chairman of the full committee.[6]

In January 1961 Anderson determined that he would take a more activist role than his predecessor in managing the committee's internal affairs. He divided the existing staff into three categories. The first consisted of a single person. That individual's work habits were unsatisfactory to Anderson, but his cardinal sin was entering and losing a 1960 Montana senatorial primary. The victor, Senator Lee Metcalf (D), vowed to purge him from the committee staff and Anderson readily complied. Anderson gave those in the second category, including Murray's son and other patronage employees, thirty days to find other employment. Members of the third group were permitted to remain and the overall staff size dropped from twenty-five to seventeen. Forming the nucleus of the Anderson team were staff director Richard Callaghan, chief counsel Stewart French, forestry specialist Robert Wolf, and the Senate's expert on wilderness and water legislation, Benton J. Stong.[7] Anderson's legislative assistant, Jerry Verkler, moved over to the committee as its chief clerk.

In the wilderness battles ahead, Anderson would have no better counsel than Ben Stong. Before joining the committee's staff in 1955, Stong had worked for newspapers in Iowa and Tennessee. In 1942 he became an organizer in the Rocky Mountain states for the Farmer's Union under the dynamic leadership of James G. Patton.[8] In 1946 Patton, a believer in high farm production levels, broke with agriculture secretary Anderson who was then advocating severe restraints on production. Patton eventually demanded that President Truman fire Anderson as a consequence of his "fumbling, fluctuating policies."[9] Anderson remembered Stong's association with Patton and that memory may have accounted for the aide's being paid under a temporary annual funding resolution rather than on the permanent payroll with ten of the committee's seventeen staff. Nonetheless, Anderson quickly came to respect Stong's sound advice and no-nonsense style.[10]

Anderson valued the expertise he found in Stong and other members of the reorganized staff. He insisted on regular briefings from those he trusted, turning aside those not directly under his control. His suspicion of outside counsel surfaced several years earlier when, in a discussion of the Interior Committee budget, one member suggested they rely more on Library of Congress specialists. Anderson opposed that approach, in a classic remark, noting "If you send for a copy of the Lord's Prayer, they would send you the Declaration of Independence, and all of the documents that led up to it, but never include the thing you want."[11]

Anderson entered his chairmanship with a talented staff and a large measure of experience, confidence, and collegial respect. By then he had served two terms as chairman of the prestigious Joint Committee on Atomic Energy and six years as head of Interior's

Reclamation Subcommittee. He also enjoyed the prospect, denied to his predecessor, of working with an administration of his own party. As a former senator, the new president appeared to appreciate the Senate's policy-making role and, in matters outside his immediate range of interest, he instinctively deferred to the judgment of that body's elders, particularly Chairman Anderson.[12]

On February 13, with the confirmation of key Interior appointees accomplished, Anderson met with the president to discuss the administration's natural resources agenda and, specifically, the chief executive's forthcoming special message to Congress on that topic. The natural resources message served to set and support the Interior Committee's agenda. Dealing with the statement's principal recreation features—wilderness and shoreline legislation—the committee established a pattern of holding hearings in the spring, revising and polishing each bill's language in the early summer, and obtaining full Senate approval at summer's end.[13]

Anderson introduced the revised Wilderness Bill on January 5, 1961—his first substantive act as Interior Committee chairman. Weeks earlier, during the Christmas holidays, Anderson aide Claude Wood met with Interior Committee staff as well as Interior Department and interest group representatives to refine further the bill that had succumbed to the Allott-O'Mahoney onslaught in mid 1960. The working group produced for Anderson an introductory statement clearly designed for an audience wider than the United States Senate. The Wilderness Society, whose imprint was evident therein, purchased 15,000 copies of Anderson's remarks, as they appeared in the *Congressional Record*, for mailing to supporters across the nation. Anderson sent several thousand copies to other conservation organizations, even providing some in sealed postage free envelopes to reduce the expense of their subsequent redistribution.[14]

Committee clerk Jerry Verkler suggested that the most opportune time for public hearings on the Wilderness bill would be February 27 and 28, to coincide with the annual meeting in Washington of the National Wildlife Federation. In the same vein, Verkler noted that hearings on shoreline preservation might be scheduled for March 8, the final day of the Washington convocation of the North American Wildlife Conference. Anderson followed both suggestions, ensuring a large and sympathetic turnout for those key hearings.[15]

Anderson owed much of his legislative effectiveness to an appreciation for careful orchestration and timing. The president agreed to send his natural resources message to Congress on the Thursday before the scheduled start of the Interior Committee's Monday wilderness hearings. In addition to help from the White House, Anderson received substantial aid from the media. The February issue of the *Atlantic Monthly* contained a cover story under the banner "Our National Parks in Jeopardy." In that series, Devereux Butcher, the former executive secretary of the National Parks Association who had been ousted at Conrad Wirth's initiative, slammed Wirth's "Mission 66" program. Echoing the preservationists' line, he charged that "to popularize and commercialize the national parks is to cheapen them and to reduce them to the level of ordinary playgrounds. To cherish them for their primeval splendor," Butcher continued, "and give them the protection the pending wilderness bill would afford is to realize the enduring value they have for us and those who will follow us."[16]

On the day before the hearings began the *Washington Star* carried an article entitled "Renewed Vigor in Congress' Drive To Enact Legislation For Parks." The article predicted a favorable future for the bill due to the administration's backing, the extensive educational efforts of the Wilderness Society, and the "vigorous sponsorship" of committee chairman Anderson.[17]

Anderson opened this first legislative hearing under his chairmanship with the assertion that the committee would focus on the bill's specifics—how much land would be preserved, and how rigidly it would be maintained in its natural state—rather than its philosophical underpinning, about which there was general agreement. He anticipated that the opposition, principally the mining, grazing and lumbering interests, would build its case on three basic objections.[18]

The opposition argument that most annoyed the chairman and in his view had the least merit called for deferring action on the Wilderness bill until the Outdoor Recreation Commission's final report was available for study, presumably later in 1961. On that point, Anderson agreed with the Sierra Club's David Brower who charged that this tactic was essentially "a search for time and not for information."[19] He reminded those who held this view that he was the principal author of both measures. In his judgment, the Wilderness bill would facilitate the commission's work.

From the time of the recreation commission's creation, Anderson had taken an active part in its work. By the end of 1960, however, he recognized that the seventeen-member panel was in trouble. Delays of more than a year in receiving its first major appropriation and in selecting an executive director caused the commission's timetable to slip badly. Factions quickly emerged among its members and neither chairman Laurance Rockefeller nor executive director Francis Sargent seemed able to calm the waters. One of the most outspoken commissioners was Prudential Insurance Company vice president M. Frederik Smith. Smith also had been director of the influential Council of Conservationists, and he and Anderson had been acquainted for many years through their mutual involvement in the insurance business. In 1958 Smith had hoped in vain that President Eisenhower would name him chairman. By the beginning of 1961 that disappointment fueled his frustration with chairman Rockefeller's "academic" approach. He commended Anderson on his efforts "to get the commission back on a straightforward and practical course, instead of mushing along in the intellectual malted milk course that I am afraid is settling in."[20]

Smith reflected Anderson's own "pragmatic" approach to the commission's work, in noting that "the lower echelon of the staff is very busy making and enjoying studies of all sorts and the top echelon is busy drawing conclusions, and their lines of communications are not very good." By the time of the Interior Committee's February 1961 hearings, Anderson feared that the commission might either toil on indefinitely or produce a superficial and misleading final report. Recalling the difficulties of the commission's contractors in agreeing on a working definition of "wilderness," Anderson observed "that it is hard to study what you have not been able to delineate." In that spirit, he argued for passage of a Wilderness Act to guide the drifting commission, and he introduced a bill to extend the commission's reporting date from September 1961 to January 1962.[21]

The second source of contention at the February wilderness hearings promised to be the most crippling. It centered on a proposal to remove from the bill's coverage forty primitive areas covering eight million acres. This would leave only previously designated "wilderness" and "wild" areas. The controversy over inclusion of primitive areas cut to the very heart of the bill, from the time of its earliest versions in 1955. At one end of the range of options was the developers' plan to have Congress consider, in separate bills, each primitive area on its merits. In direct opposition, the Wilderness Society proposed that all existing primitive areas be included in the single bill, subject to subsequent removal only by the affirmative vote of both houses of Congress.

The bill before Anderson's committee provided a period of fifteen years from the date of its enactment for the secretary of Agriculture to review each primitive area, under Forest Service jurisdiction, and to recommend to the president either its conversion to permanent wilderness status, or its removal from the system. The president, in turn, would review the individual recommendations and forward them to Congress. If Congress, during the session following submission, failed to override a recommendation for conversion, the area would be added to the wilderness system, with removal possible only by a future presidential declaration of national need for its timber or mineral resources. Developers feared that provision would lock up large, potentially valuable tracts for at least fifteen years. Both sides recognized that review of primitive areas would be difficult and time-consuming.[22]

The third objection to the Anderson Wilderness bill centered on the specific mechanism by which Congress would review primitive areas. Even Senator Frank Church (D-ID), a strong supporter of the bill's overall objectives, expressed strong reservations on this feature. He believed that allowing a president's recommendation to take effect unless both houses specifically rejected it diminished the powers of Congress. In the normal legislative process, he argued, a single house could block or alter a proposal either through inaction or substitution. Church presented his case during the hearings logically and effectively. In so doing, he briefly irritated the chairman who wished to conclude the formality of public hearings and move into the crucial committee "mark up" phase. When the youthful Idaho senator requested that the "experts on the detail of the drafting of the bill" be made available to answer his questions, Anderson assured him that the experts were indeed present. "You just have to ask those of us who sat in the office hour by hour and crossed out word by word and decided what we would put in and what we would not," the chairman responded defensively. Church insisted that the bill's ambiguities, of which this was a prime example, might make a "charade" of the wilderness system concept. He explained that the president could favorably recommend conversion of a primitive area to wilderness status and that Congress, for its own good reasons, might overrule the president. As the bill stood, the area in question would simply retain its "primitive" status and remain under the broad protection of the wilderness system. With an eye on the large federal land holdings in Idaho, Church wanted to avoid the inadvertent locking up of lands more suitable to development than to preservation. He urged the committee to revise the bill to ensure that once an area had been rejected by the president or Congress, it would be dropped from the system altogether.[23]

Anderson seemed uncharacteristically slow to grasp the well-briefed Idahoan's point. After extended and heated discussion, he lamely admitted that such ambiguities frequently creep into much-revised legislation, thus underscoring the value of public hearings. Then, in an effort to move to the offensive, he made a statement that close associates had come to recognize as a hallmark of his intention for further mischief. Anderson observed that he "would not attempt to argue with my friend, who is a lawyer." At first glance, the remark, which had little bearing on the substance of Church's position, seemed to belie a sensitivity over Anderson's lack of a law degree within an institution that placed a premium on legal training. To the contrary, associates viewed the comment as a precursor of trouble, and in this instance the chairman directed it at the freshman senator's seeming impertinence.

Throughout his congressional career, Anderson had carefully honed his interrogatory skills. His pattern was to begin his questioning of a witness with straightforward inquiries. If he thought a witness was not being totally candid, he would continue briefly with simple factual questions, then he would slip in a tough question, prefaced by "Isn't is true . . ." He would then shuffle his papers, peering under a stack of them apparently examining one that may or may not have had the refuting information. Anderson's innate decency seldom restrained his penchant for stiletto-like attacks on the unwilling and uncooperative.[25]

As the hearings continued, Wallace Bennet (R-UT) also took issue with the Wilderness bill's provision requiring a concurrent resolution of both houses of Congress to block a presidential recommendation. Representing a state where seventy percent of the lands were under federal control, Bennett feared the proposed act would further weaken the ability of states to open land to mineral and other commercial development. He argued that the burden of proving specific tracts worthy of inclusion within the wilderness system should be placed on those who advocated such action. Under the bill's provisions, in his view, the House of Representatives, constituted on the basis of population, could for "procedural, circumstantial, or vindictive" reasons permit the addition of questionable areas to the system through inaction. "Since nearly all Western states have a relatively small population, we in the West could be effectively preserved for the East, with no real voice for ourselves because the Senate would forfeit legislative control to the House." Bennett believed the bill would erase any possibility of power and reclamation development within Dinosaur National Monument and Echo Park adjacent to the Colorado-Utah border. Charging that this action would lock up Utah's right to a half-million acre feet per year of the Colorado River's flow, he returned to a familiar theme in observing "Wilderness may be good for the soul, but we cannot drink it."[26]

Anderson's impatience with Bennett's testimony became evident when the Utah senator incorrectly stated that the bill made no provision for proper wildlife management in wilderness areas and suggested that it would bar hunting. Anderson quickly responded by asking Bennett if he was a hunter. Receiving a negative answer, the chairman noted that he himself was a hunter and that he occasionally pursued that avocation with Forest Service assistant chief Edward Crafts and that Crafts had no problem with the bill in that regard. Bennett quickly backtracked. At the conclusion of his testimony, the committee's chairman and members sat in stony silence.[27]

Colorado's senior senator, Gordon Allott (R) proved to be a more formidable opponent. With the departure of Joseph O'Mahoney (D-WY) due to ill health, Allott remained to spearhead western opposition to the bill. In 1960, Anderson had become frustrated over his delaying tactics. Now as chairman, he was prepared to respond decisively at the first sign of their reemergence. The opportunity presented itself during the hearings when Allott informed Anderson of what he considered a fatal flaw in the legislation. The Colorado senator announced that the Senate's parliamentarian had confirmed his own suspicion that the majority leader had the authority to keep a resolution of Senate disapproval from being called up for floor consideration. He cited this possibility to support his view that the proposed system of congressional review was devised to favor wilderness advocates, for lack of positive action by both houses would result in permanent wilderness status for areas receiving presidential approval.

On hearing Allott's statement, Anderson abruptly left his chair at the rostrum and disappeared into the adjacent committee office. Within a few minutes he returned with Assistant Parliamentarian Floyd Riddick in tow. Riddick, a scholarly authority on Senate rules and procedure, quickly realized that his earlier conversation with Allott's legislative assistant had been misinterpreted. He confirmed Anderson's understanding that a resolution of disapproval of a presidential action, under the provisions of the 1949 Reorganization Act, was indeed a privileged matter and had to be considered immediately on its arrival in the Senate. Anderson later noted that the exchange with Allott "did not amount to a hill of beans except in illustrating how precipitously temperatures had risen within the committee." Certainly Allott's temperature was elevated, as he fired his hapless legislative assistant later that day.[28]

Although the committee received highly supportive testimony from most concerned executive branch agencies, the quasi-independent Federal Power Commission raised a dissenting voice, the sound of which further irritated Anderson. He believed that the bill would make it more difficult for the commission, in issuing power site licenses, to ignore Agriculture Department objections in cases where construction of a dam was clearly in conflict with the basic purpose of the wilderness area in which it was to be located. The commission's chief counsel, John Mason, agreed that his agency might have difficulty setting aside such objections. He maintained, however, that it might be possible to argue for compatibility of purposes in specific areas. In response to Anderson's question about the possibility of such a finding in the case of New Mexico's Gila Wilderness, Mason concluded that a license could be granted.

Coyly observing that he was probably "relying on insufficient evidence," Anderson said he had always believed such action was impossible. He pressed Mason and other commission representatives to cite examples of dams in existing wilderness areas. After several incorrect answers, Mason admitted that none existed. Accordingly, Anderson asked the commission to prepare an amendment to his bill stipulating that the 1920 Power Act's review and licensing process would apply only to primitive areas until such time as they had been reviewed and accepted as wilderness areas. The remainder of the hearings ran a predictable course, repetitive of earlier sessions. Periodically, as the testimony became tedious, Anderson held up a large bound volume of transcripts saying that this was the testimony already accumulated, welcoming witnesses to "make as many copies as you'd like, but nobody's being brief." He made it clear that he intended to finish within the allotted time, noting that he had his "telescope on the clock."[29]

In the four-and-a-half month interval between the end of the hearings and the committee's "mark up" session, the panel and its staff attempted to resolve five basic points of disagreement that had emerged during the February hearings. The first to be settled was Allott's amendment calling for specific descriptions within the bill of all areas to be designated as wilderness. The Forest Service, in opposing that change, pointed out that Allott's descriptions contained more than one hundred typographical errors and several significant omissions. After examining a Library of Congress study that raised serious legal objections to such specific delineations, Allott accepted a compromise providing that maps and other technical descriptions would be deposited for public inspection with the appropriate congressional committees and elsewhere across the nation.[30]

Among other opposing western members, Senators Alan Bible (D-NV) and Henry Dworshak (R-ID) presented a stronger challenge with their amendment to make all national forest areas subject to federal mining laws including prospecting, patenting, and location of claims. This would have opened national forest portions of the wilderness system to extensive mining operations, and conservationists asserted it would make a mockery of the legislation. Frank Church, Dworshak's Idaho colleague, settled the matter by offering alternate language to allow mining surveys in forest wilderness areas by means "not incompatible with the preservation of the wilderness environment." This apparent middle course undercut the amendment's force and ultimately won acceptance with the grudging approval of conservationists such as Howard Zahniser.[31]

The most difficult negotiations occurred on the subject of primitive area reviews. All sides wanted to ensure that the majority of these areas not remain in an indeterminate status during the entire fifteen-year review period set forth in the bill. Howard Zahniser feared that the Forest Service intended to turn over to developers many primitive areas simply by failing to review them so that at the end of the statutory period they would automatically revert to ordinary forest status. Committee wilderness expert Ben Stong prepared an amendment, with Anderson's encouragement, that reduced the review period to ten years and required the Forest Service to review promptly each primitive area. It gave the president authority to adjust area boundaries as long as the total acreage within each area remained unchanged. In this connection, Anderson agreed to a change in the procedure for congressional disapproval of presidential recommendations. He accepted Church's contention that a single house of Congress, not both, should be able to block a presidential determination by means of inaction or explicit disapproval. This brought a strong protest from Zahniser who argued that Congress should take positive action to remove primitive areas. He posed the extreme example of a president recommending that an area be eliminated and Congress rejecting that recommendation. That would result, he argued, in the area's elimination under the proposed statute.[32]

The committee accepted a final significant modification with little discussion. To forestall objections from senators sympathetic to the grazing interests, Anderson agreed to a provision that precluded the reduction or termination of grazing in those wilderness areas where it was already "well-established."

Despite these modifications, Senator Allott continued his campaign to weaken the measure. On July 13, 1961, as the committee assembled behind closed doors to mark up the bill in preparation for its journey to the full Senate, Allott offered what the chairman considered to be a fatal amendment. His provision required that both the Senate and the House take separate *affirmative* action on each primitive area. Anderson saw this as "double jeopardy." After the wilderness proponents had fought the many battles necessary to pass the basic bill, which in Allott's version would include only existing wild and wilderness areas, they would have to renew their campaign all over again, on a case-by-case basis, for each of the primitive areas. Given the regional peculiarities associated with each area and Congress' limited attention span for such legislation, the chances of salvaging the proposed system intact would be exceedingly dim.

Several minutes before noon on July 13, Anderson put the Allott amendment to a vote. To his consternation, it passed by a 9 to 8 margin. The chairman looked around the committee table and announced that as far as he was concerned the wilderness bill was dead. He then recessed the committee until 2:00 p.m. As Anderson was leaving the room, aide Ben Stong, a former Iowa newspaperman, told him he thought he could generate pressure on Senator Jack Miller (R-IA) to change his vote.

With Anderson's approval, Stong contacted Spencer Smith, secretary of the Citizens' Committee on Natural Resources, and a native Iowan. Smith quickly called an influential member of the Morrell packing family, one of Senator Miller's principal campaign contributors, who, in turn, urged the freshman senator to reconsider his vote. Anderson was also not idle during the luncheon break. He phoned the veteran political cartoonist of the *Des Moines Register,* J. N. "Ding" Darling. In 1936 Darling had served as first president of the National Wildlife Federation and designed federal "duck stamps" sold to wildfowl hunters. Darling immediately urged influential Iowans to flood Miller's office with telegrams.[33]

Anderson, an instinctively cautious man, was unwilling to permit the vote of a single senator to jeopardize years of legislative toil. Frank Moss (D-UT) had also voted with Allott, but in his two years in the Senate he had established himself as a thoughtful champion of conservation legislation. Anderson believed that Moss would reconsider his vote on the issue when reminded that the Allott amendment's principal backers included the cattle and mining interests who had worked so hard to prevent Moss' Senate election. What Anderson considered a "purely political pitch" succeeded, and Moss took the lead during the afternoon session in calling for a reconsideration of the earlier vote. Both Moss and Miller voted to kill the Allott amendment, and by an 11 to 4 vote the bill was then cleared for the Senate's consideration.[34]

Anderson subsequently told California Republican Thomas Kuchel, also a stalwart supporter of the measure, that he "would have preferred to let the bill die in committee than put it before the Senate butchered as it was." To conservationist Ira Gabrielson he expressed his frustration at the seemingly endless roadblocks, noting that the committee mark-up session "was the hardest day I've put in in a long time." He continued that "if we don't pass the Wilderness bill this year, I hope it will be sent to some other committee and let that chairman wrestle with it for a while." Howard Zahniser was euphoric at the outcome, thanking the chairman for "a national contribution that will be long recognized in conservation history."[35]

As Anderson waited for Majority Leader Mike Mansfield (D-MT) to schedule Senate debate on the bill, he drafted his opening statement. He emphasized that the measure required no new outlays from the federal treasury, but that inaction would necessitate a vast expenditure to reclaim those prime lands at a later time from developers' ravages. Anderson stressed that there would be no change in federal agency jurisdiction over individual lands, always a source of concern among pressure groups who were not eager to build new alliances with unfamiliar bureaucracies. He reiterated that the bill's passage would benefit rather than impede the work of the Outdoor Recreation Committee, and that the measure was the product of a bipartisan effort, citing the strong support of the Senate's assistant Republican floor leader, Thomas Kuchel.[36]

Anderson never delivered that statement. Once again, at a time of stress, his chronically poor health undermined his legislative plans, forcing him in this instance to return to New Mexico for gall bladder surgery.[37] Before departing late in August, he turned to Frank Church, the committee's fourth-ranking Democrat, and successfully prevailed upon him to serve as the bill's floor manager.[38]

Debate in the Senate opened on September 5, 1961, and lasted two days. Church began with the assertion that this bill and measures providing for Alaska and Hawaii statehood were the three most important measures to have come from the Interior Committee during his five years in the Senate. He followed Anderson's strategy in emphasizing the bill's modest objectives. It would not affect existing timbering, grazing, or mining operations in wilderness areas. It would not impede fire and insect control, nor would it interfere with Indian lands or with state jurisdiction over water resources or control of fish and wildlife. Church reminded his colleagues that he represented a state two-thirds of which was owned by the federal government and that he would be the first to oppose a threat to the development of that land.[39]

The bill's supporters stood in strategic locations throughout a sparsely populated Senate chamber. Lee Metcalf and then Frank Moss took turns in the presiding officer's chair. Yet the measure's allies might have taken concern from the presence on the floor of three of the four dissenting committee members. The opposition strategy became apparent when Agriculture committee chairman Allen Ellender (D-LA) suddenly rose to move that the bill be committed to his panel for further study. He argued that the majority of lands in the proposed wilderness system were under Forest Service control and thus within the jurisdiction of the Agriculture Committee. Observing that the House was not planning to act on the bill in the few remaining weeks of the 1961 session, Ellender reasoned that additional review would not seriously delay the measure. He pledged that his committee would report it back to the Senate by the following March.

Illinois Senator Paul Douglas (D) jumped to the bill's defense, asking Ellender why he had waited so long to assert his committee's claim to jurisdiction. Ellender responded, with questionable sincerity, that he had been too busy and had only recently noticed the bill on the Senate calendar. At that point, Majority Leader Mansfield made a motion directing the sergeant-at-arms to summon all absent members to establish a quorum and presumably to bring in reinforcements to kill the Ellender motion.

The counterattack began with Mansfield who correctly pointed out that the Senate rules gave the Interior Committee jurisdiction on legislation affecting "forest reserves and national parks created from the public domain," the very lands that fell within the scope of the wilderness bill. After more than an hour of heated debate, the Ellender motion failed by a vote of 32 to 41.[40]

Colorado's Gordon Allott continued, during the floor debate, as the bill's most persistent and effective opponent. His amendment requiring the approval of both houses for the inclusion of primitive areas failed (32 to 53), as did his proposal to allow the secretary of agriculture, rather than the president, who would be less responsive to developers' pressure, to grant exemptions to the bill's mining restrictions.

With the emotions and energies of both sides spent, the legislative clerk called the roll. Ten years after Howard Zahniser's first draft and five years after Hubert Humphrey's first legislative embodiment of that concept, the Wilderness Act passed the Senate by a decisive 78 to 8 majority.[41] Frank Church won immediate and widespread praise for his skillful handling of a bill that his colleagues might easily have misconstrued. He wrote to Anderson and graciously observed that "the fact that you were the chief sponsor of the bill was in large measure responsible for the big endorsement it received on final passage." Anderson expressed deep appreciation for Church's courage. In the face of a tough reelection battle the following year, the Idaho senator had championed a bill that was extremely unpopular with his state's powerful lumber and mining interests. During the debate, as Church later told Senator Henry Jackson in strained metaphor, he felt every time he opened his mouth to speak in the bill's defense, he was putting another shovel of dirt on his political grave.[42]

The honor roll of members responsible for Senate passage included names such as Humphrey, Kuchel, Mansfield, Metcalf, and Church, but Anderson, as many senators acknowledged, deserved principal credit for breaking the five-year log jam. Committee aide Stong earlier had observed that he could not "recall any bill that has produced more mail more consistently with stronger feelings." Anderson's careful redrafting of the earlier versions, his insistence on bringing all sides into the strategy discussions, and his reputation for moving only after careful deliberation accounted for the bill's unexpectedly overwhelming Senate margin. Anderson knew that the House of Representatives was watching and that its leaders would examine with care the final Senate vote in setting their own priorities for the 1962 session.[43]

Ten weeks before the Senate approved the Wilderness Act, it routinely passed the Cape Cod National Seashore Act, a measure dear to President Kennedy's heart. This was the first in a series of five bills designed to preserve endangered shoreline areas for recreation. The president's active interest ensured that the Cape Cod bill would pass both houses without difficulty. Supporters of the remaining measures hoped their bills would swim through the legislative channels with comparable ease. When the Senate adjourned in September 1961, it had cleared for House action two others, the Shoreline Recreation Area Act and the Point Reyes [California] National Seashore Act. These measures were significant in that they authorized the first areas under National Park Service jurisdiction to be acquired largely through purchase of private land and, unlike other Park Service units, their principal purpose was recreation.[44]

As early as 1935 the National Park Service had recommended the acquisition of twelve national seashore recreation areas along the Atlantic and Gulf coasts. At that time the service estimated a cost of $15 million to purchase 600,000 acres along 400 miles of shoreline. Twenty years later, in 1955, only at Cape Hatteras, North Carolina, had portions of recommended lands been converted to park status. The Park Service at that time warned that "almost every attractive seashore area from Maine to Mexico that is accessible by road has been developed, has been acquired for developmental purposes, or is being considered for development."[45]

In 1960 the Eisenhower administration asked Congress to authorize acquisition of three shoreline areas it believed to be in imminent danger of destruction. The Senate Interior Committee decided that each of these areas had problems that would require further detailed study and separate legislation. Not wishing to lose sight of the broader issue of shoreline preservation, Anderson introduced an omnibus bill at the beginning of the 1961 session.

Anderson's Shoreline Recreation bill had three objectives. It authorized $400,000 to undertake detailed studies of twelve prime areas identified by the National Park Service. The measure further designated $10 million in matching funds to assist states in acquiring shoreline areas. Finally, it provided $400,000 for the Forest Service to examine national forest lands in an effort to identify areas worthy of special shoreline preservation. Anderson scheduled committee hearings on the bill in March 1961. There he argued that quick action would reduce the time needed to respond to the forthcoming recommendations of the Outdoor Recreation Commission. Noting that further delay could prove to be excessively expensive, he cited figures showing that in 1935, at the time of the original Park Service study, prime shoreline cost $9,000 per mile. By 1960 that cost had escalated to $110,000. In that spirit, he urged the bill's adoption as an "economy measure."[46]

Following an examination of the shoreline bill, the Interior Committee turned to the Cape Cod legislation. Massachusetts Senators Leverett Saltonstall (D) and John Kennedy first introduced the measure in 1959. It provided for the acquisition of 10,000 acres of public and private land to preserve a region considered to be unsurpassed in its geological, biological, and historical value. The measure's supporters shrewdly noted that the area lay within one day's drive of one-third of the nation's population. By 1961, with one of the initial sponsors in the White House, the Cape Cod bill had been expanded at the Park Service's recommendation to 30,000 acres with eighty-four miles of shoreline, and its authorization had grown to $16 million.

During the Senate's hearings, a classic division in attitude emerged between the measure's House and Senate sponsors. Representative Hastings Keith (R), whose district included all of Cape Cod, served as the principal House supporter. He argued strongly for a greater local option in land selection and urged that affected towns be allowed to withdraw up to ten percent of the acreage incorporated in the National Park Service's ever-expanding plan, which had formed the basis of the Senate's version of the bill. The Senate, on the other hand, appeared less sensitive to the immediate concerns of local townspeople. President Kennedy wished to see the measure become law without further bickering over a few acres.[47]

Although Alan Bible's subcommittee on Public Lands was the forum for the Cape Cod hearings, Anderson, as chairman of the parent committee, asserted his prerogative to guide the hearing through its initial stages. At that session he demonstrated his skills as prodder and conciliator. He lectured Representative Keith on the consequences of the Massachusetts delegation's failure to compromise on legislation of such importance to the state and the nation. He warned that the alternatives would not be pleasant. If necessary, the committee would make its own changes and hope to prevail in conference with the House, or, as he put it, "This is not the first time that a Cape Cod bill has been before the Congress. And it may not be the last time."[48]

Interior Secretary Udall told the subcommittee that the president regarded this as pioneering legislation, a model for the preservation of shorelines elsewhere in the nation, but particularly in the East. This, the administration hoped, would counter the view of many urban congressmen that federal recreation spending principally benefited the rural West. Udall emphasized that the full resources of his department would be directed to the achievement of the president's goal.[49]

As the hearings moved slowly onward, Anderson became increasingly impatient with Representative Keith and also Park Service Director Conrad Wirth. At one juncture, he led the congressman and the director through a point-by-point review of the seashore's specific boundaries, probing for areas of softness in the adversaries' respective positions. Anderson understood that Keith had to stage a performance for his constituents in the audience and at home. He demonstrated less tolerance for the redoubtable Wirth, bearing down and extracting concessions where the director had pleaded that nothing else could be dropped from the plan without destroying the seashore's integrity. At one point, Wirth's temper flared in response to Keith's reference to Devereux Butcher's article in *Atlantic Monthly* charging the Park Service with mismanagement. Wirth told Keith that he had chosen to ignore that allusion when the congressman had made it earlier in the House hearings. Wirth exploded, charging that the article, "written by one Butcher, I believe," was a slur on the Service's integrity and he defied "anyone to show that the parks are not being managed properly." At that juncture, Anderson took up his conciliatory demeanor, suggesting that Butcher meant only that "Congress does not give you enough money" to properly run the parks, citing the success of New Mexico's Carlsbad Caverns whose federal funding he had personally overseen.[50]

Several weeks later Anderson attended, but did not actively involve himself in, hearings on a second specific seashore measure. The Point Reyes National Seashore bill was designed to recover nearly 53,000 acres of privately owned seashore located thirty-five miles north of San Francisco. Interior Secretary Udall testified that the federal government was in a life-or-death race with area developers, noting "they are actually trenching and laying sewerpipe," and he warned of the consequences of the Bay area's population explosion from 4.5 million to a projected 8 million by 1980.[51]

The three shoreline bills moved quickly from the Interior Committee to the Senate floor. Late in June, the Cape Cod bill passed by a routine voice vote, and the president signed it at the height of the summer tourist season. Shortly before Anderson returned to New Mexico for surgery at the end of August, he sent the Point Reyes bill to the full Senate. Unfortunately, as was the case with the Wilderness Act, Anderson's medical problems prevented him from participating in the final stage of the Senate's consideration for the shoreline and the Point Reyes measures. The Senate agreed to the shoreline bill on August 28 just after its floor manager, Alan Bible, announced to the Senate that Anderson had withstood his operation "very successfully." The upper house then approved the Point Reyes bill on September 7, the day after the successful wilderness vote.[52]

Throughout the course of the 1961 wilderness and shoreline deliberations, Anderson became aware that many influential senators were not content to follow the new Kennedy administration's lead in the shaping and conduct of natural resources policy. Since the Hoover Commission's recommendations in 1949, the idea of a new cabinet-level department of natural resources to reduce the fragmentation of federal policy in that area had attracted powerful support. By 1960 the numerous practical difficulties associated with the implementation of that proposal had forced its supporters to devise an alternative. In January 1960 Interior Committee chairman James Murray held hearings on his bill to establish, within the executive office of the president, a "Council of Resources and Conservation Advisers" patterned after the President's Council of Economic Advisers. During his 1960 election campaign, candidate John Kennedy pledged to establish the council Murray advocated.[53]

In his February 1961 natural resources message, however, the new president backed away from his campaign promise and substituted an advisory committee on natural resources under the jurisdiction of the Council of Economic Advisers. This led California Senator Clair Engle (D) to call for hearings on a reintroduced version of former Chairman Murray's bill. Engle had served as chairman of the House Interior Committee during the four years before he moved to the Senate in 1959. He enjoyed considerable standing among conservationists and, although not a member of the Senate Interior Committee, he posed at least an indirect threat to Anderson's leadership. Engle's bill would have established a council of resources advisers in the executive branch as well as a Joint Congressional Committee on Resources and Conservation.

Both proposals, the administration's and Engle's, raised jurisdictional problems for Anderson. Under the Kennedy plan, which placed responsibility with the Council of Economic Advisers, congressional oversight of natural resources would have to be shared with the Joint Economic Committee. Anderson asserted it would be unacceptable for that committee to have control over matters more properly assigned to the Interior Committee. He predicted that Engle's plan for a joint resources committee would run into fatal opposition from House speaker Sam Rayburn, who roundly hated joint committees. Anderson's own experience during four years as chairman of the Joint Committee on Atomic Energy soured him on the effectiveness of such combined panels. When serving on the 1960 platform committee of the Democratic party, he rejected the joint resources committee idea but did support the future president's pledge for a resources council. He pointed out that the less busy House members of a joint committee had more time to become actively involved in its work, often outnumbering and overwhelming the one or two senators who find time to attend meetings. Chairmanships rotated between houses from Congress to Congress. The body controlling the chair, in Anderson's experience, seldom concerned itself with the other body's convenience in scheduling meetings.[54]

The administration's proposal, with its suggestion of a major role for the Bureau of the Budget in coordinating the resources agenda, placed Anderson in a difficult position. He was committed to advancing the administration's resources program, yet his aversion to the Budget Bureau extended back to his service as Secretary of Agriculture. He demonstrated the depth of those feelings earlier in the year during the confirmation hearings of the Interior Department's undersecretary. When the nominee volunteered that he would return to private life if he found himself unable to abide by the intent of Congress in discharging his responsibilities, Anderson offered an alternative. "If you ever get to where you cannot follow the congressional intent," said the chairman, "you should go to work for the Bureau of the Budget."[55]

Engle's resources council bill received a courteous but inconclusive hearing before Anderson's Interior Committee on April 13, 1961. The Interior and Agriculture departments withheld comment pending the president's elaboration of his February Natural Resources message. The Budget Bureau stated that it believed a new resources council would be unnecessary. When the hearings adjourned, Anderson decided to let the matter rest for the time being.[56]

The matter did not rest long. Five days later, a draft presidential executive order on resources and public works reached Anderson. That order, if promulgated, would have strengthened the Budget Bureau's control over natural resources policy, empowering it to schedule "a progressive and orderly sequence of surveys, investigations, plans and developments," with the power to recommend to the president "policies, standards, and criteria for resource programs."[57] Among its added responsibilities, the Budget Bureau would oversee federal participation in river basin planning activities. The Council of Economic Advisers would also acquire a greater coordinating role, but one clearly subordinate to the Budget Bureau.

Ben Stong believed the proposed order had disastrous implications for future resources policy development, particularly from the legislative perspective. He advised Anderson that the order would place the Budget Bureau astride established communications channels between executive resources agencies and Congress, and that increased responsibility for the Council of Economic Advisers was simply an illusion masking the bureau's greater role.[58] He told Anderson that the order represented an ill-conceived attempt to enhance the congressionally devised mandate of the Budget Bureau by means of presidential administrative powers, a clear usurpation of Congress's role and intent. Stong warned that Congress might respond with far more detailed legislative standards, criteria and regulations, in effect preempting the proper role of executive agencies.[59]

Anderson agreed with Stong's feeling that President Kennedy might not be fully aware of the likely "congressional, political, and practical reaction" to the order. On April 21, twenty senators, all involved in resources policy matters, sent a telegram to the president reminding him of his campaign pledges to push for a separate council on natural resources. They pointed out that the proposed order would negate those pledges, and they urged Kennedy to consult with Anderson before acting further on the order.[60]

On that same day, Anderson prepared a six-page letter to the president in which he expressed shock at the order's contents and his doubt that it could have received the chief executive's careful attention.[61] Observing that Kennedy was the first president since Andrew Johnson to have served in both houses of Congress, Anderson volunteered that he could appreciate "better than any previous president in nearly a century the reaction in both the House and the Senate to an executive order which codifies and extends the Bureau of the Budget's role in policymaking, scheduling, and administration of resources and public works planning and developments, and in river basin planning." Anderson warned that "serious conflict will inevitably arise between you and the Congress immediately if the proposed executive order is issued." He continued that "it is an extremely bad issue—an unnecessary and needless one—on which to start a fight." Anderson further warned that the order would result in subordination of Kennedy's cabinet officers to the Budget Bureau and also "reopen all the old sore spots—and many new ones—between Congress and the Executive Office."[62]

Anderson sent a copy of the letter to budget director David Bell, whom he believed, along with the president, had been overly influenced by Harvard professor Richard Neustadt's theories of administrative centralization. These views were contained in his recently published book *Presidential Power,* known to some critics as the "Bible for the cult of the presidency."[63] The administration responded quickly, agreeing to send White House natural resources adviser Lee White to meet with Anderson and other concerned members. Anderson assembled a high-powered force for that session. It included House Interior Committee chairman Wayne Aspinall, whose views on the indispensability of congressional autonomy in resources matters and the need for direct consultation with cabinet agencies were well known and often reiterated. Also present were senators and representatives holding key committee positions on resources matters.[64]

Several days after the meeting, Kennedy invited Anderson to the White House for a late afternoon "coffee" and discussion on the proposed executive order. Despite administration congressional liaison chief Lawrence O'Brien's private assessment that Anderson was "now more a debtor than a creditor in the Senate" as a result of the 1959 Lewis Strauss confirmation fight, Kennedy quickly yielded to Anderson's protest.[65] Shortly thereafter budget chief Bell wrote advising Anderson that the administration had desired only to codify, not enlarge, the Budget Bureau's responsibilities. Accordingly, he believed "the simplest solution is to eliminate the offending provisions entirely from the draft order, and I have directed that this be done."[66] Anderson later told Bell that "the points [he] had made were pleasing to all of us," but he also hoped that the Bureau would give cautious attention to its related proposals to expand the role of the Council of Economic Advisers in resources matters. In a hand-written postscript, Anderson advised the budget chief that he had declined requests from the press for copies of his earlier letter to the president and he hoped Bell could see his way clear to refuse also.[67] Thus Congress, led by Anderson, had won a strategically-important battle with the fledgling administration in a crucial test of wills over the basic direction of natural resources policy.

As the 1961 session of Congress drew to an end late in September, the Kennedy administration recognized that the goals of its February natural resources message were close to being realized in the Senate. The landmark Wilderness Act has passed by a margin that would surely impress undecided House members. The president's campaign to rescue endangered shoreline areas had also made great strides in the upper chamber. The Outdoor Recreation Resources Review Commission was moving closer to its reporting deadline, and its conclusions would lead to a new round of legislative activity in both houses of Congress. By September, however, many conservationists conceded that the administration's honeymoon with Congress was nearing an end. The new year promised renewed testing at the hands of congressmen who, with an eye on the high stakes involved in resources development, were dissatisfied with what they perceived to be a reluctance by the administration to follow through with earlier promises. Anderson's skill as conciliator and prodder, as administration counselor and legislative leader would undoubtedly be tested as never before.

# 6

# Chairman's Apogee
## Outdoor Recreation, Wilderness, and Parklands, 1962

We New Mexicans did reserve the right to start off first. A man has to have some privileges for being chairman of a committee.

Clinton P. Anderson
May 24, 1962

In 1962 Clinton Anderson reached the apogee of his effectiveness as a national conservation leader. The Kennedy administration viewed him as a creative and determined legislative strategist with a sense of timing and understanding of the limits of the possible unexcelled among his congressional colleagues. From January through May, Anderson played a major role in the rapid succession of conservation policy events. The action began on January 31 with the presentation at the White House of the Outdoor Recreation Resources Review Commission's final report. One month later, on March 1, President Kennedy sent Congress the first comprehensive conservation program since the administration of Theodore Roosevelt. In quick succession, on April 2, the new Bureau of Outdoor Recreation began operation within the Interior Department.[1] Early in May Anderson convened Senate hearings on legislation to strengthen the new recreation bureau and to fulfill the promise of the recreation commission report. That month ended with a full-scale White House Conference on Conservation, the first of its kind since 1908. As the Eighty-seventh Congress came to an end in October 1962, Clinton Anderson could accept, as more than conventional flattery, Interior Secretary Udall's expressed hope that "the people of the United States realize what tremendous conservation leadership we have had from you and your committee during this Congress."[2]

At the White House ceremony for the Outdoor Recreation Commission's report, Anderson appeared to be in unusually good humor. Standing between the president and commission chairman Laurance Rockefeller, he believed that event would sweep aside a major obstacle to passage of the Wilderness Act in the House of Representatives. Those who had made their support of the act conditional on the outcome of the commission's deliberations now had their report. It appeared, as an official of the Sierra Club observed, that "a three-year moratorium on conservation is over."[3]

The commission had "found" that the nation was unprepared to meet the likely outdoor recreation demands of the year 2000. Reporting that sixty-five percent of Americans customarily traveled less than 250 miles from home for their recreation, the commission urged immediate planning for facilities to be located in metropolitan areas. It discovered that the most popular outdoor activities were also the simplest. They ranged, in order of preference, from pleasure riding in the family automobile, to walking, picnicking, swimming, boating, birdwatching, hiking and camping.[4]

The commission offered two principal recommendations. The first called for creation of a program of matching federal grants for states to finance planning of new outdoor recreation sites. Of greater long-range significance, the second proposal urged establishment of a Bureau of Outdoor Recreation within the Interior Department. This office's mission would be to coordinate the multiplicity of recreation-related programs scattered throughout twenty federal agencies.[5]

A look beyond these general recommendations revealed serious deficiencies in the commission's work effort. The 250-page final report itself was a product of compromise, haste, and a less than fully articulated sense of that panel's mission. Chairman Rockefeller wished to avoid the divisiveness inherent in advisory bodies representing broad constituencies. To that end, he purposely steered away from considerations of cost and financial allocation. He also wanted his report to appear on schedule. The result was a bland compendium of oversized photographs and understudied generalities.[6]

Anderson appeared more interested in the report's form than substance. He believed that its simple existence would remove the final argument of Wilderness bill opponents that they could not reasonably consider that measure until they had examined the results of this $2.5 million study. Wayne Aspinall (D-CO), chairman of the House Interior Committee, had repeatedly refused to schedule hearings on the bill until the commission had concluded its work. Under these circumstances, Anderson reacted with irritation when the report received mixed press reviews. The presence on the commission of Marian Sulzberger Dryfoos, daughter of the *New York Times'* board chairman and wife of its publisher, underscored that paper's ongoing interest in natural resources policy. Not unexpectedly, the *Times* praised the report's conclusions.[7] *The Washington Post,* to the contrary, took a darker view, expressing disappointment that the commission had failed to set forth both a specific program and cost estimates. To this complaint, chairman Rockefeller weakly responded that the panel sought only to provide the "tools and principles, leaving to others how best to use the money."[8]

Most interested periodicals reviewed the commission report in terms that were descriptive rather than analytical. *Field & Stream* provided a notable exception with an article entitled "The ORRRC Report: A Glittering Blunder." The magazine's editors argued that the commission, faced with a "golden opportunity" to shape outdoor recreation policy for decades to come, had merely produced a "goldbrick."[9] They directed their most destructive salvo at the proposal for a new recreation agency, charging that "an obscure bureau, tucked away in the corner of the Interior Department, is the flimsy, jerry-built foundation on which the whole brave new world of the ORRRC rests." The editors predicted that the bureau, "without power or prestige, would earn nothing but the contempt of the leather-tough bureaucrats of the cabinet departments."[10]

Anderson led the commission's response to the *Field & Stream* attack.Chairman Rockefeller had been sidelined with gall bladder surgery and Joseph Penfold, father of the recreation review concept, had just suffered a serious heart attack. Anderson sent a carefully documented rebuttal to the magazine's editors. When it became apparent that they had little interest in publishing his letter, the senator took his case directly to a friend who was chairman of the periodical's parent company. "I was wondering," he wrote with undisguised irritation, "if the matter of the article concerning the

ORRRC report might not be the subject which might be discussed at the next meeting of the board."[11]

Criticism of the proposed recreation bureau struck a sensitive chord for Anderson. He knew that commissions could issue reports and legislatures could pass laws, but executive agencies would ultimately determine the effectiveness of those studies and statutes. As the commission's recommendations were taking shape, a year earlier, Anderson had vigorously opposed its staff's apparent predisposition to propose a new agency, particularly one placed in the Interior Department subject to National Park Service influence. He warned that the work plan was establishing "a conclusion toward which we are going to start assembling facts," and he urged the staff not to propose "an agency which Congress might not agree to establish, in order to administer a [grant-in-aid] law Congress might not agree to pass, to take care of a situation which the statistics might show didn't exist."[12]

In reviewing a draft version of the report that seemed to favor an expansion of Park Service prerogatives, Anderson complained that his initial effort to create a broad review of recreation resources was ending up as a "drive to give [Park Service Director] Connie Worth [sic] the power of a czar over the parks, the forests, the lakes for fishing and wildlife, and the seashore!"[13] He predicted open strife if the commission's report supported the Park Service's designs on the administration of lands under the jurisdiction of the rival U.S. Forest Service in the Department of Agriculture. Anderson agreed with aide Claude Wood's observation that those two agencies had "done a pretty fine job of providing for the recreation needs of the country with the limited amount of money provided them in the past." Wood advised the senator to pursue alternatives to creating a new bureau, such as giving permanent status to the recreation commission, or creating an interagency coordinating committee on recreation resources "to promote harmony between the agencies."[14]

As the commission's studies advanced, however, it became clear that the Interior Department would be the least objectionable location for outdoor recreation planning functions. At the same time, sentiment also ran toward making the new bureau independent of that agency's Park Service.[15] The more that Director Wirth fought the concept of a separate division, the more convinced Anderson was that it would serve as a realistic solution to a difficult bureaucratic situation. Laurance Rockefeller assured Anderson that despite Wirth's vigorous efforts to expand the Park Service's recreation role, the distinction between its function and that of the new recreation bureau would be carefully and clearly drawn in the commission's final report. Anderson ultimately agreed and then advised the chairman not to take too seriously the howl of protest likely to issue from the Agriculture Department on behalf of its Forest Service."[16]

At the commission's White House ceremony in January 1962, a shadow of concern may well have crossed Anderson's outwardly sunny demeanor. A crucial supporting study, one of twenty-seven, remained unfinished. Entitled "Wilderness and Recreation," the study had been the target of much of Anderson's attention over the previous year. More than any other product of the commission, this report was likely to determine whether House Interior Committee chairman Aspinall would keep his promise to move ahead with consideration of the stalled Wilderness Act. Anderson feared that a weak or contradictory wilderness study would provide Aspinall with justification for additional, and thus possibly fatal, delay.[17]

The commission's Washington staff had procrastinated before awarding the wilderness report contract to the Wildland Research Center within the University of California at Berkeley. As a result of the delay, the contract had to be negotiated in great haste, giving the research center less than adequate time, barely a year, and vague guidelines for the study's completion. Incredibly, the most serious omission in the charge to the contractor was a definition of "wilderness." Left to its own devices, the contractor adopted a flawed and unrealistic definition. It included only public or Indian lands within the continental United States "of *at least* 100,000 acres containing no usable roads and possessing a reasonably unified boundary configuration."[18]

Anderson called the contractor's definition "parochial and inadequate," clearly in contradiction of the commission's broad objectives. He calculated that such a standard would exclude eighty-two of the 120 wilderness-type areas already incorporated in the Senate-passed version of the Wilderness bill, and he protested that the contractor had failed to consider the value of wilderness areas' scenic, scientific, historical, and educational qualities.[19] The 100,000 acre limitation arbitrarily excluded all potentially attractive eastern areas as well as many choice smaller western sites.

The New Mexico senator was further concerned by the possible consequences of a hostile response from the Forest Service. Well aware of that agency's powerful political base with foresters scattered in nearly one thousand ranger districts across the country, he had once quipped, "God help the Secretary of Agriculture who crosses the Forest Service."[20] Yet he sympathized with Forest Service charges that the contractors had naively assumed wilderness was desirable in its own right without attempting to set down criteria against which specific tracts of national forest land could be evaluated. The agency complained that the contractor lacked both the time and competence to justify its conclusion that seven million acres of unclassified Forest Service land should be set aside in the wilderness system without additional study. Although Forest Service officials generally supported the aims of wilderness preservation, they did not wish to do so at the expense of removing productive timber lands from sustained yield harvesting.[21]

Anderson feared that the research center's report would strengthen the hand of the mining interests, for it contained specific information on wilderness area mineral possibilities while offering only vague generalities on wildlife and aesthetic values. He also took issue with the contractor's use of public opinion sampling, arguing that limiting a major study to individuals visiting areas larger than 200,000 acres merely proved that "people who go to 200,000 acre wilderness areas like 200,000 acre wilderness areas."[22] He concluded that the overall impact of the study was "a gathering together of available data on wilderness by a group who had little information or knowledge about planning techniques, or the essential planning role of the agency that employed them."[23]

While the commission staff tried to salvage the wilderness report, the Kennedy administration put the finishing touches on a major conservation message to Congress, the first of its kind in more than a half century. Both Anderson and Aspinall were involved in the preparation of that message, for without their support, it was unlikely to transcend the bounds of inspirational rhetoric.

Anderson played a greater role than Aspinall. Personally closer to both the president and Secretary Udall than was the acerbic Colorado chairman, he was also less subject to the pressures of hostile mining and timber interests. Accordingly, Anderson became the proposal's advance spokesman, appearing on NBC's "Today Show" on the day before the message was delivered. He used that opportunity to repeat his contention that the Wilderness Act would decidedly not "lock up" the nation's vital mineral and timber resources, and he indirectly urged the House of Representatives to follow the Senate's lead in passing the measure.[24]

In his message, the president announced plans for a White House Conference on Conservation, establishment of a cabinet-level Outdoor Recreation Advisory Council, and creation of the Bureau of Outdoor Recreation.[25] For that latter agency, Anderson took a direct interest in the choice of a director. A month before the president's message, he had heard rumors that Secretary Udall intended to recommend Francis Sargent, the recreation commission's executive secretary. Anderson believed Sargent was not the best choice. The senator's experience with the commission's administrative direction confirmed his view of such bodies as inefficient vehicles for advancement of public policy, with little value beyond that of consensus building. In Anderson's opinion, Sargent had become too closely associated with the commission's inefficiencies to be entrusted with the direction of a promising, but fragile, new agency.[26] Word quickly passed to White House congressional liaison chief Lawrence O'Brien that Anderson has grown "considerably agitated" at the prospect of Sargent's appointment and that he intended to take the matter up with the president at the earliest opportunity. Udall quickly called the senator to assure him that Sargent would not be selected.[27]

Anderson decided that Edward Crafts, the Forest Service's director of legislative liaison, should have the position. The senator appreciated the symbolic value of naming such a key Agriculture Department official to a major Interior Department post, particularly one that required a high level of cooperation between the two traditionally antagonistic agencies.[28] Crafts, however, had other career plans. He hoped to succeed his boss, Richard McArdle, as head of the Forest Service. Late in 1961 McArdle had announced his plans to retire after a decade as the nation's chief forester. McArdle, whose gruff manner belied an amiable personality and informal manner of operation, decided not to recommend Crafts as his replacement. Although Crafts was highly regarded for the quality of his intellect and his ability to get things done on Capitol Hill, his straightforward, no nonsense manner earned him a reputation for having "icewater in his veins." A well-oiled campaign by Assistant Chief Edward Cliff for the top post also doomed Crafts' chances.[29]

Sierra Club executive secretary David Brower, unaware of these

barriers to Crafts' promotion, launched a campaign to block his elevation, fearing a major setback for the objectives of the preservationists if Crafts succeeded. He enlisted Supreme Court Justice William O. Douglas to dissuade Udall and the president from making
the appointment. Brower regarded Crafts as "probably the bright-
est person they ever had in the Forest Service." He believed that
Crafts' "extreme skills, his ability to maneuver, to work with Congress, his cleverness, his good footwork were so frightening, that
we were afraid any attempt at preservation would be put back a
long, long time if he were made chief of the Forest Service."[30]

Anderson shared Brower's view of Crafts' ability, but not of his
aloofness. Several months later, he professed surprise on learning
that Crafts possessed a doctorate, and jokingly apologized for calling him "Ed" in the past. Anderson admired the forester's folksy
manner, noting that Crafts was the "sort of person that comes in,
sits down beside you and visits with you as if he ran the blacksmith's
shop next door to your store."[31] After several discussions with Udall
on Crafts' behalf, Anderson learned that his candidate would receive the recreation bureau post.[32]

At early April ceremonies in Udall's office to announce Crafts' appointment and to inaugurate the new bureau, Anderson commended
the secretary on his masterstroke of reaching into the Agriculture
Department for the director. He recalled his own efforts, while secretary of Agriculture, to promote interagency harmony by giving
the Secretary of the Interior at least two days' advance notice of
any decision affecting that agency, noting "You'd be surprised how
much stealing that cuts down."[33] Observing that Crafts faced a "very
delicate job," Anderson remarked that the forester would "start it
out on a decent basis and not on the basis of what we can steal."[34]

Within forty-eight hours of the festivities in Udall's office, Anderson introduced two administration drafted bills designed to advance
the work of the new recreation bureau. The first provided the
bureau with statutory authority to extend its planning and coordination functions to all federal agencies with recreation-related programs. The measure also established a $50 million, five-year grant-
in-aid program to spur states in the development of comprehensive outdoor recreation plans.[35]

The second measure provided for creation of a "Land Conservation Fund" to finance federal acquisition of lands for "park, recreation, forest, and certain fish and wildlife purposes." It authorized an

advance allocation of $500 million in federal funds to begin the pur-
chase program.[36] Ultimately, half the acquisition costs were to be
repaid through the fund's ongoing revenue sources. These included user charges collected at federal recreation areas, proceeds from
the sale of surplus nonmilitary lands, a two-cent-per-gallon tax on
motorboat fuels, and an annual levy on the use of recreation boats.

Within days of the Land Conservation Fund bill's introduction,
recreation boat owners angrily attacked the proposed tax, shower-
ing the White House and Congress with telegrams of protest. Consequently, Anderson decided to shelve the fund bill pending "further
study" and to concentrate instead on the more modest grant-in-aid
and recreation bureau authority measure. This strategy allowed him
to maintain the momentum of popular and congressional support
for the recreation commission's findings and to capitalize on the
obvious popularity of a grant-in-aid proposal among state governors. Citing recreation commissioner Fred Smith's view that the
first priority should be attached to a review of existing outdoor
recreation areas to ensure their effectiveness, Anderson contended
that "haste makes waste" and that his objective would be to get
the bureau "funded, staffed, and functioning" and the "states moving ahead with their planning and program development."[37] Ultimately, Anderson feared that premature consideration of the more
costly and ambitious measure, in the face of a broadly based and
highly vocal boating lobby, would seriously undermine the chances
of passing the grant-in-aid bill. Worse, it might also muddy the waters for prompt House consideration of the Wilderness Act.[38]

In March 1962, as the Senate Interior Committee prepared for
hearings on the recreation bills and sought to influence House action on the Wilderness Act, its chairman became embroiled in a
press attack on the size and partisan complexion of Senate committee staffs. Anderson's response further illuminated his philosophy of committee leadership and his intolerance of distortion for
partisan political gain.

Using information supplied by Senator Carl Curtis (R-NE), syndicated columnist Roscoe Drummond charged that the Senate's
Democratic leadership had conspired against that body's Republican members by hiring Democratic committee staff members at a
ratio of more than ten to one over the Republicans. For Anderson's
Interior Committee, the columnist listed seventeen Democrats and
only one Republican.[39] Anderson directed committee aide Jerry

Verkler to survey the staff's political affiliation and also to draft a
response to Drummond. Verkler reported finding twelve Democrats, three Republicans, and two "Independents." He noted that
most of the staff worked in a purely fact-finding capacity and that
few of the issues before the committee were considered partisan
in the traditional sense. He cited the Wilderness Act as a good example of a measure that drew support and opposition from within
both parties.[40]

In his response to Drummond, Anderson suggested that the columnist had been misinformed by Senator Curtis who may have written "out of good intentions if not good information." He continued,
"I suppose that Senator Curtis was trying to maintain that as a result of the strong preponderance of Democrats, Republican bills
do not get fair hearings. Ask him how he has come along with his
reclamation bills. Ask him if he has not personally thanked me several times for the consideration I have given him."[41]

Anderson's anger at the charges' partisan derivation continued
for several months. Senate Majority Leader Mike Mansfield (D-MT)
asked Anderson to join him in accepting a Republican proposal for
a Library of Congress study of committee staffing. Anderson told
Mansfield, "I'm afraid that I do not view this as calmly as you do,
but I tried to do what you have. I wrote Everett [Dirksen, the Minority Leader] a nice, conciliatory letter."[42] In that letter, Anderson asked Dirksen to understand that he was "not bitching, and
not griping, and not mad." He asserted, however, that the charges
were "badly out of line and were used to criticize committees and
committee chairmen where no criticism was due."[43] As the force
of his vindictive campaign against Lewis Strauss three years earlier
demonstrated, Anderson could tolerate honest error, but he never
forgave intentional distortion or outright lies. He believed that this
incident embodied more than honest error. He told Mansfield that
he had taken great pains to be fair in the treatment of Interior Committee staff when he took over as chairman. Although he dismissed
a large number, they were all Democratic proteges of Chairman
James Murray and were clearly distinguishable in the quality of their
job assignments from those with substantive professional responsibilities. He recalled that in 1953, when Senator Hugh Butler (R-
NE) became chairman of that committee, "he tore up the staff fast
and insisted that it be a Republican staff." Anderson continued, "I
don't think I ever had any help from staff members during that

time."[44] The New Mexico senator urged the majority leader to convene a special legislative hearing to expose what he believed to be groundless charges, promising that such a forum would allow a "slugging match from start to finish in which I would be delighted to participate."[45] Despite Anderson's call, the leadership chose the Library of Congress study to defuse the controversy.[46]

April and May of 1962 brought a renewal activity on the Wilderness bill. On April 6 House Interior Committee Chairman Aspinall announced that the long-delayed hearings would begin on May 7.[47] The recreation commission had agreed to pay a supplemental charge to the Government Printing Office to ensure that the Wilderness and Recreation study report would be available several weeks before the start of those hearings.[48] At the Interior Department, plans went ahead for the White House Conference on Conservation scheduled for May 24 and 25.

The House hearings on the Wilderness bill consumed an entire week early in May. They provided a forum for ninety witnesses on all sides of the wilderness issue and confirmed Anderson's pessimism that Chairman Aspinall had no intention of clearing for action by the full House a bill similar to the one the Senate had passed the previous September. Although the hearings were under the direction of Representative Gracie Pfost (D-ID), Aspinall interceded at crucial points to challenge advocates of the Senate version. Contrary to the demeanor of their Senate colleagues, who cloaked their antagonism in a veil of congeniality, the participating House members lashed out at one another in plain and direct language.[49] Representative John Saylor (R-PA), the fiercely independent conservationist and sponsor of an identical version of the Senate-passed bill, began the hearings with an eloquent plea for prompt action in which he quoted former Park Service Director Newton Drury's admonition that "surely we are not so poor that we need to destroy [the remaining parks and wildlands], or so rich that we can afford to lose them."[50] Saylor concluded his testimony by inserting into the hearing record the complete text of Anderson's 1961 statement introducing the Senate version.[51]

Aspinall argued that the Saylor-Anderson bill favored a narrow elite of nature lovers at the expense of the nation's strategic and material needs. Throughout the hearings and several weeks later at the White House conservation conference, Aspinall hammered away at his theme, borrowed from the Gifford Pinchot tradition, that conservation meant "wise use" of natural resources rather than the locking up, in his view, of materials essential to the lumber and mining industries.[52]

With the House hearings concluded, attention shifted to the White House Conference, another exercise designed to buoy the Wilderness bill's prospects. Proposed ten weeks earlier in the president's conservation message, the conference bore the marks of hasty planning. For reasons that were not entirely clear, the Kennedy administration invited as participants only government officials, both federal and state, while relegating private sector representatives, including industry and conservation group lobbyists, to observer status. What they observed were four carefully orchestrated consecutive sessions conducted for the 300 delegates who gathered in the State Department auditorium on May 24 and 25.

Anderson chaired the session entitled "Conservation and Congress." The conference's lack of careful planning and absence of sharply defined purpose was reflected in Anderson's panel. Two of the senators among the five congressional panelists failed to attend, as the Senate was then in the midst of a heated debate on a major farm bill. Anderson and Senator Lee Metcalf (D-MT) departed shortly after completing their own formal presentations. This left the heart of the discussion to the foremost House protagonists, Aspinall and Saylor.[53]

Anderson seemed to view the conference as merely another vehicle to advance the Wilderness bill in the House. The fact that the meeting was being held was of greater import than any new paths that it might be expected to blaze. Consequently, Anderson assumed the demeanor of a charming and self-confident showman rather than that of earnest persuader. His prepared address, distinguished only by its brevity, stressed the preeminence of Congress in the field of natural resources conservation. He noted, with a touch of irony, the basic cordiality of his own relationship with the chairman of the House Interior Committee. Aspinall responded in kind, observing that their willingness to agree was demonstrated in their frequent meetings. Anderson would agree to have their meetings in his own Capitol hideaway office, and Aspinall would agree to walk to that office![54]

At the time of the White House conference, Anderson displayed a particularly sunny disposition as House and Senate conferees had just approved his bill to authorize New Mexico's San Juan-Chama

water project. This long-sought victory led Anderson to rejoice pub-
licly in his prerogatives as committee chairman. He told the audience that the success of the New Mexico project ought to be "good
news" for all the Rocky Mountain states, for when the chairman's
"projects get on the road, and additional money is available, work
can be started on other projects in that area." Nodding in the direction of the governor of Utah, Anderson declared, "We New Mexican did reserve the right to start off first. A man has got to have
some privileges for being chairman of a committee."[55]

The White House conference accomplished little more than providing an opportunity for like-minded individuals to meet and compare notes. It produced no formal conclusions or recommendations.
Representatives of private industry and conservationists complained
about their exclusion as participants. Secretary Udall responded with
a hasty promise to convene a follow-up session at some future time.
Hobbled by insufficient time for planning and inundated by the existing high tide of conservation sentiment within both Congress
and the Kennedy administration, the conference and its published
proceedings were quickly forgotten.[56]

The conference did nothing to alter Aspinall's position on the
Wilderness Act. On August 9, 1962, while Anderson was sidelined
in New Mexico with a heart ailment, the House Public Lands Subcommittee finally acted on the bill. Following Aspinall's lead, it abandoned the Saylor-Anderson measure for a far more restrictive version.
The substitute bill removed from the proposed wilderness system
all thirty-nine "primitive areas" encompassing 8 million of the 14.6
million acres in the Senate act. It further required affirmative congressional action before any of the primitive areas or other lands
not then carrying formal designation as wilderness could be added.
Where the Senate bill prohibited all new mining activity and sanctioned only nondisruptive prospecting, the House bill permitted
prospecting for twenty-five years and allowed the use of heavy
"mechanized ground or air equipment."[57]

At the end of August, Aspinall maneuvered his bill out of the full
Interior Committee. With the measure came a highly unusual in-
struction from a majority of the committee's members, "directing"
Chairman Aspinall to seek floor consideration under a "suspension"
of House rules. This procedure, used primarily for minor and non-
controversial bills, placed severe limits on debate, permitted no
amendments, and required a two-thirds majority of those voting to

secure passage. Aspinall recognized that under normal floor procedures, his bill would have been quickly amended to incorporate
the abandoned Senate version. This potential scenario mirrored the
earlier action in the Senate where the western-dominated Interior
Committee barely approved the measure, only to have the full body
accord it an overwhelmingly favorable majority.[58] Speaker John Mc-
Cormack (D-MA), sensitive to the Kennedy administration's wishes
and a flood of telegrams inspired by conservation lobbies, refused
to permit Aspinall's tactics to succeed. In a virtually unprecedented
rebuff to a committee chairman, the speaker insisted that the bill
be considered on its merits with opportunity for full debate and
appropriate amendments. Under those circumstances, Aspinall simply packed his bags and left town, blocking further action on the
measure for the remainder of the 1962 session.[59]

Early in 1962 many leading conservationists believed that the
Eighty-seventh Congress, coinciding with the first two years of the
Kennedy administration, would earn the distinction of being labeled
"the Conservation Congress." The deadlock, in mid-September, over
the Wilderness bill extinguished those hopes. With only a few weeks
remaining before adjournment, dispirited ranks of conservationists
looked ahead to January 1963 when they again would have to marshal their arguments and their limited financial resources in the
halls of Congress.[60]

Despite this bleak outlook, the month of September brought a
number of positive accomplishments for conservation that ranked
only slightly behind the Wilderness bill in degree of importance.
These developments included dedication of the Navajo Dam to harness the scarce water resources of northern New Mexico, signing
of acts to create national seashores at Point Reyes, California, and
Padre Island, Texas, reporting of a bill in the Senate to establish
Canyonlands National Park in southern Utah, and a hearing in Santa
Fe, New Mexico, on an Anderson bill to create Valle Grande National Park. The Valle Grande hearing occurred on the same day
that the Wilderness bill died in the House. Although the hearing
did not lead immediately to Senate action on the New Mexican park
bill, it revealed an attitude among key legislative and administrative figures that boded well for the success of conservation legislation during the upcoming Eighty-eighth Congress in 1963.[61]

During the 1961-62 congressional sessions, influential members
of Congress pressured the Kennedy administration to designate and

fund new national parks within their respective states. Each summer, millions of American shattered old attendance records as they jammed national and state parks. Interior Secretary Udall had reportedly promised Colorado, home of Chairman Aspinall, prompt action on studies preliminary to legislative consideration of new parks there. As he demonstrated at the White House conference, Anderson was not reluctant to assert his own prerogatives to the advantage of his home state. As of 1961, New Mexico had ten areas under the jurisdiction of the National Park Service, but only one of them, Carlsbad Caverns, enjoyed national park status and the accompanying financial support.[62]

The Jemez Mountains of northern New Mexico offered several potentially attractive sites for new national parks. In the face of financial stringencies, the New Mexico legislature in its 1961 session canceled plans to fund the expansion of Rio Grande Gorge State Park in that region. Robert McKinney, Anderson associate and publisher of the *Santa Fe New Mexican,* suggested editorially that the state seek federal funds for this purpose.[63] In April 1961, as McKinney began to sound out the state's congressional delegation to this end, a large tract of land became available for purchase. Amounting to nearly 100,000 acres, the tract was situated in the Valle Grande region near Los Alamos. Known as the Baca Location #1, the parcel was surrounded on three sides by national forest land and on the fourth by lands under the jurisdiction of the Atomic Energy Commission. The main feature of the area was the Valles Caldera, one of the world's largest and best understood collapsed volcanic summits. Fifty miles in circumference, the caldera ranged from five hundred to two thousand feet in depth.[64]

The trustees of the estate controlling the Baca location approached Anderson to determine whether the federal government wished to purchase the property for either the Park Service or the Forest Service. Anderson at once became interested.[65] The tract had the dual advantages of excellent recreational potential and a vital watershed for the Rio Grande Valley. It was situated approximately one hundred miles from the rapidly growing Albuquerque metropolitan area and less than half that distance from Santa Fe. Anderson calculated that a national park in the region would attract more out-of-state visitors and could extend their average stay in New Mexico by at least one day. Assuming that each visitor spent $10.00 per day, that the tourist season lasted three months, and that approximately ten thousand visitors toured the Santa Fe region daily, Anderson happily concluded that a national park could pump an additional $100 million per year into the state's economy.[66]

By mid-1961, Anderson had assumed a mediatory role in the negotiations over the tract's selling price and federal agency jurisdiction. Difficulties with both of these issues threatened to sabotage the deal. The trustees made it clear that although they would like to see the land preserved, they would also consider selling to cattlemen or developers. The senator doubted the tract's value as a cattle ranch as the 8,000 to 11,000 foot elevation limited its use to summer grazing, and there was no suitable winter range in the vicinity. Furthermore, the Baca location offered grazing land of only marginal quality. He urged the executors to settle on a price that reflected values of comparable land rather than an inflated notion of its grazing potential. Anderson considered the entire tract to be worth between $1 million and $2 million. Initially, the executors did not dispute his estimate, so he asked Secretary Udall to have the Park Service begin work on a formal appraisal.[67]

The question of agency jurisdiction also proved delicate, both in Washington and among Anderson's New Mexico constituents. The senator favored a plan under which the Park Service would acquire the entire tract. Then that agency would turn over two-thirds of the area to the Forest Service, retaining the approximately 35,000 acres that encompassed the Jemez Crater for development as a national park. He advocated a leading role for the Park Service because it had greater flexibility in accepting private funds for such acquisitions. He recognized that speed was essential, for the owners were reluctant to expose their offering to extensive public scrutiny out of fear that it would erode the property's market value. He also recognized that the label "national park" served to attract more tourists and greater revenues than would be the case in an area administered by the Forest Service. Timber prices at that time were particularly depressed, so Anderson saw little advantage in having the entire area fall under the Forest Service's control.[68]

New Mexico state hunting and fishing interests strongly disagreed with Anderson's plan to give the initiative to the Park Service. Control by that agency, even over a small portion of the entire tract, implied fences, hunting restrictions, and paved roads that would bring high speed traffic, clutter, and "a shattering of the natural, slow atmosphere of nature as undisturbed as possible."[69] The prime advocates of turning the land over to the Forest Service were the New Mexico Wildlife and Conservation Association and the local chapters of the Izaak Walton League. They cited a recent crisis in Yellowstone National Park where Park Service bans on hunting had resulted in the expansion of elk and deer herds. This overpopulation had led to a depletion of the natural food supply, starvation of the herds and destruction of foliage vital to the maintenance of effective watersheds. At Yellowstone, park rangers were called in to slaughter hundreds of animals to relieve this pressure. Sportsmen argued that controlled hunting in national parks or, in the case of the Baca tract, ownership by the Forest Service, under the supervision of the state game and fish agency, would prevent the problem.[70]

Anderson responded to those who advocated this approach with his characteristic blend of anger and resignation. He told the local Izaak Walton chapter, "I have worked hard on all sorts of conservation this year. I was hoping that we might acquire the Baca location for the federal government, but I have to admit that the attitude of your chapter . . . coupled with the position taken by the American Forestry Association, which is opposed to wilderness in any form, makes the task of acquiring this for the federal government a rather difficult one."[71]

By April 1962 the executors had grown impatient with the pace of the Park Service's survey and with the prospect of extended legislative proceedings. They also realized that the federal government was unlikely to pay more than the $1.5 million that Anderson had advised the owners to accept. The executors then told Anderson that they had decided to seek a commercial buyer. By that time, the senator was willing to go to great lengths to prevent such an outcome. He counseled the owners that the time would never be better to make a deal with the federal government. He alluded to his own influential position on the Senate Interior Committee, to the strategic placement of other members of the New Mexico congressional delegation on the key authorizing and funding committees, and to the active support of the Interior Department. Anderson warned them to avoid the temptation of various "sell-it-by-the-acre schemes," hinting that Texas oil interests were posed to carve up New Mexico for their own financial gain. Although the owners might hope to realize as much as $50 million in that manner, Anderson warned that "the Department of Justice is really at work in our part of the world," and he told the owners to hope that they got their funds "before the U.S. Marshal gets the salesmen."[72] He concluded with the observation "that recreation brings in the most dollars of any use of water, and I would like to live long enough to see a little of that developed in New Mexico."[73]

The executors yielded to Anderson's counsel. He moved quickly and introduced a bill to establish the Valle Grande National Park.[74] To resolve the conflict between the game interests and those who wanted the increased economic benefits associated with a new national park, Anderson scheduled field hearings of the Senate Interior Committee in Santa Fe. He timed the hearings to follow the mid-September 1962 dedication of the Navajo Dam, for he knew that event would bring Secretary Udall and other Washington dignitaries to New Mexico.

Although illness kept Anderson from attending the Navajo Dam ceremony, he was sufficiently recovered to preside at the Santa Fe hearings two days later. The hearing, featuring Anderson, Udall, and Senators Frank Moss (D-UT) and Lee Metcalf, attracted an audience of two hundred. Earlier in the day, Udall, Moss, Metcalf, accompanied by committee and agency staffs, had flown over the Valle Grande for a first-hand inspection of its scenic beauty. With the administration's chief conservation officer and two of the region's senators at his side, Anderson, in an impressive display of political muscle, offered an unparalleled forum for his constituents. From the most prominent to the most obscure, they capitalized on the opportunity to express their views. The New Mexico senator returned to Washington the next day confident that the hearing had provided an effective safety valve for the frustrations of the various local interests.[75]

Soon after his return to Washington, Anderson directed his attention to a Senate Interior Committee draft report recommending approval of legislation that would establish a major new national park in southeastern Utah. The proposed Canyonlands National Park, the handiwork of Utah Senator Frank Moss, was planned to encompass 330,000 acres "filled with mazes of canyons, gigantic standing rock formations, towering buttes, natural bridges or arches, balanced rock formations and other evidences of mighty geologic forces and millions of years of erosion."[76] As the draft report warned, "Canyonlands may be the nation's last opportunity to establish a national park of the Yellowstone class—a vast area of scenic wonders and recreational opportunities unduplicated elsewhere on the American continent or in the world."[77]

As with Anderson's Valle Grande proposal, the Moss bill raised basic questions as to the composition, control, and development of federal park lands. In each case, opponents charged that bestowing national park status would "lock up" the region to badly needed economic development, particularly that related to mining, hunting, and grazing. In each case, to undercut this opposition, the bill's principal sponsors were obliged to modify their original proposals, to the point of developing major exceptions to existing Park Service management policies. Unlike Valle Grande, however, all but 27,000 acres of Canyonlands belonged to the federal government, so the cost of developing the area would be nominal.[78]

The Interior Department had initiated preliminary studies of the Canyonlands region in 1959, but the proposal's chances of legislative success increased greatly in July 1961 when Senator Moss conducted an inspection tour for Interior Secretary Udall. Impressed by the area's stark and unparalleled beauty, Udall made an on-the-spot commitment of Interior Department support for legislation to add Canyonlands to the country's inventory of thirty national parks.[79]

The Moss bill, which had Anderson's active support, stimulated an immediate and hostile response from Utah's commercial interests. Governor George Clyde (R) appointed a "bipartisan" commission to investigate the impact of Moss' proposal to set aside the Canyonlands area, the equivalent of 500 square miles. The commission, weighted on the side of the developers, recommended the establishment of three smaller parks, totalling one-third the acreage of the Moss plan. The parks would be surrounded by a "national recreation area" in which multiple-use development would be encouraged.[80]

Anderson scheduled hearings for March 1962 on a revision of the original Moss proposal. Moss had agreed to modify the bill to permit mining activity subject to specific regulations preserving the area's scenic recreational values. This revision did little, however, to blunt the force of the opposition, led by Governor Clyde and the state's senior senator, Wallace Bennett (R).[81] Both men reacted to the proposal's threat to restrict further the growth of the area's sagging uranium industry. In 1953 the assessed value of land in San Juan County had been $3.4 million. By 1960 it had escalated to $132 million thanks to a late 1950s uranium boom. This reflected an increase in the mineral industry's value from $128,000 to more than $115 million during that period. By the time of the hearing, however, the bubble had burst with the government's termination of uranium purchases. This foreshadowed an acute economic crisis for southeastern Utah.[82]

The Moss bill's opponents sought to extract major concessions from the federal government. These included the exchange of state-owned school lands within the proposed park area for a proven and producing oilfield on federal property elsewhere in the state. They also demanded a guarantee from the Park Service that it would not interfere with mining, grazing, and hunting in the area.[83]

Anderson encouraged Moss to ignore what he considered to be political posturing by Governor Clyde in an election year, insisting as he had in the past, that the development of national parks ought to be a bipartisan matter.[84] During the hearings, Anderson and Moss teamed up with Public Lands Subcommittee chairman Alan Bible (D-NV) to cross examine the proposal's opponents. Bible, low-keyed but clever, acted as the fair-minded chairman, calling witnesses, summarizing testimony, probing for areas of agreement among contradictory positions. Moss, as the sponsor, provided factual information, remained open to suggested modifications, and struck a tone of moderation in the face of those who sought to misconstrue his intent. Anderson took a less direct, but equally significant role. As chairman of the full committee, he exercised his prerogative to interrupt the proceedings with questions and observations. He grilled hostile witnesses, searching for inconsistent or illogical views and challenging vague and inaccurate statements. Anderson took particular umbrage at the conduct of Utah's senior senator, Wallace Bennett.[85]

Bennett, in his prepared statement, attacked the original version of the Moss bill and an even wider ranging Interior Department proposal, circulated for discussion, but not formally introduced. Anderson interrupted the proceedings several times to urge Bennett to discuss the bill before the committee rather than a nonexistent "Udall Bill." Bennett agreed, but continued, to Anderson's and Bible's consternation, to tear apart the "Udall Bill."[86] Anderson then took issue with Bennett's proposal for a tripartite review of tracts proposed to be included in the park area. His plan would involve the governor, county commissioners, and the National Park Service. Chairman Anderson responded that county commissioners were not likely to favor much scenic preservation and he argued that this was "a dangerous way to set up criteria for establishing a national park," particularly considering that the land belonged to the federal government.[87] To Bennett's proposal that a multiple use "national recreation area" surround three small parks, Anderson countered by wondering "what they would play out there."[88] Finally, the chairman attacked the notion that the adjacent area, lacking in vegetation or significant rainfall, had appreciable hunting or grazing value. He observed that as few as forty-one deer had been taken during the previous year and that only $2,700 had been realized in grazing fees. He resisted Governor Clyde's proposal for a system that would give the state control over hunting on federal lands, noting that Wyoming had worked out a satisfactory plan in cooperation with the National Park Service. He asked Clyde whether he thought "Utah people are so stupid that they can't do it as well as Wyoming people do it?"[89] The governor agreed that his constituents could meet the challenge.

Shortly after the hearing ended, Interior Committee aide Ben Stong cautioned Anderson of the precedent-setting implications of the Moss bill and its substitutes. For the first time in recent memory, a state was seeking concessions from the federal government to allow that government to use its own lands as a park. Rather than following the practice of several states of donating land to the federal government in return for an economically desirable grant of national park status, Utah was seeking a donation of federal land in return for its cooperation.[90] Stong was aware that Moss wanted the Senate to act on his bill before the 1962 election "to separate the sheep from the goats" on an issue of major importance to Utah. Nonetheless, he advised the chairman to delay action until 1963 to ensure careful handling of an area that had the potential of becoming one of the country's greatest national parks.[91]

At that time conservation groups such as the Wilderness Society and the National Parks Association, as well as organizations representing sportsmen, heatedly advised the committee not to permit grazing, hunting, and mineral development in areas under the jurisdiction of the National Park Service. This, they believed, would distort the Service's mission and call into question the integrity of its entire management program. Stong's counsel of delay was contrary to that of Secretary Udall who suggested to Anderson that the president, under his existing authority, ought to simply proclaim the entire area to be a "national monument," thereby settling "an essentially stupid argument over boundaries."[92] This would leave Congress to consider whether the protected area deserved the additional status of a national park.

The recommended delay occurred. Committee staff prepared a revised version of the Moss bill following the March 1962 inquiry. Field hearings, a time-honored device for extending legislative consideration, were held in April. Finally, in late September, as Anderson returned from New Mexico and the Valle Grande hearings, and with only three weeks remaining in the 1962 congressional session, the Interior Committee reported the Canyonlands bill favorably to the full Senate. This served Moss' political purposes and set the stage for action early in 1963.[93]

September 1962 also brought two additional conservation victories for the Kennedy administration with the enactment of legislation to create a national seashore at Point Reyes, California, and at Padre Island, Texas. Anderson assumed no direct role in the Point Reyes measure, but he took an active interest in the Texas bill, partly because of Padre Island's proximity to his own state and out of loyalty to the measure's principal advocates, his former Texas colleague Vice President Lyndon Johnson and Senator Ralph Yarborough (D-TX).[94]

Padre Island was a 117-mile long, three-mile wide uninhabited barrier reef along the Texas Gulf coast near Corpus Christi. Bills for its establishment as a national seashore had been in the hands of the Senate Interior Committee since 1958, and hearings had been conducted in 1959, 1960, and 1961. Finally, in March 1962 the committee recommended to the Senate a bill that provided for an eighty-eight-mile park and authorized $4 million to acquire land from private owners.[95] The measure permitted continued private ownership of the extensive oil and gas resources within the park's boundaries. Anderson scheduled Senate floor debate for mid-April. His allies on that occasion were Public Lands Subcommittee chairman Bible and Ralph Yarborough, the measure's principal sponsor and Texas' senior senator.

As debate began, that state's junior senator, John Tower (R), in an effort to kill the bill, made a motion to recommit it to the Interior Committee. Tower argued that the area was too large and the funding for acquisition was unrealistically low. He noted that much of the area served as a naval bombing range, adding facetiously that the only suitable substitute in the vicinity would be the middle of the 865,000 acre King Ranch. Tower said he "trembled to think what might happen if we tried to take over a portion" of that ranch, a source of fantastic yearly earnings for Texas' powerful Kleberg family.[96] Anderson countered heatedly that the Interior Committee had spent enough time on the bill, more than on all the other seashore proposals combined. He saw no problem in dividing ownership of the surface land and subsurface mineral rights, leaving the latter in private hands. Anderson suggested that a House-Senate conference committee could resolve the dispute over the park's total area, even if it meant accepting the shorter sixty-five-mile tract in the House version.[97]

When Tower proposed that the bill be referred to another committee, Anderson retorted that he did not want his committee's jurisdiction invaded. Jokingly, he professed to be tired of Yarborough's persistent entreaties to move the bill onto the floor, adding "I do not want him back again. I want to be footloose from him."[98] Anderson agreed that $4 million might be insufficient, but with a veiled reference to the financial resources of Texas oil interests, he suggested that private funds could be found, as they had in other proposed national park areas, to supplement the federal appropriation.[99]

Under the pressure of a pending adjournment deadline, the Senate and House passed separate versions of the Padre Island legislation, resolved their differences, and the president signed the measure on September 28.[100] On that same day, as Anderson entered Bethesda Naval Medical Center for treatment of an inner ear infection, Hubert Humphrey addressed the Senate in commemoration of the first anniversary of that body's passage of the Wilderness bill. He noted that the event was "a tribute to Anderson's leadership and reasonableness" and he urged the House, particularly Aspinall, to come to terms with the Senate version.[101]

In the weeks following the adjournment, as Anderson recuperated in New Mexico, he had little reason to believe that Humphrey's call would be answered. A letter he received from Secretary Udall made it clear that the campaign for enactment would continue to be directed from the Senate. Although Udall acknowledged that the Wilderness issue would be the number one conservation priority of the coming congressional session, he confessed that he had omitted reference to it in a letter to Aspinall because of the House chairman's "sensitivity" to the matter.[102] A disabled Anderson, an intransigent chairman, and a reluctant secretary—unlikely confederates moving toward the "Conservation Congress."

Anderson in 1956. *(Fred Maroon)*

Adversaries. Anderson shares witness table on May 5, 1959 with Lewis Strauss as he testifies in opposition to Strauss's nomination as secretary of commerce. *(Washington Star)*

Western senators united. Joseph O'Mahoney (D-WY), Anderson, Wayne Morse (D-OR), and Gale McGee (D-WY) in an early morning celebration following defeat of the Lewis Strauss nomination, June 19, 1959. Later that day O'Mahoney suffered a stroke that hastened the end of his Senate career. *(Library of Congress)*

During a break in hearings of the Senate Interior Committee Anderson confers with Interior Secretary Stewart Udall and Agriculture Secretary Orville Freeman. *(Library of Congress)*

Anderson shown at January 19, 1962 swearing-in ceremony for Robert G. McConnell as assistant secretary of interior for congressional liaison. From left: Rep. Joseph Montoya (D-NM), Rep. Wayne Aspinall (D-CO), Interior Secretary Stewart Udall, McConnell, and Anderson. *(Library of Congress)*

Chairman Laurance Rockefeller presents Outdoor Recreation Resources Review
Commission report to President Kennedy on January 31, 1962 as Anderson and other
commissioners look on. *(Library of Congress)*

Anderson beams as Navajo Tribal Council Chairman Paul Jones assists President Kennedy at the June 13, 1962 signing of legislation authorizing the San Juan–Chama Diversion and the Navajo Indian Irrigation projects. Pictured from left are Rep. Joseph Montoya (D-NM). Rep Thomas Morris (D-NM), Interior Secretary Stewart Udall, Anderson, Jones, Council Secretary Maurice McCabe, and Sen. Dennis Chavez (D-NM). *(UPI Photo))*

# Sidewalk Saboteurs!

An opposition view of Anderson's efforts to preserve the Indiana Dunes, February 13, 1963.
*(Indianapolis Star)*

Facing page: President Kennedy honors Anderson for his conservation achievements at
Rose Garden ceremony on May 20, 1963. From left: Fairfield Osborne, the Conservation
Foundation; Fred Hornaday, American Forestry Association; Joseph Penfold, Izaak Walton
League; Interior Secretary Stewart Udall; Clarence Cottam; National Parks Association;
Tom C. Kimball, National Wildlife Federation; President Kennedy; Ira Gabrielson, Wildlife
Management Institute; Anderson; Mrs. Anderson; Sherburne P. Anderson; Mary Elizabeth
Roberts (Anderson's granddaughter); James Carr, undersecretary of interior; Nancy Roberts
(Anderson's daughter). *(Special Collections, Zimmerman Library, University of New Mexico)*

Among the 600 who gathered to honor Senator Anderson at his National Conservation Testimonial Dinner on May 20, 1963 were (left to right) Clinton R. Gutermuth, Wildlife Management Institute; Orville Freeman, Secretary of Agriculture; Tom Kimball, National Wildlife Federation; Senator Anderson; and Stewart Udall, Secretary of Interior. *(Special Collections, Zimmerman Library, University of New Mexico)*

Anderson at May 21, 1963 hearing on Cochiti Reservoir legislation with Sen. Frank Moss (D-UT) and New Mexico Governor Jack M. Campbell. *(Library of Congress)*

Anderson at Roswell, N.M., with Interior Secretary Stewart Udall, June 1, 1963. *(Library of Congress)*

Anderson huddles with Speaker of the House John McCormack (D-MA) and Senate Majority Leader Mike Mansfield (D-MT), May 8, 1964. *(Library of Congress)*

As Anderson looks on, Rep. Wayne Aspinall (D-CO) accepts pen from President Lyndon Johnson at September 3, 1964 Rose Garden signing of the Wilderness Act and the Land and Water Conservation Fund Act. *(White House photo)*

Anderson embraces Sen. Richard Russell (D-GA) at January 7, 1965 meeting of the Senate Democratic Caucus. *(Senate Historical Office)*

Anderson places on his automobile bumper a Land and Water Conservation Fund sticker purchased from Edward Crafts, director of the Interior Department's Bureau of Outdoor Recreation. Sales of the stickers were expected to provide $35 million annually for the fund. *(Library of Congress)*

Anderson conducts a news conference outside his Senate office on June 23, 1965. *(Library of Congress)*

Interior Secretary Stewart Udall, on June 28, 1965, prepares to present Anderson the first check issued under the Land and Water Conservation Fund Act. Anderson later transmitted the check for $4,737.17 to New Mexico Governor Jack M. Campbell to assist the state in its outdoor recreation planning. House Interior Committee Chairman Wayne Aspinall (D-CO) is seated at left. Standing from left: Senate Interior Committee staff director Jerry Verkler; Assistant Secretary of the Interior for Mineral Resources John M. Kelley; Sen. Joseph M. Montoya (D-NM); Rep. Thomas G. Morris (D-NM); Rep. E. S. Johnny Walker (D-NM); Max N. Edwards, Interior Department Legislative Counsel; and Robert G. McConnell, assistant interior secretary for congressional liaison. *(Library of Congress)*

Anderson greets his former boss on May 8, 1964, at a Senate celebration in honor of Harry Truman's eightieth birthday. *(Senate Historical Office)*

# 7
# The Conservation Congress
## 1963–1964

Without Clinton Anderson there would have been no
Wilderness Law.

Richard McArdle
Chief, U.S. Forest Service,
1952–62

The Eighty-eighth Congress convened on January 9, 1963, and adjourned on October 3, 1964. During its term, the Kennedy administration achieved maturity and then shattered at the force of an assassin's bullets. A new regime under the more steady political hand of Lyndon Johnson was borne aloft on a wave of popular sympathy for the objectives of a martyred president. The result was a record of extraordinary congressional accomplishment. The *Washington Post* concluded that the Eighty-eighth Congress was,"on balance, a great Congress. Its members worked long, hard, and effectively on issues of the greatest complexity and difficulty."[1] As Clinton Anderson reported to his constituents, it was a Congress that "faced up to its responsibilities across a wide range of national problems— from school dropouts to mass transportation."[2]

Anderson underscored the Eighty-eighth Congress' most notable characteristic in an end-of-the-session address to the Sierra Club. In his view, it was "the most conservation-minded Congress in history."[3] Interior Secretary Udall concurred, noting that the Congress "wrote brilliant new chapters and established wholesome new principles."[4] Among its major accomplishments were the Wilderness Act, the Land and Water Conservation Fund Act, the Outdoor Recreation Act, the Public Land Law Review Commission, the Water Resources Research Act, and measures establishing Canyonlands National Park, and, in the Senate, the Indiana Dunes National Lakeshore.

Although the "Conservation Congress" was the product of many hands, the two principal architects of that achievement were unquestionably Senator Clinton Anderson and Representative Wayne Aspinall (D-CO). When these two men disagreed, wilderness and recreation legislation failed to move. In the face of increasing pressures for the resolution of long-standing issues, and recognizing that time for effective compromise was slipping away, they yielded, traded, and ultimately produced legislation that served as the foundation for the continuing struggle to preserve beleaguered natural resources in the face of overwhelming population pressures.

Anderson and Aspinall, born within six months of one another, shared common career experiences. Both were present at the 1922 meetings in Santa Fe, New Mexico, where Commerce Secretary Herbert Hoover helped to shape the original agreement among Colorado River basin states for the allocation of that river's vital resources. Each man owed his election in 1948, in part, to a pledge to ensure that his state received the most favorable terms under that earlier agreement. Anderson and Aspinall sought and achieved membership on their respective houses' Interior Committees as freshmen and quickly rose to positions of influence. By 1955, each man had become chairman of his chamber's powerful reclamation subcommittee. From that position, both members moved toward the chairmanship of the Interior Committees, Aspinall reaching his goal in 1959 and Anderson achieving his two years later. Anderson and Aspinall also served together on the Joint Committee on Atomic Energy, which the former chaired for four years between 1955 and 1960.[5] Ultimately, both men would leave Congress in 1973.

As principal spokesmen for their respective committees on wilderness and recreation legislation during the Eighty-eighth Congress, Anderson and Aspinall clearly understood each other's personal limitations and institutional constraints. Aspinall frequently complained that his House Interior Committee was far different in composition from its Senate counterpart. States east of the Mississippi

River were well represented on the panel and their interests were often at odds with those of the western-dominated Senate committee. Aspinall's own western-slope Colorado constituency was more heavily influenced by mining and timber interests than Anderson's. As a House member, Aspinall had to stand for reelection every two years. He lamented that his district included twenty-two mountain passes with elevations in excess of 10,000 feet—a severe impediment to late fall campaigning. In the Eisenhower landslide of 1952, Aspinall had survived with a margin of only twenty-nine votes out of 85,000 cast. In 1962, partly as a result of intensive lobbying by disaffected conservationists in response to his successful efforts to bottle up wilderness legislation, Aspinall took a modest fifty-eight percent of the vote, down from seventy-one percent two years earlier. Anderson suffered under no such constraints. At the beginning of the Eighty-eighth Congress, his 1966 reelection bid lay more than three years in the future, and after his 1948 campaign he was never to face a serious reelection challenge for the remainder of his career.[6]

Such was the background of the two men who met on August 14, 1964, in Anderson's private Capitol office to forge a compromise on the Wilderness bill, the capstone of the conservation program of three presidential administrations. That meeting broke the impasse. Of the two men, it was Anderson who yielded the most. He gave more than he would have two years earlier. Under the burden of chronic and debilitating illnesses, faced with serious doubts about his own ability to carry on the battle much longer, he apparently saw no realistic option. What he could not obtain legislatively, he intended to pursue through tougher administrative agency regulation, an area in which he had become equally well accomplished during his quarter century in Washington.[7]

In the initial days of the Eighty-eighth Congress, Anderson took advantage of a perquisite available to senior members, the opportunity to reserve low and otherwise memorable numbers for his pet bills. Accordingly, his Water Resources Research legislation became "S.2." The Wilderness bill was designated S.4. The measure designed to confer broader statutory powers on the Bureau of Outdoor Recreation received S.20, and the Water Resources Planning Act became S.1111. The only key measure that departed from this system, designed for ease of recall, was S.859, the Land and Water Conservation Fund bill. The story of the Conservation Congress unfolded as these measures moved toward enactment. Their fruition also coincided with the end of Anderson's active role in the shaping of natural resources policy.

As 1962 had drawn to a close, Anderson realized that Aspinall would not cooperate on any conservation-related legislation until he received administration and Senate assurances that the Wilderness bill would provide for a positive congressional determination before public lands could be converted from normal use to wilderness status. Aspinall noted that the administration was stepping up its activity, by executive fiat, to reclassify primitive areas as wilderness.[8] In October 1962, he wrote to the president and to the secretaries of Interior and Agriculture to insist that they stop all land withdrawals until Congress addressed the matter.[9] Senate Interior Committee aide Ben Stong advised Anderson to consider Aspinall's view seriously, as there was "considerable sympathy" on the Senate panel for stronger checks on executive power to make such withdrawals.[10] Anderson, however, appeared to have little interest in playing to Aspinall's concerns at that point. When Secretary Udall suggested that the negotiations "will get bitter unless Wayne backs off," Anderson retorted that perhaps "the battle ought to get a little bitter."[11] Aspinall had just completed a relatively difficult reelection campaign. Anderson believed that the Colorado representative realized that his recent election difficulties stemmed in part from a vigorous effort by conservationist organizations to defeat him and he hoped that Aspinall's intransigent attitude might have softened accordingly.

Anderson's own intransigence bothered Recreation Bureau chief Edward Crafts who feared that a renewal of the standoff over the Wilderness bill would cause Aspinall again to sidetrack legislation giving the Bureau of Outdoor Recreation broadened powers and also the measure creating the Land and Water Conservation Fund, an indispensable source of revenues for new recreation planning and development. Anderson ignored Crafts's repeated counsel of conciliation and decided to push for Senate enactment of a Wilderness bill identical to that passed in 1961. He knew that Representative John Saylor (PA), the ranking Republican on the House Interior Committee, was going to sponsor a House version of the earlier Senate bill, and he suspected that Aspinall had already decided to "use recreation bills as trading stock in his fight for withdrawal legislation and it makes little difference whether wilderness is in the package or not."[12] In Anderson's judgment, Aspinall would be more likely to compromise if he were under pressure than if he were not.

In January 1949 Lyndon Johnson (D-TX) and Robert Kerr (D-OK) had joined Clinton Anderson as newcomers to the Senate. The three shared vast political acumen, commanding physical presence and an ever-conscious pride in their southwestern heritage. In January 1961 Johnson gave up his seat on the Senate floor for a place at the Senate presiding officer's desk and the other less well specified duties of the vice-presidency. Two years later, on January 1, 1963, Robert Kerr, "the uncrowned king" of the Senate died. Several weeks earlier Dennis Chavez (D), New Mexico's senior senator and a member of that body since 1935, also died. These developments reinforced Anderson's growing seniority. Before the Eighty-eighth Congress, Anderson occasionally operated in the shadows of all three men.

Chavez and Anderson, respectively chairmen of the influential committees on Public Works and Interior, often found themselves working as cross purposes. Chavez was quick to claim credit for Anderson initiatives, and Anderson was equally prepared to retaliate. Senators of the same state and party often experienced a fundamental rivalry not found among those of differing parties, and Chavez and Anderson were no exception. Each man represented a separate faction within New Mexico's Democratic party. But the Anderson-Chavez antagonism had deeper roots. Anderson never forgot a blistering tongue lashing that Chavez administered to him on the Senate floor in mid-1951. It occurred when the junior senator sought to amend an agricultural appropriations bill to provide $4 million for construction of access roads to uranium deposits in New Mexico, Colorado, and adjacent states. His action violated Senate rules forbidding authorizing legislation on appropriations bills and it totally by-passed the panel that held primary jurisdiction for such matters, the Public Works Committee, of which Chavez was chairman. Anderson justified his action as an emergency measure to begin construction before winter weather set in and claimed that the issue was within his jurisdiction as member of the Joint Atomic Energy Committee. Chavez jumped to his feet. Glowering at Anderson, he exclaimed, "I appreciate the importance of what he is trying to do, but I also wish to inform my colleague that I am not going to agree to have him or any other senator try to legislate for my committee. We might as well understand that now." A heated private discussion ensued, after which Anderson withdrew his amendment. On the following day he returned to Albuquerque complaining of "extreme fatigue." He failed to appear in his local office for nearly two weeks.[13]

In 1961, Anderson directed his staff on the Interior Committee to monitor closely all Chavez-sponsored bills referred to that panel. Sensing their chairman's wariness, several aides occasionally took the liberty of calling the Interior Department where committee requests for evaluations had been sent to instruct the responsible official to ignore the request. When Chavez, whose losing battle with throat cancer had reduced his persistence, subsequently inquired about the progress of his legislation, the staff responded that it had not yet heard from the Interior Department.[14]

Kerr's death opened the coveted chairmanship of the Senate Aeronautical and Space Sciences Committee, a post originally held by Johnson. Both Johnson and Kerr had used their stewardship of the Space Committee to their home states' advantage in channeling funds associated with the growing aerospace industry. Anderson decided to follow their path, even though it meant that he would have to give up his chairmanship of the Interior Committee. In effect, he was giving up little. He would continue to dominate that panel's important Reclamation Subcommittee, and his influence with committee colleagues and staff was not likely to diminish. This was evident in the forthcoming decision to retain Jerry Verkler as staff director. Verkler had come to that post from Anderson's personal staff. Next in line for the Interior Committee chair was Henry Jackson (D-WA). Anderson and Jackson had been close, in the sense of father to son, during the period of their Senate service. Jackson first met his future wife in Anderson's Senate office, where she worked as a receptionist.[15] During the coming Congress, from his vantage point as the committee's second-ranking member, Anderson would remain well equipped to shepherd his pet measures onto the Senate floor and thence to the president's desk.

Anderson did not formally turn over the Interior Committee's reins until late February 1963. In the interim, he and Aspinall worked to establish their committees' respective agendas. To that end, President Kennedy held separate meetings with each chairman. At his session on January 28 Anderson discussed his forthcoming duties as Space Committee chairman and several aerospace projects of particular interest to New Mexico. He took the opportunity to review the administration's strategy to dislodge the Wilderness bill from Aspinall's grip, and concluded the session with "a long unrequested and probably unappreciated lecture based on [his] contacts with Presidents Roosevelt and Truman."[16]

A month passed before Wayne Aspinall's trip to the Oval Office. Characterized as a "cry-baby session," the meeting gave the House chairman the opportunity to complain that his committee was too large and unwieldy to keep pace with its Senate counterpart. He expressed frustration with Anderson's tactics, which he perceived were to keep the House committee constantly blanketed with twelve to twenty "must" bills. The acerbic chairman told the young president that there was little likelihood of moving the Wilderness bill without a provision for affirmative control of wilderness area designation by Congress. He urged the chief executive to set a more modest course. Aspinall's recommended agenda included bills to establish the Land and Water Conservation Fund and to expand the Bureau of Outdoor Recreation, as well as one or two measures for the creation of new national parks.[17]

Aspinall took special aim at Anderson's water resources research and planning bills, suggesting that the administration and Congress were doing too much to aid research and not enough of direct benefit to western producers. The chairman suggested that the administration had been unwise to raise grazing fees. To that, Kennedy responded sharply that the fee increase was his idea and that Aspinall was mistaken if he thought the administration was going to knuckle under to western "pressure groups." Aspinall complained that the western cattle, mining and lumber industries had "gone to pot," but was unable to give the president specific suggestions for relief. He took the opportunity to suggest, however, that members of his committee might look more favorably on the administration's programs if they were given patronage positions to distribute. The meeting ended, producing little more than irritation on both sides.[18]

Two days after the Aspinall-Kennedy meeting, the Senate Interior Committee convened for the tenth series of hearings on wilderness legislation in nearly as many years. Although Henry Jackson had at that point taken over as committee chairman, he was greatly preoccupied with legislation affecting major contracts for the Boeing Aircraft Company in his home state of Washington. Accordingly, Anderson took control of the two-day session. Tired of hearing familiar arguments rehashed, he urged witnesses to remember that the committee had the benefit of more than 2,500 pages of testimony on the subject. "We are here today," said Anderson, "to determine if there is anything new which can be said on this subject." Interior Secretary Udall offered little that was new, as he sought to place the legislation in broader perspective, noting that it, along with the Land and Water Conservation Fund bill, would rank with the nine "great conservation decisions" in the history of the United States.[19]

Anderson knew that the opposition was holding emergency strategy sessions in a desperate effort to derail the Senate bill. As was the case in the House, a Colorado member directed opposition forces. Anderson described Gordon Allott, the committee's second-ranking Republican, as a "vigorous but honorable battler." Allott followed Aspinall's strategy of claiming to support wilderness legislation.[20] He added that he hoped Congress would act quickly to place the more than six million acres of Forest Service lands already carrying a wilderness designation under the protection of federal statute. His concern, he avowed, was over the process by which an additional eight million acres of "primitive lands" would enter the system. In response to Allott's contention that the proposed legislation gave Congress only a "negative role" in the review process, Anderson argued that Congress presently had no role at all. He cited a recent case in which the Secretary of Agriculture, "with the stroke of a pen," converted the Selway-Bitterroot primitive area in Montana to wilderness status with little direct regard for the views of the area's congressional delegation. When Allott claimed that his amendments would permit greater public involvement in the redesignation process, Anderson countered that both wilderness and primitive areas had been treated more or less interchangeably since designation of the last primitive areas in 1939. After a quarter of a century, the primitive areas were well known, and Anderson believed that their wilderness character had been established in fact if not by administrative fiat. In his opinion, the distinction between the two terms was more directly attributable to historical accident than qualitative differences.[21]

Paul Brooks, editor-in-chief of the Houghton Mifflin publishing company, reinforced Anderson's argument with a biting article in the March 1963 issue of *Harper's Magazine.* Entitled "Congressman Aspinall vs. the People of the United States," the article charged that during the 1962 session the House chairman ensured that the

Wilderness bill was "hogtied and butchered in committee, and not even the spare ribs got to the House floor."[22] Concluding that Aspinall's chief ally was not so much public apathy as the complexity of the problem, Brooks took exception to the Aspinall plan for extensive affirmative review of each primitive area. He argued that that process was as inappropriate in its application to public lands as it would be to a sinking ship. Aspinall's approach suggested "you don't rescue a sinking ship unless you have an official report on its tonnage, radar system, horsepower, electric wiring, and value as scrap metal . . . and don't, for heaven's sake, scoop a single survivor out of the water until he had shown a passport and vaccination certificate, and convinced a majority of the rescue squad that he is worth saving anyway."[23]

The leadership of the Senate Interior Committee resolved to resist the mining industry's strenuous efforts to amend the bill before sending it to the Senate floor. Anderson and Jackson agreed with staff director Jerry Verkler that those who wanted modifications should deal with the House committee "where the issue is by no means settled."[24] Both were aware that if the House passed a bill, it would be weaker than the Senate version and a conference committee would be formed to work out the differences. Anderson insisted on leaving the Senate conferees "a fair amount of trading territory" by holding firm at that point.[25] This strategy was designed to relieve the pressure on the committee of such potent groups as the American Mining Congress and promoters of a ski resort in a wilderness area near Los Angeles. The mining lobby, in its zeal to kill the Senate bill, falsely claimed that "66 million acres having a high potential for mineral deposits would be sterilized as far as mineral production was concerned."[26] Anderson regarded the statement as patently dishonest and told James Boyd of the organization that he "often wondered if witnesses really regard members of committees so stupid that they are influenced by statements like that one."[27] He reminded Boyd that reclassification of primitive areas usually resulted in "a considerable reduction of acreage," and cited the Selway-Bitterroot example where only 1.1 million of a total 1.9 million acres were proposed as wilderness, 549,000 were returned to normal forest land status, and 189,000 acres were left in primitive status subject to further review. He told the lobbyist that the Senate bill was actually more favorable to the mining industry than was the existing situation, for it would open to prospecting lands then protected by "stringent regulations."[28]

The Senate committee also rejected efforts by Los Angeles area developers who wished to carve 3,500 acres out of the San Gorgonio Wilderness area for a ski resort. The tract's proximity to the metropolitan area and its elevation, ensuring plenty of late spring skiing, accounted for the heavy volume of mail that committee members received. Anderson saw the issue as bad precedent and told its supporters that they would be better off to try to reach an accommodation with the Forest Service on an administrative basis rather than on a statutory level. He viewed the matter as a struggle between a handful of skiers and a much larger number of campers, similar to the conflict he witnessed at Yellowstone where "the hot rod youngsters with their motorboats have almost ruined a section of the park for those people who love to get into a canoe and paddle leisurely along the shores."[29] Anderson emphasized that, contrary to some reports, he was not "violently opposed" to commercial development. Characteristically, he focused on his critics' careless language. "I hope," he said, "I am not violent—at least not to the point where somebody is going to have to lock me up. I hope I am still reasonable, and whoever thought that I was violent might have been looking at me with a faint trace of prejudice."[30] He turned aside the argument that the ski area would cost the federal government nothing with the analogy of his taking a franchise to operate the Senate galleries. "I could collect a half a dollar a head probably and my selling of tickets wouldn't cost the Government a penny, but it would enrich me tremendously."[31]

Although the Senate committee turned aside the pressures for amendment by the mining and ski interests, it did make several recommended changes in the bill's text to undercut the opposition further. The most significant was a provision for public hearings before the secretaries of Interior and Agriculture submitted their recommendations for wilderness area acquisitions to the president. The committee also added language to make clear that state and private lands surrounded by wilderness tracts would receive protection and that the owners would be allowed full access and the enjoyment of their mineral rights.[32]

In 1961 illness had prevented Anderson from acting as the Wilderness bill's manager when it reached the Senate floor. Senator Frank Church (D-ID) had taken on that task reluctantly, but effectively. In April 1963 Anderson again turned to Church partly because of the Idaho senator's experience and partly because Anderson was recuperating from a recent illness. Nonetheless, Anderson remained on the floor during most of the two-day debate and, with Senator Lee Metcalf (D-MT), provided Church ample substantive and moral support. Colorado's Gordon Allott (R) led the opposition on the first day. The death of his mother, however, forced him to turn over the reins to that state's less skilled junior senator, Peter Dominick (R). As Allott left, Anderson, in a display of senatorial courtesy, agreed to "pair" his own vote in support of the committee's bill with Allott's in opposition. That gesture effectively removed both senators from the final tally with each being recorded as "Not Voting."[33]

Although deprived of a vote, Anderson was able to influence the votes of others by his presence and his extensive experience with the bill. He took as the central focus of his case the report of the Outdoor Recreation Commission. He recalled that in 1961 the bill's opponents called for a delay in its consideration until the commission had had an opportunity to complete its survey and to release its report. Anderson brightly noted that the report had now appeared and that it had in fact gone much farther in its recommendations than had the bill itself. The bill, he emphasized, dealt only with lands specifically reserved as primitive by long standing action of the Department of Agriculture. The commission, however, had recommended that previously unreserved lands be set aside for wilderness protection as well. Taking a page from the opposition's strategy manual, Anderson agreed with their argument that unreserved lands should indeed receive a case-by-case review and be brought into the system by separate and affirmative acts of Congress in a manner similar to that of new reclamation projects and new national parks. He added that even areas incorporated as wilderness tracts would not be forever immune from reexamination if "one of the two highest authorities in the land, the president or the Congress, determines that the other use is in the greater public good."[34]

When three Allott amendments were put to a vote, it became clear to the bill's supporters that another sizeable victory was at hand. The first amendment, the Aspinall plan to require affirmative congressional action on each presidential recommendation, lost by a vote of 35 to 49. Amendments allowing mineral prospecting to continue for fifteen years and excluding primitive areas from the initial system were beaten even more decisively. Finally, on April

9, the full Senate, for the second time in two years, passed the Wilderness bill by an impressive 73-to-12 margin.[35]

The Senate had cleared the Wilderness bill a mere three months into the term of the Eighty-eighth Congress, an impressive display of the busy and productive pace of its Interior Committee. By that time, the committee had also recommended for Senate action the Water Resources Research measure, S.2, the bill to broaden the powers of the Bureau of Outdoor Recreation, S.20, and S.1007, the Northwest Power bill. Aspinall complained to committee chairman Henry Jackson that, once again, the Senate was smothering him with an abundance of major bills and that it was time to let the House take the initiative on a few measures. Jackson recognized Aspinall's plight and agreed to follow a subordinate role on the bill establishing the Land and Water Conservation Fund. Both Anderson and Jackson realized that there would be little likelihood of House action on the Wilderness bill or the broader range of outdoor recreation legislation until the House cleared the conservation fund bill.[36]

In the 1962 congressional session, the conservation fund bill had been linked to the measure expanding the Recreation Bureau's authority. When heated opposition developed concerning the sources of taxation to generate revenues for the fund, Anderson removed the bill from active consideration. His plan was to get the relatively uncontroversial authority bill enacted quickly to sustain the momentum sparked by the recreation commission's report and to lay the foundation for more ambitious outdoor recreation planning efforts. Neither measure had cleared the previous Congress. Accordingly, at the beginning of the Eighty-eighth Congress in 1963, the Senate Interior Committee voted to remove from S.20 a section providing for modest planning grants and to place that provision in the larger conservation fund bill. That strategy worked, and S.20 was quickly enacted by both the Senate and the House.[37]

The Kennedy administration sent to Congress in mid-February a revised version of its Land and Water Conservation Fund bill. The bill was designed to establish, over a period of twenty-five years, a $2 billion fund to underwrite accelerated purchase of rapidly disappearing lands suitable for outdoor recreation. Revenues would be produced from a variety of sources including admission and user fees collected by federal agencies, sale of surplus federal real property, proceeds from an existing tax on motorboat fuels, and—for the third through eleventh year of the fund's existence—an annual federal interest-free loan of up to $60 million. Of the amount collected, sixty percent would be used for matching grants to states to cover up to half the cost of state planning, purchase, and expansion of outdoor recreation facilities. The provision for state involvement represented a major addition to the 1962 bill. The remaining funds would be used by federal agencies, but in all cases the funds could not be spent without specific case-by-case congressional authorization. Starting in the fund's eleventh year, half of its revenues would be turned over to the federal treasury to repay the monies previously appropriated. The remainder would continue to go to the states for programs that were in harmony with the broader federal activity.[38]

The Senate Interior Committee lost no time in scheduling hearings on the administration bill. Chairman Henry Jackson put in a brief appearance and then turned over the proceedings to Anderson. During the two-day hearings, most witnesses supported the measure's general objectives, but many clashed heatedly over the details of financing.[39]

The three most hotly disputed issues involved the percentage of total revenues allocated between the federal and state governments, the required percentage states would have to raise to qualify for matching grants, and the administration of federal entrance and user fees. On the first point, the Outdoor Recreation Commission recommended that the federal agencies administer all the monies. The administration bill, however, allocated sixty percent to the states. Anderson went even further by suggesting that the rate might be set as high as seventy-five percent for the states. Secretary Udall diplomatically indicated that a sliding scale could be devised to reach that level as needed.[40]

On the question of state contributions to qualify for matching grants, Anderson recalled that the Recreation Commission had suggested that the federal government contribute seventy-five percent of planning grants and up to fifty percent of acquisition and development costs. The administration bill reduced those levels to fifty percent for planning and thirty percent for acquisition and development. Of the latter category, states could use no more than ten percent for development. This upset many western senators more than it did Anderson. They argued that western states already had an abundance of public lands and were not likely to want to purchase more. Their need, instead, was for development of those lands.

Secretary Udall countered that the bill was designed as an acquisition measure and that even metropolitan areas in western states had needs to acquire lands close to their heavily populated areas.[41]

On apportionment of funds to states, Anderson was similarly undemanding. According to the bill's formula, one-fifth would be distributed among the states equally, three-fifths according to population, and one-fifth according to a case-by-case determination of the Interior Secretary. Anderson advised a friend, concerned over the apparent discrimination of this formula against western states, to consider that the Recreation Commission had originally suggested apportioning by population and area, after subtracting federally owned lands from each state's area. This would have had a more severe impact on New Mexico than the provisions of the administration's bill. Anderson also noted that western states needed southern and eastern support to pass legislation favorable to their peculiar needs. He candidly reminded those who complained that "we get quite a few resources development projects [San Juan-Chama, for instance] financed out of the Federal Treasury, and we cannot be too demanding or it might react on established programs of great benefit to us."[42]

Anderson's breezy attitude over the specifics of the conservation bill was evident as the committee concluded its first morning of hearings. On the issue of user charges, he asked Agriculture Secretary Freeman whether an outdoor recreation facility use sticker would be required for a visit to a house of ill repute, assuming one were located in a national forest. Freeman countered that for such difficult questions he always sought the advice of former secretary Anderson. Anderson "ruled" that he would not include such a facility among those requiring stickers.[43]

When the hearings concluded, Chairman Jackson fulfilled his pledge to Aspinall by refusing to take further action on the bill until the House Interior Committee had cleared its version for floor action. Meanwhile, the Colorado congressional delegation went to work to modify the bill. In the Senate, Peter Dominick prepared an amendment, in the nature of a substitute to the entire bill, that would limit the fund to admission and user fees, excluding boat fuel taxes and surplus land sales revenues. This would have reduced its annual income from $155 million to as little as $30 million. Dominick's amendment would also have limited use of the federal share of the fund to development, forbidding further acquisition of lands by federal agencies. On the House side, Dominick's Colorado colleague, Aspinall, sought to amend the administration's version to funnel fifty percent of the revenues to the Treasury's general fund to offset the politically sensitive federal reservoir recreation cost write-offs. He hoped, thereby, to appeal to the sizeable constituency of reclamationists in his home state.[44]

With Aspinall's intransigence slowing the momentum behind the Land and Water Fund bill and the Wilderness bill, the Kennedy administration and an assortment of conservation lobbyists got together, at the instigation of Secretary Udall, to plan an event to underscore the need for action on both measures. The occasion was Anderson's recent retirement as chairman of the Interior Committee. The date selected was May 20, 1963. On that day, shortly after noon, President Kennedy received Anderson, the senator's family, and representatives of twelve national conservation organizations in the White House Rose Garden. He saluted the senator for a lifetime of dedication to natural resources conservation and announced that he would soon visit a number of the nation's wilderness areas in support of the objectives of the pending Wilderness bill.[45]

That evening, in the main ballroom of Washington's Statler Hilton hotel, 650 conservationists and other friends of Anderson attended a dinner at which the senator was to receive the National Conservation Award. Among those present were thirty-three of Anderson's Senate colleagues, cabinet secretaries Udall, Orville Freeman, and Luther Hodges, as well as many members of the House and other dignitaries. The dinner's planners had originally expected 325 guests and were forced to close the reservation list when it reached twice that number.[46]

Anderson was hardly a reluctant participant in the evening's events. Several weeks earlier he had directed his staff to compile a list of his principal conservation achievements. That list included fifty major bills, of which twenty had become law during his fourteen years in the Senate. Of that number, ten had been under Anderson's principal sponsorship.[47] In the evening's speeches, Secretary Freeman told of Anderson's legacy, from his days as secretary, of expanding the Department of Agriculture's focus to one of conservation as well as of production. Secretary Udall pointed to Anderson's essential traits of sensitivity and fairness, commending his "daily deeds in behalf of wilderness, water, parks and forests." Udall concluded his remarks by citing the words of Anderson's conservation mentor, Aldo Leopold, that "we abuse the land because we regard it as a commodity belonging to us. When we see land as a community to which we belong, we may begin to use it with love and respect."[48] For his part, Anderson told Udall that all he needed to say, and all that the secretary needed to know, was embodied in two lines of a popular song, "As long as he needs me, I know where I will be."[49]

Anderson pursued the theme of being a prominently-placed facilitator of other men's ideas throughout his address, singling out "a large number of people who have repeatedly taken advantage of the inability of the subject of this evening to say no and stick to it."[50] Howard Zahniser, who revealed that his own seldom used middle name was "Clinton," presented an award to Anderson's wife, Henrietta. The citation, in part, read "her husband's repeated health problems, his impatience with inactivity, his refusal to excuse himself from responsibilities, his consequent, almost continuous expenditure of energies—which in his case are unusually precious—have through the years tested her resources and have in truth proved her conservation of this great man to be truly phenomenal."[51]

Several days later the *Washington Post,* a consistent supporter of natural resources legislation, took editorial notice of the Anderson dinner. Observing that the senator "eminently deserved" that recognition, the paper urged the House to begin action on the Wilderness bill to follow the pace that Anderson had set in the Senate.[52]

Several weeks after the testimonial, President Kennedy met with Aspinall to work out terms that would free the administration's conservation program from its bondage within the House Interior Committee. Aspinall complained that Agriculture Secretary Freeman was busy reclassifying primitive areas into wilderness status despite his own repeated requests for a cessation of such action until the Wilderness bill cleared the House. Kennedy agreed that Freeman's action was in violation of previous agreements and observed that the secretary acted like a "millionaire" who had no problems at cabinet meetings. He promised to try "to slow him up a little on reclassification" and he urged Aspinall to work with Anderson in that connection. Aspinall responded that "Clint put a bill through the Senate early in the session and I assume that is the last word from him."[53] Kennedy told Aspinall that Anderson might be willing to change the bill a little, and he asked the chairman to take responsibility to get the machinery of compromise in motion. Although Aspinall agreed to hold "informal discussions" with Anderson, little of immediate consequence resulted.[54]

By the middle of 1963 Aspinall had settled on a new strategy—one that would tie the passage of the Wilderness bill to a massive review of the nation's laws governing the administration and disposition of its public lands. He believed that the essence of the dispute between his committee and the Senate was over the ground rules for withdrawal of wilderness-quality lands from multiple-use status. The controversy over the extent of the executive branch's authority to reclassify lands merely demonstrated how conflicting and vague were the five thousand land-use statutes and the administrative regulations designed for their implementation. Arguing that Congress should address "first things first," Aspinall met with assistant secretary of the Interior John Carver to draft a bill that would create a public land law review study commission. The commission would recommend modernization of management and disposal laws applying to the nation's 770.8 million acres of public land holdings. Carver had previously worked for Senator Frank Church, an ardent supporter of the version of the Wilderness bill passed by the Senate in 1961 and 1963. Although sympathetic to his former boss's desire for a Wilderness bill, he was more keenly interested in land law reform and he supported Aspinall's view of the reform as a precondition to the extensive land withdrawals necessary to bring the wilderness system to fruition.[55]

Aspinall unveiled his reform plan in an address to a Chicago meeting of the American Bar Association on August 4, 1963. Arguing that "there is little relationship between the management and administration of the public lands and the policies enunciated by Congress in enacting the great body of public land laws," he set forth a six-part proposal that would encompass all non-Indian public lands and would in effect tie the hands of the Interior and Agriculture departments in future determinations of which lands were to be withdrawn for wilderness preservation.[56] His plan offered a greater degree of protection to public land mineral prospectors in recognition of the large sums required for modern exploration efforts. During the three-and-a-half year period to be devoted to the study of land law reform, Aspinall's plan would prevent executive agencies from undertaking extensive and irrevocable modifications of land use patterns. Finally, Aspinall reiterated his support for a limited Wilderness bill that would confer statutory protection on the eight million acres already converted by administrative action to wilderness status, while ignoring the additional nine million acres of primitive lands incorporated in the Senate's version. The Public Land Law Review Commission stood as the centerpiece of Aspinall's proposal. In legislation introduced on the day of his Chicago speech, Aspinall recommended a nineteen-member body that would require $4 million and nearly four years to complete its work. The commission would include six members from each house of Congress and would be assisted by a twenty-five member advisory council.[57]

Up to that time, several members of the Senate had introduced related land law reform legislation, although none of the bills was as comprehensive as Aspinall's. In 1949, the Hoover Commission had recommended reform of the amorphous tangle of conflicting and disjointed statutes, but that proposal did not take legislative form until 1955 when Senators Warren Magnuson (D) and Henry Jackson, responding to the pleas of sportsmen's groups in their state of Washington, sponsored a broad-gauged bill. It received adverse reviews from various executive agencies within the Eisenhower administration and consequently went nowhere.[58] In subsequent Congresses, both senators reintroduced that measure, although the initiative was clearly that of Warren Magnuson, who would routinely add Jackson as a cosponsor. When Jackson learned of his colleague's action, he complained that this was not the way that he wished to approach the problem. Magnuson reportedly apologized and then went on to repeat the transgression in the following Congress.[59] By 1963, with Jackson chairman of the Interior Committee, Magnuson's earlier liberties assumed greater significance, especially to Aspinall, who was looking for influential Senate support for his bill. On the eve of the introduction of Aspinall's bill, his legislative counsel Milton Pearl called Senate Interior Committee land specialist Robert Wolf and invited him to come to the House chamber to witness the introduction of the "Chairman's bill." Wolf declined, noting that Aspinall was not his chairman and that he had better things to do. Pearl countered that it indeed was similar to the bill nominally cosponsored by Wolf's own chairman and that he ought to be interested.[60]

Wolf then approached the key members of the Senate Interior Committee to assess their sentiments on the Aspinall proposal. Alan Bible (D-NV), chairman of the Public Lands Subcommittee, alluding to the recent example of the Outdoor Recreation commission, told Wolf that another commission would be a waste of money. Jackson was particularly upset when Wolf told him of Aspinall's bill and of the House chairman's efforts to associate him with its objectives. He ordered Wolf to "Get my name off" the measure and to make it clear to the House members who were impressed by Jackson's apparent support that he simply did not believe it would be an effective approach.[61]

Finally Wolf approached Anderson. After hearing Wolf's explanation, Anderson sat back in his chair, placed his hands behind his head and asked, "Do you think Aspinall really wants the commission?" When Wolf responded affirmatively, Anderson added, "And I want a Wilderness bill!" Later that day, Wolf recounted the story to his office mate Ben Stong. Stong agreed that a trade was in the works, observing that "Clint's been waiting for something that Wayne really wants." The logjam appeared to have been broken.[62]

Several days later, an article entitled "Aspinall, Anderson Continue Duel Over Wilderness Bill," appeared in the *Albuquerque Journal.* Paul Wieck, a reporter close to Anderson, pointed to Aspinall's efforts to move his land law review bill as the price of cooperation for subsequent consideration of the Wilderness bill. He noted that Anderson was tiring of Aspinall's tactics and that he would not hesitate to "play rough" with Aspinall's proposed review commission to get action on the Wilderness bill. The article posed what may have been a planted question, "Will Senator Henry M. Jackson, as chairman of the Senate Interior Committee, play the game on this bill? If he will," the article concluded, "wilderness legislation may pass before June 30, 1964."[63]

During the late summer and early fall of 1963, the pace of behind-the-scenes meetings on the conservation stalemate slowed to a crawl. Anderson spent much of that period in New Mexico, and Aspinall refused to yield on his view that primitive areas should not be accorded preferential treatment in the process of their consideration for wilderness status. Anderson urged the Forest Service to remove a symbolic but otherwise insignificant roadblock to the positive consideration of primitive areas.

Aspinall frequently cited the Uncompahgre Primitive Area in his state of Colorado as an example of why such regions should not be allowed to slide, unchecked, into wilderness status. Spread across its 53,000 acres on a patchwork of private and public lands were more than two thousand separate mining claims. The Forest Service previously had been unresponsive to calls to reclassify that area, and Anderson believed that its continuation in a primitive area status needlessly aggravated Aspinall.[64] By mid-October, in response to congressional and Interior Department pressures, the Forest Service had set the necessary machinery in motion to remove this singular source of Aspinall's irritation, downgrading the region to the "scenic area" category.

At the same time, Aspinall met with conservation lobbyist Spencer Smith to seek assurances that the Wilderness bill, if reported by his committee, would not be "tampered with" on the House floor. He indicated that he intended once again to seek floor consideration under a suspension of House rules, a move that would preclude such "tampering." Neither Smith nor representatives of the Budget Bureau to whom Aspinall turned were able to give him such assurances or to propose alternate language that would satisfy all parties. Ben Stong advised Anderson in mid-September to simply "sit and wait some more."[65]

In mid-November the White House took up the initiative on the Wilderness bill in an effort to obtain House passage by the end of the 1963 congressional session. Lee White, presidential advisor on natural resources, met with Aspinall and later reported to the president that he believed the administration could meet all of Aspinall's "major requirements" in a way that would be suitable to Anderson and the major conservation groups. White suggested that the president ask Aspinall to use his influence to get Walter Baring (D-NV), chairman of the House Subcommittee on Public Lands, to cancel forthcoming western hearings, removing an additional obstacle to the measure's consideration by year's end. White argued that prompt action would provide western congressmen additional time in which to explain the bill before their 1964 reelection campaigns. Passage would also bolster the administration's record of legislative achievements as the bill had been high on its list of "must" accomplishments. Finally, White noted that quick passage would forestall a widening split in views between the administration and the organized conservationists.[66]

At that point Anderson began to take issue with the administration over its record of achievements since 1961. White House legislative aide Mike Manatos sent Anderson the draft of a speech entitled "America's Natural Resources—An Administration Report."[67] Anderson picked up the theme he had so clearly enunciated during the 1962 White House conservation conference—the active and underappreciated role of Congress in shaping conservation policy legislation. "Whatever happened to Congress?," asked the senator after reviewing the draft. Anderson took issue with the administration's efforts to create an image of inaction in resources matters during the 1950s. He branded as "totally wrong" the assertion that growth in the demand for outdoor recreation resources went "unnoticed" in the Eisenhower years, citing his own role in the establishment of the outdoor recreation commission. Anderson suggested that the report be turned over to Interior Committee aide Ben Stong for additional review.[68] Here the Kennedy administration's efforts ended, for a week later the president traveled to Dallas to meet his fate at the hands of an assassin.

True to Chairman Jackson's earlier promise, members of the Senate Interior Committee made no effort to consider the Land and Water Conservation Fund bill until it had cleared Aspinall's committee. That action came on November 14, 1963 after President Kennedy wrote to Aspinall expressing the administration's strong endorsement. The president and Secretary Udall touted the measure as the most important piece of park and recreation legislation to come before the Congress.[69]

The principal opponents of the bill were members of the National Waterways Users Association and the Army Corps of Engineers. Both groups feared that the assessment of fees for recreation use would set an unfortunate precedent threatening the traditional policy of free commercial use of federally constructed inland waterways. To set these "misrepresentations, misconceptions, and mistakes" to rest, Anderson prepared an article entitled "Why We Need The Land and Water Conservation Fund Bill" for the March 1964 issue of *American Forests.*[70] In it he explained that the legislation did not amount to double taxation and did not have the effect of limiting the use of public lands to those able to pay, noting the fees were already collected at more than fifty areas under the jurisdiction of the National Park Service. "Admission charges," said Anderson, "don't keep people away. They even encourage the use of given areas, because not too many people want to rough it any more and they equate an admission charge with developed facilities such as running water, sanitary installations, and the like."[71] He emphasized that the bill, as reported to the House, was amended specifically to exclude levies on nonrecreation uses of public waterways. These changes occurred, he noted, without the active participation of the waterways lobby, even though it was located in Washington only a few blocks from Capitol Hill. Assuming the unlikely role of speaking for Aspinall's committee, Anderson expressed regret that the lobby had not taken the trouble to make its objections known to that panel. The organization's concerns reminded the senator of "a spooked horse that shies without reason,"[72] and he told its president that the charges contained in the association's letters were "so far afield from the true nature of the proposal that you will not want to let them stand as statements of fact over your signature."[73]

Much of the opposition came from amateur rock collectors who had been incited by the *Lapidary Journal* to believe that if they set foot on federal property without having paid a fee, they would be subject to a fine of $500 and a possible sentence of a year in prison.[74] Also in the vanguard was the Army Corps of Engineers who cherished the public relations value of free public recreation use of its reservoirs and did not want to have the federal government impose admissions charges. Representative Ed Edmondson (D-OK) led the House opposition against user fees, recalling the backlash occasioned by the Oklahoma state legislature's "Red Worm" tax passed several years earlier. A sales tax on sporting goods, including fishworms, that measure had led to the defeat of every member that had voted in its favor. Edmondson feared that every resident of his district who had to pay to use a Corps of Engineers reservoir, of which there were many in Oklahoma, would vote against him unless he vigorously worked to defeat the measure.[75] Ben Stong suggested to Anderson that the best way to put an end to the opposition's misstatements was to threaten retaliation. "If someone filed an amendment to the tax bill to levy tolls on inland waterways or just discussed that recourse publicly," noted Stong, "I suspect he could get some of the navigationists in to talk about compromise."[76]

Anderson returned to Washington for the beginning of the 1964 congressional session on January 7. On the following day Secretary Udall went to Anderson's office to discuss the new Johnson administration's legislative agenda, including the Land and Water Conservation Fund Bill.[77] Udall, with the support of Interior Committee staff director Jerry Verkler, urged Anderson to press for action on the fund bill so that it would be ready for Senate floor debate as soon as the upper chamber received a House-passed bill. This, argued Udall and Verkler, would avoid having the measure ensnared in the civil rights debate that threatened to dominate the Senate's schedule.[78] Anderson held a particularly strategic position as a member of both the Interior and Finance Committees. Earlier, Finance Committee chairman Harry Byrd (D-VA) had agreed to a proposal in the conservation fund bill permitting the transfer from the highway trust fun of motorboat fuel tax revenues. Verkler urged Anderson to use his influence with the powerful Byrd to obtain the necessary letter of agreement, thus avoiding referral of the bill to a second committee and the consequent potentially fatal additional delay.[79]

On March 27, 1964, a devastating earthquake rocked Alaska and set off violent tidal waves that claimed more than one hundred lives. At the time, Anderson had been in New Mexico for the dedication of the "Clinton P. Anderson Hall" at the New Mexico State University and for medical treatment.[80] On his return trip to Washington he had stopped in Denver to tour an aerospace plant. There he received a call from President Lyndon Johnson who urged him to take command of the Alaskan relief and rehabilitation efforts. Anderson explained that his fragile health and legislative duties would limit his effectiveness in such a task. Johnson, not easily dissuaded once he had set his mind to a project, told the senator that his relief work in New Mexico during the Depression and his experience with famine relief in Europe while agriculture secretary made him the perfect choice.

Anderson later admitted that "secretly, I was thrilled at the prospect of being involved in such an exciting undertaking."[81] His ties to Alaska had been strong. He had been one of the leading proponents of statehood as well as for the preservation of its natural resources. Johnson conferred cabinet-level rank on the reconstruction commission, not at all troubled by the constitutional indelicacy of having a member of the legislative branch serving in such an executive capacity. Anderson agreed to take the Alaskan assignment not only for the "thrill" of the experience, but also to accumulate credit with the new president. The senator told David Brower that Johnson realized "he gave me an unusual burden when he asked me to take a responsibility in the Alaska rehabilitation, but he is always more than fair with me, and he would not ask me to do something for him and not be willing to do something in return."[82]

During the Eighty-eighth Congress, Anderson's stature as a national conservation leader received wide recognition. In September 1963, the American Political Science Association bestowed on the New Mexico senator its "distinguished service award" for his "eloquent and persuasive leadership in the struggle for conservation—wise use, not misuse—of the nation's resources."[83] In May 1964 he traveled to Portland, Oregon, to receive the Garden Club of America's "Francis K. Hutchinson Medal for Outstanding National Conservation Service." Earlier winners of that citation included Hugh Bennett, father of the Soil Conservation Service, Walt Disney, Jay "Ding" Darling, and Rachel Carson.[84]

At the time Anderson received the Hutchinson Award, the House Rules Committee held the Land and Water Conservation Fund bill hostage after the measure had emerged from Aspinall's Interior panel. With it rested the Johnson administration's entire conservation program. Aspinall persisted in his refusal to move on related legislation—most of which required funding that the land and water bill was designed to provide—until the bill reached the House floor. Earlier in 1964, White House congressional liaison Mike Manatos warned the President not to include Aspinall in a meeting on the Wilderness Bill with Senators Anderson, Jackson and administration officials. He noted that "Aspinall has no use for Stewart Udall and I am not sure he has much use for Anderson's and Jackson's version of the bill. He is a very difficult individual who might well resent a broad approach."[85]

Upon returning to Washington, Anderson found an urgent appeal from Recreation Bureau Chief Edward Crafts. Crafts feared that time was running out on the conservation fund bill, the cornerstone of his entire recreation planning effort. He took the risky step of circumventing his boss, Stewart Udall, in approaching Anderson directly. Crafts told the senator that he believed Secretaries Udall and Freeman, despite their hard work, had "shot their wad." He reported that President Johnson had told Udall "to get it passed" without offering to intervene directly. Aspinall also had taken "a passive attitude." The White House recognized that Aspinall's irritation resulted in part from the President's favoring of Anderson with responsibility for the Alaska relief effort. Although the Colorado chairman wanted the bill "badly," he was unwilling to try to pressure the crusty head of the Rules Committee, "Judge" Howard Smith (D-VA). Crafts concluded that "the bill will go down the drain unless there is some heavy lifting from higher quarters—meaning you, the president, and the House Speaker."[86]

Less than a week after Anderson met with Crafts, Judge Smith agreed to release the conservation fund bill for floor consideration. On the day that Smith's Rules Committee acted, Anderson was serving as floor captain for the opponents of the civil rights filibuster that had been tying up the Senate for more than two months.[87] Later that afternoon he met with Aspinall on the Senate floor to discuss strategy. The House chairman feared that his body's leadership would continue to block action on the conservation fund bill in deference to signal callers at the White House who calculated that they lacked sufficient votes for a clear-cut victory.[88]

In an effort to neutralize the waterways lobby's opposition to the conservation fund bill, Ben Stong of the Senate Interior Committee staff engineered some mischief at the annual meeting of the Rivers and Harbors Congress, then being held in Washington. He urged C.R. "Pink" Gutermuth of the Wildlife Management Institute to attend the session of that body's Recreation and Wildlife Committee, whose chairman was Oklahoma Representative Ed Edmondson, one of the leading foes of the fund bill. When Gutermuth arrived, he discovered that Edmondson was absent. He quickly realized that the staff had failed to prepare the resolutions the committee was expected to offer on the bill. As Claude Wood later reported to Anderson, "Pink got busy and got Dr. [Spencer] Smith [of the Citizens Committee on Natural Resources] to act as temporary chairman, and they put out a report endorsing the . . . fund bill and also the wilderness bill." Wood continued, "The report went to the floor and was adopted. Ben Stong and I have not been saying anything about this, but I've got an idea that Edmondson may have a stroke when he finds this out."[89]

Late in June, Stong appealed to Anderson to use his influence with House Speaker McCormack and the president to dislodge the fund bill from its stationary position on the House calendar. Stong pointed out that time was running out with recesses coming up for the Fourth of July and the Republican National Convention. He speculated that if the bill were not passed before that first recess, there would not be enough time to complete Senate action, which had been deferred at Aspinall's request.[90] Shortly thereafter, Anderson met with Udall who assured him that the administration was then convinced that it did have enough votes in the House to resist crippling amendments from opponents of the user fee provision.[91]

When Congress returned from the Republican Convention break

late in July, the House, by a voice vote, easily passed the fund bill. Various procedural votes prior to the final tally indicated that the opposition lacked the strength to kill the measure. Recovering in New Mexico from prostate surgery, Anderson wrote to chairman Jackson, urging him to ignore what he believed to be minor differences between the House-passed bill and its Senate counterpart. Noting that "it is urgent that a fund bill be passed," Anderson sent his proxy to vote in committee against any amendments.[92]

Although Anderson's operation sidelined him from early July until mid-August, he applied his influence with the Johnson administration and the leadership of both houses of Congress at strategically sensitive times. Not involved in the day-to-day maneuvering, he knew the issues by virtue of long association with them and he certainly knew when and where to exert pressure. This low-profile approach often went undetected by the press, but not by the conservation lobby and not by those members responsible for moving or blocking the legislation.

The movement of the conservation fund bill onto the House calendar cleared the way for action by the House Interior Committee on the long stalled Wilderness bill. On July 2, 1964, the committee reported that measure to the full House. Two months earlier, on April 28, Wilderness Society executive director Howard Zahniser appeared before the House Interior Subcommittee on Public Lands to testify in support of the Wilderness bill for the nineteenth time over a period of seven years. He told chairman Walter Baring that he hoped it would be his final appearance—and it was. A week later he was dead.[93]

In announcing Zahniser's death to their respective houses, Anderson and Aspinall emphasized a point that the redoubtable conservationist had made at the hearings a week earlier—that the long battle was nearly over and that relatively minor differences should not be allowed to shift their attention from the bill's broad objectives.[94] in that spirit and with time running out on the session, both men began to probe for areas of compromise. The Democratic leadership wanted a substantial record of achievement to carry to the electorate in the fall. Anderson's health was deteriorating and he began to question whether he would be able to conduct another campaign for reelection in 1966. Wayne Aspinall considered retiring at the end of the session to become chairman of the House-passed Public Land Law Review Commission. As summer approached, he awaited Senate action on that bill, so dear to him. The climate for serious bargaining never looked better.[95]

Anderson finally agreed to concede on the major point of contention between the House and Senate versions, the provision governing the incorporation of primitive areas. This was the amendment that Senator Gordon Allott narrowly missed having adopted in mid-1961 and had pursued ever since. At a meeting in Anderson's finely appointed private Capitol office, the senator told Aspinall, "If you give us a bill, I am ready to yield on the provision for affirmative action by both chambers."[96] As Anderson later recalled the encounter, "Wayne smiled with pleasure and, somewhat to my surprise, took my offer. He seemed delighted that he could finally settle the dispute on terms favorable to himself and end the bitter antagonism of the conservationists."[97] Anderson was disappointed over the concession, but he stoically observed that without it there would have been no bill at all.

On June 10, 1964, the Senate, by a margin of four votes, broke the seventy-five-day civil rights filibuster, marking the first time cloture had been invoked on a civil rights measure and only the sixth success for the debate-limiting device in the Senate's history.[98] On the same day, the House Interior Subcommittee on Public Lands approved a version of the Wilderness bill sponsored by Representative John Saylor and similar in its fundamentals to that passed in the Senate.[99] Several weeks later the full Interior Committee favorably reported that version to the House for floor consideration. The measure, as refined by the Interior Committee according to the Anderson-Aspinall agreement, differed from the Senate bill in two important respects. It permitted mineral leases for the next twenty-five years, while the Senate version had prohibited them altogether. The House Committee bill included only existing national forest tracts that bore the designation "wild," "wilderness," or "canoe" areas. This amounted to 9.1 million acres, 5.5 million acres less than the Senate version that included national forest primitive areas. Under the House bill's provisions, an act of Congress would be necessary to add primitive areas and National Park Service units to the wilderness system. The Senate bill had simply required a resolution of either house to block a presidentially recommended addition. Finally, the House committee agreed to set aside 3,500 acres within the San Gorgonio Wild Area for development as a commercial ski resort.[100]

In an effort to mollify conservation organizations, the House committee included a provision stipulating that existing primitive areas would continue to be treated as wilderness until respective department secretaries made recommendations to Congress, through the president, as to their future status. This quieted fears about the possibility that areas would be immediately despoiled, removing them from further consideration. At the same time, the committee bill would have allowed the Secretary of Agriculture, with the president's approval, to declassify primitive areas when such further study indicated that they were not of "wilderness" quality. To ensure that this review process did not lapse, the bill included a requirement that all primitive areas were to be evaluated in specific stages over a ten-year period.[101]

Faithful to his agreement with Jackson, Aspinall called up the Wilderness bill for House floor debate in late July, one week after that body had passed the Land and Water Conservation Fund bill. House debate centered on two amendments proposed by John Saylor.[102] Both were adopted. The first removed the exemption for the San Gorgonio ski area on the grounds that carving out portions of wilderness areas would set a dangerous precedent against the integrity of the entire system and that the area was one of the few of its kind still available to southern Californians. The second Saylor amendment removed the provision allowing the Secretary of Agriculture to declassify primitive areas. Saylor turned Aspinall's congressional supremacy argument against the chairman, declaring that Congress should have "complete control" over the disposition of these areas. With the adoption of these key amendments the House approved the Wilderness bill by a resounding 373 to 1 margin.[103] The Senate, however, refused to accept the House version, so both bodies appointed members to a conference committee to resolve the differences. Clinton Anderson was designated as that committee's chairman.

On the morning of August 14, following a five-week sojourn in New Mexico, Anderson met with Aspinall once again in his Capitol hideaway office. There the two men retraced the familiar outlines of the bill in preparation for that afternoon's meeting of the conference committee. In an earlier meeting, he had reluctantly accepted the Aspinall-Allott plan to exclude the Forest Service's primitive areas from the initial system.[104] Now he was faced with a decision on the House's provision to permit prospecting in Wilderness areas for an additional twenty-five years. A face saving device was needed, and Anderson found it in the Forest Service's assurance that it had controlled mining entry in wild, wilderness, and primitive areas over the past quarter century through administrative regulation and that it would continue to do so with even tougher agency rules. Aspinall added that the House proponents of the prospecting provision did not intend to permit mechanized access or the building of permanent roads to facilitate the prospector's work. Resting his faith on the strengthened Forest Service regulations, Anderson agreed to drop his opposition to this second House provision.[105]

The conferees met for two days. Representative John Saylor observed that he knew of "no conference between the House and the Senate in which the version of the two bills passed by the separate bodies have been as far apart."[106] Saylor joined Anderson and Frank Church as the Senate version's principal proponents, but Anderson's agreement with Aspinall set the tone for the conferees' discussion. The Aspinall forces yielded on several points of moderate importance in return for that agreement. They reduced the period during which prospecting would be allowed from twenty-five years to nineteen. The House version also had placed a 5,000 acre minimum limit on individual wilderness areas, but the conferees agreed to eliminate specific acreage in lieu of a statement of intent that a tract should be of "sufficient size to make practicable its preservation and use in an unimpaired condition."[107] The conferees also deleted the provision of the House version that would have required the president to identify specific values in an area that would justify its preservation as wilderness. They included primitive areas under the nineteen-year prospecting limit, a significant recognition of the favored position of these lands that had been denied immediate "wilderness" status.[108]

Ultimately, the most troublesome matter before the conferees was the San Gorgonio Wilderness ski area proposal. The House Interior Committee had recommended that 3,500 acres be carved out of the wilderness for commercial uses. The full House had reversed this provision and the Senate had never considered it at all. The conference committee strongly resisted efforts by two of its California members, Senator Thomas Kuchel (R) and Representative Harold Johnson (D), to reinsert this exemption. Anderson later explained to critics of that deletion that the bill would have been subject to a point of order on the floor of the House or the Senate as that provision had not been included in either chamber's version as passed. In a show of characteristic impatience against ill timed and misinformed lobbying efforts, Anderson began his form letter response to those critics with the observation, "Apparently you do not understand how bills are passed through Congress."[109]

On the final day of the congressional session, before the scheduled recess for the Democratic National Convention, Anderson and Aspinall carried the conferees' handiwork back to their respective houses. Both emphasized the bill's long-range benefits and commended all involved for their willingness to set aside short range considerations for the good of future generations. Each man paused to praise Howard Zahniser who, in Aspinall's view "like the patriarch of old was denied the opportunity to experience his moment of victory."[110] In the Senate, Anderson focused on the contributions of Hubert Humphrey who, with Zahniser's inspiration and counsel, began the struggle eight years earlier.[111] Both Houses quickly adopted the conference report, and their clerks readied the measure for its journey to the White House.

September 3, 1964, brought four major milestones on the long road toward a modernized national conservation policy. At 10:30 that morning in the White House Rose Garden, President Johnson placed his signature on the Wilderness Act and the Land and Water Conservation Fund Act. At his side were Senators Anderson and Jackson, Representative Aspinall, and Secretary Udall. The president chose to single out Anderson for special commendation, remarking that he had been "in the forefront of conservation legislation since he first came to the House in 1941."[112] As that ceremony ended, the Senate approved legislation establishing Utah's Canyonlands National Park and the Public Land Law Review Commission. The Senate Interior Committee had taken little active interest in the review commission, regarding it as the price that had to be paid for Aspinall's agreement to dislodge the Wilderness bill.[113]

Over the following two weeks both measures would follow the Wilderness and Conservation Fund acts to the White House for the presidential signature. Senator Frank Moss had almost singlehandedly guided the Canyonlands bill from proposal to law, neutralizing opposition within Utah and building support among other members who sympathized with the need for such facilities within their own states. Later, Moss observed, "It was my baby . . . in the hearings, I really had my way . . . . I drew the boundaries and added and subtracted areas. I guess I wheeled and dealed on it."[114]

This left unsigned two significant conservation measures that Anderson had actively supported during the Eighty-eighth Congress. They were the Valle Grande National Park bill and a proposed statute to establish the Indiana Dunes National Seashore. The Valle Grande measure had become ensnared during the previous Congress in a dispute over the willingness of area land owners to sell their property to the federal government. That property and a tract held by the Atomic Energy Commission were essential in the creation of a geographically contiguous and manageable site. In 1962 Anderson had decided to wait until the president issued a proclamation transferring the AEC tract to the National Park Service. That action occurred early in 1963, a week after Anderson's conservation award testimonial dinner.[115] The New Mexico senator then introduced a modified bill, which reduced the overall size of the proposed park from nearly 100,000 acres to one-third that area. The revised measure also incorporated the adjacent Bandelier National Monument to increase the attractiveness of the site to tourists in New Mexico and supporters in Washington.[116]

The Senate Interior Committee held hearings on the Valle Grande bill late in May 1964. There Anderson recounted his four decades of familiarity with the area and his four-year campaign to encourage private land holders to sell their tract at a reasonable price. In spite of his testimony, the bill died. Unlike the Moss Canyonlands measure, with which it shared many similarities, the Valle Grande bill became entangled in the private land issue and in conflicting jurisdictions among federal agencies. Unlike Moss, Anderson lacked the time and motivation to straighten matters out. The apparent greed of private interests offended him, so he simply let the matter slide until another day.[117] His willingness to abandon the Valle Grande bill, while simultaneously placing considerable political capital behind an effort to create a national park in the increasingly industrialized Chicago metropolitan area, underscored his stature as a legislator whose conservation interests transcended his southwestern regional base.

Early in 1963, as Anderson was preparing to step down as chairman of the Senate Interior Committee, an editorial cartoon appeared in the *Indianapolis Star.* Labeled "Sidewalk Saboteurs!," it depicted

Anderson, Senator Paul Douglas (D-IL), and Representative John Blatnik (D-MN), mischievous smiles on their faces, in the process of attacking a construction site from the safe platform of an adjacent sidewalk. Anderson held an armful of stones, Douglas operated the slingshot to apparent good effect, and Blatnik took aim with a rifle. In the background a sign stood designating the area as a Bethlehem Steel plant construction zone. A distant city appeared on the far side of a body of water. The cartoon was the price Anderson paid for exercising his customary mediatory role in an uncharacteristically public manner, a slip that he would not soon duplicate.[118]

At issue was the imminent destruction of the Indiana Dunes, located along a twenty-five-mile stretch of Lake Michigan shoreline between East Chicago and Michigan City. To Anderson and other supporters, principally Paul Douglas, the Dunes provided an excellent example of the type of recreation area the Outdoor Recreation Commission had in mind a year earlier when it urged preservation of lands adjacent to large metropolitan areas. By the early 1960s, more than 9 million persons in the region lived within 100 miles of the Dunes, including the population of Chicago, one hour's drive away.[119]

A Senate report described the threatened area as "an unusual complex of exceptional sand dunes, numerous marshes, swamps and bogs with greatly diversified flora and fauna and an attractive white sand beach." The report noted that the "sand dunes rise to heights of 200 feet in a series of ridges and valleys, simulating miniature mountain ranges. Because there are over 1,000 different flowering plants and ferns found in the dunes, a meeting ground for northern and southern species, botanists and biologists consider the area to be an outstanding scientific laboratory."[120] In the spirit of this report, Anderson was determined to use his influence to bring the area under the protective shelter of national park status.

The controversy over the Indiana Dunes had long roots. In 1916, at the time the National Park Service was established, its first director, Stephen Mather, had recommended measures to ensure the area's preservation. That goal met increasingly strong resistance over the years from industrial interests, particularly steel companies, who viewed the region as the best possible site of a new deepwater port. In 1929 Midwest Steel purchased a large tract of dunes land and petitioned the Army Corps of Engineers to conduct a feasibility study, an essential prerequisite for federal assistance with the costs of land acquisition and port construction. The issue smoldered along for the next three decades until the completion, in 1959, of the Saint Lawrence Seaway.[121] That facility held great promise for the economic development of the northern Indiana region and particularly for the steel companies that had been quietly buying up land in the area. In 1960 the Corps of Engineers finally reported that a port located at a site known as Burns Ditch would be economically justifiable. The State of Indiana then moved quickly to issue revenue bonds to finance its share of the anticipated $70 million construction cost. Of this amount, the federal government was expected to provide $25 million.[122]

In 1958, at the urging of the Izaak Walton League, Senator Paul Douglas had entered the fray, introducing legislation that would establish the Indiana Dunes National Monument consisting of 3,800 acres in the unspoiled Central Dunes. Several years later Douglas expressed his complete dedication to the measure in commenting, "If we get this bill through, I will feel that my life had not been in vain. Until I was thirty, I wanted to save the world. Between the ages of thirty and sixty, I wanted to save the country. But since I was sixty, I wanted to save the Dunes." His efforts came to naught until 1962. Early in that year, President Kennedy committed his administration to support preservation of the Dunes, using the Recreation Commission's report as justification.[123]

The Senate Interior Committee's Public Land Subcommittee held hearings on the Douglas bill late in February 1962.[124] Anderson maintained a low profile, recognizing that there was little chance to move the bill out of committee as long as both Indiana senators, sympathetic to the area's economic development needs, remained firmly opposed. There was no doubt among Anderson's closest advisers, however, of his sympathy for Douglas' objectives. Later, Anderson cast the issue in the classic mold of preservationists versus developers. He wrote, "There is no monetary scale on which the timeless grace of a sand dune can be weighed, though it seems to count less to so many people than the profits of an ore field, the receipts from a cut of timber, or the payroll of a thousand new jobs." In this, Anderson echoed the conservationist's classic refrain captured in Carl Sandburg's earlier observation that the dunes constituted "a signature of time and eternity—once lost the loss would be irrevocable."[125] For the moment, however, he withheld his direct support, determined to serve later in a mediatory role.

The opportunity came quickly. At the Senate hearings, Bethlehem Steel and other proponents of the Burns Ditch deepwater port site were told to prepare detailed surveys of alternate sites as the price for further congressional consideration.[126] Within a month, however, Bethlehem boldly announced a contract to sell two million tons of sand from the dunes as fill for a project to extend the campus of Northwestern University. Immediately, steam shovels began to level dunes within three miles of existing Dunes State Park. This action clearly jeopardized the seven miles of unspoiled dunes remaining from the original twenty-five–mile tract. Douglas responded with a flurry of telegrams to prominent potential supporters including President Kennedy, poets Sandburg and Robert Frost, Anderson and others.[127] Charging Bethlehem with a "deliberate and wanton act," Douglas demanded that the Army Corps of Engineers end its delay in considering his earlier request to provide studies of three alternate sites. He also insisted that the Bureau of the Budget scrutinize the Engineers' plans to provide $26 million for Burns Ditch harbor.[128]

At that point Anderson decided that the time had come to enter the dispute. He met with subcommittee chairman Alan Bible, Indiana Governor Matthew Welsh (D), Indiana Senator Vance Hartke and representatives of Bethlehem Steel to test the possibilities for a compromise bill. Anderson proposed that the existing 2,000-acre Dunes State Park be transferred to federal ownership. He agreed that the transfer could be effected by the state legislature to take some of the developers' pressure from Democratic Governor Welsh who was facing a difficult reelection contest. He insisted that sections of Dunes known as Unit 1 and Unit 4 be included, but he agreed that portions of Units 2, 3, and 5 could be dropped.[129]

Douglas reacted to a report of the Anderson meeting with a sense of betrayal.[130] Previously Douglas had argued that saving Unit 2 was the "crucial issue." In his view, if that unit fell into the hands of the developers, the remainder of the area would soon be despoiled, and there would be nothing left to preserve. Anderson quickly assured Douglas that his own role at the meeting had been misreported. He claimed that, as chairman of the Interior Committee, he was simply trying to express to the Indiana delegation what he believed would be the Senate's minimum acceptable position. Anderson denied that he had offered an outright proposal and wistfully added that "I probably would have been better advised to have kept still and indicated that the only thing any of us would take would be the Douglas bill."[131]

The matter continued to fester through the end of 1962 without further significant congressional attention. On February 7, 1963, Douglas advised Anderson and several other sympathetic members that he had just learned that Bethlehem Steel had completed stripping the vegetation on 250 acres of its key Dunes holdings in the eastern part of Unit 2. Douglas further informed his colleagues that the Indiana State legislature had refused to vote an additional three-cent tax on cigarettes to finance an outer breakwater for the proposed Burns Ditch harbor. Douglas concluded that this signalled the death of the Burns Ditch project. He urged Anderson and several others to wire the chairman of Bethlehem Steel to request a halt in the bulldozing until a meeting could be held in the Secretary of Interior's office to discuss options.[132]

On February 11, Anderson sent the requested telegram. His action ignited a firestorm of criticism.[133] The Indiana house of representatives passed a resolution of condemnation telling the federal government to "keep its nose out of Indiana's sovereign business."[134] Letters and telegrams reflecting the sentiment of the *Indianapolis Star's* cartoon poured in Anderson's office, charging him with "arrogance" and "contemptible tactics."[135] White House press secretary Pierre Salinger disavowed any administration connection with Anderson's action.[136] In Albuquerque for a congressional recess, Anderson instructed his personal secretary to write Bethlehem's chairman to explain that he had subsequently learned "that the harbor is not as dead as it had been represented" and that, under the circumstances, he would be willing to meet with representatives of the firm when he returned to Washington.[137] Anderson acknowledged that his telegram "could have been improved," but he refused to yield in his contention that he was playing the honest broker in a tangled and complex issue. Although he was about to step down as chairman of the Senate Interior Committee, Anderson saw the consequences of inaction to be a continued erosion of the priceless Dunes, with time on the side of the developers.

For the remainder of the Eighty-eighth Congress, Anderson followed a path in support of the Douglas bill that was less visible to the public, but ultimately more effective. On September 24, 1964,

Douglas wrote a personal note to Anderson. "My appreciation for your efforts can never be fully expressed. Suffice it to say that this is one of the most memorable days in my life and I am extremely grateful for your help."[138] The Indiana Dunes bill had passed the Senate. With less than a week remaining before the end of the Eighty-eighth Congress, the battle would have to be renewed in 1965, but the Senate had expressed itself, with Anderson's active assistance, and the chances for saving at least a significant portion of the Dunes remained very much alive.[139]

Unlike most western senators, Clinton Anderson transcended his background and constructively devoted himself to issues that rose above a regional base. That ability was clearly evident in his efforts to promote natural resources policy legislaton. His conflict with Wayne Aspinall, who epitomized the western desire for resources development at the expense of their long term conservation, underscored Anderson's national focus. The campaign to establish a national wilderness preservation system also highlighted Anderson's ability to transcend the narrow claims of specific regions and interest groups.

His success as a legislator was attributable to his sense of timing and his ability to keep his attention on the long range objective. Anderson had little interest in the short term symbolic victory and he had little patience with the staff member or lobbyist who pleaded that the time was right to act or that a specific action was politically appropriate. When an aide told Anderson, "from a political point of view, I think . . .," the senator cut him off in mid-sentence with the admonition, "You don't think, you tell me the facts, and I will worry about the political side."[140] When Howard Zahniser appeared on his doorstep, he would put his arm around the man universally described as a "fine Christian gentleman," converse with him for a brief time, and then guide him to a waiting staffer, who would take down the substance of the lobbyist's familiar message.[141]

Anderson's sense of timing accounted for his unwillingness to participate in Hubert Humphrey's pre-1961 campaign for the Wilderness Act. After Anderson became Interior Committee chairman in 1961, that measure took on a more "realistic" tone. Anderson held firm to his goals, specifically the inclusion of primitive areas and the prohibition of mining, through three years of debate and maneuver. Twice, under his leadership, the Senate passed Wilderness bills embodying his basic objectives. As chairman and colleague, he knew when to let other senators air their views and he also knew when the time had come to end the discussion and act.[142] That time had come by mid-1964. A devotee of poker and gin rummy, Anderson played his legislative hand down to the last card. To avoid a potentially fatal stalemate, he then yielded advantage that he would not have given earlier in the game. The result was the Wilderness Act and a series of related legislation that had been, for a time, hostage to the immediate interests of Aspinall's western constituency. The Wilderness Act was, in many respects, flawed. For the next two decades, members of Congress and succeeding administrations would struggle with its ambiguities. Nonetheless, it gave permanent statutory protection to a large body of primeval land and it established, as national policy, the intention to add to that priceless store before the possibility of such additions had vanished forever.

During the Eighty-eighth Congress, Anderson was less able to devote a significant portion of his time to natural resources legislation due to illness, his intense involvement with Medicare legislation, the Alaska reconstruction effort, and the demands of the Joint Atomic Energy and Aeronautical and Space Sciences committees. While the quantity of his attention diminished, the quality did not. He relied more heavily on talented staff, familiar with his objectives, to focus the competing issues for his attention. When Ben Stong, Claude Wood, or Jerry Verkler suggested that the time had come for him to intercede with Aspinall, the speaker of the House, or the president, Anderson reviewed their arguments and moved as he thought most appropriate. As necessary, his weapons were humor, logic, political credit, or intimidation.[143] In this respect, as the speakers at his 1963 testimonial dinner affirmed, Anderson had moved to the role of prominently placed facilitator of other men's ideas. This he did against the background of a life long commitment to natural resources conservation.

For the remaining eight years of his Senate term, Anderson's deteriorating health and other legislative interests kept him out of the conservation policy limelight. Allowing his staff to act, with increasing frequency, as his surrogate, Anderson could rest assured that his contributions had been of a distinctive and enduring nature. This he expressed, with reference to the Wilderness Act, shortly before his retirement. He said, "I felt a sense of positive achievement. It was the kind of imperfect compromise that often comes out of Congress, leaving a certain uneasiness in its trail, but it was important nonetheless. I felt that we had done something significant for the generations of Americans who will follow us."[144]

# 8
# Water Conservation at Home
## Navajo–San Juan Projects, 1956–1962

I did not initially seek to push legislation for those who love nature in its various forms. My compelling motive was a healthy desire to bring about a beneficial use of New Mexico's contractual share of the waters of the Colorado River.

Clinton P. Anderson
Address to the Sierra Club
November 7, 1964

In mid-1962, while recuperating from a heart ailment, Clinton Anderson told novelist Oliver LaFarge, "I have many times wondered how I would feel if I had to leave Congress because of ill health and dozens of times I have said that if I could just get the Navajo Irrigation–San Juan–Chama diversion project through Congress, I would be perfectly willing to leave."[1] Six weeks earlier, Anderson's wish had come true when President Kennedy signed legislation authorizing construction of a $135 million irrigation project for 110,000 acres of Navajo Indian land in northwestern New Mexico and a related $86 million project to divert water from the Colorado River to New Mexico's Rio Grande basin. These combined projects constituted the final phase of Anderson's thirteen-year legislative campaign to ensure that his state harnessed its maximum entitlement of the Colorado's flow. More than any other New Mexico official, Anderson singlehandedly fashioned a fragile but enduring network of agreements within his state, his region, and the government in Washington to achieve a goal that in 1956 seemed to have little chance of realization.

When President Eisenhower signed the Colorado River Storage Project Act in April 1956, the statute's immediate value to New Mexico remained uncertain. Earlier, Anderson had threatened to block the measure unless Congress and the administration supported his proposal to include the Navajo Dam as one of the project's major facilities. Anderson got his way. Of the four dams authorized, only the Navajo was to be devoted exclusively to irrigation storage. The others were to produce power and consequently the revenues to finance the entire basin-wide storage project.[2] With the project's authorization secure, its supporters turned to the equally critical task of getting it funded. To Anderson's consternation, the Eisenhower administration's $8 million request to fund initial construction activity contained no reference to the Navajo Dam. Anderson reacted bitterly, telling Senate Appropriations Committee chairman Carl Hayden (D-AZ) that he was "disappointed, chagrined, and hurt by the apparent slap at New Mexico."[3] He warned Acting Interior Secretary Clarence Davis that the administration's action clearly violated congressional intent and the good faith of Navajo Indians whose active lobbying for the entire project had been crucial in building support among urban liberals in Congress. He argued that irrigation dams traditionally had enjoyed bipartisan support and cited the case of a GOP-backed facility, on Nebraska's Republican River, that in 1946 had won the Truman administration's endorsement.[4]

In mid-1956, Anderson had two objectives in his dealings with the Senate Appropriations Committee as it considered funding for the storage project. First, he sought to insert $1 million for preliminary work on the Navajo Dam. Second, he tried to add $150,000 for the related Navajo Indian Irrigation Project. The 1956 act had not specifically authorized that facility, but had directed the Secretary of the Interior to give it priority status for future consideration as available funds allowed. Although the legislative process dictated that such projects had to be separately authorized before they could be funded, it was not uncommon to find authorizing language within appropriations bills. Considered an abuse of proper legislative procedures, this practice was often condoned when it suited the purposes of those in power. When it didn't, as with Anderson's 1951 effort to add funding for uranium access roads, the ploy set off howls of indignation from chairmen of authorizing committees. Appropriations Committee staff turned aside Anderson's stratagem, warning that his efforts on behalf of the irrigation project could easily jeopardize larger funding for the Navajo Dam.[5] Anderson yielded, recognizing that neither New Mexico state officials nor their counterparts within the Interior Department had completed essential engineering studies for the irrigation facility and the related inter-basin diversion project. Consequently, the Appropriations committees added funding only for the Navajo Dam. Preliminary excavation and engineering work was scheduled to begin early in 1958.[6]

By itself, the Navajo Dam would serve no useful purpose. Without prompt congressional action on the Navajo Irrigation Project that dam was designed to feed, the Eisenhower administration would have a credible case against completing the dam on schedule and thus would succeed in its original objective of blocking the entire project. At the start of the Senate's 1957 session, Anderson responded to the glacial pace of background work on the irrigation and diversion projects by assigning staff aide Doyle Kline to monitor that effort.[7] He feared an extended impasse until the Interior Department specifically apportioned between its Reclamation and Indian bureaus responsibility for planning, construction and operational phases of the Navajo irrigation facility. Anderson recognized that neighboring states, particularly Colorado and Texas, watched uneasily as New Mexico formulated specific plans for allocation of its share of Colorado River water. Finally, divisions within New Mexico's state bureaucracy concerned him. The senator told Kline that he expected federal agency officials to take advantage of the latter problem with predictable expressions of, "Well, we are not able to do it because you didn't know what you wanted." He advised his aide, "If we do know what we want, then we can criticize somebody if a supplementary budget is not sent up from the White House, and I would be in a position to release a news story inviting the White House to send up such a supplementary budget."[8]

Division between the Interior Department's Indian and Reclamation bureaus particularly troubled Anderson. The Indian Bureau expressed reluctance to seek appropriations for the irrigation project because the Reclamation agency appeared to be in no hurry to proceed with construction of the Navajo Dam, source of the project's water. Conversely, the Reclamation Bureau justified its relaxed pace by reference to the dim prospects for authorization of the irrigation project, for which the dam was being constructed.[9] Recognizing this as a classic bureaucratic stalemate, Anderson became determined to force these agencies to resolve several potentially troubling issues. Foremost among them was need for agreement on an exchange of Navajo reservation land for adjacent federal property, creating a tract that could be irrigated more efficiently. By eliminating long fingers of land described in the initial project plan, Anderson argued that per-acre irrigation cost would drop from $3,750 to less than $1,000, a reduction that would not be lost on the project's potential opponents.[10]

Early in 1958, Anderson decided the time had come to begin legislative action on these irrigation and diversion projects so crucial to conservation and effective use of New Mexico's water resources. He introduced the Navajo–San Juan bill on April 21 and scheduled hearings before his Irrigation and Reclamation Subcommittee for mid-July.[11] Anderson's bill specifically authorized a Navajo Indian Irrigation project designed to ensure an annual flow of 508,000 acre feet [163 billion gallons] to irrigate 110,000 acres of Navajo Reservation land on two large tracts south of the San Juan River in northwestern New Mexico. Of the estimated $135 million in construction costs, water users would be expected to repay only $21 million over a fifty-year period. Under statutes providing for underwriting of Indian irrigation facilities, the federal treasury would absorb all remaining costs. Interior Department planners estimated that the project would create more than one thousand new farms, raising the standard of living for 16,000 of the reservation's 85,000 inhabitants.[12]

The second portion of the Anderson bill authorized the San Juan–Chama diversion project. As of 1958, New Mexico had been able to capture only ten percent of the Colorado River water to which it was entitled under the 1948 upper basin compact. Twenty years earlier, Colorado had agreed to permit New Mexico access to the San Juan River, the Colorado River's second largest tributary. The Anderson bill provided the specific plan for removal of only 110,000 acre feet [36 billion gallons] although New Mexico would retain its right ultimately to withdraw more than twice that volume. Diverting water from three of the San Juan's feeder streams, the project would transport it through concrete tunnels under the Rocky Mountains and into the Rio Grande basin. Of the diverted amount, 57,000 acre feet, approximately half its volume, would be

sent down the Rio Grande to Albuquerque to relieve severe demands by municipal, commercial and defense users on that city's
already limited supply. Cost of the initial construction was estimated
at $86 million of which irrigation users would repay merely $8 million over fifty years. New Mexico's entitlement to surplus power
revenues from the three main power dams of the Colorado River
Storage Project would fund the balance of the diversion project's
costs.[13] For New Mexico, the financing scheme promised a massive economic gain and a tremendous political dividend for those
elected officials who could bring it to pass.

Tourists searching the Senate Office Building for legislative activity during the morning of July 9, 1958, might have been puzzled
upon entering Room 224. There, in an ornate setting, an epic unfolded that might have reminded the casual observer more of a Senate salute to New Mexico than a legislative hearing. The morning's
events were under the direction of New Mexico's Anderson, chairman and only member of the Irrigation Subcommittee in attendance.
Principal congressional witnesses included Dennis Chavez (D), the
state's senior senator, and Representative Joseph Montoya (D). Republican Governor Edwin Mechem flew in from Santa Fe to give
the meeting a bi-partisan flavor. Accompanying the governor were
state engineer Steve Reynolds and nearly a dozen officials and residents of various New Mexico cities and towns. The Interior Department supplied a supporting cast of reclamation and Indian affairs
specialists.[14]

The chairman concisely set a tone for the morning's hearings by
explaining that the "purpose of the Navajo Irrigation Project and
the San Juan–Chama project [was] to provide water for municipal
use, water for agriculture, and water for the development of oil
and gas, coal, uranium, and the many other minerals and resources
that are found in the northwest part of New Mexico and that are of
strategic importance to the safety and welfare of the entire country."[15] Anderson noted with approval Governor Mechem's earlier
commitment to link the two projects. Observing that supplies from
the Rio Grande near Albuquerque were fully appropriated, the senator argued that it was "essential" to use "surplus" San Juan waters
by bringing them across the Rockies, particularly to ensure water
supplies for that area's rapidly growing defense establishment. Anderson continued that such a diversion would simply not be possible until the Navajos living near the San Juan could be guaranteed

ample supplies for their own irrigation needs. The Navajo Irrigation Project was to be both collateral and fulfillment of that guarantee.[16]

The only discordant notes at an otherwise harmonious hearing came, predictably, from California representatives. They argued that New Mexico would be in violation of the Colorado River compact if it permitted even a drop of Colorado flow to enter Texas, as would happen as a result of diversion to the Rio Grande. Anderson retorted that it was nonsense to worry about where specific water came from as long as New Mexico consumed "equivalent" amounts of imported water. He suggested that California had enjoyed the surplus that upper basin states had been unable to harness. Now these states were finally preparing to take what was rightfully theirs.[17]

Anderson knew that insufficient time remained in the congressional term to enact his bill. By calling hearings six weeks before a scheduled adjournment, he sought to force recalcitrant executive agencies and affected states to complete review of both projects. If the Senate could be prevailed upon to approve the bill in the remaining weeks of 1958, chances would increase for speedy Senate passage and early House consideration at the start of the 1959 session.

Anderson's subcommittee approved the Navajo–San Juan bill, with minor amendments, after two days of hearings. The measure quickly moved to the Senate floor where, on August 15, 1958, it passed in less than three minutes.[18] Joining Anderson on the floor were Majority Leader Lyndon Johnson (D-TX) and Minority Leader William Knowland (R-CA). Anderson presented the bill with amendments to reassure Johnson's Texas and Knowland's California that the project would not threaten water rights guaranteed under existing compacts. Anderson spoke briefly, emphasizing that crops produced in newly irrigated areas would not contribute to existing surpluses and that added water in the Rio Grande basin was vital to continued secure operation of three Albuquerque-area military installations.[19]

After the bill passed under a routine unanimous consent agreement, Anderson took the floor to lend the authority of his Reclamation Subcommittee chairmanship to a California irrigation project important to Minority Leader Knowland. Staged as part of a mutual support agreement, Anderson's statement sounded uncustomarily generous, particularly in light of his earlier sustained efforts to block the project until California's senators agreed to support his measure.[20] Speaking to prejudices of senators outside the public lands

states, as well as those competing with New Mexico for federal reclamation dollars, Anderson "confessed" that he had been "very skeptical about the [San Luis] project in the beginning because [he] did
not understand it." Noting that he had recently flown over the area,
Anderson concluded, "I am very happy to say now that I believe it
is one of the finest projects I have ever seen. It will pay out without question. It is of great economy value."[21] Such was the pattern
of legislative reciprocity!

The 1958 congressional elections produced large margins for
Democrats in reaction to the "Eisenhower Recession" and that administration's apparent inability to deal effectively with the nation's
mounting social and economic problems. In the Senate, Democrats
increased their lead over Republicans from two in the 1957–1958
Congress to thirty at the beginning of 1959, their widest margin
since World War II. In seniority, Anderson moved up ten places
to thirtieth position. In the House, Democrats added forty-eight seats
to their majority. Several important House committee chairmanships changed hands. Among them, that of Interior and Insular Affairs panel passed to Colorado's Wayne Aspinall.[22]

Aspinall had spoken plainly during the 1958 congressional session about his priorities for water development in the southwestern Colorado–northwestern New Mexico region. The Colorado
projects would take priority in the House! Particularly frustrating
to Aspinall was the situation in which Colorado, whose territory
spawned nearly three-quarters of the Upper Basin's waters, had
harnessed less than half of its allocation of fifty-one percent of those
resources. This he contrasted to New Mexico, a state that, after a
period of hesitation in the early 1950s, had moved ahead swiftly
with detailed plans to capture its eleven percent entitlement. Aspinall
feared that New Mexico's claims to a full quota, in years of diminished flow, and Indian claims to prior and superior rights under the
Winters Doctrine, would leave Colorado with a crippling deficit.[23]

Colorado's plans for developing its water resources, through the
proposed Fryingpan–Arkansas Transmountain Diversion Project, had
run afoul of the House of Representatives' eastern-urban bloc during every Congress since 1954, although the Senate had routinely
passed the measure. Similar in conception to New Mexico's San
Juan–Chama project but twice as costly, the measure authorized
$169 million to divert water from the Fryingpan basin of the Colo-
rado River eastward across the Continental Divide to Colorado's

Arkansas River Basin. The project would provide nearly 70,000 acre feet of water to the Colorado Springs and Pueblo areas and would control flooding of the Arkansas River.[24] Critics in the House argued that the plan exceeded all previous cost standards, running to about $23 per acre, almost five times the estimated revenue from the project's irrigation water. This measure also suffered under opposition from Aspinall who feared that it would drain water away from his western slope constituency.[25]

Similar difficulties lay in the path of a second Colorado undertaking. The Animas–La Plata Irrigation Project had been designed to water 66,000 acres in Colorado and 20,000 acres in New Mexico. A supporter of this plan, Aspinall feared that reduced flows of the Colorado River might interfere with New Mexico's ability to draw sufficient water to develop its portion of the Animas project, causing that state to abandon its share. If New Mexico lands were not included, the project's cost effectiveness would be called into question, threatening its further development. Citizens of Durango, Colorado, who expected to receive the additional water, were particularly vocal in their concerns that New Mexico projects would deny the Animas project its essential flows. To reduce these fears, Anderson directed Senate Interior Committee staff to prepare an analysis of the impact of New Mexico's withdrawals on water availability for Colorado projects.[26] That study, released early in March 1959, indicated that more than a quarter of New Mexico's 838,000 acre-foot entitlement would remain for future developments on completion of the Navajo and San Juan projects.[27]

With the staff study in hand, as well as supportive letters from the Reclamation Bureau, Anderson convened hearings on the Navajo–San Juan bill on March 16, 1959. Consolidating it with several related bills that also had passed the Senate late in the previous Congress, Anderson expected no delay in returning the measure to the Senate floor.[28] In less than an hour, the subcommittee received testimony designed, in Anderson's words, to provide "concrete affirmation" that nothing in the Navajo–San Juan bill would adversely affect the Colorado project.[29] Ominously, Interior Department witnesses were unable to assure the subcommittee that the Animas project would continue to be feasible without participation of New Mexico lands included in the existing project plan.[30] To sidestep this possibility, the panel in its report pointed to the Interior Department's assertion that New Mexico's overall entitlement to Colorado River water would not be reduced, thus assuring sufficient flows for the Animas project. Conclusions to the contrary were based on "compact interpretations and resultant water supply studies" that the Interior Department considered unacceptable.[31] From such tenuous assurances, Aspinall drew little comfort.

In 1958, the Navajo–San Juan bill had encountered no resistance on the Senate floor. In May 1959, prospects suddenly dimmed thanks to President Eisenhower's call for a moratorium on new water development projects for the coming fiscal year. Accordingly, neither the Interior Department nor the Bureau of the Budget was in a position to provide the committee with a favorable report. Interior acknowledged that planning reports were completed but they had not been returned by the affected states where they were under review. Anderson argued that many states, having no objection, simply never bothered to respond. Colorado's failure to reply seemed to him, however, to be a delaying tactic. In the light of the administration's "no new starts" policy, Anderson feared that the absence of these reports would sidetrack his bill indefinitely.[32]

With the support of Appropriations Committee chairman Carl Hayden, Anderson tried to weaken the opposition case by observing that the measure simply authorized funds, but did not specifically appropriate them. Moving to the offensive, he declared that Congress had the ultimate right to work its will, regardless of executive agency recommendations. By linking New Mexico's two projects to the $40 million Navajo Dam, already under construction, Anderson sought to distinguish them from new proposals. He asserted that the prime beneficiaries of the dam's impounded water would be the Navajo Indians, most of whom lived not in New Mexico, but in Chairman Hayden's Arizona. Anderson turned aside arguments that the additional water would increase the production of crops already in surplus with the explanation that, for the San Juan diversion, the principal beneficiaries would be Albuquerque-area defense installations. "I only know," said the senator innocently, "that the Defense Establishment has requested this project." Thus, Anderson couched his arguments in an appeal to congressional prerogatives, Democratic hostility to the Eisenhower program, the nation's obligation to its exploited Indians, demands of national security, and an altruistic sense that his concern transcended the mere interests of his own state. Anderson's tactics succeeded. With only a handful of senators participating in the voice vote, the measure carried with six or seven members nodding in the affirmative and two in opposition.[33]

Shortly after Senate passage, Wayne Aspinall set three conditions that New Mexico would have to meet before he would schedule hearings on the Navajo–San Juan bill.[34] As his first requirement Aspinall sought assurances from the Reclamation Bureau that the San Juan–Chama project would display a favorable benefit-cost ratio. Preliminary studies had indicated an undesirable ratio of 0.81 to one based on direct costs over a fifty-year repayment period. Calculated to include indirect costs and extended over twice the period, the figure rose to a more respectable 1.26 to 1. New Mexico State Engineer Steve Reynolds advised Anderson that those apparently marginal ratios were not likely to encounter serious resistance from other basin state members of Congress. He noted that none of the eleven participating projects previously authorized as part of the Colorado River Storage Project, including those in Aspinall's state, had ratios as great as one to one on a fifty-year, direct cost basis. Reynolds counselled Anderson and New Mexico Governor John Burroughs (D) against requesting a new Reclamation Bureau cost study. This would reflect adversely on the measure and would certainly add to the delay under the no-new-starts policy.[35]

Aspinall's second condition grew out of the concern of his western slope constituents that New Mexico might pull out of the Animas project due to an inability to draw on its full Colorado River entitlement. He wanted a formal written agreement between the governors of both states that water would be provided. Reynolds assured Anderson and Burroughs that the Colorado Water Conservation Board director had agreed informally to discuss the matter with that state's governor. The governor, in turn, would try to convince Aspinall that the states intended to agree on an amendment to the bill guaranteeing Colorado's rights.[36]

In his final requirement, Aspinall sought assurances that New Mexico's share of net power revenues from the Upper Colorado project would be sufficient to cover costs that users of the Navajo and San Juan projects could not pay directly. Reynolds responded that this question would not be in order until construction appropriations for the projects were considered. He added that it should not be allowed to delay the authorization process.[37]

Aspinall's conditions led Anderson and other key New Mexico

officials to increase pressure on Colorado Governor Steve McNichols (D) to complete that state's review of the New Mexico projects' planning reports. New Mexico Governor Burroughs served
as point man, but his assault faltered and he turned to Anderson for
guidance in the face of Colorado's growing intransigence.[38] Anderson urged Burroughs to remind McNichols that costs of the Navajo
irrigation project were nonreimbursable under the statutes providing federal payment of Indian water costs. Thus, the facility would
not draw upon power revenues from the Glen Canyon dam that
could be assigned to repay construction costs of Colorado's projects. The senator also suggested that Burroughs tell McNichols of
New Mexico's commitment not to separate the Navajo and the San
Juan projects from a single authorization bill. He advised Burroughs
to hint that New Mexico might be willing to consider delaying construction of the San Juan diversion project until Colorado had the
opportunity to secure funding for its own projects. The short-term
goal for New Mexico was simply to secure authorization for both
measures, delicately entwined in a single piece of legislation.[39]

In January 1960 the Colorado governor proposed to Burroughs
a set of potentially troublesome amendments for the Navajo–San
Juan bill. Anderson's aide, Claude Wood, observed that the amendments appeared to strike at the substance of rights already guaranteed New Mexico in the Colorado River compact. Noting that
Colorado was preparing to request funding for its previously authorized Curecanti storage unit, Wood recommended that Anderson and Chavez "sit down on Colorado's projects for a while and
see how they like it. Maybe they will try to be a little more cooperative."[40] In an effort to reach agreement between the two states
and the Interior Department to clear the way for House hearings
during 1960, Anderson called a meeting in his office on March 9.
Key Reclamation Bureau officials and representatives of Colorado's
state water board joined Anderson and his staff. Anderson sought
to pressure Interior Secretary Fred Seaton to release a study indicating the amount of water from the Navajo reservoir needed to
protect Colorado's Animas project.[41] At the same time, New Mexico agreed to Colorado's request to earmark among the principal
uses of the Navajo Dam, "exchange storage releases" for the Animas project.[42]

Colorado continued to delay its response as the congressional
session wound down in the face of the upcoming 1960 presiden-

tial nominating conventions and House and Senate races. Following Claude Wood's suggestion, Anderson joined with Dennis Chavez, chairman of the Senate Public Works Committee, in an attack on the funding of two Colorado projects. The 1956 Colorado River Storage Act had authorized both the Curecanti and Florida projects. The New Mexico senators asked Senate Appropriations Committee chairman Hayden to defer consideration of these projects pending resolution of the New Mexico–Colorado disputes.[43] They argued that each project was interrelated with, and would affect the overall development of all upper basin water resources. Specifically, the Curecanti Storage Unit would have to be financed at interest rates considerably higher than anticipated before 1956 when the Colorado Storage Project's feasibility was calculated. Anderson and Chavez noted that the higher rate would deplete the Basin Fund, to which power revenues were credited to repay irrigation costs for all upper basin projects.

Anderson expressed frustration that his separate legislation to place a ceiling on project interest rates had been passed by the Senate but blocked in Aspinall's House Interior Committee. He urged Hayden to sit on the legislation until the House, presumably under Aspinall's lead, moved to settle the maximum interest rate issue. Similarly, the New Mexico senators objected to the Florida project, as it would draw water from the San Juan River. They labored to block that project "until such time as agreement is reached with our sister state with reference to the uses of *all* of the San Juan system."[44]

The Anderson-Chavez appeal succeeded. Within five days Aspinall announced that the House Irrigation and Reclamation Subcommittee would hold hearings on the New Mexico projects on May 20. Late in the evening of May 19, negotiators from New Mexico and Colorado reached agreement on the language of an amendment to the Senate passed bill. Colorado, however, made that agreement contingent upon an Interior Department finding that the New Mexico project would not adversely affect the water supply of the Animas project.[45]

Although the House hearings were ostensibly under the direction of subcommittee chairman Walter Rogers (D-TX), Aspinall took an active role, sitting as chairman in Rogers' absence and guiding the course of the day's discussion. At the outset, Aspinall made clear his support of the broad outlines of the legislation. He remarked, however, that the Budget Bureau and the Interior Department had taken a year to respond to his request for reports and that the Budget Bureau opposed the measure.[46] He reminded representatives of the Navajo tribe that, unlike the Senate, the House and its Interior Committee had to move cautiously on such measures. "I want you folks to realize," he told Navajo Tribal Council Chairman Paul Jones, "that there is a whole lot more to shepherding one of these projects through the House of Representatives than just the mere wishes and hopes of the people or representatives of the area."[47] Observing that the House committee had not "lost one of these big projects" over the past decade, he reiterated his decision to withhold the bill from House floor consideration until 1961.[48]

Aspinall's chief concern at the hearing was to build a record in support of his view that the Navajo project must be operated strictly as an Indian project, under separate appropriations, and have no claim on revenues of the closely guarded Basin Fund. To that end, he suggested that the Navajo and the San Juan projects be separated, within a single bill, into two titles.[49]

A month later, in mid-June 1960, the Interior Department announced that its further investigations of the Navajo–San Juan Projects, as requested by Aspinall, had been completed and that they supported the measure's enactment.[50] Shortly thereafter, New Mexico's State Board of Finance gave Colorado $10,000 to accelerate a Reclamation Bureau feasibility study for the Animas project. The Colorado Water Conservation Board responded with gratitude and predicted that the study would be completed by the middle of 1961.[51]

The Navajo Dam issue entered the 1960 New Mexico political campaign as Anderson, running for a third Senate term, and Republican Edwin Mechem, seeking a return to the Governor's mansion after a two-year absence, traded charges about each other's degree of responsibility for the project. Speaking at a rally on the dam site, Anderson recounted his own role in having the facility included in the 1956 storage project. Mechem countered that Anderson had placed faith in a "faltering memory" in outlining the project's construction history. Mechem claimed that he was the first of New Mexico's elected officials, in 1953, to support the project.[52] Anderson acknowledged Mechem's assistance in having an access road constructed but recalled the governor's silence in the four years following the project's authorization in the face of fellow Republicans' efforts to prevent or limit its funding. Anderson discounted Mechem's claims that he made frequent calls to the Eisenhower White

House, noting that such claims were easy to make because, "nobody keeps carbon copies of phone calls." Anderson concluded his rebuttal asserting that "I am one of the sponsors of the legislation that authorized the project. Credit for the Navajo Dam belongs to the men who got the law on the books, who fought for the money for construction, and who kept construction going—not to letter writers and telephone callers."[53]

The Kennedy administration had barely settled into office when Anderson, on January 27, 1961, in his new role as chairman of the Senate Interior Committee, wrote Interior Secretary Stewart Udall to urge prompt action on a departmental report concerning the reintroduced Navajo–San Juan bill.[54] That report arrived less than twenty-four hours before the start of the March 15 Senate hearing. Anderson's desire to expedite the report compelled the Interior Department to send its favorable recommendation without customary prior approval of the Budget Bureau. Secretary Udall testified that the measure fit the pattern of "wise and beneficial resource development" that President Kennedy had set forth in his natural resources message to Congress.[55]

Following Udall's brief statement, Anderson inserted in the hearing record a telegram that the San Juan County New Mexico Farm and Livestock Bureau had sent to Wyoming Senator J. J. Hickey (D). Residents of the northwestern New Mexico region claimed they had been blocked in their efforts to submit testimony in opposition to the San Juan diversion. Anderson responded that his committee had received neither the request nor the written testimony. He added, "I am shocked at the telegram. I can not believe it."[56] Although Anderson professed shock over the telegram, he could not have been particularly surprised. Two months earlier, his office had received a resolution adopted by "the 250 farm families" that composed the bureau. The bureau members saw the San Juan diversion measure as part of a "thinly disguised plot" by Albuquerque interests eventually to take large amounts of water from the region, thus crippling the economy of northwestern New Mexico. They urged Congress to pass the Navajo project independently of the diversion project, allowing the latter to "stand on its own merits."[57] In a note to Anderson, Claude Wood volunteered, "This makes me 'sorta' sick. After all the work to have this bunch start 'kicking over the traces'."[58]

Late in January, Anderson wrote to Lincoln O'Brien, publisher of

San Juan County's *Farmington Daily Times,* to inquire whether the area's opposition was serious and broadly based. O'Brien reported that there was "no appreciable body of intelligent opinion" opposed to the diversion project as part of the favored Navajo project. O'Brien added there were "a few cranks, but they are of no consequence."[59] Claude Wood wrote to another influential San Juan basin resident, I. J. Coury, chairman of the New Mexico Interstate Stream Commission and the state's director of the National Reclamation Association. He told Coury that Anderson had agreed to his offer of written questions in the event dissident area residents attended the hearing.[60] Later Coury reported on a March 1 area meeting that he characterized as heatedly "anti-Anderson" and filled with charges that the "Middle Rio boys" were out "to steal our water."[61] Coury wrote again to Wood, several days after the mid-March hearing, to obtain a copy of the bureau petition. Anticipating that his neighbors' opposition would surface at a House hearing set for April, Coury promised, "With the petitioners' names before me, I believe I can wreck their playhouse between now and the hearing date."[62]

Following negotiations between Colorado and New Mexico, Anderson agreed to introduce a revised version of the measure he had sponsored in 1960. The 1961 bill made clear that the San Juan–Chama project would include only the "initial stage," diverting an average 110,000 acre feet per year. The balance of the 235,000 acre-foot entitlement would be subject to additional authorization at a later time. Refusal of water users on New Mexico's lower Rio Grande to participate in the diversion project made this important limitation possible. They contended that when water was in short supply on the Rio Grande, it was also less available on the San Juan. Accordingly, they were not interested in bearing a share of the diversion's expenses.[63] The second major change limited the total volume diverted over a ten-year period to 1.35 million acre feet. This was set to assure Colorado that sufficient water would remain for other authorized projects.[64]

Anderson took great pains during the hearings, and two weeks later when the bill was taken up on the Senate floor, to protect comity with his California colleagues. He agreed to add language reaffirming that state's rights to all protection offered by existing compacts and guaranteeing it legal recourse if the project caused those agreements to be violated.[65] Anderson was particularly solicitous of Senator Thomas Kuchel (R-CA). Kuchel had cooperated with Anderson when the measure passed the Senate in 1958 and 1959. Anderson cited the Californian's support to assure potentially skeptical senators from the Colorado's upper and lower basins that the Navajo–San Juan bill would not undercut their long-term access to that river's flow.

During the 1961 hearings, Kuchel called to Anderson's attention language in the December 1960 report of the special master, a court appointed investigator, who had developed facts surrounding the long-running litigation between Arizona and California over their respective Colorado river rights. Kuchel noted that in one conclusion affecting the entire Colorado basin, the special master was "woefully wrong."[66] The master's report indicated that the upper basin states' total draw upon the river, once all their project units specified in the 1956 act were completed, would not be more than 4.8 million acre feet per year. Implicit in the report was the right of lower basin states to sue over conflicting compact interpretations with the expectation of receiving a major portion of the unclaimed 2.7 million acre feet of the upper basin's 7.5 million total.[67] Kuchel believed the master's opinion could be interpreted to mean that the upper basin states had voluntarily placed a ceiling on the amount of water intended for future development. This would please the lower basin states, particularly California, but Kuchel courageously rejected the argument as specious. Anderson joined Kuchel in a hearty condemnation of that interpretation, observing that he had written much of the 1956 act's language, as well as legislative history, and that there was no possible way to expect that upper basin states would accept such a tenuously based limitation.[68]

Shortly before Senate floor debate began, Anderson received the long awaited Budget Bureau recommendation. That agency reaffirmed an earlier report that the San Juan–Chama project had only a 0.81 to 1.0 benefit-to-cost ratio over a fifty-year period. While cautioning that such an adverse balance was generally unacceptable, the Bureau made an "exception" for the San Juan facility because its project report disclosed that tributary irrigation units were "suffering economic distress as the result of increasing population pressures, erratic water supplies, deterioration of existing irrigation works, and subdivision of ownerships among heirs."[69]

Anderson served as the Navajo–San Juan bill's floor manager, as he had the two previous times it passed the Senate. In 1961, as in 1959, his principal adversaries were Senators Frank Lausche (D-

OH) and John Williams (R-DE). The Ohio senator emphasized the Navajo project would result in a per acre expenditure of $1,250 to reclaim land Anderson acknowledged to be worth no more than five dollars. Lausche tried, with little apparent success, to demonstrate the irony of such an effort a week after the Senate had acted to reduce farm acreage for the production of feed grains. Anderson countered that this was a different situation in view of the impoverished state of the Navajos and the numerous Indian suits against the United States for treaties not honored.[70] He also responded to Lausche's charge that the San Juan–Chama project provided practically no water for farming by explaining that reclamation projects were taking a new direction toward supplying water for municipal use in areas where individual communities were unable to afford such works.[71] This new direction may also have been influenced by cost accounting considerations in determining project feasibility. If the San Juan–Chama project had been dedicated chiefly to irrigation purposes, the benefit-to-cost ratio, assuming a fifty-year life span, would have remained at 0.81 to 1.0. If, however, its principal uses were for more valuable municipal purposes, for which higher assessments could be made, the ratio would rise to more acceptable levels, particularly if indirect costs related to national defense were added.[72]

Williams of Delaware, in alliance with Minority Leader Everett Dirksen (R-IL), sought to send the bill to the Senate Agriculture Committee in view of its potential contribution to existing crop surpluses. Williams pointed out that, of the $86 million cost of the San Juan project, only $29 million had been earmarked for municipal and industrial use. The bulk of the remaining portion, approximately $53 million, was to support irrigation uses. Implicit in the latter figure was the likelihood that only a small portion, perhaps $8 million, would actually be repaid to the federal treasury.[73]

Anderson responded with less than compelling candor by noting that the proportion of municipal to irrigation uses would undoubtedly prove to be much greater. He argued that the San Juan project had been designed in the 1940s when the population of Albuquerque hovered near 35,000 in contrast to the 1960 rate of 200,000. The New Mexico senator claimed that the municipal portion could rise to as much as $70 million, ensuring a greater percentage of repayment. Williams wondered how Anderson reconciled that figure with the project report's $29 million estimate. Anderson called Williams's attention to the use of the qualifier "tentatively," saying that actual costs could not be allocated until contracts were negotiated with individual municipalities.[74] Such vagueness of calculation refired Williams' desire to return the bill to committee until the Agriculture Department had the opportunity to analyze the measure. If, as Williams argued, $53 million was allocated to irrigation of 121,000 acres, the per-acre cost would be a staggering $445. If users could only repay $8 million, the per-acre federal subsidy would amount to $378.[75]

Williams next turned to the sensitive question of the interest rate to be charged against the project. He noted that the federal government was then paying an average of four percent on its long term debt obligations, while this bill permitted the government to receive from project users only 2.63 percent, the actual cost of money at the time of the project's inception. The difference between the two rates, he argued, resulted in a substantial additional subsidy to the project's beneficiaries.[76] Anderson responded sharply. The question of calculation of interest rates lay at the heart of the water project funding debate. Until the passage of the 1956 Colorado Storage Project Act, delicate benefit-cost ratios had been figured on the average *rate* of interest paid on long-term government debt at the time funds were set aside for construction. The Colorado project departed from this practice by charging a rate based on the average *yield,* or amount the government had to repay over the life of the project.[77] In 1959 Anderson had moved successfully to correct the damage done under the Colorado measure. He attached an amendment to a bill authorizing construction of a water project in Norman, Oklahoma. His amendment reversed the interest rate calculation procedure, moving once again to the less costly average of the initial rate rather than the long-term yield.[78] The exchange sent Anderson and Wiliams in search of financial pages from the morning's newspapers. Williams got the best of the argument when he produced *Wall Street Journal* data indicating current long-term yields to be running as high as 3.82 percent. Anderson countered by noting that there was no way to predict what rates would be at the time of the project's completion, nor what the actual construction costs would amount to.[79]

In this assertion rested the ultimate difference in orientation between western senators and those from other regions. For all the estimates of Interior Department and committee specialists, calculation of western water project costs more closely approximated an art form than a precise science. At this art Anderson displayed skills of a master. The Senate, on March 28, by a vote of 17-68, defeated Williams' motion to send the measure to the Agriculture Committee and then, by a voice vote, quickly passed the Navajo–San Juan bill for a third time in four years.[80] Anderson believed that the action, coming so early in the congressional session, boded well for the measure's ultimate success in the House.[81]

By 1961 House Interior Committee chairman Wayne Aspinall had become a strong advocate of the Fryingpan-Arkansas diversion project. Earlier versions of that measure had seriously divided Colorado's eastern and western slope residents. Western slope inhabitants, including Aspinall, feared that the proposed diversion would leave insufficient supplies for their own uses. A revised version, drafted in 1961, expanded the size of a planned western slope reservoir, ensuring that it would contain more than enough water to replace that diverted as well as sufficient supplies for western Colorado's future development projects.[82]

The Senate had passed earlier versions of the Fryingpan project with little debate, only to see them die in the House. By 1961, with Anderson as chairman of the Senate Interior Committee, Aspinall recognized that the past scenario might be reversed. Without sympathetic House treatment of Anderson's Navajo–San Juan bill, Aspinall had little hope of seeing the Fryingpan bill advance out of the Senate Interior Committee. Accordingly, Aspinall scheduled hearings on the Navajo bill less than a month after it passed the Senate.[83] On July 10, 1961, the Aspinall committee favorably reported the measure to the full House with two significant amendments. The first took the Senate authorization figure of $221 million and divided it to $135 million for the Navajo irrigation project and $86 million for the San Juan diversion. This was intended to emphasize that the bulk of the Navajo project costs fell under existing statutes exempting Indians from repaying them. The second amendment prohibited production on newly irrigated lands of crops considered to be surplus. This restriction would run for ten years after the completion of each project. Fearing that the Navajos would invoke the Winters Doctrine to claim an unlimited amount of water from the San Juan, Aspinall included an amendment stipulating that water shortages would be shared by all users. Reluctantly, the

Navajos agreed to waive their preferential rights as the price for obtaining this much-desired legislation.[84]

In March 1962, as Colorado's and New Mexico's projects awaited action of the Rules Committee preliminary to House floor debate, Aspinall announced that he was prepared to "pull out all the stops this year to get favorable action" on the Fryingpan bill.[85] He believed the Appropriations committees of Congress would agree to not more than $400–$600 million in new reclamation projects over a two-year period. Both pending measures would amount to approximately $391 million, well within that limit.[86] After overcoming eastern-based opposition within the Rules Committee, the measures' supporters prepared carefully for action in the House chamber.

In mid-May 1962, on the week before the scheduled House vote, New Mexico Governor Edwin Mechem and State Engineer Steve Reynolds arrived in Washington to join a contingent of Navajo Indian leaders and the New Mexico congressional delegation. In a carefully organized campaign, these advocates went to work on likely pockets of congressional opposition. Their major tactical objective was to have the bill passed without a roll call vote.[87] This would retain the passive support of lower basin and California members who were in no position to appear on the record favoring legislation so apparently beneficial to the upper basin. Anderson later expressed his admiration for the effectiveness of his state's Republican governor and lieutenant governor in convincing key House Republicans that this was not a "political issue." He also greatly respected the Navajos' lobbying skills. A number of House members told Anderson they would announce their support for the bill if he would "call off the Indians."[88]

On May 23, 1962, Anderson walked to the House chamber to observe the final vote and to do what he could to calm any wavering members. When Speaker John McCormack (D-MA) put the question as to whether there was sentiment for a roll call vote, thirty-five hands rose. The Speaker later told Anderson, "I gave them an honest count, but a fast count." Deeming that an insufficient expression of interest in a recorded vote, the Speaker called the question and pronounced the bill passed.[89]

Anderson did not like the House amendments but feared if the Senate insisted on its earlier version, the resulting conference between the two bodies would give House opponents another chance to kill the bill.[90] Accordingly, he urged the Senate to yield. In doing so, however, Anderson added to the record of the measure's legislative history his own reservations. He warned that the ten-year moratorium on surplus crop production and a provision arranging for affirmative congressional review of water delivery contracts created unwelcome new precedents.[91] Nonetheless, he expediently determined that those actions had enough basis in past reclamation policy to warrant their acceptance. Both Anderson and Aspinall recognized that time was running out on the Eighty-seventh Congress and that further delay could be fatal. The Senate agreed to Anderson's recommendation and quickly accepted the House version.[92] On June 13, 1962, the House passed Colorado's Fryingpan measure and President Kennedy signed New Mexico's Navajo–San Juan act. Within a month the Senate Interior Committee approved the Fryingpan bill. It quickly passed the Senate and received the President's signature.[93]

Newspapers in New Mexico reflected the state's jubilation over the economic benefits of the long-desired legislation. *The Albuquerque Tribune* carried a representative headline, "Grand Design for New Mexico: Anderson's Water Battle Long One."[94] At the height of his legislative effectiveness as the Eighty-seventh Congress drew to a close late in 1962, Anderson could reflect with satisfaction on the application of his political power and skills in the service of his state's water needs. He had successfully steered the Navajo–San Juan legislation past competing New Mexico interests, past antagonistic Colorado and California officials, into the national legislative arena. There, from his cockpit in the Senate Interior Committee, Anderson singlehandedly propelled his measure to enactment using arguments based, as appropriate, on statistical analysis, cost effectiveness, national defense, Indian treaty obligations, and resources conservation. Anderson saved his shots. He was not accustomed to launching trial balloons. When he spoke, his colleagues listened. When he decided that New Mexico could gain no more by prolonged debate, he settled for the best package available. When he attached to a legislative measure the full weight of his intellect and prestige, doubting solons set aside their skepticism, and he prevailed.

# 9
# Water Resources for the Nation
*Senatorial Initiative,
1955–1964*

I hope this assurance will permit you to sign the Water
Resources Research bill because it has been very close to my
heart for several years, and I would hate to lose it after the
long fight I have made for it.

Clinton P. Anderson to
Lyndon B. Johnson
July 8, 1964

Authorization and funding of the Navajo–San Juan projects marked
the culmination of Anderson's active campaign to associate critical
water needs of his state with regional and national well being. His
success in weaving local imperatives into the fabric of the country's military and economic self sufficiency came in the face of
strongly entrenched contradictory interests at the local, regional,
and national levels. At approximately the same time Anderson engineered another state-federal linkage. In this instance, however,
he focused principally on the nationwide benefits of water resources
planning and development. Although he saw that New Mexico got
its fair share of those benefits, Anderson's chief concern rested with
the nation's long range ability to command water supplies essential to sustained and secure growth. In casting for solutions at the
national level, he drew not only on his New Mexico experience,
but also on a vast body of concern and experience among western
states and their congressional representatives in dealing with wa-

ter scarcity. Anderson's overriding legislative genius lay in his ability to provide a constructive linkage between western issues and national issues to the greater benefit of both constituencies.

In the late 1950s, as the nation at large began to experience water supply crises similar to those endemic to the West, Anderson used his position as chairman of the Senate's Irrigation and Reclamation Subcommittee to intensify the search for enduring national solutions. He envisioned a program of legislative and administrative remedies that incorporated basic and applied research, construction of new basin-wide facilities and, most essentially, a more vigorous role for the federal government of coordination and funding. Anderson also looked to creation of new supplies through cost effective desalinization programs. Viewed across the perspective of a quarter century, his initiatives were noteworthy not for their uniform success, for some have yet to be fully proven, but for the consistency with which they nourished creative new programs from the laboratory of the West's experience.

Widespread water shortages plagued the nation during 1957. Water taps ran dry in Emporia, Kansas and Dallas Texas. Residents of New York City and Orange, New Jersey, struggled with severe curtailments.[1] A year later the Eisenhower administration, in a perplexing display of poor timing, announced a "no new starts" policy that threatened to end all federal assistance for water supply project construction.[2] Democratic political strategists seized on this policy as a major campaign issue in the light of predictions that the nation's water consumption would expand by fifty percent over the next fifteen years. Although the administration may have had sound technical reasons for its policy shift, it would have difficulty explaining them against the specter of 1930s dust bowl conditions. A chronic problem for western states suddenly loomed as a national nightmare.[3]

Montana's Mike Mansfield, assistant Democratic leader of the Senate, set political machinery in motion to respond to this problem at the start of the 1959 congressional session. With the endorsement of the Conference of Western Senators, he introduced legislation to establish a fact finding Senate Select Committee on National Water Resources. The seven-member panel would have two years to survey "the amount, the character, and the timing of water resources development necessary to meet the national requirements by 1980." Its final report would be due on January 31, 1961, just in time for a new, and presumably Democratic, administration to implement its recommendations.[4]

As chairman of the Senate Interior Committee's Subcommittee on Irrigation and Reclamation, Clinton Anderson had principal jurisdiction over the Mansfield proposal as well as over any legislative recommendations such a panel might formulate. Mansfield sought Anderson's assistance in obtaining prompt clearance for the select committee and he asked him to consider serving as its chairman. Anderson agreed to facilitate the resolution, but told Mansfield that Dennis Chavez (D), New Mexico's senior senator, had a better claim as chairman of the Public Works Committee. Chavez, whose relations with Anderson were correct but less than cordial, jealously guarded his prerogatives and could be expected to meet his junior colleague's appointment with hostility. Mansfield was unwilling to consider Chavez, whose battle with throat cancer and other health problems left him little energy for such initiatives. Anderson then suggested Oklahoma's Robert Kerr (D), whose seniority equaled his own. He knew that Kerr was eager for a full committee chairmanship.[5] As former governor of a state once famous for its dust storms, Kerr had ample experience in water resources management, and he could be counted on to keep the needs of his state and region well in mind.

The popularity of the select committee among the Senate's newly enlarged Democratic majority became evident as the measure establishing it was amended to include three members each from the committees on Agriculture, Interior, Commerce, and Public Works, all having related jurisdictional interests. To provide regional balance, five eastern and midwestern senators were added, as well as Interior Committee chairman James Murray (D-MT), bringing Mansfield's originally trim seven-member panel to a structurally and geographically expanded body of seventeen.[6] Interior Committee members included Anderson, Henry Jackson (D-WA) and assistant Republican floor leader Thomas Kuchel (CA).

With Robert Kerr as chairman, the Select Committee spent the remainder of 1959 recruiting a small staff and commissioning studies by various federal, state, and private agencies. Shortly after Congress recessed for the year in September, the panel began a series of twenty-two field hearings in nineteen states, gathering more than three thousand pages of testimony from over eight hundred witnesses. Chairman Kerr, rising to the task, attended nearly all of the hearings, including one in Albuquerque just before Thanksgiving.[7]

Anderson opened that session warning of a "clear and unmistakable need for an early meeting of the minds on a coordinated national program" of water resource development. "I fear," he said, "that we in America have indulged ourselves in gross waste of our limited water resources, waste similar to that which we have experienced in the case of some of our other natural resources."[8] The four-hour hearing provided Anderson an opportunity for a full-scale review of New Mexico's water problems in the context of past or proposed federally sponsored solutions. He reminded Kerr, a valuable Senate ally, of New Mexico's progress and continuing needs. State Engineer Steve Reynolds rendered a characteristically authoritative statement of New Mexico's efforts to salvage up to one-third of its water from such nonbeneficial uses as channel losses and transpiration by uneconomic vegetation. Reynolds pointed out that the state's population had increased by fifty percent over the past nine years and that it was expected to increase another 150 percent by 1980.[9] The problem for New Mexico lay in the character of the population shift, away from agricultural pursuits toward those requiring greater amounts of municipal and industrial water supplies.[10] Reynolds added that ninety-three percent of the state's water was then devoted to irrigation. To double the amounts available for municipal and industrial use, the state would need only to reduce the irrigation allotment by seven percent.[11]

Aside from helping to compile a full record at the Albuquerque hearing, Anderson took little direct role in the Select Committee's routine work. When Kerr asked his opinion on staff selection, he diplomatically conceded that he would be content to follow the chairman's lead, noting, "The best job I have done for the water supply of America is to get out and let you take this on because you'll do a fine job on it."[12]

Anderson's attitude shifted markedly late in 1960, following his own successful reelection campaign and that of the Democratic presidential ticket. Kerr set December 10 for the drafting subcommittee to make its final adjustments to the committee's report. Anderson found the draft poorly written and lacking in focus. He and other members were disturbed that the draft omitted specific and forceful legislative recommendations. Senator Gale McGee (D-WY) agreed and suggested that the committee hire a professional writer to increase the report's clarity and impact, removing the cloak of obscurity from the study's most interesting revelations.[13]

At a more substantive level, Anderson became upset over an assertion in the draft that federal ownership claims over unappropriated waters in western states tended to "retard state plans and projects for development of their own water resources to meet local needs and conditions."[14] Recalling that Solicitor General J. Lee Rankin had once testified against such a position, Anderson asked Rankin for a statement of what he remembered to be Rankin's "very wonderful attitude" on the matter.[15] At the December drafting session Anderson read into the record Rankin's entire nine-page response in support of the need for federal supremacy in control of unappropriated waters within individual states. Anderson recommended that the committee "would do well to put a little of Rankin's analysis in the report instead of this awful language that must have come from [California water lobbyist] Northcut Ely. No one else would write this." When a colleague suggested that Thomas Kuchel might have submitted that language, so openly supportive of California's claims on unappropriated Colorado River water, Anderson responded that his close friend Kuchel was "too sensible a person to be the original author of that much sin."[16] He recalled that Kuchel had once agreed with Ely's idea that states should have individual jurisdiction within their segments of river basins, but that the California senator had "finally calmed down" when he realized that the Senate Interior Committee was not going to recommend legislation requiring the federal government to put up several hundred million dollars and support the Ely theory. In Anderson's words, Kuchel "took the several hundred million and surrendered the principle. Now it is back in here again."[17] Agreeing that on the subject of federal-state water jurisdictional relations, "the less said the better," Kerr and Anderson removed the offending passage.[18]

In the midst of his campaign for House passage of the San Juan–Chama transmountain diversion, Anderson reacted strongly to the draft report's negative appraisal of such interbasin transfers. It characterized them as so "fraught with legal, financial and political problems of such great magnitude, that they can not be considered as a major solution to problems of unequal water distribution."[19] Staff director Theodore Schad promised Anderson a more positive statement.

Anderson's final major grievance with the draft involved the practice of mixing, in a single budget, figures for long term capital investment and routine operating expenses. He resorted to a familiar theme, used extensively in congressional floor debate by western members who wished to assure eastern and urban colleagues that water project costs were actually loans, repayable with interest over a project's lifetime. At a time when the Eisenhower administration, in its campaign for a balanced budget, sought to kill projects priced as low as $50,000, Anderson recognized the value of separate bookkeeping for a capital investment program likely to cost $10 billion. Such investments, in Anderson's view, were "the most productive things the federal government can do for its people."[20]

The Select Committee released its final report on schedule in January 1961. Although the Senate had appropriated $325,000 to complete the study, the panel spent less than $100,000, borrowing heavily from existing staff resources of other Senate committees and federal agencies. It published thirty-two separate background papers drawing together nearly one hundred reports by federal, state, and private groups. On balance, Anderson felt disappointed that Kerr had failed to develop the committee as an aggressive instrument for promoting basic research in the nation's water resources. He concluded Kerr used the panel as "a device for drumming up support for heavier federal expenditures in western water projects."[21]

The Select Committee predicted that the nation's water demands would double by 1980 and triple by the year 2000. Accordingly, it recommended a three-pronged approach that included construction of additional storage facilities, more effective conservation and use of existing supplies, and development of new sources through programs of desalinization, weather modification and other artificial means. To achieve these broad goals, the panel specified five federal policy actions focusing on improved federal-state coordination of river basin development and management. To stimulate cooperation, the committee urged Congress to approve a ten-year program of water resources planning grants to states and accelerated federal research into all phases of water use and development. Through the end of the century, the entire program called for an expenditure of more than $80 billion.[22]

Chairman Kerr had originally intended to let the select committee's study reports speak for themselves, without specific recommendations. Panel members Frank Moss (D-UT), Clair Engle (D-CA),

Gale McGee, and Philip Hart (D-MI) strongly disagreed, urging the committee to recommend a "crash program" of pollution abatement research as well as accelerated construction of municipal water supply systems, navigation facilities, irrigation projects and hydroelectric power plants.[23] Anderson, anticipating his elevation to chairmanship of the Interior Committee, took a more active role in the select committee's final days, as indicated by his involvement in the work of the subcommittee charged with drafting the final report. He convinced Kerr to include general recommendations and laid plans for specific legislative remedies.[24]

In April 1961 Anderson introduced his Water Resources Planning Act. Staff of the Senate Interior Committee fashioned the bill to address the second of the select committee's five specific recommendations. It provided for a ten-year grant-in-aid program funded at $5 million per year to assist states in preparing long range water development programs. The measure's preamble affirmed the primacy of state initiative in planning, but its text made clear that close federal review would be expected in return for annual grants of up to $200,000. Anderson believed that a decade would be sufficient time for states to achieve significant planning progress, and he expected that each state could use the funding to hire up to ten professional engineers, economists, or planners.[25]

On July 10 Anderson conducted a two-hour hearing on his bill. He introduced letters from twenty-six state governments, most of whom favored his proposal. Anderson noted with pleasure the interest of eastern and mid-western states in matters that had been the traditional concern of the West. A memorandum from New Mexico State Engineer Steve Reynolds reflected the advanced level of western state preparation in response to that concern. Reynolds noted that there was little in the Anderson bill likely to be of direct benefit to his state, where planning programs were well under way.[26] Spencer Smith of the Citizens' Committee on Natural Resources took issue with the measure's language supporting state primacy in resources planning, observing that it should heavily underscore the dominant position of the national government.[27] Anderson sought to draw what he believed to be an essential distinction between federal aid for site evaluation and construction on one hand, and the states' rights to control allocation of the resulting water resources.[28]

On the day of the Senate committee hearing, Anderson learned that the Kennedy administration planned to submit an expanded version of his own bill, encompassing three additional recommendations of the select committee. The president, in his February 19 natural resources message, endorsed the select committee's call for coordinated river basin planning programs. His proposed bill provided for a Federal Water Resources Council as well as commissions for each of the nation's major river basins. The council's membership would include the secretaries of Interior, Agriculture, Defense and the Department of Health, Education and Welfare.[29]

Anderson immediately became suspicious of the proposed council, seeing it as a vehicle for a renewed Budget Bureau campaign to wrest control of natural resources planning from cabinet agencies. Although he had succeeded three months earlier in killing a proposed executive order that would have expanded the bureau's role, Anderson believed that bureau director Elmer Staats had not slackened his efforts to achieve that goal.[30] Senior officials in various executive agencies reinforced his concerns by privately referring to the measure as the "Elmer Staats bill," in recognition of the director's likely influence over any such interdepartmental committee.[31]

Hearings on the revised administration bill began shortly after Anderson announced he would set aside his own measure in deference to the president.[32] He questioned Interior Secretary Udall, for the record, on the relationship between the proposed council and Budget Bureau, recalling the adverse impact of the notorious December 1952 Budget Circular A-47. That document had been used to ill effect by successive administration budget directors as basis for evaluating costs associated with multiple purpose water projects. It had become synonymous with redirection of Interior Department objectives by bureau personnel so lacking in subject expertise that in Anderson's view, they "would not know a cow from an elephant."[33] Udall assured him that the council would strengthen his agency's position against the ill effects of A-47, although it would not eliminate Budget Bureau involvement. Jocularly, he offered to burn the offending document, and Anderson agreed they would enjoy the funeral oration.[34]

When U.S. Chamber of Commerce representatives testified in opposition to the council, Anderson bristled. They argued that it would "nationalize all water resources planning and development," depriving states of control of water and related land areas.[35] Anderson exploded, "This is the type of testimony that always bothers me, because you know that is not what the bill means. But in order to try to get a newspaper story out of it, to take a slap at it, you go into something that you know is a distorted opinion of the bill."[36] When the witness unwisely persisted, claiming a trend among federal agencies to interfere with state water allocation activities, Chairman Anderson asked him to be specific. "I am afraid I can't, Senator." "I am afraid you can't either," retorted Anderson. "You can not do it this afternoon, you can not do it tomorrow afternoon."[37] When the flustered witness later wrote Anderson, citing two court decisions allegedly upholding federal powers over state allocation rights, the senator referred the letter to the Attorney General for review. The response confirmed Anderson's view that "neither of the mentioned cases could in any way change the power of the states 'to allocate, to take water,' nor was either brought for such a purpose."[38]

Threat of federal domination through the Water Resources Council and regional control through river basin commissions generated a huge volume of state-based pressure on Congress and the administration to sidetrack the Water Resources Planning bill. Accordingly, when hearings concluded in August, Anderson made no attempt to have his committee act on the measure. The Kennedy administration similarly dropped its push for action. Interior Secretary Udall briefly considered a proposal to establish a departmental Water Research Bureau, but abandoned the idea for lack of congressional sanction. Then, to the secretary's surprise, the president took steps to set up an informal water resources council, naming Udall as chairman.[39]

Ben Stong, the Senate Interior Committee's water expert, emerged as a leading candidate for the position of council staff director. Representatives of three cabinet secretaries contacted him within days of the President's decision. Stong told Anderson that he would be interested in the job if the senator thought it was a good move and if he could be convinced that the Budget Bureau would not dominate the council. Stong sought to strengthen the case for his leaving by reporting that there were two other possible candidates. One was an employee of the Army Corps of Engineers, suggesting an orientation not altogether compatible with the aims of the Interior Department's Reclamation Bureau. The other was rumored to be Elmer Staats, who allegedly had the original draft of the Water Resources Planning bill amended to increase the salary of the Council director in the event he needed a "featherbed to land on if the

Budget job got too hot for him"[40] Anderson responded in a curiously equivocal fashion, considering the value of Stong's expertise to the Interior Committee. He told committee staff director Jerry Verkler that the decision was up to Stong and that "it would be nice to have him in this water planning work."[41] Undoubtedly, the senator realized that he would continue to benefit from Stong's counsel regardless of his decision. Also, Anderson characteristically refused to acknowledge his dependence on any staff member, particularly in matters as familiar to him as water resources policy.

Stong never had to make his decision. The Kennedy administration spent its energies elsewhere early in 1962, particularly in foreign policy crises and in a continuation of its costly confrontation with the old-guard leadership of the House Rules Committee in an effort to clear a logjam of its priority legislation.[42] For a while, presidential advisors suggested establishing the council and the river basin planning commissions by executive order. This plan foundered on House Interior Committee chairman Wayne Aspinall's insistence that the commission receive explicit congressional approval. Natural resources advisor Lee White suggested to Stong that Anderson might use his influence with Aspinall to change the latter's mind, at least with respect to the council.[43]

With action on water planning legislation temporarily sidetracked, Anderson turned his attention to a recommendation of the water resources select committee that the Kennedy administration submit to Congress by January 1962 a review of the existing water research programs and recommendations for future expansion. In his February 1961 natural resources message, the president had told Congress of his request to the National Academy of Sciences for a broadly based study of "the present state of research underlying conservation, development, and use of natural resources."[44] Kennedy also pledged to direct his Council for Science and Technology to review federal research activities in these fields. In mid-1962, presidential resources advisor Lee White confessed to Stong that he had lost track of these studies.[45] Stong told Anderson that when White got around to checking on their progress, he would find that "the Water Resources Subcommittee of the Council on Science and Technology has rejected three drafts of a report . . . and expects to meet again in late July or August [1962] to consider a fourth draft." Stong continued, "He will find that the Academy Research Council expects to hold a meeting 'in a month or so' on its recommendations."[46]

Columnist Neal Peirce once dubbed Anderson "one of the most creative legislators ever to serve in Congress."[47] With regard to water research, Anderson paradoxically exercised his creative powers through direct imitation. In July 1962 he introduced a bill whose basic language was seventy-five years old.[48] The Hatch Act of 1887 established agricultural experiment stations at the nation's land grant colleges. This measure over the years had become enormously successful and was particularly popular with conservative rural legislators. In drafting his research bill, Anderson followed his favorite tactic of grafting a new program onto an existing and proven bureaucratic structure. He had used a similar ploy in suggesting that the controversial Medicare program be administered within the Social Security Administration to avoid creation of a costly separate bureaucracy. He anticipated that a proposal to establish a handful of regional centers would face opposition from members whose states were not included. By following the land grant college model, Anderson hoped to capitalize on a ready-made constituency of university officials and their supporters in Congress to goad a quiescent administration into constructive action.[49] He also intended the model to underscore the partnership quality of the federal-state relationship in water resources research, a relationship that many state officials, in view of their recent experience with the water planning bill, were beginning to fear was tending in the direction of Washington.

Title I of Anderson's imitative measure authorized an appropriation of $75,000 to each state, increasing to $100,000 by the third year and extending over a decade. With these funds, states were to establish within their designated land grant institution a college-wide water research institute. Additional funds would be available, up to a total of $5 million each year, for the Secretary of the Interior to distribute to match state, local, or donated funds for specific research projects at these institutes. Title II would establish a Water Resources Service in the Interior Department, similar to the Agriculture Department's Cooperative State Experiment Station Service, to administer the program.[50]

Anderson had been a consistent supporter of coordinated basic research since his days as Secretary of Agriculture. He recalled his efforts to establish a research bureau within that agency. On one occasion he learned of two university-sponsored research investigations into the dyeing characteristics of irrigated cotton as opposed to the rainbelt variety. The department's contribution to the effort was merely to inform both projects of the other's existence with the suggestion that they might wish to compare notes.[51] His later experience with legislation to establish saline water conversion and weather modification research programs intensified his belief in university-based basic and applied research. Anderson argued that any private industry that allocated as small a portion of its development expenditures to supporting basic research as the federal government did in the water field would be in serious trouble. Even his bill, with its maximum $20 million annual appropriation for research, would only amount to two percent of the $10 billion the federal government was then spending for water development. Combining all public and private outlays for water development, the research investment would amount to only two-tenths of one percent.[52]

As background for Anderson's bill, staff of the Senate Interior Committee sent a draft of that measure to more than one hundred state universities, foundations, corporations and individuals involved in water research. A majority of the respondents lauded the measure, noting that the field was becoming increasingly fragmented and specialized. Tied to their support for accelerated research was a call for intensified training programs to meet "a genuine shortage of well qualified personnel for water resources planning, research, and administration."[53] In land grant colleges, Anderson had found an apparently ideal environment for blending research, training and outreach to ultimate users along the agricultural experiment station and extension service model.

Anderson waited until the start of the Eighty-eighth Congress in January 1963 before launching his campaign for Senate approval of the water research bill. He obtained a coveted low number—S.2—for the measure and set hearings for mid-February. As expected, the National Academy of Sciences and the Federal Council for Science and Technology hastened their reviews and pronounced the Anderson bill highly acceptable.[54] Affected cabinet agencies, with the notable exceptions of the Agriculture Department and Budget Bureau, signalled their approval. In opposition, Agriculture Secretary Orville Freeman argued that the bill would "complicate" his department's longstanding relationship with land grant colleges. Citing more than a half century of departmental experience in water research and watershed management, Freeman also took issue with the Interior Department's role as prime coordinator of such research.[55] The Budget Bureau also disagreed with the "coordination" function for Interior, presumably wishing to retain that activity for itself.[56]

The revised bill differed in one significant respect from the 1962 discussion draft. Title II included authority for the Interior Secretary to make grants to water research centers in addition to land grant colleges. Five million dollars would be available in the first year and would increase to $10 million by the program's fifth year. Anderson recognized that many states, including his own, had several centers of water research competence.[57] This was particularly true when the field was broadly defined to include economic and social considerations of water allocation and development. Economist Nathaniel Wollman of the University of New Mexico supplied a timely reinforcement of Anderson's point in his late 1962 study of comparative economic values of water in alternative uses. He found that water from the San Juan–Chama project used for recreation would add up to five times as much to New Mexico's gross product as if it had been used for irrigation agriculture. If used by industry, according to Wollman, that same water would increase the state's gross product by as much as fifteen times more than if used for recreation. New thinking on optimal combinations of water uses was clearly in order.[58]

Public hearings on Anderson's bill opened before the Senate Interior Committee on February 19, 1963. That session marked Anderson's final appearance as chairman and the arrival of three new committee members—one a fifty-year congressional veteran, the others freshmen with significant prior experience as conservationists. With particular satisfaction, Anderson welcomed Appropriations Committee chairman Carl Hayden to committee membership, recalling his own experience as a House member in the early 1940s. He reminded Hayden that whenever a big city delegation managed to remove a provision dear to western members, "we would get together around the crying towel and cry a little bit, and then we would would say, 'Well, Senator Hayden will put it back in.'" Anderson added, "He almost always did."[59] Accompanying Hayden were newly elected Senators George McGovern (D-SD) and Gaylord Nelson (D-WI).

The Senate committee received predictably supportive testimony on Anderson's research bill from Interior Secretary Udall and representatives of the nation's land grant colleges. The Agriculture De-

partment sent the director of its Cooperative State Experiment
Station Service to object to an increased role for the Interior Department. Anderson assured him that the latter agency would act
simply as collector of information, rather than as active coordinator. He cited the experience of the Agriculture Department, in the
wake of the 1946 Agriculture Research Act, of not intruding into
established programs of other federal agencies. Anderson pledged
that Interior would have no involvement with the Department of
Health, Education and Welfare's water pollution control activities
or with traditional research programs of the Agriculture Department.[60] Spencer Smith of the Citizens' Committee on Natural Resources captured the hearing's generally upbeat tone in observing
that upon turning the nation's water problems over to state colleges, "we will soon have enough water surpluses to match our
grain surpluses in storage."[61]

Floor debate on Anderson's water research bill began on April
22, 1963, two months after Interior Committee hearings concluded.
Majority Leader Mansfield took the opportunity to announce the
forthcoming conservation testimonial dinner in Anderson's honor.
He underscored the reasons for the dinner by observing that the
pending measure was Anderson's third major piece of legislation to
come to the Senate floor at such an early point in the congressional
session. The first two, the Wilderness Act and the Outdoor Recreation Act, had passed quickly and with decidedly large margins.[62]

Anderson presented a near classic case for the bill's passage. In
his brief opening statement, he demonstrated that there existed a
crisis of broad national proportions. As he had noted on introducing his measure in January, "We are right now eye-ball to eye-ball
with shortages, and in many areas we cannot afford enough time to
blink. We must invest in water development and research or stag-
nate."[63] Having described the crisis, Anderson moved swiftly to an
exposition of the proposed solution. Of greatest importance to the
Senate, an institution that gave great weight to actions enmeshed
in precedent, was the bill's kinship to the 1887 Hatch Act, a statute
that had weathered the storms of 75 years. Finally, the measure
bore the seal of approval of a consensus-building Senate study group,
the Select Committee on National Water Resources. The main criticism of that panel's work had been its lack of bold, imaginative,
and immediate recommendations. Anderson's proposal more than
filled that deficiency. By waiting to schedule hearings as long as

seven months after introducing the "study bill" in July 1962, Anderson forced the Kennedy administration to fulfill its commitment to have prestigious national advisory panels evaluate the specific proposal. On April 22, 1963, he was able to stand on the Senate floor and announce that his bill had been "strongly endorsed" not only by the federal agencies whose work formed the basis of the select committee's report, but by the National Academy of Sciences and the Federal Council for Science and Technology.[64] To these impressive credentials, the New Mexican added the measure's "modest cost," its emphasis on research and training at a time of rapidly escalating national commitment to higher education, and its contribution to the welfare of every state in the union. Finally, Anderson pointed to a wide spectrum of support from soil and water organizations, conservationists, the League of Women Voters, and conservative Republican senators. Even the U.S. Chamber of Commerce, seldom an ally of federal involvement in local matters, added its qualified endorsement.[65] After two days of debate, in which the most serious threat to the measure came from Colorado's Gordon Allott, who tried unsuccessfully to limit the program's budget and lifespan, the measure passed by voice vote.[66]

The Kennedy administration's 1961 Water Resources Planning bill had drawn mixed reviews. Officials within the Interior Department pushed for the concept of a coordinating body housed within that agency. Senate Interior Committee members and individual states supported strongly the provision of a ten-year $5 million annual matching fund for state water resources planning. The greatest controversy surrounded Title II, authorizing the president to establish river basin planning commissions. Members of the commissions, as proposed in the original Kennedy bill, would be appointed by the president on recommendation of governors of the affected states. A similar proposal had been offered in the waning days of the Eisenhower administration, so Anderson and its other supporters felt safe in declaring the measure to be broadly bipartisan.[67]

More than a half century earlier, on February 3, 1908, President Theodore Roosevelt's Inland Waterways Commission recommended "prompt and vigorous action" by federal and state governments to develop comprehensive plans for the nation's river basins.[68] In 1962, Clinton Anderson stood in the vanguard of a legislative campaign to convert that ancient commission's recommendations to reality.

With the notable exception of the Tennessee Valley Authority in the 1930s, river basin development had proceeded on a piecemeal basis, victimized by federal and state squabbling over respective rights and jurisdictions.[69]

The draft legislation may have appealed to leaders of both political parties at the national level, but no such harmony existed between that level and state governments. Through the Interstate Conference on Water Problems, a unit of the Council of State Governments, states objected vigorously to the nature and mechanics for establishing individual river basin commissions. Specifically, they took issue with the provision allowing a single state within a basin to initiate action to establish a basin-wide planning commission. They contended that two-thirds of the involved states should participate in such an action. Secondly, states argued that governors rather than the president should have the power to appoint commissioners, who would then be loyal to individual states and not the powers in Washington.[70]

To air states' grievances, Anderson convened a second committee hearing in March 1962. There, representatives of various states presented an extensive revision of the proposed bill. Several committee members believed this would amount to a complete surrender of federal prerogatives in the water field. Anderson viewed with disdain extremists on both sides of the issue, charging that those who would "prefer to waste our water resources than to concede a drop of authority of jurisdiction to their antagonist . . . are hopelessly behind the times."[71] He argued that water within a river basin cannot be reasonably separated into "state water" and "federal water" for which separate plans exist. Water planning, in his view, should be an engineering matter, not a political contest. Accordingly, he endorsed revised legislation that emerged from numerous federal-state discussions during 1962.

Anderson introduced the revised bill in the Senate on March 15, 1963. The only significant alteration came in Title II, concerning the appointment of basin commissions. Under that title, the president would establish a basin commission when the Federal Water Resources Council and one-half the involved states agreed to it. The president would appoint representatives of participating federal agencies, and the states would name their own representatives. The chairman, designated by the president, would have one of the two votes permitted each commission. The vice chairman, elected by the commission's state representatives, would have the other vote. If commissions failed to reach agreement on substantive matters, the issues would be referred to the involved states, and to the president and Congress for resolution. Anderson believed that such referrals would be rare, for "if studies are done thoroughly, then the facts make the decisions—not philosophical points of view."[72]

Ben Stong did not think much of the proposed river basin commissions, believing they would be only slightly less cumbersome than existing interstate compact organizations. He saw them rather as the price to be paid to salvage Anderson's original legislation providing for a state matching grants program and a coordinating Federal Water Resources Council. Where the basin commissions failed to work, traditional routes would still be available. They included commissions specifically authorized by Congress, interagency committees, Interior Department and Army reports to Congress, and action by the proposed water resources council.[73]

Budget Bureau chief Elmer Staats opposed the Anderson revision, preferring the original administration bill with its greater federal role. Staats specifically wanted to place control of river basin planning with the Army Corps of Engineers. To do so would require a total estimated appropriation for that agency of $400 million. That figure included funds for additional planning in Louisiana, where powerful Senate Agriculture Committee chairman Allen Ellender thought that planning had been completed and projects were ready to be constructed. Ben Stong reported to Anderson that Ellender's resulting unhappiness and the large amount of anticipated funding for the Engineer Corps would defeat Staats's strategy.[74]

Staats's opposition, in the face of favorable reports from the departments of Agriculture and the Army, deepened Anderson's animosity towards the budget director. The Senate Interior Committee could not move ahead on the legislation until it received reports from key federal agencies. Staats held up their transmission while attempting to convince the Interior Department, whose concurrence was vital, to recommend deletion of the basin planning provisions of Title II.[75] Representatives of state government water agencies refused to agree to Staats' demand that they compromise in advance of Senate hearings, arguing that the governors or key water officials of forty states had already endorsed the revised measure. These representatives felt that Staats was being presumptuous in his promise that the bill would not move without his agency's clearance.[76] Growing impatient, Interior Committee Chairman Jackson asked Ben Stong in early August to see if Anderson would be willing to begin hearings without agency reports. Stong advised Anderson to defer to Senator Frank Moss, who was reportedly willing, if not eager, to handle the measure then resting before the Subcommittee on Irrigation and Reclamation.[77] All parties agreed and the hearings began on September 12, 1963.

The Moss hearings proceeded smoothly with a broad range of support registered by states and water-related organizations.[78] The most notable departure came in testimony from the National Association of Manufacturers. Its representatives attacked the measure, but Chairman Moss, in his questioning, made clear that the attack had been prepared for the discarded earlier version, and that the Association's witnesses were unaware that a substantively new bill lay before them. Stong called it the "worst job I ever saw them do."[79]

Anderson was not present for the September hearings, but he took over as the bill's Senate floor manager when it was called up for debate on December 4, 1963. He noted that the measure, along with the Senate-passed Water Resources Research bill, would take the recommendations of the Senate Select Committee on National Water Resources one large step closer to fruition. He emphasized that the bill was not intended to alter existing state water rights and that no state could be forced to participate in a basin commission, to pay its expenses, or abide by its decision.[80] The commissions would simply function to draw up water development plans that the states and Congress could accept or reject. After extended debate and the passage of minor amendments, the Senate approved the Anderson bill by voice vote.[81]

Water research and planning legislation in the House lacked the committed leadership that had propelled it through the Senate. Wayne Aspinall, at a moment of strategic importance, observed that supporters of the water research bill "had better get someone more interested in that bill than I am, or it is dead."[82] The river basin planning bill's chief sponsor, Representative Leo O'Brien (D-NY) was the second ranking Democrat on the House Interior Committee, but not a member of the Irrigation Subcommittee that controlled its fate. Subcommittee chairman Walter Rogers (D-TX) supported the measure but, in Ben Stong's judgment, was not well briefed. Additionally, proponents in the Senate had to contend with elements of guerrilla warfare by lower-ranking agency and House committee staff who felt both bills upset existing bureaucratic relationships. On the river planning measure, Stong noted that "subordinates" within the Army Corps of Engineers "aren't behaving" and "we've seen their tracks."[83]

In mid-1963, with the water research bill safely past Senate review, Ben Stong checked with Aspinall's staff about the measure's chances for quick House approval. He learned, not to his surprise, that Aspinall seemed to be resorting to tactics similar to those he used against the Wilderness bill. By complaining that the Senate-passed bill did not bring about coordination of federal water research, he would "raise a related but not actually relevant matter."[84] During summer hearings, Aspinall seemed to be building a case against the Anderson bill by noting that it looked more like an aid to education bill than a research measure and accordingly should be referred to another committee.[85] He also remarked that providing funds for basic research would not solve the problem of attracting competent professionals to select water research as a career the way that others had been drawn to the fields of atomic energy and space exploration. Finally, Aspinall questioned whether the administrative costs of water programs might not be out of proportion to direct benefits.[86]

Early in 1964 the House Interior Committee accepted the conclusions of its Irrigation and Reclamation Subcommittee and recommended an extensively rewritten version of the Anderson bill. Arguing that research programs should begin modestly, the Committee followed Aspinall's lead in agreeing to limit the program to ten years, to restrict funding to a single land grant college in each state, and to remove coordinating and auxiliary grant making authority from the Interior Secretary's jurisdiction. These recommendations went to the heart of Aspinall's principal objection, that there already existed too much duplication in federal water research and that the bill would promote further division among land grant institutions throughout fifty states. He would not support further "dissipation" of research funds.[87]

Aspinall's attitude became evident late in February 1964 when he appeared before the House Rules Committee seeking clearance for legislation establishing his Public Land Law Review Commission and the Land and Water Conservation Fund. His failure to make a strong case for the water research bill resulted in a 5–3 vote to deny the essential "rule" leading to House floor consideration. Committee Chairman Howard Smith (D-VA) took the license to argue that the program would cost $125 million, failing to mention that the figure represented a ten-year authorization. In Smith's view, that was $50 million too much and the administration's budget contained no provision for such expenditures, so he saw little reason to clear the measure.[88]

Anderson sought to undercut House resistance in several ways. He obtained from Theodore Schad, the Library of Congress' water expert and former staff director of the Senate water resources select committee, an evaluation of the House committee changes. Schad pointed out that a ten-year limitation would make it difficult for state colleges to justify construction of permanent research facilities. Schad's great reservation, however, dealt with House elimination of Title II, providing the Secretary of the Interior with authority to make research grants of up to $10 million per year to institutions and individuals outside of land grant colleges.[89] The Budget Bureau joined Schad in supporting a restoration of Title II, noting that the Interior Department should have the same unrestricted grant authority in the field of water research as was then available to other federal agencies in their fields of responsibility. Accompanying that opinion was a strong repudiation of Rules Committee Chairman Smith's view that the administration's budget contained no provision for the research program. Anderson had sought such assurances, and they accounted for a rare reversal, early in May, of that committee's earlier decision.[90]

Despite Anderson's behind-the-scenes efforts to restore Title II, on June 2 the House passed by voice vote the measure as reported from its committee.[91] Less than a week later, the Senate rejected the House version and appointed Anderson and other Interior Committee members to a joint conference committee. When the conferees met on June 30, Anderson prevailed in his view that the program should be made permanent to encourage the capital investment essential to university-based research. He also succeeded in a partial restoration of Title II. His original version had authorized $5 million in research grants for the first year, increasing to $10 million after the fifth year. The conferees reduced the amount to $1 million per year for ten years, but removed the House stipulation that funds go only to land grant colleges. This would permit the Interior Department, for example, to contract with the New

Mexico School of Mines for weather modification research, although that state's water research center would be located at New Mexico State University. To obtain this concession, Anderson reluctantly agreed to a provision for a legislative veto, allowing either the House or Senate Interior Committees the right to overrule individual grants within a sixty-day period. This raised fundamental separation of power questions, putting legislative committees into activities considered the responsibility of executive agencies.[92]

Shortly after both chambers cleared the compromise version for the president's signature, Anderson learned that the Budget Bureau was considering a recommendation that the president veto the measure because of the Aspinall-inspired committee review provision.[93] That addition had placed Pres. Lyndon Johnson in a difficult position as he had included the bill on his June 23 list of measures that were essential for passage before the end of the congressional session.[94] Anderson told the president that he shared his misgivings and that he would introduce legislation before the end of the session to remove the constitutionally offensive provision. "I hope," said Anderson, "this assurance will permit you to sign the bill because it has been close to my heart for several years, and I would hate to lose it after the long fight I have made for it."[95] At a White House ceremony in mid-July Johnson signed the bill, declaring that although it was "not technically subject to constitutional objection," it violated the "spirit" of separation of power. He paused to pay special tribute to Anderson's "vision and wisdom," noting, "He has long recognized the problems. He developed the program. He guided it through Congress."[96]

Anderson returned to Washington in mid-August following his prostate surgery to preside over Senate-House final negotiations on the Wilderness Act. With those activities brought to a successful conclusion, he wrote to Laurance Rockefeller expressing his pleasure at the prospect of wrapping up the river basin planning bill. That measure, he observed, was "about the last one of our bills that could be called a conservation program."[97] Anderson's hopes went unrealized for this final item in the Eighty-eighth Congress' remarkable conservation record. Time simply ran out in the face of forthcoming election campaigns. Poor attendance crippled the House Interior Committee and forced it to reschedule meetings for the bill's consideration. Finally, on September 2, that panel cleared the river basin planning bill for floor action.[98] A distracted House leadership, its inability to produce necessary quorums, and the intensified pace of the pre-election period doomed the measure. Shortly after final adjournment, Aspinall acknowledged that the House had been "tardy" in its approach to the bill and promised swift action at the beginning of the 1965 session.[99]

Anderson's water research and planning bills provided a well funded, carefully devised mechanism for effective national water conservation. Each measure permitted extensive state and regional discretion in determining solutions of water resource problems. Conversion of saline water, however, was a problem of such magnitude and complexity that Anderson believed it required separate and directed federal encouragement. He recognized that if California had the ability to convert sea water, the Upper Colorado Basin states would be able to claim a much larger share of that river's total flow. Drawing on his experience with legislative programs for atomic energy development, Anderson set out in 1957 to accelerate research in conversion to domestic uses of both sea water and brackish inland supplies. Within a year the president had signed a pathbreaking measure creating five demonstration plants for testing the feasibility of saline water conversion, and by 1961 that legislation received the validation of expanded funding and scope. Once again, Anderson provided the imagination and legislative muscle to ensure realization of two far reaching conservation measures.

Anderson's interest in desalinization extended back to 1951 when he conducted hearings on the extent and nature of research programs.[100] A year later, Congress enacted a $2 million, five-year saline water research program "to provide for the development of practicable low-cost means of producing from sea waters, water of a quality suitable for agriculture, industrial, municipal and other beneficial consumptive uses." At that time existing conversion methods cost approximately four dollars per 1,000 gallons, far in excess of the thirty-five–cent going rate for production and delivery of natural fresh water. Its sponsors, including Anderson, hoped the 1952 program would bring the conversion cost closer to the existing market rate. The act entrusted research coordination to a new Office of Saline Water within the Interior Department.[101]

In 1955 Congress extended the research program through 1963 and increased its funding authorization to $10 million. During that same year Anderson served simultaneously as chairman of the Joint

Committee on Atomic Energy and the Interior Subcommittee on Irrigation and Reclamation. One morning he listened as a nuclear physicist explained to the Joint Atomic Energy panel the use of coolants in atomic reactors. The scientist noted that when water was circulated within a reactor, its temperature rose to 1400° F.[102] That afternoon, a witness told the Irrigation subcommittee of efforts to find an inexpensive source of energy to heat salt water to 1400° F to distill out impurities.[103]

Anderson quickly made the connection. An inquiry to New Mexico's Los Alamos Scientific Laboratory disclosed an existing plan for a facility that would produce a billion gallons of fresh water a day at a cost of only fifteen to twenty-five cents per thousand gallons. The plant's reactor would produce vast amounts of energy at a tiny cost in fuel. The only flaw was the facility's anticipated construction cost—a minimum of $600 million. Anderson recognized that Congress would not subsidize such an effort, despite its great promise, without more specific analytical data. In his judgment, the next most feasible step would be the construction of a large "demonstration" plant to test several promising conversion processes.[104] At that time members of his Irrigation subcommittee realized that no single conversion process would "provide fresh water for all purposes at all locations and under all circumstances."[105] This suggested a dynamic and fast-paced research and development program.

The Interior Department's Office of Saline Water had failed to grasp the challenge, due partly to uninspired leadership, limited funding, and close control from the Eisenhower Interior Department. By 1957 Anderson had become irritated with that Office's apparent unwillingness to move from basic to applied research. Office Director David Jenkins told an inquiring Anderson aide that six years of research had produced no new conversion process capable of supporting a full-scale test in a demonstration plant. He added that the Interior Department would hotly oppose an effort by Anderson to legislate such a test facility.[106]

Not only was Anderson aware of developments at Los Alamos, but several private water research firms were keeping him abreast of their activities. A Boston firm had successfully developed an electric ion exchange membrane system for treating brackish water. Unlike expensive sea water treatment processes requiring the removal of water from salt through distillation, the membrane process withdrew salt ions from water, a less costly task considering the lower salt content of inland brackish water. This process had great potential for the arid southwest, and Anderson became impatient to put it to a larger scale test.[107]

Soviet success in launching the space satellite "Sputnik" in October 1957 and a concurrent announcement by South African scientists of an ionic membrane conversion system capable of producing potable water at 30 cents per thousand gallons intensified Anderson's interest in moving swiftly to counter foreign technological advances.[108] These events failed, however, to dissolve the Interior Department's opposition to demonstration plants. Tired of waiting for cooperation from the Office of Saline Water, Anderson introduced a resolution at the start of the 1958 session authorizing $10 million for the Interior Department to construct and operate a sea water demonstration plant.[109]

At hearings before the Senate Irrigation and Reclamation Subcommittee in mid-March, Interior Department representatives persisted in their opposition, arguing that plans for a demonstration plant were premature and would signal a concentration of effort on two or three promising processes when in fact such processes could not then be positively identified. The Department urged the subcommittee to allow the Office of Saline Water to continue its wide ranging exploratory pattern with existing funds.[110] Anderson responded that a solution to the saline and brackish water problem "is the most important objective in the field of water development that has confronted this country since the enactment of the reclamation law in 1902."[111] He expressed irritation over the last minute cancellation of Interior Secretary Fred Seaton's planned testimony and predicted that agency's "delaying tactics will be obliterated."[112]

After a month's deliberation, Anderson's subcommittee approved a revised version of his original resolution. In unusually strong language suggestive of forthcoming election contests, the panel criticized the Interior Department for lack of determined leadership and called for a new demonstration phase to "be executed with boldness, imagination and urgency—attributes not normally associated with the methodical, painstaking, careful approach required for fundamental research and development."[113] Anderson's original resolution had called for a single sea water demonstration plant. A second measure, sponsored by Senator Francis Case (R-SD) provided for a brackish water plant to be located in the upper Great

Plains, perhaps in South Dakota, the state in which Anderson spent his childhood. As approved by the full Interior Committee, Anderson's resolution was revised to include two sea water plants, one on the Atlantic and one on the Pacific coast. It also provided for two brackish water plants, one in the upper Great Plains and one in the Southwest, perhaps in New Mexico.[114]

Several weeks passed. The Senate's Democratic Policy Committee ignored Anderson's request to clear the bill for floor action. One day Anderson approached Majority Leader Lyndon Johnson to ask about the delay. Johnson responded, "Have you read [the bill]?" Anderson countered, "Hell, of course I read it. I wrote it." Johnson, whose own water interests were well established, retorted in an icy tone, "Well, read it again," and added, "Clint, haven't you ever heard of the Gulf Coast?" Anderson quickly arranged to include a fifth plant in the Gulf Coast region, perhaps Texas, and the measure sped on to the Senate floor where it passed by voice vote in mid-June.[115] The measure moved easily through the House where, as in the Senate, it was viewed as an example of Democratic leadership in the face of Eisenhower administration paralysis. Despite this partisan tone, the measure had attracted many influential Republican supporters, and President Eisenhower reluctantly signed it on September 2, 1958.[116]

Six weeks later Lyndon Johnson wrote Anderson, encouraging his efforts to convince the Interior Department that Texas should have one of the demonstration plants. Johnson added, "With you on the job, I feel much better about the whole project. Since you are the daddy of intelligent water programs in this country, I have a great deal of confidence that your efforts will produce results." Johnson took no chances. Several days later he wrote Anderson again. Said the majority leader, "I know that you will ultimately see that one of these plants will be located in Texas and I have no doubt that you will be as efficient with the Executive Department as you were with Congress when you piloted the bill through both houses."[117] Anderson responded that he would do what he had promised in that connection.[118]

Within six months the Secretary of the Interior had selected five construction sites from among 200 applicants. They included Freeport, Texas; Webster, South Dakota; San Diego, California; Roswell, New Mexico; and Wrightsville Beach, North Carolina. The Texas facility was completed first, in mid-1961, at a cost of $1.2 million.

While it concentrated on distillation techniques, the Roswell plant, the most expensive at $1.8 million, specialized in a process of vapor compression similar to that under study at Los Alamos.[119]

In 1960 Senator Lyndon Johnson sponsored a bill to extend the saline water research program to 1969 and provide $20 million in loans to help local governments finance saline conversion plants. This measure, which passed the Senate in June, would "have made more difficult the foot-dragging-to-save-money procedure that sometimes has characterized" the Interior Department's saline water policy, as an Interior Committee aide reminded Anderson.[120] The bill died in the House, but it set off a flurry of rhetoric during that year's presidential election campaigns as both parties sought to claim credit for their foresight. Ailing Senate Interior Committee chairman James Murray (D-MT) attributed the "Democratic Saline Water Program's" major advances to Anderson, citing his lead in passing the 1958 and 1960 measures.[121] Finally, in the fall of 1961, President Kennedy affixed his signature to a revised version of the 1960 Johnson-Anderson measure. The act extended the life of the five demonstration plants to 1970 and continued basic research programs through June 1967 with a total authorization of $75 million.[122]

With the research program's existence and funding assured and work on construction of the demonstration plant at Roswell, New Mexico underway, Anderson monitored developments within the Interior Department's Office of Saline Water. From time to time, he placed supportive statements in the *Congressional Record* as individual programs made promising gains. His greatest occasion for satisfaction came in March 1964 with release of a report by the President's Office of Science and Technology. Entitled "An Assessment of Large Nuclear Powered Sea Water Distillation Plants," the study concluded that plants combining nuclear electricity generation and desalinization processes could, by 1975, make large quantities of water available in coastal areas "at prices that are reasonable to pay for municipal and industrial purposes."[123] This confirmed Anderson's 1955 inspiration that such a combination would eventually become economically and technically feasible. By midsummer, President Lyndon Johnson added his prestige and power to the study by ordering the Interior Department, the Atomic Energy Commission, and his science office to develop a plan for an "aggressive and imaginative program" to advance the progress of sea water desalinization. Once again, Anderson and Johnson had combined inspiration and power to promote solutions to critical water shortages.[124]

In 1955, the Democratic party regained control of both Houses of Congress. For the decade that followed, water resources policy emanated from Congress, rather than from presidential administrations adrift in a sea of options and conflicting proposals. Clinton Anderson, in association with other well-placed southwestern members such as Carl Hayden and Lyndon Johnson, set the pace for consideration of major water legislation. By the time he became chairman of the Senate Interior Committee in 1961, natural resources policy initiatives stood little chance of success without his approval and support. After 1964, with Johnson in the White House and Anderson in increasingly poor health, policy focus shifted back to the executive branch.

Anderson, to great effect, blended his assets of intelligence, creativity, sense of timing, collegial respect, and his fortunate combination of committee assignments. He appreciated the tactical value of undergirding legislation with scientific research and analysis. He also knew when to call a halt to a study and commence action. Once committed to action, he moved ahead resolutely without becoming ensnared in petty detail or jurisdictional struggles. When the focus of activity moved to executive agencies, he also knew how to watch actively from the legislative sidelines. There is no better summary of Anderson's legislative effectiveness at the state and national levels than his combined campaigns for the Navajo–San Juan projects and for statutes establishing water research and river basin planning on secure foundations.

# Notes

## Preface

1. Clinton P. Anderson, "Changing Public Opinion—As A Legislator Sees It," Address to the Sierra Club Rio Grande Chapter, Santa Fe, New Mexico, November 7, 1964, Clinton P. Anderson Papers, Library of Congress, Box 988.
2. Claude E. Wood to Howard Bray, April 19, 1966, author's files. (Author's files will be donated to the Anderson Papers, Library of Congress.)

## Introduction

1. For a discussion of the institutional constraints during the 1950s and 1960s on Congress's ability to plan and initiate policy reform, see James L. Sundquist, *The Decline and Resurgence of Congress* (Washington, D.C.: Brookings Institution, 1981), pp. 158–60, 190–95.
2. William C. Everhart, *The National Park Service* (New York: Praeger, 1972), p. 182.
3. Samuel T. Dana and Sally K. Fairfax, *Forest and Range Policy* (New York: McGraw-Hill, 1980), p. 81.
4. Sundquist, p. 190.
5. Interview with Maurice Rosenblatt, June 29, 1982.

## Chapter I

1. *Congressional Record* (hereafter cited as *CR*), June 13, 1963, pp. 1069–73; Luna [Diamond] to Lorella [Salazar], May 21, 1963; Clinton P. Anderson Papers, Library of Congress, Washington, D.C. (hereafter cited as AP), Box 437; *Albuquerque Tribune,* May 21, 1963; *Albuquerque*

*Journal,* May 16, 1963; testimonial dinner program in Anderson Scrapbook Collection, Anderson family custody, Albuquerque, NM.

2. Clinton P. Anderson, *Outsider in the Senate* (New York: World Publishing Co., 1970), pp. 3–5. This memoir provides the best single account of Anderson's early years. In April 1957, Anderson began to dictate an account of the major events of his career. He decided to borrow a theme that had impressed him in Colin Wilson's *The Outsider* (Boston: Houghton Mifflin, 1956), noting that Wilson had defined the "outsider" as a "man who can not live in the comfortable, insulated world of the bourgeois, accepting what he sees and touches as reality. He sees too deeply and too much, and what he sees is essentially chaos."("Memo on Material Dealing With My Senate Experiences," author's files). In 1963, Anderson asked his press secretary, Howard Bray, to help him compile a memoir that would be of interest to the senator's grandchildren and would focus on the accomplishments of which he was proudest. Bray worked on the memoir over the next five years, drawing heavily from Anderson's excellent collection of office files and personal papers. Writer Milton Viorst further polished the manuscript for publication in 1970.

3. Anderson, *Outsider,* pp. 5–7; quoted in the *Daily Argus-Leader* [undated clipping from December 1950 in Anderson Scrapbook Collection].

4. Anderson, *Outsider,* p.7.

5. Ibid., pp. 7–8.

6. Ibid., pp. 8–9.

7. Ibid., p. 11.

8. Clinton P. Anderson, "Senator Waited for Patient to Die to Get Room in Sanitarium," *Albuquerque Tribune,* December 5, 1957; Anderson, "The Best Advice I Ever Had," *Reader's Digest,* July 1953, pp. 51–52.

9. Anderson, *Outsider,* pp. 12–13; recollections cited in *Washington Post,* March 14, 1948 and *Albuquerque Journal,* December 2, 1951.

10. The legislative session lasted from January 13, 1919, to March 16, 1919. Typical of Anderson's coverage was a dispatch that appeared in the *Albuquerque Evening Herald,* January 17, 1919, p. 1; Anderson, *Outsider,* pp. 14–17.

11. Anderson, *Outsider,* p. 18; cited in background statement for the Clinton P. Anderson Award, American Lung Association of New Mexico [1983], 216 Truman, N.E., Albuquerque, NM 87108.

12. Morris Werner and John Starr, *Teapot Dome* (New York: Viking Press, 1959), pp. 64–66; David Braaten, "The Teapot Dome Muckraker," *Washington Star,* April 2, 1972. There is some question as to the precise circumstances of this encounter. Anderson confirmed its details to officials of the Albuquerque Rotary Club, but told a *Washington Star* reporter in 1972 that he could not testify to its accuracy.

13. Milton C. Nahm, *Las Vegas and Uncle Joe: The New Mexico I Remember* (Norman: University of Oklahoma Press, 1964), pp. 145–48; Anderson, *Outsider,* pp. 20–21; Interviews with Jack F. Walton, July 23, 1982 and Thomas McCaffrey, July 24, 1982.

14. Anderson, *Outsider,* pp. 20–21; "First American, Inc.," Minute Books,

April 23, 1928–November 25, 1929, Albuquerque Chamber of Commerce, Albuquerque, NM.

15. Anderson, *Outsider,* pp. 222–23; Anderson to Arthur Carhart, January 24, 1964, AP, Box 670; Samuel P. Hays, *Conservation and the Gospel of Efficiency: The Progressive Conservation Movement, 1890–1920* (Cambridge, MA: Harvard University Press, 1959), pp. 1–2.

16. *Albuquerque Evening Herald,* December 12, 1918; Interview with Claude E. Wood, November 20, 1981.

17. *Albuquerque Journal,* November 9, 1928, p. 1 and November 10, 1928, p. 1; *Washington Star,* October 9, 1944.

18. Anderson, *Outsider,* pp. 22–23; *New York Times,* June 22, 1932, p. 41; *Albuquerque Journal,* June 25, 1932. An account of Anderson's participation in the 1931 international convention in Vienna, Austria appears in *CR,* February 27, 1941, pp. A876–78; also cited in article on Anderson, "Human Dynamo," that appeared in numerous Rotary publications including *The Health City Sun,* September 11, 1942, copies in Anderson Scrapbook Collection.

19. Anderson, *Outsider,* p. 27; Interview with Jack F. Walton, July 23, 1982; Arthur Thomas Hannett, *Sagebrush Lawyer* (New York: Pageant Press, 1964), pp. 149–51.

20. Anderson, *Outsider,* pp. 29–30; quoted in *Albuquerque Journal,* December 2, 1951.

21. Interview with Jack F. Walton, July 23, 1982.

22. A spirited exchange on the significance of the 1934 Chavez-Cutting contest appears in William H. Pickens, "Bronson Cutting Vs. Dennis Chavez: Battle of the Patrones in New Mexico, 1934," *New Mexico Historical Review* 46 (January 1971): 5–36 and in T. Phillip Wolf, "Cutting Vs. Chavez Reexamined: A Commentary on Pickens' Analysis," *New Mexico Historical Review* 47 (October 1972): 317–35. Also see William H. Pickens, "Cutting Vs. Chavez: A Reply to Wolf's Comments," *New Mexico Historical Review* 47 (October 1972): 337–59.

23. Anderson, *Outsider,* pp. 32–33.

24. Ibid., pp. 34–35.

25. Ibid., p. 36; *Amarillo [TX] News,* June 30, 1941; *Albuquerque Times-Herald,* January 18, 1942.

26. Anderson, *Outsider,* pp. 36–37.

27. Ibid., pp. 37–38; *CR,* February 18, 1941, pp. 1124–26.

28. Anderson, *Outsider,* pp. 39–40; Alfred Steinberg, *Sam Rayburn* (New York: Hawthorn, 1975), pp. 195–96.

29. Anderson, *Outsider,* pp. 46–50.

30. *Albuquerque Journal,* January 25, 1944; *Albuquerque Tribune,* August 17, 1943; Drew Pearson, "Washington Merry-Go-Round," *Washington Post,* May 29, 1945, p. 2B.

31. U.S., House, Special Committee to Investigate Food Shortages, *Food Shortages,* hearings, April-June 1945, parts 1–3; *New York Times,* March 28, 1945, p. 1; *New York Times,* June 11, 1945, p. 10.

32. "Anderson Has Record Better Than Average," *PM,* May 24, 1945;

*St. Louis Star-Times,* May 23, 1945; *Chicago Tribune,* May 24, 1945; *Santa Fe New Mexican,* May 24, 1945; *Washington Post,* May 24, 1945, p.4.

33. *New York Times,* May 24, 1945, p. 1; David S. McLellan and David C. Acheson, eds., *Among Friends: Personal Letters of Dean Acheson* (New York: Dodd, Mead & Co., 1981), pp. 54–55; Anderson, *Outsider,* p. 57; "Clinton P. Anderson," *Current Biography,* June 1945, pp. 3–5.

34. Anderson, *Outsider,* pp. 94–99; James L. Forsythe, "Clinton P. Anderson: Politician and Businessman As Truman's Secretary of Agriculture." (Ph.D. dissertation, University of New Mexico, 1970), pp. 570–95; Allen J. Matusow, *Farm Policies and Politics in the Truman Years* (Cambridge: Harvard University Press, 1967), pp. 36–37.

35. Anderson, *Outsider,* pp. 94–97; Forsythe, "Anderson," chapters 10 & 14; Matusow, *Farm Policies,* pp. 68–71.

36. Anderson, *Outsider,* p.97; Forsythe, "Anderson," pp. 577–78.

37. Anderson to Thomas Donnelly, June 21, 1949, AP, Box 1046; Anderson, *Outsider,* pp. 86–89; Forsythe, "Anderson," p. 579.

38. *New York Times,* March 14, 1948, p. 39; U.S., *Public Papers of Harry S. Truman, 1948,* p. 179; Anderson, *Outsider,* p. 87; Forsythe, "Anderson," pp. 578–80; Anderson to Donnelly, June 21, 1949, AP, Box 1046; Anderson, "Memo on Material Dealing With My Senate Experiences," April 1957, author's files. Late in 1952, Truman expressed a contrary view as he evaluated his various cabinet secretaries. He observed that Anderson quit when "the going became rough in 1948" but that Charles Brannan, Anderson's successor and nemesis on the issue of agricultural price support policy, was "the best one we've had since I've been in Washington." "List of Cabinet Members and White House Aides with Notes," n.d. [Late 1952], Longhand notes File, Harry S. Truman Library, Independence, MO.

39. *New York Times,* May 11, 1948, p. 6; *Albuquerque Journal,* June 10, 1948, p. 1.

40. Anderson to Jouett Shouse, August 26, 1948, AP, Box 1046.

41. Anderson, *Outsider,* pp. 91–93; Russell D. Buhite, *Patrick J. Hurley and American Foreign Policy* (Ithaca: Cornell University Press, 1973), p. 299.

42. Anderson to Shouse, August 26, 1948, AP, Box 1046; *Albuquerque Journal,* November 3, 4, & 7, 1948.

43. Interviews with Eloise de la O, January 30, 1980; and Luna Diamond, October 27, 1980.

44. Interview with Claude E. Wood, November 20, 1981.

45. Ibid.; Claude E. Wood to Howard Bray, April 19, 1966, author's files.

46. Interviews with Claude E. Wood, November 20-21, 1981; Lorella Montoya Salazar, July 20, 1982; Luna Diamond, October 27, 1980; Richard Pino, July 20, 1982; and note, Eloise de la O to author, November 27, 1984, author's files.

47. Interviews with Lorella Salazar and Richard Pino, July 20, 1982.

48. Interviews with Claude E. Wood, November 20-21, 1981, Lorella Salazar, July 20, 1982, and Luna Diamond, October 27, 1980.

49. Interviews with Claude E. Wood, November 20-21, 1981, and Ruby Hamblen, January 30, 1980,

50. Interviews with Richard Pino, July 20 and 23, 1982.

51. Interviews with Claude E. Wood, November 20-21, 1981.

52. Ibid.

53. Ibid.

54. Interviews with Luna Diamond, October 27, 1980; Lorella Salazar, July 20, 1982; Ruby Hamblen, January 30, 1980; and Howard Bray, April 22, 1980.

55. Interview with Lorella Salazar, July 20, 1982.

56. Ibid.

57. Ibid.

58. Ibid.

59. Commencement address, Missouri Valley College, May 31, 1949, AP, Box 939.

60. Clinton P. Anderson oral history interview, John F. Kennedy Library, Boston, Massachusetts, April 14, 1967, in AP, Box 1111.

61. Interviews with Claude E. Wood, November 20-21, 1981 and Robert Wolf, January 26, 1982.

62. Interviews with Maurice Rosenblatt, June 29, 1982; Claude E. Wood, November 20-21, 1981; Jack F. Walton, July 23, 1982; and Thomas McCaffrey, July 24, 1982.

63. Interview with Robert Wolf, January 26, 1982; For an analysis of the "outsider's" role in the Senate of the 1950's, see Ralph K. Huitt, "The Outsider in the Senate: An Alternate Role," *American Political Science Review* 60 (September 1961): 566–75; William S. White provides a view of the "insider" or "Senate type" of the mid-1950's in *Citadel: The Story of the U.S. Senate* (New York: Harper Bros., 1957), pp. 81–94.

64. Interview with Maurice Rosenblatt, June 29, 1982.

65. Interview with Robert Wolf, January 26, 1982.

66. Ibid.

67. *CR,* May 5, 1959, pp. 7474–76.

68. *CR,* April 22, 1963, p. 6708.

## Chapter 2

1. "A West Texan in Washington," *El Paso Times,* November 13, 1949.

2. *Congressional Quarterly Almanac, 1949* (Washington, D.C.: Congressional Quarterly, 1950), pp. 20–21; Rowland Evans and Robert Novak, *Lyndon B. Johnson: The Exercise of Power* (New York: New American Library, 1966), pp. 26–29.

3. U.S., Commission on the Organization of the Executive Branch of the Government, *Organization and Policy in the Field of Natural Resources,* Task Force Report, January 1949, pp. 1–29.

4. U.S., *Public Papers of President Harry S. Truman, 1949,* p. 5; Gordon B. Dodds, "Conservation and Reclamation in the Trans-Mississippi West:

A Critical Bibliography," *Arizona and the West* 13 (Summer 1971): 143–47; Lawrence Rakestraw, "Conservation Historiography: An Assessment," *Pacific Historical Review* 41 (August 1972): 271–88.

5. U.S., Senate, Committee on Interior and Insular Affairs, *Natural Resources Policy,* hearings, January 31–February 7, 1949, pp. 1–5.

6. U.S., Senate, Committee on Appropriations, *Civil Functions, Department of the Army Appropriations Bill, 1950,* hearings on H.R.3734, April 5, 1949, pp. 1400–1402; Erna Fergusson, *New Mexico: A Pageant of Three Peoples* (New York: Alfred A. Knopf, 1971), pp. 355–56.

7. *Natural Resources Policy,* pp. 5–32; For a provocative assessment of the Interior Department during the Truman administration, see Clayton R. Koppes, "Environmental Policy and American Liberalism: The Department of the Interior, 1933–1953," *Environmental Review* 7 (Spring 1983): 26–33.

8. *Natural Resources Policy,* p. 13.

9. *New York Times,* May 29, 1948; June 13, 1948; June 15, 1948; July 1, 1948; March 23, 1949; April 4, 1949; May 13, 1949; David Arlin Kathka, "The Bureau of Reclamation in the Truman Administration: Personnel, Politics, and Policy" (Ph.D. dissertation, University of Missouri, 1976), pp. 151–64; Clayton R. Koppes, "Public Water, Private Land: Origins of the Acreage Limitation Controversy, 1933–1953," *Pacific Historical Review* 47 (November 1978): 620–21.

10. *Natural Resources Policy,* p. 194.

11. Ibid., pp. 426–27.

12. Ibid., pp. 191–95.

13. Ibid., p. 209.

14. Ibid., pp. 425–26.

15. U.S., Commission on the Organization of the Executive Branch of the Government, *Department of the Interior: A Report to Congress,* March 1949, pp. 4–6.

16. Ibid., pp. 26–27.

17. U.S., Department of the Interior, Bureau of Reclamation, *Plan for Rehabilitation, Vermejo Project, Canadian River Basin, New Mexico: Project Planning Report, 5–12, 15–1,* February 1949, pp. 11–18; U.S., Senate, *Construction of Vermejo Reclamation Project,* Report 81–813, March 23, 1949, Clinton P. Anderson Papers, Library of Congress (hereafter cited as AP), Boxes 489–91.

18. *Natural Resources Policy,* p. 194.

19. *Plan for Rehabilitation, Vermejo Project,* pp. 11–13.

20. Ibid.; A full account of the complexities of cost-benefit calculations as applied to federal reclamation projects appears in Daniel Swartzman, Richard A. Liroff, and Kevin G. Croke, eds., *Cost-Benefit Analysis and Environmental Regulations: Politics, Ethics, and Methods* (Washington, D.C.: Conservation Foundation, 1982).

21. *Plan for Rehabilitation, Vermejo Project,* pp. 11–13.

22. Anderson's bill was S.1382, AP, Box 489.

23. U.S., House, *Veto Message on Bill to Construct Vermejo Project, New Mexico,* Document 81–316, August 23, 1949.

24. Ibid., AP, Box 490.

25. *Albuquerque Journal,* September 6, 1949.

26. Anderson to James E. Barber, August 30, 1949, AP, Box 490.

27. Anderson to John Thaxton, August 30, 1949, AP, Box 490.

28. Anderson to Harry S. Truman, August 31, 1949, AP, Box 490.

29. Harry S. Truman to Anderson, September 21, 1949; David Bell to Anderson, undated, AP, Box 490.

30. *New York Times,* November 13, 1949.

31. Anderson introduced his revised bill, S.3517, on May 1, 1950. The president signed it on September 27, 1950, as Public Law 81–848.

32. An acre foot of water amounts to 325,851 gallons, the volume covering an acre of land at a depth of one foot.

33. U.S., Department of the Interior, Bureau of Reclamation, *Plan for Development: Canadian River Project, Texas, Project Planning Report 5–12, 22–1,* June 1949, pp. 1–8.

34. U.S., Senate, *Authorizing Construction of the Canadian River Project,* Report 81–2110, July 20, 1950, pp. 3–9.

35. Anderson to Homer Grant, August 19, 1949, AP, Box 481.

36. John Bliss to Anderson, August 17, 1949, September 23, 1949, AP, Box 481.

37. Anderson to Joseph O'Mahoney, February 27, 1950, AP, Box 481; General Correspondence, AP, Box 481.

38. Anderson to Will Harrison, June 15, 1950, AP, Box 481.

39. Anderson to John Bliss, December 19, 1950; Bliss to Anderson, December 28, 1950, AP, Box 481.

40. Clinton P. Anderson, *Outsider in the Senate* (New York: World Publishing Co., 1970), pp. 236–38.

41. For an insider's account, from the Arizona perspective, of these complex negotiations, see Rich Johnson, *The Central Arizona Project, 1918–1968* (Tucson: University of Arizona Press, 1977); A more balanced and scholarly study appears in Norris Hundley, *Water and the West: The Colorado River Compact and the Politics of Water in the American West* (Berkeley: University of California Press, 1975).

42. Ibid.

43. U.S., Senate, Committee on Interior and Insular Affairs, *Central Arizona Project and Colorado River Water Rights,* hearings on S.75 and S.J. Res.4, March 21-May 2, 1949, pp. 30–51; Dean E. Mann, *The Politics of Water in Arizona* (Tucson: University of Arizona Press, 1963).

44. *Central Arizona Project and Colorado River Rights,* pp. 64–75.

45. Ibid., p. 63.

46. Ibid., pp. 87, 115, 135, 153, 155.

47. Ibid., p. 88.

48. Ibid., pp. 183–85, 248–52; U.S., Senate, *Dam in Main Stream of Colorado River at Bridge Canyon,* Report 81–832.

49. John Bliss to Anderson, April 29, 1949, AP, Box 507.

50. 207 US 564; Norris Hundley, Jr., "The 'Winters' Decision and Indian Water Rights: A Mystery Reexamined," *Western Historical Quarterly* 13 (January 1982): 17–42; Norris Hundley, Jr., "The Dark and Bloody Ground of Indian Water Rights: Confusion Elevated to Principle," *Western Historical Quarterly* 9 (October 1978): 455–65; Robert G. Dunbar, *Forging New Rights in Western Waters* (Lincoln: University of Nebraska Press, 1983), pp. 194–201; Michael L. Lawson, "The Navajo Indian Irrigation Project: Muddied Past, Clouded Future," *The Indian Historian* 9 (Winter 1976): 20–21.

51. *Congressional Record* (hereafter cited as *CR*), July 31, 1950, pp. A5487–88.

52. John Bliss to Anderson, April 29, 1949, AP, Box 507.

53. Anderson to Julius Krug, June 24, 1949, AP, Box 507.

54. Ibid.

55. Julius Krug to Anderson, August 16, 1949; Anderson to Krug, August 17, 1949, AP, Box 507.

56. Anderson to Kenneth Markwell, August 15, 1949, AP, Box 507.

57. Fred Wilson to Anderson, September 14, 1949, AP, Box 507.

58. A well documented account of Chapman's operating style and relationship to Anderson is found in Clayton R. Koppes, "Oscar L. Chapman, A Liberal at the Interior Department, 1933–1953" (Ph.D. dissertation, University of Kansas, 1974), pp. 168–88; *CR* July 31, 1950, pp. A5487–88; William Warne to Oscar Chapman, July 26, 1950, AP, Box 507.

59. *CR,* July 31, 1950, pp. A5487–88.

60. Oscar Chapman to Anderson (September 1950), AP, Box 507.

61. *Farmington Times,* September 7, 1950.

62. Radio Broadcast, September 17, 1950, transcript in AP, Box 507.

63. Anderson's bill, S.353, became Public Law 81–94 on June 10, 1949.

64. The "Anderson-Mansfield Act," S.J.Res 53 was signed on October 11, 1949; U.S., Senate, *Reforestation and Revegetation of Forest and Range Lands of National Forests,* Report 81–97; Public Law 81–348.

65. U.S., Senate, Committee on Agriculture and Forestry, *Forestry and Timber Access Roads,* hearings on S.282 and others, May 25 and 31, 1949, pp. 1–4.

66. General correspondence in AP, Box 494.

67, *Santa Fe New Mexican,* September 25, 1949; *CR,* October 19, 1949, pp. 15029–30.

68. *New Mexico Stockman,* June 1949, copy in AP, Box 494.

69. Anderson to Horace Henning, June 17, 1949, AP, Box 494.

70. *Forestry and Timber Access Roads,* pp. 1–4; the Senate passed H.R. 2296, which became Public Law 81–392 on October 26, 1949.

## Chapter 3

1. U.S., House, Committee on Interior and Insular Affairs, *Colorado River Storage Project,* hearings on H.R. 4449, January 18–28, 1954, pp. 249–55; U.S., Senate, Committee on Interior and Insular Affairs, *Colorado River Storage Project,* hearings on S. 1555, June 28–July 3, 1954, pp. 52–56.

2. U.S., Bureau of Reclamation, *Colorado River Storage Project: Project Planning Report,* 4–8a, 81–2 (Salt Lake City, 1950), pp. 8–15, Clinton P. Anderson papers, Library of Congress (hereafter cited as AP), Washington, D.C., Box 1064.

3. Ibid.

4. Memorandum prepared by Anderson's staff in 1954 to refute charges of his senatorial campaign opponent, Edwin Mechem, that the latter's interest in saving the Navajo Dam antedated Anderson's; contains text of letter from Clinton Anderson to Arthur Watkins, April 16, 1952, AP, Box 1065.

5. Gary W. Reichard, *The Reaffirmation of Republicanism, Eisenhower and the Eighty-Third Congress* (Knoxville: University of Tennessee Press, 1975), pp. 179–80; George Van Dusen, "Politics of 'Partnership': The Eisenhower Administration and Conservation, 1952–1960" (Ph.D. dissertation, Loyola University, 1974); James L. Sundquist, *Politics and Policy: The Eisenhower, Kennedy, and Johnson Years* (Washington, D.C.: Brookings Institution, 1968), p. 323.

6. From the *Idaho Statesman,* November 22, 1952, cited in Elmo Richardson, *Dams, Parks and Politics: Resource Development and Preservation in the Truman-Eisenhower Era* (Lexington: University Press of Kentucky, 1973), p. 85.

7. See Eighty-third Congress bills: S.1555, H.R. 4443, H.R.4449, H.R. 4463, AP, Box 955.

8. *Colorado River Storage Project,* pp. 244–55.

9. U.S., Bureau of Reclamation, *Supplemental Report on the Colorado River Storage Project and Participating Projects,* Upper Colorado Basin, October 1953, pp. 4–5.

10. *Colorado River Storage Project,* pp. 249–55.

11. Ibid., pp. 79–81.

12. White House press release, March 20, 1954.

13. AP, Box 955.

14. John U. Terrell, *War for the Colorado River,* Vol. 2. (Glendale, California: Arthur H. Clark Co., 1965), pp. 116–18; U.S., House, *Authorizing Construction, Operation and Maintenance of Initial Units of Colorado River Storage Project,* Report 83–1774, pp. 1–5.

15. U.S., Senate, Committee on Interior and Insular Affairs, *Colorado River Storage Project,* hearings on S.1555, June 28–July 3, 1954, pp. 30, 52–56.

16. Richard A. Squires, "Reverberations from Echo Park," *American Forests,* February 1954, pp. 34–35; *Colorado River Storage Project* [Senate], pp. 47–48; the definitive account of the Echo Park battle appears in Owen Stratton and Phillip Sirotkin, *The Echo Park Controversy* (University, Alabama: University of Alabama Press, 1959); an excellent interpretive study is found in "Just a Tiny Dinosaur," in Richardson, *Dams, Parks and Politics,* chapter 7; Mark W. T. Harvey, "Echo Park: An Old Problem of Federalism," *Annals of Wyoming* 55 (Fall 1983): 9–18.

17. Squires, pp. 39–40; Bernard DeVoto, "And Fractions Drive Me Mad," *Harper's Magazine,* September 1954, pp. 10–11; Raymond Moley, "Water, Land, and Bookkeeping," *Newsweek,* April 12, 1954, p. 112; Moley, *Newsweek,* May 10, 1954, p. 108, Moley, *Newsweek,* May 17, 1954, p. 84; Harvey, "Echo Park," pp. 12–13.

18. *Colorado River Storage Project* [Senate], pp. 464–69.

19. Ibid., pp. 496–522.

20. Ibid., pp. 61–66; Richardson, *Dams, Parks and Politics,* pp. 138–39; Norris Hundley, Jr., *Water and the West: The Colorado River Compact and the Politics of Water in the American West* (Berkeley: University of California Press, 1975), p. 170; Harvey, "Echo Park," pp. 13–15.

21. *Colorado River Storage Project* [Senate], pp. 584–610.

22. Clinton Anderson to Lincoln O' Brien, July 19, 1954, AP, Box 1062.

23. U.S., Senate, *Authorizing the Secretary of the Interior to Construct, Operate, and Maintain the Colorado River Storage Project and Participating Projects,* Report 83–1983, July 26, 1954, p. 9.

24. Clinton P. Anderson, *Outsider in the Senate* (New York: World Publishing Co., 1970), p. 238.

25. *Congressional Record* (hereafter cited as *CR*), July 26, 1954, p. 11941.

26. Paul Douglas presented the most carefully documented summary of this position, *CR,* April 18, 1955, pp. 4575–80; *CR,* April 19, 1955, pp. 4634–41.

27. "Aqualantes Correspondence," AP, Box 1062; *Farmington Daily Times,* March 6, 1956.

28. U.S., Senate, *Colorado River Storage Project,* hearings on S.500, February 28–March 5, 1955, p. 1.

29. Ibid., p. 15.

30. Ibid., pp. 162 ff, 243 ff.

31. U.S., Senate, *Secretary of Interior to Construct Colorado River Storage Project and Participating Projects,* Report 84–128, pp. 1–9.

32. *CR,* April 18, 1955, pp. 4541–42.

33. Ibid., pp. 4546–47.

34. Ibid., April 19, 1955, p. 4641.

35. Ibid., p. 4645.

36. Ibid., April 20, 1955, p. 4813.

37. *Washington Post,* June 5, 1955; John Bliss to Clinton Anderson, June 3, 1955, AP, Box 1062; Harvey, "Echo Park," p. 15.

38. "Albright Controversy" folder in AP, Box 1061, letters dated July 7, 12, 15, 20, 22, and 28, 1955.

39. Donald C. Swain, *Wilderness Defender: Horace M. Albright and Conservation* (Chicago: University of Chicago Press, 1970), pp. 302–304.

40. Anderson to Horace Albright, July 20 and 28, 1955, AP, Box 1061; Albright to Anderson, July 15 and 22, 1955, AP, Box 1061.

41. Clinton Anderson to Lincoln O'Brien, AP, Box 1061.

42. Anderson to Fred Smith, November 3, 1955, AP, Box 1062; interview with Steve Reynolds, July 22, 1982.

43. Howard Zahniser to Anderson, January 4, 1956; Anderson to Arthur Watkins, January 10, 1956; Tom Bolack to Horace Albright, January 14, 1956; Claude Wood to Anderson, January 23, 1956; Howard Zahniser to Anderson, January 23, 1956, AP, Box 1062.

44. *CR,* March 1, 1956; "UCRP Passes," *Farmington (New Mexico) Daily Times,* March 1, 1956; *Farmington Daily Times,* March 2, 1956.

45. Craig W. Allin, *The Politics of Wilderness Preservation* (Westport, CT: Greenwood Press, 1982), p. 45.

46. Transcripts of Conference Committee, March 8, 1956, National Archives, Washington, D.C., RG 46, 84A–E9.

47. See Chapter 8.

## Chapter 4

1. The fullest sources on the creation and work of the Outdoor Recreation Commission are U.S., Senate, Committee on Interior and Insular Affairs, *Outdoor Recreation Resources Commission,* hearings on S.846, May 15, 1957 and U.S., Outdoor Recreation Resources Review Commission, *Outdoor Recreation for America: A Report to the President and Congress,* (Washington, D.C.: Government Printing Office, 1962). For the early legislative stages of the Wilderness Act, see U.S., Senate, Committee on Interior and Insular Affairs, *National Wilderness Preservation Act, hearings on S.1176,* June 1957 and U.S., Senate, Committee on Interior and Insular Affairs, *National Wilderness Preservation Act, hearings on S.4028,* July 23, 1958; Edward C. Crafts, "Saga of a law: Part II," *American Forests* 76 (July 1970): 35; Dennis Roth, "The National Forests and the Campaign For Wilderness Legislation," *Journal of Forest History* 28 (July 1984): 112-25; Albert Dixon, "The Conservation of Wilderness: A Study in Politics" (Ph.D. dissertation, University of California at Berkeley, 1968), p. 61; Donald Nicholas Baldwin, *The Quiet Revolution: The Grass Roots of Today's Wilderness Preservation Movement* (Boulder: Pruett Publishing Co., 1972), pp. 153–65; Joel Gottlieb, "The Preservation of Wilderness Values: The Politics and Administration of Conservation Policy" (Ph.D. dissertation, University of California at Riverside, 1972), pp. 121–32.

2. J. Michael McCloskey, "Natural Resources—National Forests—the Multiple Use–Sustained Yield Act of 1960," *Oregon Law Review* 41 (December 1961): 49–79; Harold Steen, *The U.S. Forest Service* (Seattle: University of Washington Press, 1976), 278–314.

3. Clinton P. Anderson, *Outsider in the Senate* (New York: World Publishing Co., 1970), p. 227; in the two decades since his death, Howard Zahniser's stature as a preeminent conservationist has increased as recently demonstrated in Stephen Fox, *John Muir and His Legacy: The American Conservation Movement* (Boston: Little Brown, 1981), p. 270; see also "Howard Clinton Zahniser, 1906-1964," *Living Wilderness,* Winter-Spring,

1964, pp. 3–6; Interviews with Robert Wolf, January 26, 1982 and Claude E. Wood, November 21, 1981; Roth, p. 118.

4. Analyses of this longstanding conflict are plentiful. Two of the best are found in William C. Everhart, *The National Park Service* (New York: Praeger, 1972), p. 182 and John Ise, *Our National Park Policy: A Critical History* (Baltimore: Johns Hopkins Press, 1961), chapter 25.

5. *Our National Park Policy,* pp. 525, 557; David R. Brower oral history, University of California, Berkeley, Bancroft Library, p. 64; Howard Zahniser to Frank Church, April 11, 1961, Clinton P. Anderson Papers, Library of Congress (hereafter cited as AP), Box 641. Despite the Agriculture Department's recommendation, no logging took place in the Three Sisters Wilderness and the designated acreage was added to the wilderness system in 1977, Samuel T. Dana and Sally Fairfax, *Forest Range Policy* (New York: McGraw-Hill, 1980), pp. 179–198.

6. U.S., Senate, Committee on Interior and Insular Affairs, *Natural Resources Policy,* January 31–February 7, 1949, pp. 260–70.

7. Ibid.

8. Elmo Richardson, *Dams, Parks and Politics: Resource Development and Preservation in the Truman-Eisenhower Era* (Lexington: University Press of Kentucky, 1973), pp. 58–67; Clayton R. Koppes, "Oscar L. Chapman: A Liberal at the Interior Department, 1933-1953" (Ph.D. dissertation, University of Kansas, 1974), pp. 348–59.

9. Conrad Wirth's term as chief of the National Park Service abounded in controversy. Some claimed he saved the agency by attracting congressional support and increased funding. His detractors view his years as a "Disneyland Era" filled with inappropriate construction, tourist development and agency aggrandizement, *Forest Range Policy,* p. 192. Wirth tells his side of the story in Conrad L. Wirth, *Parks, Politics and the People* (Norman: University of Oklahoma Press, 1980).

10. *Congressional Record* (hereafter cited as *CR*), June 1, 1955, pp. A3809–12; a classic study on the impact of the concept of wilderness on American thought is found in Roderick Nash, *Wilderness and the American Mind* (New Haven: Yale University Press, 1967); *National Wilderness Preservation Act,* hearings on S.4028, p. 158.

11. *CR,* February 29, 1956, pp. 3551–54; *CR,* June 7, 1956 pp. 9772–82

12. See Eighty-fourth Congress bill S.4013; for a summary of the military land withdrawal issue, see *CR,* August 20, 1957, pp. 15297–98, AP, Box 595.

13. S.E. Reynolds to Arthur Watkins, May 15, 1956, AP, Box 599.

14. John Bliss to S.E. Reynolds, July 11,1956, AP, Box 599.

15. Claude Wood to Anderson, undated memo (December 1956), AP, Box 599. Prepared in advance of Penfold's December 13, 1956 meeting with Anderson, it outlines process of negotiation that led to modification of Penfold's original proposal.

16. *CR,* January 25, 1957, pp. 958–59.

17. Revised draft of April 3, 1957 speech, AP, Boxes 599 and 967.

18. *Outdoor Recreation Resources Commission,* pp. 11–12, 43–48.

19. Ibid.

20. Horace Albright to Anderson, June 6, 1957, AP, Box 599.

21. Claude Wood to Anderson, June 7, 1957; Anderson to Horace Albright, June 11, 1957, AP, Box 599.

22. Horace Albright to Anderson, June 12, 1957, AP, Box 599.

23. *Outdoor Recreation Resources Commission,* pp. 109–110.

24. Joseph Penfold to Benton Stong, June 8, 1957, AP, Box 599.

25. "Various Bills," transcript of executive session, June 18, 1957, pp. 3–7, Senate Committee on Interior and Insular Affairs, Box 18, 85A–F9, RG 46, National Archives.

26. *CR,* June 26, 1957, pp. 10319–21.

27. *Parks, Politics and the People,* pp. 251–52.

28. John McPhee, *Encounters with the Archdruid* (New York: Farrar, Straus, and Giroux, 1971), pp. 5–6, 95.

29. David Brower to Conrad Wirth, April 11, 1957; Brower to Sierra Club Board of Directors, May 8, 1957; Brower to Board, July 5, 1957, Office files series, Sierra Club papers, Bancroft Library, University of California, Berkeley; Brower oral history, Bancroft Library, pp. 58–61.

30. Unsigned memorandum to Claude Wood, July 25, 1957, AP, Box 594.

31. Claude Wood to Anderson, July 31, 1957, AP, Box 594.

32. Anderson to Fred Seaton, August 1, 1957, AP, Box 594.

33. Transcript of executive session, July 9, 1957, Senate Committee on Interior and Insular Affairs, Box 5, 85A–E9, RG 46, National Archives.

34. Conrad Wirth to Anderson, August 16, 1957, AP, Box 594, *CR,* June 16, 1958, pp. 11367–78; *CR,* June 17, 1958, p. 11431.

35. U.S., Senate, Committee on Interior and Insular Affairs, *National Wilderness Preservation Act,* hearings, June 19, 1957, pp. 17–25.

36. Ibid., pp. 8–11, 90–107.

37. Ibid., pp. 13–17, 107–111.

38. Ibid., pp. 16, 150, 295, 298, 339, 397, 414, 416.

39. Ibid., pp. 152–275.

40. *CR,* June 18, 1958, pp. 11551–58.

41. Claude Wood to Anderson, April 8, 1958, AP, Box 622.

42. Claude Wood to Anderson, July 1, 1958, AP, Box 622.

43. *National Wilderness Preservation Act,* July 23, 1958, pp. 107–110, 131–32.

44. *CR,* July 10, 1958, p. 11347.

45. Anderson to Joseph Penfold, July 14, 1958; Penfold to Anderson, July 15, 1958, AP, Box 878.

46. *New York Times,* September 16, 1958; Fred Smith to Anderson, September 16, 1958, AP, Box 877.

47. Edward Crafts to Anderson, September 16, 1958, AP, Box 877.

48. Claude Wood to Anderson, n.d. (pre-August 1958), AP, Box 878.

49. U.S., Senate, Committee on Interior and Insular Affairs, *National Wilderness Preservation Act,* November 1958, p. 908.

50. Ibid., p. 919; Interview with Steve Reynolds, July 22, 1982.

51. Ibid., *National Wilderness Preservation Act,* p. 926.

52. Ibid., pp. 934–38.

53. Ibid., p. 953.

54. Ibid., p. 921.

55. Benton Stong and Victor Reinemer oral history, February 15, 1978, University of Montana Library, p. 13; Hubert Humphrey to Anderson, January 26, 1959, January 27, 1959, AP, Box 619; Carl Solberg, *Hubert Humphrey: A Biography* (New York: W.W. Norton, 1984), p. 461.

56. Claude Wood to Anderson, February 2, 1959; Anderson to Hubert Humphrey, February 3, 1959, AP, Box 619; Wood to Howard Bray, April 19, 1966, Wood Collection.

57. Anderson to Hubert Humphrey, February 9, 1959; Anderson to Harvey Broome, April 9, 1959, AP, Box 619.

58. Elliot Barker to Anderson, February 5, 1959; Oliver LaFarge to James Murray, April 17, 1959, AP, Box 619; New Mexico Legislature (House) Joint Memorial #3, March 1959 (reprinted in *CR*, 9/5/61), p. 18100.

59. Odd Halseth to Anderson, April 22, 1959, AP, Box 619.

60. Howard Zahniser to Claude Wood, April 29, 1959, AP, Box 619.

61. *Outsider in the Senate,* pp. 184–221; interviews with Richard Pino, July 20, 1982 and Hugh Scott, September 14, 1982. In his memoirs, Lewis Strauss could not bring himself to mention Anderson by name, referring to him as "The Junior Senator from New Mexico." Lewis Strauss, *Men and Decisions* (Garden City, NY: Doubleday, 1962). Frances Freedle concludes that Strauss's refusal to take members of Congress into his confidence led Anderson to decide that a person who behaved that way should not become a cabinet officer. Frances D. Freedle, "The Ninth Rejection: Senator Anderson VS. Lewis Strauss," (MA thesis, University of New Mexico, 1964) pp. 13, 43, 46–49, 65. "A Most Controversial Man," *Newsweek,* June 16, 1958, p. 27; Stephen E. Ambrose, *Eisenhower: The President* (New York: Simon and Schuster, 1984), p. 530.

62. Hugh Woodward to Claude Wood, June 29, 1959, AP, Box 619.

63. Claude Wood to Anderson, July 7, 1959, AP, Box 619.

64. Steve Reynolds to Anderson, AP, Box 619.

65. Anderson to Charles Murray (Administrative Assistant to James Murray), July 25, 1959, AP, Box 622.

66. AP, Box 619; Carl Moore, "Joseph Christopher O'Mahoney: A Brief Biography," *Annals of Wyoming* 41 (October 1969): 185–86.

67. Joseph O'Mahoney to James Murray, August 27, 1959, AP, Box 622.

68. Charles Callison, William Zimmerman and Howard Zahniser to Anderson, August 13, 1959, AP, Box 622.

69. Arthur Johnson to Anderson, December 26, 1959; David Brower to Anderson, January 19, 1960, AP, Box 877; David Brower to Thomas Kuchel, April 13, 1960; Brower files, Sierra Club Papers.

70. Anderson to David Brower, January 20, 1960, AP, Box 877.

71. Anderson to (members of Congress from Western states), January 27, 1960; Warren Magnuson to Anderson, February 22, 1960; Henry Jack-

son to Anderson, February 9, 1960; Wallace Bennett to Anderson, February 19, 1960; Frank Moss to Anderson, February 23, 1960, AP, Box 877.

72. Wayne Aspinall to Anderson, February 8, 1960; Claude Wood to Anderson,February 3, 1960, AP, Box 877.

73. Howard Zahniser to Leslie A. Miller, January 28, 1960; Brower files, Sierra Club Papers.

74. William Zimmerman, Jr., to David Brower, February 10, 1960; Brower files, Sierra Club Papers.

75. AP, Box 619; *Outsider in the Senate,* p. 226.

76. William Zimmerman, Jr. to William L. Losh (Trustees for Conservation), May 7, 1960; Brower files, Sierra Club Papers.

77. Richard E. McArdle, "Why We Need the Multiple Use Bill," *American Forests* 76 (June 1970): 10, 59; McArdle, "Wilderness Politics: Legislation and Forest Service Policy," *Journal of Forest History* 19 (October 1975): 177.

78. Edward C. Crafts, "Saga of a Law: Part I," *American Forests* 76 (June 1970): 18–19.

79. Ibid., 18, 52; "Half a Century of Conservation: A Biography and Oral History of Edward P. Cliff," March 1981, U.S. Forest Service History Section, pp. 202–206.

80. David Brower to Howard Zahniser, May 26, 1960; David Brower to Alex Hildebrand, July 7, 1960; Brower files, Sierra Club Papers.

81. *CR,* July 2, 1960, pp. 15563–69.

## Chapter 5

1. U.S., President, *Public Papers of John F. Kennedy, 1961,* p. 114.

2. The fullest accounts of Anderson's relations with Kennedy and Johnson are found in Clinton P. Anderson, *Outsider in the Senate* (New York: World Publishing Co. 1970), Chapter 10; Clinton P. Anderson oral history, April 14, 1967, John F. Kennedy Library; Clinton P. Anderson oral history, May 20, 1969, Lyndon B. Johnson Library. For a survey of the Democratic party's Senate power structure in the mid-1950s, see William S. White, "Democrats' 'Board of Directors,' " *New York Times Magazine,* July 10, 1955, pp. 10–11.

3. Anderson oral history, Kennedy Library; Rowland Evans and Robert Novak, *Lyndon B. Johnson: The Exercise of Power* (New York: New American Library, 1966), p. 281. George Reedy, a close Johnson aide, speculates that Rayburn urged Johnson to accept the vice presidency to strengthen the ticket and deny the election to Richard Nixon, whom he detested. George E. Reedy, *Lyndon B. Johnson, A Memoir,* (New York: Andrews and McNeel, 1982), p. 129.

4. Anderson oral history, Kennedy Library; James MacGregor Burns, oral history, Kennedy Library, May 14, 1965, p. 10; Robert Sam Anson, *McGovern: A Biography* (New York: Holt, Rinehart and Winston, 1972), pp. 98–101; interviews with Maurice Rosenblatt, June 29 and July 8, 1982.

5. Interview with Paul Wieck, July 12, 1982; interview with Maurice Rosenblatt, June 29, 1982. A vastly different and less plausible version of this account comes from Robert Kennedy as reprinted in Arthur M. Schlesinger, Jr., *Robert Kennedy and His Times* (Boston: Houghton Mifflin Co., 1978), pp. 225–26. Kennedy believed that Anderson was interested and reported that the president-elect called Anderson after agreeing to select Udall. When Anderson indicated he would be interested, Robert Kennedy claimed they were in an embarrassing position especially with "the dangers of Clinton Anderson getting in there and putting in cronies and associates, a number of whom we had seen during the course of the campaign who were rather unsavory, unquestionably, and certainly of different viewpoints, different generation, ideas and thoughts as we have." According to Robert Kennedy, the president-elect explained to Anderson the importance of his remaining in the Senate, and Anderson "bought it without any problem."

6. Interview with Robert Wolf, November 5, 1981.

7. Donald E. Spritzer, "New Dealer from Montana: The Senate Career of James E. Murray" (Ph.D. dissertation, University of Montana, 1980), pp. 483–84; U.S. Senate, *Report of the Secretary of the Senate* for the years 1952, 1953, 1954, 1955, 1960, 1961; interview with Robert Wolf, November 5, 1981.

8. Washington Post, September 8, 1980, p. C4; *Congressional Record* (herafter referred to as *CR*), September 10, 1980, pp. S12362–63 (daily edition).

9. Allen J. Matusow, *Farm Policies and Politics in the Truman Years* (Cambridge: Harvard University Press, 1967), p. 71.

10. Interview with Maurice Rosenblatt, July 8, 1982; interview with Jerry Verkler, September 1, 1982.

11. U.S. Senate, Committee on Interior and Insular Affairs, "Confidential transcript," p. 29, National Archives, Washington, D.C. Sen 85A–F9, no. 17.

12. "Democratic Steering Committee Completes Nominations to Standing Committees," *New York Times,* January 11, 1961.

13. Anderson to Fred Smith, February 14, 1961, Clinton P. Anderson Papers, Library of Congress (hereafter cited as AP), Box 641; Anderson to John F. Kennedy, February 14, 1961, AP, Box 641.

14. Claude Wood to Anderson, December 30, 1960, AP, Box 642; *CR,* January 5, 1961, p. 192; correspondence related to address and distribution list in AP, Box 641.

15. Jerry Verkler to Anderson, January 27, 1961, AP, Box 642.

16. Devereux Butcher, "Resorts or Wilderness," *The Atlantic Monthly,* February, 1961, pp. 45–51. See also Anderson's letter of support, February 16, 1961 (published in April issue), AP, Box 641.

17. *Washington Star,* February 26, 1981.

18. U.S., Senate, Committee on Interior and Insular Affairs, *The Wilderness Act,* hearings on S.174, February 27 and 28, 1961, pp. 1–2; Claude

Wood to Anderson, "Memorandum re. S.174, for use at hearing," undated, AP, Box 642.

19. *Wilderness Act,* p. 352.

20. Fred Smith to Anderson, December 15, 1960, AP, Box 642.

21. Fred Smith to Anderson, February 10, 1961, AP, Box 641; *Wilderness Act,* p. 87; see S.449 to extend the recreation commission's life and supporting letter of Laurance S. Rockefeller to President of the Senate, December 30, 1960, AP, Box 634.

22. U.S., Senate, Committee on Interior and Insular Affairs, *National Wilderness Preservation Act,* Hearings on S.1176, June 19 and 20, 1957; *National Wilderness Preservation Act,* Hearings on S.4028, July 23, 1958; *Wilderness Act,* passim.

23. *Wilderness Act,* p. 28.

24. Ibid., pp. 30–33.

25. Interviews with George Murphy, September 13, 1980, Frank Moss, April 5, 1980, and Linda Wertheimer, May 19, 1981.

26. *Wilderness Act,* pp. 33–38.

27. Ibid., pp. 39–40; transcription of telephone conversation between David Brower and Henry Romney, February 27, 1961, Brower files, Sierra Club Papers, University of California, Berkeley.

28. *Outsider in the Senate,* p. 230; *Wilderness Act,* pp. 171–74; interview with Floyd M. Riddick, October 13, 1981; U.S., Senate, *Report of the Secretary of the Senate From July 1, 1960 to June 30, 1961,* p. 99. Warren Elliot, Allott's legislative assistant, was removed from the Senate payroll effective March 12, 1961 and replaced by Donald Melbye effective February 16, 1961.

29. *Wilderness Act,* pp. 69–74.

30. Benton J. Stong, "Memorandum in regard to situation of S.174, the Wilderness Bill," June 5, 1961; Stong to Anderson, May 5, 1961, June 27, 1961, AP, Box 642.

31. Stong to Anderson, May 5, 1961 and June 27, 1961, AP, Box 642 U.S., Senate, *Establishing a National Wilderness Preservation System,* Report 87–635, July 27, 1961, see especially "Minority Views," pp. 36–43.

32. Howard Zahniser to Frank Church, April 11, 1961, AP, Box 641.

33. Anderson to J. N. Darling, July 21, 1961, AP, Box 641; *Outsider in the Senate,* p. 231; Natural Resources Council of America, *Legislative News Service,* Sierra Club Bulletin files, Sierra Club Papers.

34. Ibid.

35. Anderson to Ira Gabrielson, July 18, 1961, AP, Box 642; Anderson to Thomas Kuchel, July 14, 1961, AP, Box 641; Anderson to Lee Metcalf, July 14, 1961, AP, Box 641; Zahniser to Anderson, July 14, 1961, AP, Box 642.

36. *CR,* August 24, 1961, pp. 17016–19.

37. Anderson's departure for gall bladder surgery prompted one of his Interior Committee aides, recalling the chairman's sometimes vindictive nature, to express hope that while the surgeons were at it, they might "cut out the mean streak," as recounted by an observer, author's files.

38. *Outsider in the Senate,* p. 233.

39. *CR,* September 5, 1961, pp. 18045–47.

40. *CR,* September 5, 1961, pp. 18047–51, 18064.

41. *CR,* September 5, 1961, pp. 18400.

42. Frank Church to Anderson, September 12, 1961, AP, Box 641; *Outsider in the Senate,* p. 233; as recounted by committee aide Robert Wolf in interview, January 26, 1982.

43. John Bird, "The Great Wilderness Fight," *Saturday Evening Post,* July 8, 1961, p. 30.

44. The specific measures under consideration were: S.857 (Cape Cod), S.543 (Shoreline Recreation), and S.476 (Point Reyes Seashore).

45. Quoted in *CR,* June 27, 1961, p. 11393.

46. U.S., Senate, Committee on Interior and Insular Affairs, *Shoreline Recreation Areas,* Hearings on S.543, March 8 and 9, 1961, pp. 6–9.

47. U.S., Senate, Committee on Interior and Insular Affairs, *Cape Cod National Seashore Park,* Hearings on S.857, March 9, 1961, pp. 24–27; for a detailed account of this measure's legislative history, see Francis P. Burling, *The Birth of the Cape Cod National Seashore* (Plymouth, MA: Leyden Press, 1978).

48. Ibid., pp. 30–31.

49. Ibid., pp. 32–37.

50. Ibid., pp. 38–50.

51. U.S., Senate, Committee on Interior and Insular Affairs, *Point Reyes National Seashore,* Hearings on S.476, March 28, 30, and 31, 1961, pp. 5–18.

52. The Cape Cod Seashore Act was signed on August 7, 1961, PL 87–126. For Senate debate, see *CR,* June 27, 1961, pp. 11390–94; the Point Reyes National Seashore Act Senate debate appears in *CR,* September 7, 1961, pp. 18462-64, the House failed to act on it during 1961; the Shoreline Recreation Act appears in *CR,* August 28, 1961, pp. 17187–95.

53. U.S. Senate, Committee on Interior and Insular Affairs, *Proposed Resources and Conservation Act of 1960,* Hearings on S.2549, January 25, 26, 28, 29, 1960, passim; and *Resources and Conservation Act of 1961,* Hearings on S.239 and S.1415, April 13, 1961, p. 28. Anderson observed "facetiously" that Kennedy lost every state in which he made a campaign promise to set up a council of conservation advisers.

54. *Resources and Conservation Act of 1961,* pp. 28, 231.

55. U.S., Senate, Committee on Interior and Insular Affairs, *Interior Nomination (James K. Carr),* January 26, 1961, p. 7.

56. *Resources and Conservation Act of 1961,* p. 169.

57. Proposed Executive Order on Resources and Public Works, AP, Box 192.

58. Stong to Anderson, April 18, 1961, AP, Box 192.

59. Ibid.

60. Quentin Burdick and others to John F. Kennedy, April 21, 1961, AP, Box 192.

61. Anderson to Kennedy, April 21, 1961, AP, Box 192.

62. Ibid.
63. Stong to Anderson, April 18, 1961, AP, Box 192.
64. Jerry Verkler, April 25, 1961, AP, Box 192.
65. Memo, Lawrence O'Brien files, folder 1, John F. Kennedy Library.
66. David Bell to Anderson, May 5, 1961, AP, Box 192.
67. Anderson to Bell, May 8, 1961, AP, Box 192.

## Chapter 6

1. For a general account of Kennedy Administration conservation policy activities in 1962 and an assessment emphasizing that administration's legislative leadership role, see James L. Sundquist, *Politics and Policy: The Eisenhower, Kennedy, and Johnson Years* (Washington, D.C.: Brookings Institution, 1968), pp. 355–61, 489–93.
2. Stewart Udall to Clinton Anderson, October 3, 1962, Clinton P. Anderson Papers, Library of Congress (hereafter cited as AP), Box 184.
3. David E. Pesonen, "An Analysis of the ORRRC Report: 'Outdoor Recreation for America,' " *Sierra Club Bulletin* 47 (May 1962): 6; "President Kennedy Gets the Word," *American Forests* 68 (February 1962): 6–7.
4. U.S., Outdoor Recreation Resources Review Commission, *Outdoor Recreation for America* (Washington: GPO, 1962), pp. 1–8.
5. Ibid.
6. *New York Times,* February 1, 1962, p. 1.
7. Ibid., February 2, 1962; Eloise de la O to Mike Manatos, November 13, 1962, AP, Box 875.
8. *Washington Post,* February 2, 1962, p. A22.
9. Ross McCluskey, "The ORRRC Report: A Glittering Blunder," *Field & Stream,* April 1962, p. 24.
10. Ibid., p. 145.
11. Francis Sargent to Anderson, March 14, 1962, AP, Box 875; Lawrence N. Stevens to Anderson, March 29, 1962, AP, Box 880; Franklin Forsberg to Laurance Rockefeller, April 24, 1962, AP, Box 880; Anderson to Edgar Rigg, May 1, 1962, AP, Box 880. (There is no evidence that the board responded to Anderson's recommendation.)
12. Interview with Claude Wood, November 21, 1981; Anderson to Fred Smith, February 6, 1961, AP, Box 875.
13. Anderson's marginal notations on "Agenda Item #6" (ORRRC Meeting, May 22, 1961), AP, Box 875.
14. Ibid.; Claude Wood to Anderson, undated May 1961, AP, Box 875.
15. "Agenda Item #6"; Ben Stong to Claude Wood, June 20, 1961, AP, Box 875.
16. Laurance Rockefeller to Anderson, October 23, 1961; Anderson to Laurance Rockefeller, November 2, 1961, AP, Box 875.
17. *Wilderness and Recreation—A Report on Resources, Values, and Problems* (ORRRC Study Report 3), (Washington: GPO, 1962); "Report on

Congressional Activity," March 7, 1961, draft address for Anderson to present at ORRRC meeting, AP, Box 875.

18. Ben Stong to Anderson, August 3, 1961, AP, Box 875; Anderson to Laurance Rockefeller, September 20, 1961, AP, Box 875.

19. Anderson to Laurance Rockefeller, September 20, 1961, AP, Box 875.

20. Quoted in "Edward C. Crafts: Forest Service Researcher and Congressional Liaison: An Eye to Multiple Use," (oral history interview) Forest History Society, 1972, p. 84. Regarding the Forest Service's advocacy role, Crafts explained that "It could develop tremendous pressures if it wanted to. It had a very fine subterranean lobbying system and it took risks, gambled, and men were willing to do it." (p. 84); Edward C. Crafts, "Congress and the Forest Service, 1950–1962" (oral history interview), Regional Oral History Office, University of California, Berkeley, April 3, 1965.

21. U.S., Forest Service, "Preliminary Draft of Comments on 'Wilderness and Recreation,' " September 15, 1961, AP, Box 979.

22. Anderson to Laurance Rockefeller, September 20, 1961, AP, Box 875.

23. Ibid.

24. Transcript reprinted in *Congressional Record* (hereafter cited as *CR*), March 7, 1962, pp. 3594–95; "Today Show," February 28, 1962, Senate Interior Committee, National Archives & Records Service, Washington, D.C., RG46, 87A–F11, #190.

25. U.S., *Public Papers of John F. Kennedy, January 1, 1962 to December 31, 1962,* pp. 176–80.

26. Interview with Claude Wood, November 21, 1981; Mike Manatos to Lawrence O'Brien, February 6, 1962, O'Brien Senate file, folder #1, John F. Kennedy Library, Boston, Mass.

27. Mike Manatos to Lawrence O'Brien; Anderson to Samuel Dana, March 28, 1962, AP, Box 184.

28. Samuel Dana to Anderson, March 25, 1962, AP, Box 184.

29. Interview with Robert Wolf, November 5, 1981; Claude Wood to author, June 20, 1982, author's collection.

30. "David R. Brower: Environmental Activist, Publicist, and Prophet," (oral history) Regional Oral History Office, University of California, Berkeley, 1980, p. 81.

31. U.S., Senate, Committee on Interior and Insular Affairs, *Outdoor Recreation Act of 1962,* hearings on S.3117, May 10 and 11, 1962, p. 68.

32. Anderson to Samuel Dana, March 28, 1962, AP, Box 184.

33. Quoted in *The Portland Oregonian,* April 9, 1962, copy in *Bulletin* files, Sierra Club papers, University of California, Berkeley.

34. Quoted in "The Birth of a Bureau," *American Forests* 68 (April 1962): 64.

35. S.3117, Eighty-seventh Congress; *CR,* April 4, 1962, pp. 5873–76.

36. S.3118, Eighty-seventh Congress; *CR,* April 4, 1962, pp. 5876–77.

37. *Outdoor Recreation Act* of 1962, pp. 5–8.

38. Ibid., p. 7.

39. Copy of Drummond column in AP, Box 660.

40. Jerry Verkler to Anderson, March 19, 1962, AP, Box 660.

41. Anderson to Roscoe Drummond, March 20, 1962, AP, Box 660.

42. Anderson to Mike Mansfield, May 24, 1962, AP, Box 660.

43. Anderson to Everett Dirksen, May 18, 1962, AP, Box 660.

44. Interview with Claude Wood, November 21, 1981; Anderson to Mansfield, May 24, 1962, AP, Box 660.

45. Ibid.

46. U.S., Senate, *Senate Committee Staffing: A Survey,* Document 88–16, April 23, 1963. This report demonstrated that although committee staffing was heavily influenced by partisan considerations, the balance was not as heavily on the Democratic side as Drummond alleged. Of 140 professional staff, 79 were identified as Democrats and 28 as Republicans. Thirty-three were classified as "non-partisan" or "unknown."

47. Laurance Rockefeller to Anderson, April 6, 1962, AP, Box 880.

48. Francis Sargent to Anderson, May 22, 1962, AP, Box 875.

49. U.S., House, Committee on Interior and Insular Affairs, *Wilderness Preservation System,* hearings on S.174 etc., May 7–11, passim.

50. Ibid., p. 1092.

51. Ibid., pp. 1095–99.

52. Ibid., pp. 1105–7; U.S., White House Conference on Conservation, *Proceedings* (Washington: GPO, 1962), pp. 61–65.

53. U.S., White House Conference on Conservation, *Proceedings,* passim. For a presentation of Aspinall's and Saylor's respective views, see *CR,* September 20, 1962, pp. 20201–03 and *CR,* September 21, 1962, pp. 20266–69.

54. U.S., White House Conference, *Proceedings,* pp. 57–61.

55. Ibid., pp. 57–58.

56. *New York Times,* May 26, 1962, p. 1.

57. *New York Times,* August 22, 1962; *New York Times,* September 14, 1962; U.S., House of Representatives, *Providing for the Preservation of Wilderness Areas,* Report 87–2521, October 3, 1962.

58. *New York Times,* September 16, 1962.

59. *New York Times,* September 18, 1962; *St. Louis Post-Dispatch,* September 16, 1962; "Editorial," *Living Wilderness* 80 (Spring/Summer 1962); Paul Brooks, "Congressman Aspinall vs. the People of the United States," *Harper's,* March 1963, p. 62; Aspinall's abrupt departure is recounted in Robert Bendiner, *Obstacle Course on Capitol Hill* (New York: McGraw-Hill, 1964), p. 62. In his study of major domestic policy between 1953 and 1966, James Sundquist cites Aspinall's action as "the outstanding example of a veto by a nonrepresentative legislative committee," *Politics and Policy,* p. 520.

60. Howard Zahniser to John F. Kennedy, September 27, 1962, AP, Box 641; Laurance Rockefeller to Anderson, October 19, 1962, AP, Box 875; *New York Times,* September 16, 1962.

61. U.S., Senate Committee on Interior and Insular Affairs, *Valle Grande National Park, N. Mex.,* hearings on S.3321, September 17, 1962.

62. W. J. Scanzini to Anderson, May 4, 1961, AP, Box 637.

63. "Why Be Patient," *The Santa Fe New Mexican,* April 10, 1961.

64. *Valle Grande National Park, N. Mex.,* pp. 3–5; U.S., National Park Service, *Valle Grande* (feasibility study), July 1964.

65. W. J. Scanzini to Anderson, May 4, 1961, AP, Box 637; Anderson to W. J. Scanzini, May 23, 1961, AP, Box 637.

66. *Valle Grande National Park,* N. Mex., p. 2.

67. Anderson to Stewart Udall, May 19, 1961, AP, Box 637.

68. Anderson to Thomas Sandenaw, October 7, 1961, AP, Box 637.

69. Jerry Verkler to Anderson, June 23, 1961, AP, Box 637; Fred Thompson to Anderson, June 30, 1961, AP, Box 637; Anderson to Albert Kelley, October 3, 1961, AP, Box 637; Jess White to Anderson, October 13, 1961, AP, Box 637.

70. Doc H. Burnett to Anderson, October 24, 1961, AP, Box 637; Anderson to Thomas Sandenaw, October 7, 1961, AP, Box 637; Hugh Woodward to Anderson, June 11, 1962, AP, Box 637; Fred Thompson to Anderson, June 27, 1962, AP, Box 637.

71. Anderson to Thomas Sandenaw, October 7, 1961, AP, Box 637.

72. Anderson to George Savage, April 16, 1962, AP, Box 637.

73. Ibid.

74. Max Edwards to Anderson, May 17, 1962, AP, Box 637; Anderson to George Savage, May 23, 1962, AP, Box 637.

75. Valle Grande National Park, N. Mex., pp. 1–2; *The Santa Fe New Mexican,* September 17 and 18, 1962.

76. U.S., Senate, *Providing for the Establishment of the Canyonlands National Park,* Report 87–2121, September 24, 1962, pp. 1–6.

77. Ibid., p. 1.

78. U.S., Senate, Committee on Interior and Insular Affairs, *Proposed Canyonlands National Park in Utah,* hearings on S.2387, March 29–30, 1962, pp. 4–5, 12–15.

79. Ibid., pp. 12, 48.

80. Ibid., pp. 102–6.

81. Frank Moss to Wallace Bennett, March 21, 1962, AP, Box 662; Anderson to Frank Moss, March 22, 1962, AP, Box 662.

82. *Providing for the Establishment of Canyonlands National Park,* pp. 8–10.

83. Ben Stong to Anderson, April 26, 1962, AP, Box 662.

84. Anderson to Frank Moss, March 22, 1962, AP, Box 662.

85. Interview with Jerry Verkler, September 1, 1982; *Proposed Canyonlands National Park,* pp. 26–41.

86. Ibid., pp. 30–32.

87. Ibid., p. 38.

88. Ibid., p. 121.

89. Ibid., p. 111.

90. Ben Stong to Anderson, April 26, 1962, AP, Box 662.

91. Ibid.
92. Stewart Udall to Anderson, December 14, 1962, AP, Box 691.
93. *Providing for the Establishment of Canyonlands National Park.*
94. Point Reyes National Seashore Act, PL 87–657, September 13, 1962; Padre Island National Seashore Act, PL 87–712, September 28, 1962; *CR,* April 10, 1962, pp. 6243–44.
95. U.S., Senate, *Padre Island National Seashore,* Report 87–1226, March 6, 1962.
96. *CR,* April 10, 1962, pp. 6256–57.
97. Ibid., pp. 6257–59; Neal R. Pierce, *The Megastates of America* (New York: W. W. Norton & Co., 1972), pp. 524–525; Anderson learned at first hand of the operation of the King Ranch from its owner Richard Kleberg in 1945 as the latter testified before Anderson's House food shortages committee, U.S., House, Committee to Investigate Food Shortages, *Food Shortages,* hearings, April 20, 1945, pp. 299–316.
98. *CR,* April 10, 1962, p. 6258.
99. Ibid., pp. 6258–59.
100. U.S., *Public Papers of John F. Kennedy, January 1, 1962 to December 31, 1962,* p. 725.
101. *CR,* September 28, 1962, pp. 20097–98.
102. *News from the Capitol,* October 9, 1962 (Anderson's weekly newsletter), AP, Box 177.

## Chapter 7

1. *Washington Post,* September 4, 1964, reprinted in *Congressional Record* (hereafter cited as *CR*), September 8, 1964, p. A4634.
2. *News from the Capitol,* October 13, 1964, Clinton Anderson Papers, Library of Congress (hereafter cited as AP), Box 224.
3. "Changing Public Opinion—As A Legislator Sees It," Address to the annual meeting of the Sierra Club, Santa Fe, New Mexico, November 7, 1964, AP, Box 988.
4. "Udall Hails 'Conservation Congress' for History-making Legislation," Interior Department press release, October 13, 1964, AP, Box 988.
5. "Wayne Aspinall," (Oral History) Former Members of Congress, Inc., February 15, 1979, Library of Congress, Box 1, pp. 4–6; "Aspinall New Chairman of House Interior Committee," *Congressional Quarterly,* January 23, 1959, p. 109; Obituary, *Washington Post,* October 10, 1983, p. C10.
6. "Wayne Aspinall," pp. 7, 14; Interview with John Bingaman, August 6, 1983.
7. Clinton P. Anderson, *Outsider in the Senate* (New York: World Publishing Co., 1970), p. 236; Anderson appointment book, 1964, AP, Box 1010; Anderson press release, August 17, 1964, AP, Box 670.
8. Ben Stong to Anderson, November 14, 1962, AP, Box 670.
9. Wayne Aspinall to John F. Kennedy, October 15, 1962, reprinted in U.S., House, Committee on Interior and Insular Affairs, *Need for Revi-*

*sion of the Public Land Laws,* Committee Print No. 6, August 23, 1963, pp. 45–46.

10. Ben Stong to Anderson, November 14, 1962, AP, Box 670.

11. Stewart Udall to Anderson, November 5, 1962, AP, Box 433; Anderson to Stewart Udall, November 8, 1962, AP, Box 433.

12. Ben Stong to Anderson, November 14, 1962, AP, Box 670.

13. *CR,* July 26, 1951, pp. 8937–40; *Albuquerque Journal,* July 29, 1951; *Albuquerque Tribune,* August 11, 1951.

14. Interview with Robert Wolf, November 5, 1981; Others close to the committee firmly denied that Anderson encouraged any such sabotage; Interview with Jerry Verkler, September 1, 1982; Helene Monberg, "Mechem, Gets Jump on Senate Seniority," *Farmington [NM] Daily Times,* December 4, 1962, AP, Box 175.

15. Interview with Robert Wolf; interview with Claude Wood, November 21, 1981.

16. Anderson to Norris E. Bradbury, January 28, 1963, AP, Box 175; "Favors Granted, Clinton P. Anderson," Congressional Favors File, Box 1, Lyndon B. Johnson Library, Austin Texas.

17. Ben Stong to Henry Jackson, February 26, 1962, AP, Box 694.

18. Ibid.

19. U.S., Senate, Committee on Interior and Insular Affairs, *National Wilderness Preservation Act,* hearings on S.4, February 28 and March 1, 1963, pp. 1, 16–18.

20. Anderson, *Outsider in the Senate,* p. 20.

21. *National Wilderness Preservation Act,* p. 54.

22. Paul Brooks, "Congressman Aspinall vs. the People of the United States," *Harper's Magazine,* March 1963, pp. 59–63.

23. Ibid., p. 62.

24. Jerry Verkler to Henry Jackson, March 11, 1963, AP, Box 670.

25. Anderson to James Boyd, May 28, 1962, AP, Box 670; Anderson to Vincent X. Flaherty, April 2, 1963, AP, Box 670.

26. Ibid.

27. Anderson to James Boyd, May 28, 1962, AP, Box 670.

28. Ibid.

29. Anderson to Alex Deutsch, March 28, 1963, AP, Box 670.

30. Anderson to Vincent X. Flaherty, April 2, 1963, AP, Box 670.

31. Ibid.

32. U.S., Senate, *Establishing A National Wilderness Preservation System for the Permanent Good of the Whole People,* Report 88–109, April 3, 1963, pp. 21–22.

33. *CR,* April 9, 1963, p. 5928.

34. *CR,* April 8, 1963, p. 5885.

35. *CR,* April 9, 1963, p. 5943.

36. Jerry Verkler to Anderson, January 13, 1964, AP, Box 671.

37. *CR,* March 11, 1963, pp. 3892–94.

38. U.S., Senate, Committee on Interior and Insular Affairs, *Land and*

*Water Conservation Fund,* hearings on S.859, March 7 and 8, 1963, pp. 2–7.

39. Ibid., pp. 19–36.
40. Ibid., pp. 18–19.
41. Ibid., p. 24.
42. Anderson to John Bingaman, March 12, 1963, AP, Box 671.
43. *Land and Water Conservation Fund,* p. 46.
44. Ben Stong to Henry Jackson, May 1, 1963, AP, Box 671.
45. President's appointment book, May 20, 1963, John F. Kennedy Library; U.S., *Public Papers of John F. Kennedy,* January 1, 1963 to November 22, 1963, p. 414.
46. Luna (Diamond) to Lorella (Salazar), May 21, 1963, AP, Box 437; *CR,* June 13, 1963, pp. 19769–73; Clinton P. Anderson, "This We Hold Dear," *American Forests* 70 (July 1963): pp. 24–25.
47. AP, Box 670.
48. *CR,* June 13, 1963, p. 10771.
49. Ibid., pp. 10772–73.
50. Ibid., p. 10772.
51. Ibid., p. 10773.
52. "True Conservative," *Washington Post,* May 26, 1963, reprinted in *CR,* June 13, 1963, p. 10773.
53. Ben Stong to Anderson, June 19, 1963, AP, Box 670.
54. Ibid.
55. Interview with Robert Wolf, November 5, 1981; *Need for Revision of the Public Land Laws,* pp. 7–38 passim.
56. Wayne Aspinall, "Remarks Before the Section on Mineral and Natural Resources Law at the American Bar Association Annual Meeting, Chicago, Ill., August 13, 1963," reprinted in *Need for Revision of the Public Land Laws,* pp. 39–44 and in abbreviated form in *CR,* August 20, 1963, pp. 15505–06.
57. Ibid.; Congressional Quarterly Service, *CQ Almanac, 1964,* p. 505; U.S., House, *Establishment of Public Land Law Review Commission,* Report 88–1008, December 7, 1963, pp. 1–4.
58. *Establishment of Public Land Law Review Commission,* pp. 4–6; Interview with Robert Wolf, November 5, 1981.
59. Interview with Robert Wolf, November 5, 1981.
60. Ibid.
61. Ibid.
62. Ibid.
63. Paul Wieck, "Aspinall, Anderson Continue Duel Over Wilderness Bill," *Albuquerque Journal,* August 25, 1963, AP, Box 670.
64. Ben Stong to Anderson, September 18, 1963, AP, Box 672; Director, Bureau of Outdoor Recreation Edward Crafts to Secretary Stewart Udall, October 19, 1963, AP, Box 670.
65. Ben Stong to Anderson, September 18, 1963, AP, Box 672.
66. Lee White to John F. Kennedy, November 12, 1963, Lee White Papers, John F. Kennedy Library.

67. Mike Manatos to Lawrence O'Brien, November 8, 1963, White House Staff Files, folder 3, Clinton Anderson, John F. Kennedy Library.

68. Anderson to Mike Manatos, November 13, 1963, AP, Box 238.

69. *CR,* November 14, 1963, p. 21825.

70. Clinton P. Anderson, "Why We Need the Land and Water Conservation Fund Bill," *American Forests* 70 (March 1964), reprinted in *CR,* March 16, 1964, pp. 5365–68.

71. Ibid., p. 5366.

72. Ibid., p. 5367.

73. Anderson to G. M. Dorland, November 13, 1963, AP, Box 671.

74. Ben Stong to Anderson, December 10, 1963, AP, Box 671.

75. Ibid.

76. Ibid.

77. Anderson appointment book, 1964 (January 8), AP, Box 1010.

78. Jerry Verkler to Anderson, January 13, 1964, AP, Box 671.

79. Ibid., January 22, 1964.

80. Anderson appointment book, 1964 (March 27), AP, Box 1010.

81. *Outsider in the Senate,* pp. 250–52.

82. Anderson to David Brower, May 11, 1964, AP, Box 670.

83. Presented at the association's annual meeting in New York, N.Y., September 6, 1963, citation in AP, Box 441.

84. *CR,* May 20, 1964, pp. 11474–75; AP, Box 442.

85. Mike Manatos to Bill Moyers, March 3, 1964, LBJ Library, Name File, Box 152.

86. Edward Crafts to Anderson, May 21, 1964, AP, Box 670; Mike Manatos to Lawrence O'Brien, June 29, 1964, LBJ Library, Name File, Box 152.

87. "Senate Invokes Cloture," *New York Times,* June 11, 1964, p. 1; Anderson appointment book, 1964 (June 10), AP, Box 1010.

88. Ben Stong to Anderson, June 23, 1964, AP, Box 670.

89. Claude Wood to Anderson, June 8, 1964, AP, Box 671.

90. Ben Stong to Anderson, June 23, 1964, AP, Box 670.

91. Memorandum of conversation, July 28, 1964, AP, Box 671.

92. Anderson to Henry Jackson, July 28, 1964, AP, Box 671.

93. U.S., House, Committee on Interior and Insular Affairs, *Wilderness Preservation System,* hearings on H.R. 9070, H.R. 9162, S.4, April 28, 1964, p. 1180; *New York Times,* May 6, 1964, p. 47.

94. *CR,* May 6, 1964, p. 10214; *CR,* May 11, 1964, pp. 10473–74.

95. Interview with Robert Wolf, November 5, 1981; in mid-July Anderson announced his intention to retire in 1966 at the end of his term, *Albuquerque Journal,* July 10, 1964.

96. *Outsider in the Senate,* p. 235.

97. Ibid.

98. *New York Times,* June 11, 1964, p. 1.

99. Ibid.

100. U.S., House, *National Wilderness Preservation System,* Report 88–1538, July 2, 1964, pp. 1–6.

101. Ibid., pp. 9–10.

102. *CQ Almanac,* 1964, pp. 485–87, 491.

103. *New York Times,* July 31, 1964, p. 1.

104. Anderson appointment book, 1964, AP, Box 1010; *Outsider in the Senate,* p. 235; Anderson press release, August 17, 1964, AP, Box 670.

105. U.S., House, *Establish A National Wilderness Preservation System,* Report 88–1829, August 19, 1964, pp. 9–11.

106. *CR,* August 20, 1964, p. 20630.

107. Ibid., p. 20629.

108. *Establish A National Wilderness Preservation System,* pp. 9–10.

109. Anderson to Philip Lester, September 10, 1964, AP, Box 670.

110. *CR,* August 20, 1964, p. 20630.

111. Ibid., p. 20601.

112. U.S., *Public Papers of Lyndon B. Johnson,* Book II, July 1–December 31, 1964, pp. 1033–34.

113. *CR,* September 3, 1964, pp. 21557–61 (Canyonlands) and pp. 21568–70; Established in 1965, the commission spent five years and $7 million to produce a report. One analyst later noted, "It was Aspinall's show from the first to last. His martinet approach, keen interest, and familiarity with the subject matter kept the commission moving," William K. Wyant, *Westward In Eden: The Public Lands and the Conservation Movement* (Los Angeles: University of California Press, 1982), pp. 142–45.

114. "Frank Moss," (Oral History) Former Members of Congress, Inc., September 20, 1978, Library of Congress, Box 6, p. 11.

115. Proclamation No. 3539, June 1, 1963, 28 F.R. 5407.

116. Jerry Verkler to Anderson, June 8, 1963, National Archives & Records Service, Washington, D.C., RG 46, 88A–F11; Verkler to Anderson, June 11, 1963, National Archives, 88A–F11.

117. U.S., Senate, Committee on Interior and Insular Affairs, *Valle Grande–Bandelier National Park,* hearings on S.1870, May 29, 1964, pp. 7–11.

118. *Indianapolis Star,* February 13, 1963, p. 12.

119. For a partisan, but fair, background statement of the Dunes issue, see Paul Douglas, *In the Fullness of Time* (New York: Harcourt Brace Jovanovich, 1972), chapter 38; also William Peeples, "The Indiana Dunes and Pressure Politics," *Atlantic,* February 1963, pp. 84–88; and Frederic Sicher, "The Indiana Dunes National Lakeshore," *National Parks Magazine,* July 1964, pp. 5–7, 15; J. Ronald Engel, *Sacred Sands: The Struggle for Community in the Indiana Dunes* (Middletown, CT: Wesleyan University Press, 1983), chapter 6; Kay Franklin and Norma Schaeffer, *Duel for the Dunes: Land Use Conflict on the Shores of Lake Michigan* (Urbana: University of Illinois Press, 1983), pp. 134–37, 164–68.

120. U.S., Senate, *Indiana Dunes National Lakeshore,* Report 88–1362, August 10, 1964, pp. 3–5.

121. Peeples, "The Indiana Dunes and Pressure Politics," pp. 85–87.

122. Ibid., p. 87.

123. U.S. *Public Papers of John F. Kennedy, January 1, 1962 to December 31, 1962,* p. 179: Special Message to Congress on Conservation. March 1, 1962; *Chicago Sun-Times,* August 4, 1964.

124. U.S., Senate, *Indiana Dunes National Lakeshore,* hearings, February 26–27, 1962.

125. *Outsider in the Senate,* p. 224; Carl Sandburg to Paul Douglas, June 27, 1958, quoted in Engel, *Sacred Sands,* p. 117.

126. Sicher, "The Indiana Dunes National Lakeshore," p. 7.

127. Paul Douglas to John F. Kennedy, March 31, 1962, Douglas Papers, Chicago Historical Society, Box 672.

128. Ibid.

129. Vance Hartke to Anderson, March 24, 1962, AP, Box 662; Anderson to Hartke, May 28, 1962, AP, Box 662.

130. Anderson to Paul Douglas, June 18, 1962, AP, Box 662.

131. Ibid.

132. Paul Douglas to Anderson, February 7, 1963, AP, Box 673.

133. Text of Anderson's telegram is contained in Anderson to Hilbert Rust, February 19, 1963, AP, Box 673.

134. AP, box 673 passim.

135. Hilbert Rust to Anderson, February 12, 1963, AP, Box 673.

136. Transcript of Pierre Salinger's news conference, February 12, 1963, Douglas Papers, Box 675.

137. Eloise de la O to Arthur B. Horner, February 14, 1963, AP, Box 673; Anderson to Hilbert Rust, March 4, 1963, AP, Box 673. This is a classic Anderson letter—sharp, candid, combative and drafted without staff assistance in the heat of battle.

138. Paul Douglas to Anderson, September 29, 1964, AP, Box 673.

139. The story of the bill's final enactment in October 1966 is recounted in Paul Douglas, *In the Fullness of Time,* pp. 541–43.

140. Interview with Robert Wolf, November 5, 1981.

141. Ibid., and interview with Claude Wood, November 21, 1981.

142. Interview with Robert Wolf, November 5, 1981.

143. Ibid., and interview with Howard Bray, April 22, 1980.

144. *Outsider in the Senate,* p. 236.

## Chapter 8

1. Clinton P. Anderson to Oliver LaFarge, August 1, 1962, Clinton P. Anderson Papers, Library of Congress (hereafter cited as AP), Box 640.

2. See chapter 3 for a full account of Anderson's maneuvering to include New Mexico projects in this act.

3. Anderson to Carl Hayden, May 2, 1956, AP, Box 1061.

4. U.S., Senate, Committee on Appropriations, *Public Works Appropriations, 1957,* hearings on H.R. 11319, May 24, 1956, pp. 198–201.

5. Doyle Kline to Anderson, undated but subsequent to January 28, 1957, AP, Box 639.

6. Public Law 84–641, July 2, 1956.

7. Anderson to Doyle Kline, January 28, 1957, AP, Box 639.

8. Ibid.

9. Doyle Kline to Anderson, February 13, 1957 and February 28, 1957, AP, Box 639.

10. Anderson to Edwin Mechem, February 6, 1957, AP, Box 639.

11. U.S., Senate, *Navajo Indian Irrigation and San Juan–Chama Participating Projects,* Report 85–2198, August 5, 1958, pp. 2–5.

12. U.S., Senate, Committee on Interior and Insular Affairs, *Navajo Irrigation—San Juan–Chama Diversion,* hearings on S.3648, July 9–10, 1958, pp. 5–10, 13–14; Michael L. Lawson, "The Navajo Indian Irrigation Project: Muddied Past, Clouded Future," *The Indian Historian* 9 (Winter 1976): 19–29.

13. *Navajo Irrigation—San Juan–Chama Diversion,* pp. 11–12; Kay Collins, "The Transmountain Diversion of Water from the Colorado River" (M.A. thesis, University of New Mexico, 1965), chapter 5.

14. *Navajo Irrigation—San Juan–Chama Diversion,* p. 1.

15. Ibid., p. 2.

16. Ibid., pp. 2–3.

17. Ibid., pp. 153–61.

18. *Congressional Record* (hereafter cited as *CR*), August 15, 1958, pp. 11720–23.

19. Ibid.

20. U.S., Senate, *San Luis Unit, Central Valley Project, California,* Report 85–2202, August 5, 1958, pp. 6–8; *Outsider in the Senate,* p. 239.

21. *CR,* August 15, 1958, pp. 17725–26.

22. U.S., Congress, *Congressional Directory,* Eighty-sixth Congress, First Session, p. 216; "Aspinall New Chairman of House Interior Committee," *Congressional Quarterly Weekly Report,* January 23, 1959, p. 109; for an analysis of the impact of the Democratic "Class of 1958," see Michael Foley, *The New Senate: Liberal Influence On A Conservative Institution, 1959–1972* (New Haven: Yale University Press, 1980), pp. 26–33.

23. Helene Monberg, "New Mexico Bill's Future Uncertain," Newspaper clipping, n.d. but pre-January 23, 1959, AP, Box 639.

24. U.S., House, *Fryingpan–Arkansas Project,* Colorado, Report 87–694, July 11, 1961, p. 6.

25. Ibid., p. 24.

26. Anderson to Goodrich Lineweaver, February 27, 1959, AP, Box 639.

27. Lineweaver to Anderson, March 2, 1959, AP, Box 639.

28. U.S., Senate, Committee on Interior and Insular Affairs, *Navajo Indian—San Juan–Chama Diversion, New Mexico,* hearings on S.72, March 16, 1959, pp. 1–2.

29. Ibid., p. 10.

30. Fred Aandahl to James Murray, March 9, 1959, AP, Box 639.

31. U.S., Senate, *Navajo Irrigation and San Juan–Chama Project, New Mexico,* Report 86–155, April 8, 1959, p. 12.

32. *CR,* May 5, 1969, pp. 7474–76.

33. Ibid., p. 7476; *CR,* May 19, 1959, pp. 8462–67.

34. Helene Monberg, "New Mexico–Colorado Agreement Vital on Nav-

ajo Irrigation," *Farmington Daily Times,* August 26, 1959, p. 1. (Copy in AP, Box 639.)

35. Steve Reynolds to Anderson, September 4, 1959, AP, Box 639.
36. Ibid.
37. Steve Reynolds to John Burroughs, June 4, 1959, AP, Box 639.
38. John Burroughs to Anderson, September 9, 1959, AP, Box 639.
39. Anderson to Burroughs, September 10, 1959, AP, Box 639.
40. Claude Wood to Anderson, January 21, 1960, AP, Box 639.
41. Anderson to Fred Seaton, March 15, 1960, AP, Box 639.
42. March 14, 1969, AP, Box 639.
43. Anderson and Dennis Chavez to Carl Hayden, April 7, 1960, AP, Box 639.
44. Ibid.
45. U.S., House, Committee on Interior and Insular Affairs, *San Juan–Chama Reclamation Project and Navajo Indian Irrigation Project,* hearings on H.R. 2352, H.R. 2494, and S.72, May 20, 1960, p. 162.
46. Ibid., p. 9.
47. Ibid., p. 68.
48. Ibid., p. 9.
49. Ibid., p. 90.
50. U.S., Department of Interior, Press Release, June 18, 1960; Anderson to Wayne Aspinall, June 18, 1960, AP, Box 639.
51. Felix Sparks to Steve Reynolds, September 14, 1960, AP, Box 639.
52. *Albuquerque Journal,* October 18, 1960, p. 1.
53. Undated press release, Office of Senator Clinton P. Anderson, possibly October 18, 1960, AP, Box 639.
54. Anderson to Stewart Udall, January 27, 1961; Udall to Anderson, February 2, 1961, AP, Box 640.
55. U.S., Senate, Committee on Interior and Insular Affairs, *Navajo Indian Irrigation and San Juan–Chama Project,* hearings on S.107, March 15, 1961, p. 11.
56. Ibid., p. 12.
57. San Juan Farm and Livestock Bureau, "Resolution to All Members of Congress," January 17, 1961, AP, Box 640.
58. Claude Wood to Anderson, memo attached to San Juan resolution, January 1961, AP, Box 640.
59. Anderson to Lincoln O'Brien, January 23, 1961; O'Brien to Anderson, January 30, 1961, AP, Box 640.
60. Claude Wood to I. J. Coury, February 16, 1961, AP, Box 640.
61. Coury to Wood, March 2, 1961, AP, Box 640.
62. Coury to Wood, March 22, 1961, AP, Box 640.
63. Interview with Steve Reynolds, July 22, 1982.
64. *Navajo Indian Irrigation Project,* (S.107), p. 31.
65. *CR,* March 27, 1961, pp. 4909–10.
66. *Navajo Indian Irrigation Project,* (S.107), pp. 58–59.
67. Ibid., pp. 58–67; *CR,* March 27, 1961, p. 4910.
68. Ibid.

69. Phillip S. Hughes to Anderson, March 24, 1961 in *CR*, March 27, 1961, pp. 4910–11.

70. *CR*, March 27, 1961, pp. 4911–12.

71. Ibid., p. 4913.

72. Ibid., p. 4914.

73. *CR*, March 28, 1961, pp. 4986–89.

74. Ibid., p. 4989.

75. Ibid.

76. Ibid., p. 4990.

77. Ibid., pp. 4990–91.

78. U.S., Senate, *Authorizing the Secretary of the Interior to Construct, Operate, and Maintain the Norman Project, Oklahoma,* Report 86–872, September 2, 1959, pp. 2, 6–8; *CR*, June 2, 1960, p. 11638.

79. *CR*, March 28, 1961, p. 4992.

80. Ibid., p. 4999.

81. Anderson to Lincoln O'Brien, March 27, 1961, AP, Box 640.

82. *Fryingpan-Arkansas Project, Colorado,* pp. 2–4; *Congressional Quarterly Almanac, 1962,* p. 470.

83. U.S., House, Committee on Interior and Insular Affairs, *San Juan–Chama Reclamation Project and Navajo Indian Irrigation Project,* hearings on H.R.2552, H.R.6541, H.R.7596, and S.107, April 24–June 1, 1961, pp. 1–14.

84. U.S., House, *Authorizing Construction of Navajo Indian Irrigation Project and Initial Stage of San Juan–Chama Project as Participating Projects of the Colorado River Storage Project,* Report 87–685, July 10, 1961, pp. 1–10; Richard L. Berkman and W. Kip Viscusi, *Damming the West* (New York: Grossman Publishers, 1973), pp. 184–90; Rosalie Martone, "The United States and the Betrayal of Indian Water Rights," *The Indian Historian* 7 (Summer 1974): 3–12.

85. "Aspinall Expects House Rule on Fryingpan Bill this Week," typescript of article that appeared on Pueblo, Colorado *Star-Journal and Chieftan,* n.d., AP, Box 640.

86. "Aspinall Totals Building Costs for Water Projects," typescript of article that appeared in Pueblo, Colorado *Star-Journal and Chieftan,* n.d., AP, Box 640.

87. Claude Wood to Anderson, May 12, 1962; Anderson to Lincoln O'Brien, May 28, 1962, AP, Box 640.

88. Ibid.

89. Ibid.

90. Anderson to Oliver LaFarge, June 4, 1962, AP, Box 640.

91. *CR*, May 29, 1962, pp. 9484–85.

92. Ibid.

93. *CR*, June 12, 1962, pp. 10146–74; *CR*, June 13, 1962, p. 10388; *CR*, August 6, 1962, pp. 15683–86; U.S., *Public Papers of President John F. Kennedy, 1962,* p. 620.

94. AP, Box 640; "Anderson's Seven-Year Fight Ends," *Albuquerque Tribune,* August 20, 1964, p. 1.

## Chapter 9

1. "Water Shortage—Seven States Endure Severe Scarcity," *New York Times,* March 7, 1957, p. 1; Robert and Leona Rienow, "The Day the Taps Run Dry," *Harper's,* October 1958, p. 72; Walter Prescott Webb, "The American West, Perpetual Mirage," *Harper's,* May 1957, pp. 25–31.

2. "Annual Budget Message to Congress, January 13, 1958," in U.S, *Public Papers of Dwight D. Eisenhower,* 1958, pp. 68–69.

3. A good example of the public views of western Democratic senators on water development restrictions appeared in an address and letter to the president by Oregon's Senator Richard L. Neuberger, *Congressional Record* (hereafter cited as *CR*), January 30, 1958, pp. 1355–60.

4. *CR,* January 27, 1959, pp. 1156–64.

5. Mike Mansfield and James Murray to Clinton Anderson, February 1, 1959, Clinton P. Anderson Papers, Library of Congress (hereafter cited as AP), Box 874; Clinton P. Anderson, *Outsider in the Senate* (New York: World Publishing Co., 1970), pp. 246–47.

6. *CR,* April 24, 1959, p. 6632; *CR,* April 28, 1959, p. 6902.

7. U.S., Senate, *Report of the Select Committee on National Water Resources,* Report 87–29, January 30, 1961, pp. 72–78.

8. U.S., Senate, Select Committee on National Water Resources, *Water Resources,* hearing on S. Res. 48, part 12, November 23, 1959, pp. 1972–75.

9. Ibid., pp. 2002–4.

10. Ibid., p. 2006.

11. Ibid., pp. 2011–12.

12. Anderson to Robert Kerr, May 20, 1959, AP, Box 874.

13. Gale McGee to Kerr, November 28, 1960; James Murray to Kerr, December 5, 1960; Doyle Kline to Anderson, June 6, 1960, AP, Box 874.

14. Cited in J. Lee Rankin to Anderson, December 9, 1960, AP, Box 874.

15. Anderson to Jerry Verkler, November 25, 1960; Verkler to Anderson, November 5, 1960; AP, Box 874.

16. U.S., Senate, Select Committee on National Water Resources. Unprinted transcript of drafting subcommittee meeting December 10, 1960, p. 20, AP, Box 874.

17. Ibid., p. 21.

18. Ibid., p. 27

19. Ibid., p. 106.

20. Ibid., p. 50.

21. *Outsider in the Senate,* pp. 246–47.

22. *Report of Select Committee,* pp. 15–16.

23. Ibid., pp. 137–44.

24. Unprinted transcript, p. 67; a thoughtful and comprehensive sum-

mary of the Select Committee's work and the broader problems of water supply appears in Frank E. Moss, *The Water Crisis* (New York: Frederick A. Praeger, 1967).

25. *CR,* April 14, 1961, pp. 5914–16.

26. U.S., Senate, Committee on Interior and Insular Affairs, *Water Resources Planning Act of 1961,* hearings on S.1629, July 10, 1961, pp. 174–75; for a full account of New Mexico's water supply situation see "New Mexico Statement to the U.S. Senate Select Committee on National Water Resources, September 1959," AP, Box 874.

27. *Water Resources Planning Act,* p. 200.

28. Ibid., pp. 207–209.

29. Ben Stong to Anderson, July 11, 1961, AP, Box 217.

30. For details, see Chapter 5.

31. Stong to Anderson, July 11, 1961, AP, Box 217; U.S., Senate, Committee on Interior and Insular Affairs, *Water Resources Planning Act of 1961,* hearings on S.2246, S.1629, S.1778, August 16, 1961, p. 102.

32. *CR,* July 14, 1961, p. 12536.

33. *Water Resources Planning Act of 1961,* July 26, 1961, p. 81.

34. Ibid., pp. 17–18.

35. Ibid., p. 127.

36. Ibid., p. 129.

37. Ibid.

38. Anderson to Ramsey Clark, August 18, 1961; Clark to Anderson, August 28, 1961, in Ibid., pp. 137–38.

39. Ben Stong to Anderson, September 5, 1961, AP, Box 217; Stong to Anderson, October 16, 1961, AP, Box 432.

40. Stong to Anderson, October 16, 1961, AP, Box 432.

41. Anderson to Jerry Verkler, October 19, 1961, AP, Box 432.

42. For an analysis of the price the administration paid in legislative terms for its efforts in 1961 to "pack" the House Rules Committee, see *Congressional Quarterly Weekly Report,* September 14, 1962, pp. 1528–29 and Richard Bolling, *House Out of Order* (New York: E. P. Dutton, 1966), Chapter 10.

43. Ben Stong to Anderson, July 13, 1962; July 24, 1962, AP, Box 217.

44. U.S., *Public Papers of President John F. Kennedy,* 1961, p. 115.

45. Stong to Anderson, July 13, 1962, AP, Box 217.

46. Ibid.

47. Neal Peirce, *The Mountain States of America* (New York: Norton, 1972), p. 266.

48. *CR,* July 27, 1962, pp. 14942–46.

49. Interview with Paul Wieck, July 12, 1982.

50. *CR,* July 27, 1962, pp. 14946–47.

51. U.S., Senate, Committee on Interior and Insular Affairs, *Water Resources Research Act,* hearing, February 19–20, 1963, pp. 36, 38.

52. *CR,* July 27, 1962, pp. 14942–46.

53. Ibid., p. 14944.

54. *Water Resources Research Act,* pp. *13–16, 204.*

55. Orville Freeman to Anderson, February 19, 1962, Ibid., pp. 20–21.

56. Jerry Verkler to Anderson, December 15, 1962, AP, Box 669.

57. *CR,* July 27, 1962, p. 14945; "News from the Capitol" (Anderson's newsletter), October 16, 1962, AP, Box 177.

58. *CR,* January 14, 1963, p. 205.

59. *Water Resources Research Act,* p. 21.

60. Ibid., pp. 48–49.

61. Ibid., p. 73.

62. *CR,* April 22, 1963, p. 6706.

63. *CR,* January 14, 1963, p. 203.

64. *CR,* April 22, 1963, p. 6708; James Sundquist describes this process of legislative communication, in which Anderson excelled, as involving "a combination of factual information and emotional advocacy" that are arranged in three levels. They include: "The expert level, where the nature of the problem and the adequacy of the solution are analyzed in factual terms. The political leadership level where factual analysis is blended with emotional appeal . . . and the campaign level, where the weight of the dialogue is upon emotional appeal and factual argument may be reduced to a few symbolic words and numbers." *Politics and Policy: The Eisenhower, Kennedy, and Johnson Years* (Washington, D.C.: Brookings Institution, 1968), p. 508.

65. *CR,* April 22, 1963, p. 6714.

66. *CR,* April 23, 1963, pp. 6772–85.

67. U.S., Senate, *Preliminary Report of the Inland Waterways Commission,* February 26, 1908, Document 60–325, pp. 25–27.

68. U.S., Senate, Committee on Interior and Insular Affairs, *River Basin Planning Act of 1964,* hearings on S.1111, September 12–13, 1963, pp. 24–29.

69. For a resume of earlier planning efforts, see Congressional Quarterly, *Congress and the Nation, 1965–68,* p. 499.

70. U.S., Senate, Committee on Interior and Insular Affairs, "Water Resources Planning Act," unprinted transcript hearings on S.2246, March 2, 1962, National Archives, RG 46, 87A–F11, Box 215, no. 68.

71. Ibid., *CR,* March 15, 1963, pp. 4321–22.

72. Ibid.

73. Ben Stong to Anderson, December 14, 1962, AP, Box 669.

74. Ibid.; Stong to Anderson, April 30, 1963, AP, Box 672; Stong to Anderson, January 21, 1963, National Archives RG 46, 88A–F11 (42).

75. Stong to Anderson, January 21, 1963; Stong to Anderson, January 5, 1963, National Archives, RG 46, 88A–F11 (42).

76. Ibid.

77. Stong to Anderson, April 30, 1963, AP, Box 672. Anderson had arranged in 1962 for Moss to become chairman of the Irrigation and Reclamation Subcommittee to bolster the Utah senator's reelection chances. When Ernest Gruening (D-AK) protested that he had more seniority, Anderson refused to step aside until the Alaska senator relented. Shortly af-

ter taking over as chairman of the full committee in 1963, Henry Jackson replaced Moss with Frank Church (D-ID), whom he felt would be more diligent in ensuring that not a drop of Columbia River water left its basin. Jackson's actions greatly irritated Anderson. (Interview with Frank Moss, April 5, 1980).

78. *River Basin Planning Act of 1964,* pp. 72–99.

79. Stong to Anderson, September 18, 1963, AP, Box 672.

80. *CR,* December 4, 1963, pp. 23234–36.

81. Ibid., p. 23250.

82. Stong to Anderson, February 26, 1964, AP, Box 669.

83. Stong to Anderson, June 30, 1964, AP, Box 669.

84. Stong to Anderson, June 19, 1963, AP, Box 669.

85. U.S., House, Committee on Interior and Insular Affairs, *Water Resources Research Centers,* hearings on S.2, H.R.2683, et al., June 24–25, July 22–23, 1963, pp. 44–45.

86. Ibid., pp. 62–68.

87. U.S., House, *Establishing Water Resources Research Centers at Land Grant Colleges,* Report 88–1136, February 10, 1964, p. 1.

88. Stong to Anderson, February 26, 1964, AP, Box 669.

89. Theodore Schad to Jerry Verkler, February 19, 1964, AP, Box 669.

90. Anderson to Kermit Gordon, May 1, 1964; Phillip Hughes to Anderson, May 18, 1964, AP, Box 669.

91. *CR,* June 2, 1964, pp. 12541–69.

92. "Amendments to S.2 as passed by the House, Senate Interior Committee staff suggestions," n.d., AP, Box 669; Stong to Anderson, June 30, 1964, AP, Box 669; John Walsh, "Water Resources: Congress Votes Research Centers for States; River Basin Planning Bill Advances," *Science,* September 4, 1964, pp. 1022–24; U.S., House, *Water Resources Research Centers,* Report 88–1526, June 30, 1964, pp. 7–8.

93. Stong to Anderson, June 30, 1964, AP, Box 669.

94. U.S., *Public Papers of President Lyndon B. Johnson, 1963–64,* p. 806.

95. Anderson to Lyndon B. Johnson, July 8, 1964, AP, Box 669; Myer Feldman to Lyndon B. Johnson, July 14, 1964, LBJ Library, Name File, Box 152; Stong to Anderson, November 12, 1964, AP, Box 720.

96. White House Press Release, July 17, 1964, AP, Box 669.

97. Anderson to Laurance S. Rockefeller, August 19, 1964, AP, Box 670.

98. Stong to Anderson, September 17, 1964, AP, Box 720; Jerry Verkler to Eloise de la O, September 4, 1964, AP, Box 720; U.S., House, *Water Resources Planning Act,* Report 88–1877, September 2, 1964, p. 1.

99. Stong to Anderson, December 10, 1963, AP, Box 669; Stong to Anderson, n.d. [January 1965], AP, Box 720; the measure, reintroduced as S.21, passed early in the Eighty-ninth Congress and was signed by President Johnson on July 22, 1965.

100. U.S., Senate, Committees on Interior and Insular Affairs, Agricul-

ture and Forestry, and Interstate and Foreign Commerce, *Weather Control and Augmented Potable Water Supply,* joint hearings on S.5, S.22, and S.798, March 14–19, April 5, 1951, pp. 10–11.

101. For a convenient summary of the earlier efforts to establish a federal saline water program, see Congressional Quarterly, *Congress and the Nation* (Washington, 1965), pp. 939–42.

102. U.S., Senate, *Amending the Act of July 3, 1952, Relating to Research in the Development and Utilization of Saline Waters,* Report 84–370, May 23, 1955, pp. 2–6; *Outsider in the Senate,* p. 244.

103. *Outsider in the Senate,* pp. 244–45.

104. Ibid.

105. *Amending the Act of July 3, 1952,* p. 5.

106. Doyle Kline to Anderson, June 3, 1957, AP, Box 601.

107. Wayne Brobeck to Anderson, May 22, 1957; Kline to Anderson, May 29, 1957; Anderson to Brobeck, May 29, 1957; Kline to Anderson, June 3, 1957, AP, Box 601.

108. Kline to Anderson, November 8, 1957, AP, Box 601; Brobeck to Anderson, November 25, 1957, AP, Box 601.

109. Kline to Brobeck, January 14, 1958; Claude Wood to Anderson, December 23, 1957, AP, Box 601; U.S., Senate, Committee on Interior and Insular Affairs, *Saline Water Conversion Program, Memorandum of the Chairman of the Subcommittee on Irrigation and Reclamation,* Committee Print, March 14, 1958, p. 1.

110. U.S., Senate, Committee on Interior and Insular Affairs, *Saline Water Conversion,* hearings on S.J. Res. 135 and S.3370, March 20–21, 1958, pp. 3–6.

111. Ibid., p. 9.

112. *CR,* April 1, 1958, p. 5883.

113. Press release, Office of Clinton P. Anderson, April 24, 1958, AP, Box 601; U.S., Senate, *Saline Water Program,* Report 85–1593, May 19, 1958, pp. 6–9.

114. Ibid.

115. *Outsider in the Senate,* p. 244; interview with Paul Wieck, July 12, 1982; *CR,* June 10, 1958, pp. 10659–64.

116. *CR,* August 12, 1958, pp. 17144–51; *CR,* August 23, 1958, p. 19586; *CR,* August 21, 1958, pp. 18915–17.

117. Lyndon B. Johnson to Anderson, November 7, 1958, AP, Box 601; Johnson to Anderson, November 12, 1958, LBJ Library, Congressional File, Box 39.

118. Anderson to Johnson, November 18, 1958, AP, Box 601.

119. *Congress and the Nation,* p. 941.

120. Anderson to Lyndon Johnson, May 16, 1960; Stewart French to Anderson, September 12, 1960, AP, Box 640.

121. *CR,* August 25, 1960, p. 16349.

122. *CR,* June 27, 1961, pp. 11358–59; U.S., Senate, *Saline Water Conversion Program,* Report 87–780, August 25, 1961, pp. 2–7; *CR,* August

31, 1961, pp. 17715–36; U.S., Senate, Committee on Interior and Insular Affairs, *Saline Water Conversion,* hearings on S.2156, August 22, 1961, pp. 13–17, 19.

123. *CR,* March 12, 1962, p. 3848; *Congress and the Nation,* pp. 940–41.

124. *Congress and the Nation,* p. 941.

# Bibliography

## Interviews

Bingaman, John August 6, 1983
Bray, Howard April 22, 1980
Conway, John February 8, 1980
de la O, Eloise January 30, 1980; February 8, 1980
Diamond, Luna October 27, 1980
Hamblen, Ruby December 17, 1979; February 8, 1980
Hruska, Roman August 21, 1981
Hynes, Patrick June 21, 1982
McCaffrey, Thomas July 24, 1982
Moss, Frank E. April 5, 1980; November 4, 1982
Murphy, George September 13, 1980
Pino, Richard July 20 & 23, 1982
Reynolds, Steve July 22, 1982
Riddick, Floyd October 13, 1981
Roberts, John August 4, 1983
Rosenblatt, Maurice June 29, 1982; July 8, 1982
Salazar, Lorella Montoya July 20, 1982
Scott, Hugh September 14, 1982
Smith, Margaret Chase July 5, 1984
Verkler, Jerry September 1, 1982
Walton, Jack F. July 23, 1982
Wertheimer, Linda May 19, 1981
Wieck, Paul July 12, 1982
Wolf, Robert November 5 & 6, 1981; January 26, 1982
Wood, Claude E. November 20 & 21, 1981

# Oral History Transcripts

Anderson, Clinton P. John F. Kennedy Library, Boston, MA, April 4, 1967.
———. Lyndon B. Johnson Library, Austin, TX, May 20, 1969.
Aspinall, Wayne. Former Members of Congress, Inc. Library of Congress, Washington, DC, June 11, 1974; February 15, 1979.
Brower, David. "David R. Brower: Environmental Activist, Publicist, and Prophet." Regional Oral History Office, University of California, Berkeley, 1974–78.
Burns, James MacGregor. John F. Kennedy Library, May 14, 1965.
Cliff, Edward. "Half A Century of Conservation." U.S. Forest Service History Section, Washington, DC, March 1981.
Crafts, Edward C. "Congress and the Forest Service, 1950–1962." Regional Oral History Office, University of California, Berkeley, April 3, 1965.
———. "Forest Service Researcher and Congressional Liaison." Forest History Society, Santa Cruz, CA, 1972.
Leonard, Richard. "Mountaineer, Lawyer, Environmentalist." Regional Oral History Office, University of California, Berkeley, 1972–73.
Moss, Frank E. Former Members of Congress, Inc. Library of Congress, Washington, DC, September 20, 1978.
Riddick, Floyd M. Senate Historical Office, Washington, DC, June 1978–February 1979.
Stong, Benton J. and Victor Reinemer. University of Montana Library, Missoula, February 15, 1978.

# Manuscript Collections

## California

University of California, Berkeley
    William F. Knowland Papers
    Sierra Club Papers

## District of Columbia

Library of Congress
    Clinton P. Anderson Papers
National Archives
    RG 46 United States Senate

## Georgia

University of Georgia
    Richard B. Russell Papers

*Illinois*

Chicago Historical Society
Paul Douglas Papers
Claude A. Barnett Papers

*Massachusetts*

John F. Kennedy Library
John F. Kennedy Papers
Lawrence O'Brien Papers

*New Mexico*

University of New Mexico
Clinton P. Anderson Papers
Joseph Montoya Papers

*Oklahoma*

University of Oklahoma
Robert S. Kerr Papers

*Texas*

Lyndon Baines Johnson Library
Lyndon Johnson Papers
Mike Manatos Papers
Lawrence O'Brien Papers

## Theses and Dissertations

Baker, Richard A. "Senator Clinton P. Anderson and the Politics of Conservation, 1949–1964." Ph.D. dissertation, University of Maryland, 1982.

Collins, Kay. "The Transmountain Diversion of Water from the Colorado River: A Legal-Historical Study," MA thesis. University of New Mexico, 1965.

Dixon, Albert. "The Conservation of Wilderness: A Study in Politics." Ph.D. dissertation, University of California, Berkeley, 1968.

Freedle, Frances. "The Ninth Rejection: Senator Anderson V. Lewis Strauss." MA thesis, University of New Mexico, 1964.

Forsythe, James L. "Clinton P. Anderson: Politician and Businessman as Truman's Secretary of Agriculture." Ph.D. dissertation, University of New Mexico, 1970.

Gilligan, James P. "The Development of Policy and Administration of Forest Service Primitive and Wilderness Areas in the Western United States." Ph.D. dissertation, University of Michigan, 1954.

Gottlieb, Joel. "The Preservation of Wilderness Values: The Politics and Administration of Conservation Policy." Ph.D. dissertation, University of California, Riverside, 1972.

Kathka, David Arlin. "The Bureau of Reclamation in the Truman Administration: Personnel, Politics, and Policy." Ph.D. dissertation, University of Missouri, 1976.

Koppes, Clayton R. "Oscar L. Chapman: A Liberal at the Interior Department." Ph.D. dissertation, University of Kansas, 1974.

LeUnes, Barbara. "The Conservation Philosophy of Stewart L. Udall, 1961–1968." Ph.D. dissertation, Texas A & M University, 1977.

McBride, Conrad. "Federal-State Relations in the Development of the Water Resources of the Colorado River Basin." Ph.D. dissertation, University of California, Los Angeles, 1962.

Sayles, Stephen P. "Claire Engle and the Politics of California Reclamation, 1943–1960." Ph.D. dissertation, University of New Mexico, 1978.

Spritzer, Donald E. "New Dealer from Montana: The Senate Career of James E. Murray." Ph.D. dissertation, University of Montana, 1980.

Stewart, Ronald L. "Wilderness Heritage of the Arid Southwest." Ph.D. dissertation, University of New Mexico, 1970.

Van Dusen, George. "Politics of 'Partnership': The Eisenhower Administration and Conservation, 1952–1960." Ph.D. dissertation, Loyola University, 1974.

# Congressional Documents: House

## Committee Hearings

Interior and Insular Affairs

*Colorado River Storage Project,* HR.4449, January 18–28, 1954.

*San Juan–Chama Reclamation Project and Navajo Indian Irrigation Project* HR.2352, HR.2494, and S.72, May 20, 1960.

*San Juan–Chama Reclamation Project and Navajo Indian Irrigation Project,* HR.2552 and S.107, April 24–June 1, 1961.

*Wilderness Preservation System,* Part IV, HR.293 and S.174, May 7–11, 1962.

*Water Resources Research Centers,* S.2, June 24–25 and July 22–23, 1963.

*Wilderness Preservation System,* HR.9070, HR.9162, and S.4, January 9–May 1, 1964.

## Reports

*Authorizing Construction, Operation and Maintenance of Initial Units of Colorado River Storage Project,* 83–1774, 1954.

*Authorizing Construction of Navajo Indian Irrigation Project and Initial Stage of San Juan–Chama Projects as Participating Projects of the Colorado River Storage Project,* 87–685, July 10, 1961.

*Fryingpan-Arkansas Project, Colorado,* 87–694, July 11, 1961.

*Providing for the Preservation of Wilderness Areas,* 87–2521, October 3, 1962.

*Establishment of Public Land Law Review Commission,* 88–1008, December 7, 1963.

*Establishing Water Resources Research Centers at Land Grant Colleges,* 88–1136, February 10, 1964.

*Water Resources Research Centers,* 88–1526, June 30, 1964.

*National Wilderness Preservation System,* 88–1538, July 2, 1964.

*Establish a National Wilderness Preservation System,* 88–1829, August 19, 1964.

# Congressional Documents: Senate

## Committee Hearings

Agriculture and Forestry

*Forestry and Timber Access Roads,* S.282, May 25–31, 1949.

Appropriations

*Civil Functions, Department of the Army, 1950,* HR.3734, April 5, 1949.

*Public Works, 1957,* HR.11319, May 24, 1956.

Interior and Insular Affairs

*Natural Resources Policy,* January 31–February 7, 1949.

*Central Arizona Project and Colorado River Water Rights,* S.75 and SJRes.4, March 21–May 2, 1949.

*Weather Control and Augmented Potable Water Supply,* S.5, S.22, and S.798, March 14–19, April 5, 1951.

*Colorado River Storage Project,* S.1555, June 28–July 3, 1954.

*Colorado River Storage Project,* S.500, February 28–March 5, 1955.

*Outdoor Recreation Resources Commission,* S.846, May 15, 1957.

*National Wilderness Preservation Act,* S.1176, June 19–20, 1957.

*Saline Water Conversion,* SJRes.135 and S.3370, March 20–21, 1958.

*Navajo Irrigation—San Juan–Chama Diversion,* S.3648, July 9–10, 1958.

*National Wilderness Preservation Act,* S.4028, July 23 and November 10–14, 1958.

*Navajo Indian—San Juan–Chama Diversion, New Mexico,* S.72, March 16, 1959.

*Proposed Resources Conservation Act of 1960,* S.2549, January 25–29, 1960.

*Nomination (James K. Carr),* January 26, 1961.

*The Wilderness Act,* S.174, February 27–28, 1961.

*Shoreline Recreation Areas,* S.543, March 8–9, 1961.

*Cape Cod National Seashore Park,* S.857, March 9, 1961.

*Navajo Indian Irrigation and San Juan–Chama Project,* S.107, March 15, 1961.

*Point Reyes National Seashore,* S.476, March 28–31, 1961.

*Resources and Conservation Act of 1961,* S.239 and S.1415, April 13, 1961.

*Water Resources Planning Act of 1961,* S.1629, July 10, 1961.

*Water Resources Planning Act of 1961,* S.2246, S.1629, S.1778, August 16, 1961.

*Saline Water Conversion,* S.2156, August 22, 1961.

*Proposed Canyonlands National Park in Utah,* S.2387, March 29–30, 1962.

*Outdoor Recreation Act of 1962,* S.3117, May 10–11, 1962.

*Valle Grande National Park, New Mexico,* S.3321, September 17, 1962.

*Water Resources Research Act,* S.2, February 19–20, 1963.

*National Wilderness Preservation Act,* S.4, February 28–March 1, 1963.

*Land and Water Conservation Fund,* S.859, March 7–8, 1963.

*River Basin Planning Act,* S.1111, September 12–13, 1963.

*Indiana Dunes National Lakeshore,* S.2249, March 5–7, 1964.

*Valle Grande–Bandelier National Park,* S.1870, May 29, 1964.

Select Committee on National Water Resources

*Water Resources, Albuquerque, New Mexico,* S.Res.48, November 23, 1959.

## Reports

*Reforestation and Revegetation of Forest and Range Lands of National Forests,* 81–97, 1949.

*Construction of Vermejo Reclamation Project,* 81–813, March 23, 1949.

*Dam in Mainstream of Colorado River at Bridge Canyon,* 81–832, 1949.

*Additions of Lands to El Morro National Monument,* 81–1356, 1950.
*Authorizing Construction of the Canadian River Project,* 81–2110, July 1950.
*Authorizing the Secretary of the Interior to Construct, Operate, and Maintain the Colorado River Storage Project and Participating Projects,* 83–1983, July 26, 1954.
*Secretary of Interior to Construct Colorado River Storage Project and Participating Projects,* 84–128, 1955.
*Amending the Act of July 3, 1952, Relating to Research in the Development and Utilization of Saline Waters,* 84–370, May 23, 1955.
*Saline Water Program,* 85–1593, May 19, 1958.
*Navajo Indian Irrigation and San Juan–Chama Participating Projects,* 85–2198, August 5, 1958.
*San Luis Unit, Central Valley Project, California,* 85–2202, August 5, 1958.
*Navajo Irrigation and San Juan–Chama Projects, New Mexico,* 86–155, April 8, 1959.
*Authorizing the Secretary of the Interior to Construct, Operate, and Maintain the Norman Project, Oklahoma,* 86–872, September 2, 1959.
*Report of the Select Committee on National Water Resources,* 87–29, January 30, 1961.
*Establishing a National Wilderness Preservation System,* 87–635, July 27, 1961.
*Saline Water Conversion Program,* 87–780, August 25, 1961.
*Padre Island National Seashore,* 87–1226, March 6, 1962.
*Providing for the Establishment of Canyonlands National Park,* 87–2121, September 24, 1962.
*Establishing a National Wilderness Preservation System for the Permanent Good of the Whole People,* 88–109, April 3, 1963.
*Indiana Dunes National Lakeshore,* 88–1362, August 10, 1964.

## Exective Branch Documents

U.S. Commission on the Organization of the Executive Branch of the Government. *Department of the Interior,* March 1949.
———. *Organization in the Field of Natural Resources,* 1949.
U.S. Commission on the Organization of the Executive Branch of the Government (1953–1955). *Water Resources and Power,* 1955.
U.S. Department of the Interior. Bureau of Reclamation. *The Colorado River: A Natural Menace Becomes a Natural Resource, Interim Report on the Status of Investigations Authorized to be Made by the Boulder Canyon Project Act,* 1947.
———. *Colorado River Storage Project: Project Planning Report, 4–8a,* 1950.
———. *Plan for Development: Canadian River Project, Texas: Project Planning Report 5–12, 22–1,* June 1949.

———. *Plan for Rehabilitation, Vermejo Project, Canadian River Basin, New Mexico: Project Planning Report 5–12, 15–1,* February 1949.
———. *Supplemental Report on the Colorado River Storage Project and Participating Projects, Upper Basin,* October 1953.
———. *Water Supply and the Texas Economy,* 1952.
U.S. Outdoor Recreation Resources Review Commission. *Outdoor Recreation for America,* 1962.
———. *Wilderness and Recreation: A Report on Resources, Values, and Problems,* ORRRC Study Report 3, 1962.
U.S. White House Conference on Conservation. *Proceedings,* 1962.


# Articles

Anderson, Clinton P. "Conservation is Our Constant Task." *American Forests* 69 (November 1961): 19.
———. "Protection of the Wilderness." *Living Wilderness* 78 (Autumn-Winter 1961–62): 13–19.
———. "Reflections on New Mexico: What is Progress?" *New Mexico* 50 (March-April 1972): 16–20.
———. "Statement on the Wilderness Bill." *Living Wilderness* 74 (Autumn-Winter 1960–61): 28–34.
———. "This We Hold Dear." *American Forests* 70 (July 1963): 24–25.
———. "Why We Need the Land and Water Conservation Fund Bill." *American Forests* 70 (March 1964): 24–27.
———. "The Wilderness Act: A Constructive Measure." *Living Wilderness* 86 (Spring 1964): 3–4.
Bennett, Elmer. "A Symposium on Federal, State and Local Cooperation on Conservation and Development of Water Resources: The Role of the Federal Government." *California Law Review* 45 (December 1957): 584–98.
Bird, John. "The Great Wilderness Fight." *Saturday Evening Post,* July 8, 1961, p. 8.
Boroff, David. "A New Yorker's Report on New Mexico." *Harper's,* February 1965, pp. 72–78.
Brooks, Paul. "Congressman Aspinall vs. the People of the United States." *Harper's,* March 1963, pp. 59–63.
Butcher, Devereux. "Resorts or Wilderness?" *Atlantic Monthly,* February 1961, pp. 45–51.
Clark, Robert Emmet. "New Mexico Water Law Since 1955." *Natural Resources Journal* 2 (December 1962): 484–561.
———. "Water Rights Problems in the Upper Rio Grande Watershed and Adjoining Areas." *Natural Resources Journal* 11 (January 1971): 48–68.
Cline, Dorothy I., and Barrett, Joel V. "Concepts and Planning in the Use and Conservation of Natural Resources." *New Mexico Business* 17 (December 1946): 1–10.

Crafts, Edward C. "Saga of a Law" *American Forests* 76 (June 1970): 13–19; (July 1970); 29–35.

Dodds, Gordon B. "Conservation and Reclamation in the Trans-Mississippi West: A Critical Bibliography." *Arizona and the West* 13 (Summer 1971): 143–71.

———. "The Historiography of American Conservation: Past and Prospects." *Pacific Northwest Quarterly* 52 (April 1965): 75–81.

Harvey, Mark W. T. "Echo Park: An Old Problem of Federalism." *Annals of Wyoming* 55 (Fall 1983): 9–18.

Huitt, Ralph. "Outsider in the Senate." *American Political Science Review* 60 (September 1961): 566–75.

Hundley, Norris. "The Dark and Bloody Ground of Indian Water Rights: Confusion Elevated to Principle." *Western Historical Quarterly* 9 (October 1978): 455–65.

———. "The 'Winters' Decision and Indian Water Rights: A Mystery Reexamined." *Western Historical Quarterly* 13 (January 1982): 17–42.

Knight, Oliver. "Correcting Nature's Error: The Colorado-Big Thompson Project." *Agricultural History* 30 (October 1956): 157–69.

Koppes, Clayton R. "Environmental Policy and American Liberalism: The Department of the Interior, 1933–1953." *Environmental Review* 7 (Spring 1983): 26–33.

———. "Public Water—Private Land: Origins of the Acreage Limitation Controversy, 1933–1953." *Pacific Historical Review* 47 (November 1978): 607–36.

Lawson, Michael L. "The Navajo Indian Irrigation Project: Muddied Past, Clouded Future." *Indian Historian* 9 (Winter 1976): 19–29.

Lee, Lawrence. "One Hundred Years of Reclamation Historiography." *Pacific Historical Review* 47 (November 1978): 507–64.

Maass, Arthur. "Congress and Water Resources." *American Political Science Review* 44 (September 1950): 576–93.

McArdle, Richard. "Wilderness Politics: Legislation and Forest Service Policy." *Journal of Forest History* 19 (October 1975): 166–79.

———. "Why We Need the Multiple Use Bill." *American Forests* 76 (June 1970); 10.

McCloskey, J. Michael. "Natural Resources—National Forests—The Multiple Use-Sustained Yield Act of 1960." *Oregon Law Review* 41 (December 1961): 49–79.

———. "The Wilderness Act of 1964: Its Background and Meaning." *Oregon Law Review* 45 (1966): 288–321.

McCluskey, Ross. "The ORRRC Report: A Glittering Blunder." *Field & Stream* (April 1962): 24.

Martone, Rosalie. "The United States and the Betrayal of Indian Water Rights." *The Indian Historian* 7 (Summer 1974): 3–12.

Maxwell, Neal A. "The Conference of Western Senators." *Western Political Quarterly* 10 (December 1957): 902–10.

Moore, Carl. "Joseph Christopher O'Mahoney: A Brief Biography." *Annals of Wyoming* 41 (1969): 159–86.

Morris, Thomas G. "The San Juan–Chama Diversion Project." *New Mexico Business* 18 (June 1965): 1–13.

Peeples, William. "The Indiana Dunes and Pressure Politics." *Atlantic Monthly* (February 1963): 84–88.

Pesonen, David E. "An Analysis of the ORRRC Report." *Sierra Club Bulletin* 47 (May 1962): 6.

Pickens, William H. "Bronson Cutting Vs. Dennis Chavez: Battle of the Patrones in New Mexico, 1934." *New Mexico Historical Review* 46 (January 1971): 5–36.

———. "Cutting vs. Chavez: A Reply to Wolf's Comments." *New Mexico Historical Review* 47 (October 1972): 337–59.

Rakestraw, Lawrence. "Conservation Historiography: An Assessment." *Pacific Historical Review* 41 (1972): 271–88.

———. "Uncle Sam's Forest Reserves." *Pacific Northwest Quarterly* 44 (October 1953): 145–51.

Rienow, Robert and Leona Rienow. "The Day the Taps Run Dry." *Harper's* (October 1958): 72.

Roth, Dennis. "The National Forests and the Campaign For Wilderness Legislation." *Journal of Forest History* 28 (July 1984): 112–25.

Sicher, Frederic. "The Indiana Dunes National Lakeshore." *National Parks Magazine* (July 1964): 5–7.

Squires, Richard A. "Reverberations From Echo Park." *American Forests* (February 1954): 34–40.

Walker, J. Samuel. "The Confessions of A Cold Warrior: Clinton P. Anderson and American Foreign Policy." *New Mexico Historical Review* 52 (April 1977): 117–34.

Walsh, John. "Water Resources: Congress Votes Research Centers For States; River Basin Planning Bill Advances." *Science* (September 4, 1964): 1022–24.

Webb, Walter Prescott. "The American West, Perpetual Mirage." *Harper's* (May 1957): 25–31.

Wengert, Norman. "The Politics of River Basin Development." *Law and Contemporary Problems* 22 (1957): 258–63.

White, William S. "The Democrats' Board of Directors." *New York Times Magazine* (July 10, 1955): 10–11.

Wolf, T. Phillip. "Cutting vs. Chavez Reexamined: A Commentary on Pickens' Analysis." *New Mexico Historical Review* 47 (October 1972): 317–35.

## Books

Allin, Craig W. *The Politics of Wilderness Preservation.* Westport, Conn.: Greenwood Press, 1982.

Ambrose, Stephen E. *Eisenhower: The President.* New York: Simon and Schuster, 1984.

Anderson, Clinton P. *Outsider in the Senate.* New York: World Publishing Co., 1970.

Anson, Robert Sam. *McGovern: A Biography.* New York: Holt, Rinehart and Winston, 1972.

Baldwin, Donald Nicholas. *The Quiet Revolution: The Grass Roots of Today's Wilderness Preservation Movement.* Boulder, Colo.: Pruett Publishing Co., 1972.

Bendiner, Robert. *Obstacle Course on Capitol Hill.* New York: McGraw-Hill, 1964.

Berkman, Richard L. and W. Kip Viscusi. *Damming the West.* New York: Grossman Publishers, 1973.

Bolling, Richard. *House Out of Order.* New York: E. P. Dutton, 1966.

Brooks, Paul. *The Pursuit of Wilderness.* Boston: Houghton Mifflin Co., 1971.

Buhite, Russell D. *Patrick J. Hurley and American Foreign Policy.* Ithaca: Cornell University Press, 1973.

Burling, Francis P. *The Birth of the Cape Cod National Seashore.* Plymouth, Mass.: Leyden Press, 1978.

Clawson, Marion. *Economics of Outdoor Recreation.* Baltimore: Johns Hopkins Press, 1966.

———. *Land and Water for Recreation.* Chicago: Rand McNally and Co., 1963.

Dana, Samuel T. and Sally K. Fairfax. *Forest and Range Policy.* New York: McGraw-Hill, 1980.

Douglas, Paul. *In the Fullness of Time.* New York: Harcourt Brace Jovanovich, 1972.

Dunbar, Robert G. *Forging New Rights in Western Waters.* Lincoln: University of Nebraska Press, 1983.

Engel, J. Ronald. *Sacred Sands: The Struggle for Community in the Indiana Dunes.* Middletown, Conn.: Wesleyan University Press, 1983.

Evans, Rowland and Robert Novak. *Lyndon B. Johnson: The Exercise of Power.* New York: New American Library, 1966.

Everhart, William C. *The National Park Service.* New York: Praeger, 1972.

Fergusson, Erma. *New Mexico: A Pageant of Three Peoples.* New York: Alfred A. Knopf, 1971.

Foley, Michael. *The New Senate: Liberal Influence on A Conservative Institution, 1959–1972.* New Haven: Yale University Press, 1980.

Fox, Stephen. *John Muir and His Legacy: The American Conservation Movement.* Boston: Little Brown, 1981.

Franklin, Kay and Norma Schaeffer. *Duel for the Dunes: Land Use Conflict on the Shores of Lake Michigan.* Urbana: University of Illinois Press, 1983.

Frome, Michael. *Battle for the Wilderness.* New York: Praeger, 1974.

———. *The Forest Service.* New York: Praeger, 1971.

Gates, Paul Wallace. *History of Public Land Law Development.* Washington, D.C.: Government Printing Office, 1968.

Gillette, Elizabeth R., ed. *Action for Wilderness,* 12th Wilderness Conference, Washington, D.C., 1971. San Francisco: Sierra Club, 1972.

Graham, Frank, Jr. *Man's Dominion: The Story of Conservation in America.* New York: M. Evans & Co., 1971.

Gruening, Ernest. *Many Battles.* New York: Liveright, 1973.

Hannett, Arthur T. *Sagebrush Lawyer.* New York: Pageant Press, 1964.

Hays, Samuel P. *Conservation and the Gospel of Efficiency: The Progressive Conservation Movement, 1890–1920.* Cambridge: Harvard University Press, 1959.

Holmes, Jack E. *Politics in New Mexico.* Albuquerque: University of New Mexico Press, 1967.

———. *Science Town in the Politics of New Mexico.* Albuquerque: Division of Government Research, University of New Mexico, 1967.

Hundley, Norris, Jr. *Water and the West: The Colorado River Compact and the Politics of Water in the American West.* Berkeley: University of California Press, 1975.

Ingram, Helen M. *Patterns of Politics in Water Resources Development: A Case Study of New Mexico's Role in the Colorado Basin Bed.* Monograph Series No. 79. Albuquerque: Division of Government Research, University of New Mexico, 1969.

Irion, Frederick C. *New Mexico and Its Natural Resources, 1900–2000.* Monograph Series No. 55. Albuquerque: Division of Government Research, University of New Mexico, 1959.

Ise, John. *Our National Park Policy: A Critical History.* Baltimore: Johns Hopkins Press, 1961.

Johnson, Rich. *The Central Arizona Project, 1918–1968.* Tucson: University of Arizona Press, 1977.

Jonas, Frank H., ed. *Politics in the American West.* Salt Lake City: University of Utah, 1969.

Krutilla, John, and Otto Eckstein. *Multiple Purpose River Development: Studies in Applied Economic Analysis.* Baltimore: Johns Hopkins Press, 1958.

Lee, Lawrence B. *Reclaiming the American West: A Historiography and Guide.* Santa Barbara, Calif.: ABC Clio, 1980.

Leopold, Aldo. *Sand County Almanac.* New York: Oxford University Press, 1966.

Leydet, Francois, ed. *Tomorrow's Wilderness.* 8th Wilderness Conference, 1963. San Francisco: Sierra Club, 1963.

Lowitt, Richard. *The New Deal and the West.* Bloomington: Indiana University Press, 1984.

McCloskey, Maxine, ed. *Wilderness and the Quality of Life.* 10th Wilderness Conference, San Francisco, 1967. San Francisco: Sierra Club, 1969.

McPhee, John. *Encounters With the Archdruid.* New York: Farrar, Straus, & Giroux, 1971.

McPherson, Harry. *A Political Education.* Boston: Little Brown, 1972.

Mann, Dean. *The Politics of Water in Arizona.* Tucson: University of Arizona Press, 1963.

Matthews, Donald R. *U.S. Senators and Their World.* Chapel Hill: University of North Carolina Press, 1960.

Matusow, Allen J. *Farm Policies and Politics in the Truman Years.* Cambridge: Harvard University Press, 1967.

Maxwell, Neal A. *Regionalism in the United States Senate: The West.* Research Monograph No. 5. Salt Lake City: Institute of Government, University of Utah, 1961.

Moreell, Ben. *Our Nation's Water Resources: Policies and Politics.* Chicago: University of Chicago Law School, 1956.

Morgan, Neil. *Westward Tilt.* New York: Random House, 1961.

Moss, Frank E. *The Water Crisis.* New York: Praeger, 1967.

Nahm, Milton C. *Las Vegas and Uncle Joe: The New Mexico I Remember.* Norman: University of Oklahoma Press, 1964.

Nash, Roderick. *Wilderness and the American Mind.* New Haven: Yale University Press, 1967.

*Nation Looks at its Resources.* Report of the Mid-century Conference on Resources for the Future. Washington: Resources for the Future, 1954.

New Mexico People and Energy. *Who Runs New Mexico: The New Mexico Power Structure Report.* Albuquerque: NMPE, 1981.

Ogden, Gerald, comp. *The United States Forest Service: A Historical Bibliography, 1876–1972.* Davis: University of California, Agricultural History Center, 1976.

Peirce, Neal. *The Megastates of America.* New York: W. W. Norton, 1972.

————. *The Mountain States of America.* New York: W. W. Norton, 1972.

Pemberton, William E. *Bureaucratic Politics: Executive Reorganization During the Truman Administration.* Columbia: University of Missouri Press, 1979.

Reedy, George E. *Lyndon B. Johnson: A Memoir.* New York: Andrews and McNeel, 1982.

Reichard, Gary W. *The Reaffirmation of Republicanism, Eisenhower and the Eighty-third Congress.* Knoxville: University of Tennessee Press, 1975.

Richardson, Elmo. *Dams, Parks and Politics: Resources Development and Preservation in the Truman-Eisenhower Era.* Lexington: University Press of Kentucky, 1973.

Schlesinger, Arthur M., Jr. *Robert Kennedy and His Times.* Boston: Houghton Mifflin, 1978.

Smith, Frank E. *The Politics of Conservation.* New York: Pantheon Books, 1966.

Solberg, Carl. *Hubert Humphrey: A Biography.* New York: W. W. Norton, 1984.

Steen, Harold K. *The U.S. Forest Service.* Seattle: University of Washington Press, 1976.

Stegner, Wallace. *The Uneasy Chair: A Biography of Bernard DeVoto.* Garden City, N.Y.: Doubleday, 1974.

Steinberg, Alfred. *Sam Rayburn.* New York: Hawthorn, 1975.

Stratton, Owen and Phillip Sirotkin. *The Echo Park Controversy.* University: University of Alabama Press, 1959.

Strauss, Lewis. *Men and Decisions.* Garden City, N.Y.: Doubleday, 1962.

Sundquist, James L. *The Decline and Resurgence of Congress.* Washington, D.C.: Brookings Institutions, 1981.

————. *Politics and Policy: The Eisenhower, Kennedy, and Johnson Years.* Washington, D.C.: Brookings Institution, 1968.

Swain, Donald. *Federal Conservation Policy: 1921–1933.* Berkeley: University of California Press, 1963.

————. *Wilderness Defender: Horace M. Albright and Conservation.* Chicago: University of Chicago Press, 1970.

Swartzman, Daniel, Richard A. Liroff, and Kevin G. Croke, eds. *Cost-Benefit Analysis and Environmental Regulations: Politics, Ethics, and Methods.* Washington, D.C.: Conservation Foundation, 1982.

Terrell, John U. *War for the Colorado River.* Glendale, Calif.: Arthur H. Clark Co., 1965. 2 vols.

Udall, Stewart L. *The Conservation Challenge of the Sixties.* The Horace M. Albright Conservation Lectureship. Berkeley: University of California, School of Forestry, 1963.

————. *The Quiet Crisis.* New York: Holt, Rinehart and Winston, 1963.

Voight, William, Jr. *Public Grazing Lands: Use and Misuse by Industry and Government.* New Brunswick, N.J.: Rutgers University Press, 1976.

Waters, Frank. *The Colorado.* New York: Rinehart & Co., 1946.

Webb, Walter Prescott. *More Water for Texas.* Austin: University of Texas, 1954.

Werner, Morris and John Starr. *Teapot Dome.* New York: Viking Press, 1959.

White, William. *Citadel: The Story of the U.S. Senate.* Boston: Houghton Mifflin, 1957.

Wild, Peter. *Pioneer Conservationists of Western America.* Missoula, Mont.: Mountain Press Publishing Co., 1979.

Wirth, Conrad. *Parks, Politics and the People.* Norman: University of Oklahoma Press, 1980.

Wyant, William K. *Westward In Eden: The Public Lands and the Conservation Movement.* Los Angeles: University of California Press, 1982.

# Index